KAHANE
THE MILITANT RABBI
A Historical Drama With 127 Scenes In Four Parts

LEAH MILLER

Copyright © 2023 by Leah Miller

All rights reserved.

ISBN 978-1-63777-454-0 / 978-1-63777-455-7

No part of this book may be reproduced in any form or by any electronic or mechanical means, including information storage and retrieval systems, without written permission from the author, except for the use of brief quotations in a book review.

Contents

Location	vii
Characters	xi
Bibliography	xxv
PART 1	1
PART 2	169
PART 3	329
PART 4	451

Wherever There Is Jewish Pain

Places:

New York
Israel

Time:

1968-1999

The Dramatization Is Based On Actual Events

Characters
(IN ORDER OF THEIR APPEARANCE)

PART I:

RABBI MEIR KAHANE

WHITE MAN

BLACK MAN

HOST

HATCHETT

BUNDY

FERGUSON

REPORTER ON TV

BLACK WOMAN

SHANKER

DONOVAN

MAYOR LINDSAY

BLACK JUVENILE

MR. GOLDSTEIN

CHAIRMAN

BOARD MEMBER

JUDGE

BLACK PRINCIPAL

BLACK TEACHER

REVEREND OLIVER

RABBI

ASSISTANT PRINCIPAL

TEACHER

BLACK DEPUTY INSPECTOR

AMERICAN JEWISH CONGRESS SPOKESMAN

ADMINISTRATOR

HESTER

MARY TASHIKA

WOODS

DORE SHARY

LESLIE CAMPBELL

JDL BOYS

PAUL ANTHONY

MARY McCASSEY

GLORIA OLIVER

STERN

OGDEN VAN

DIDEON GOLDBERG

FRANK STEWART

CHAIM BIEBER

PECK

SERGEANT KILLIAN

ARTHUR GOLDBERG

MRS. BURTON LANE

SPEIVAK

PANTHER
REPRESENTATIVE BROYHILL
STEPHEN POLLACK
ADL SPOKESMAN
ELDRIDGE CLEAVER
STEIN
HOFSTADER
ELMA LEWIS
WILL MASLOW
ARNOLD FOSTER
FRANKLIN E. WHITE
PUERTO RICAN MAN
DR. JOSEPH SMITH
HENRY SCHWARTZCHILD
DR. EINHORN
PUERTO RICANS
SOL LIEBMAN
INTERVIEWER
SONNY CARSON
SHLOMO RUBENSTEIN
BOARD MEMBER A
BOARD MEMBER B
BOARD MEMBER C
COLEMAN
RABBI EISENKOPP
LARRY RIVERS (JEW)
SHEPP (BLACK)
INTERVIEWER
LEROI JONES (BLACK)

LEONARD BERNSTEIN
DONALD COX (BLACK)
MRS. BERNSTEIN
DISTINGUISHED WASP
WHITE GUESTS AT PARTY WITH PANTHERS
THOMAS HOVING
ROBERT BERNSTEIN

PART 2:
OTTO PREMINGER
WILLIAM WEXLER
ROSE HALPERIN
OFFICER REUS
ALLEN SCHOENER
NED POLSKY
ARENT
RABBI ELIEZER
RABBI STERN
BEGIN
VALERY KILMOV
RABBI WOLFE KELMAN
VASILY V. ZUGNETZOV
AMBASSADOR YOST
DMITRI KOLESNIK
JOHN KING
ELEAZER LIPSKY
JOSEPH HEFNER
AMBASSADOR DOBRYNIN
McCLOSKEY

MRS. DOBRYNIN

PRESIDENT NIXON

D. A. ROGERS

JUDGE MARRA

ROBERT MAYER

DEAN OF YESHIVA

SCHACHTER

NAT MARCONI

ABRAHAM ZALMONSON

DAVID FROST

ABBA EBAN

AMBASSADOR FROM IRAQ

MINISTER FROM JORDAN

THEODORE BIKEL

MRS. MICKEY GARELIK

SIMON BLOOM

SKINHEAD

PROSECUTOR

POLICE COMMISIONER

JOCAHIM PRINZ

SHULAMIT ALONI

LUBA ELIAV

SHUMON PERES, PRIME MINISTER OF ISRAEL

CHAIM HERZOG, PRESIDENT OF ISRAEL

MARTIN F. STERN, UJA

SHAMIR

ARTHUR HERTZBERG

RABBI HAROLD S. SILVER

PART 3:
BYRD
CALLER
MALE CALLER
FEMALE CALLER
MUHAMMED
SHARPTON
RABBI SPIELMAN
LUBAVITCH MAN
CARAMOVITCH
BORELLI
MAYOR DINKINS
RABBI HECHT
NARRATOR
REPORTER
911 OPERATOR
SUPERIOR OFFICER
FIRE DEPT DISPATCHER
FATHER
WIFE
YITZIE
GALLAGHER
DEAR
MOLLOY
GONALEZ
LYNCH
MOLLEN
POTRELL
BUTTMAN

KELLY

GIRGENTI

WHALEY

MADDOX

ROSENBAUM

FOREMAN

SLIWA

BLACK HOST

SAPERSTEIN

LEMRICK NELSON SR.

GARBER

SUSSKIND

MOSHE STERN

FOXMAN

MODERATOR

PODHORETZ

KANTROWITZ

RABBI SCHEERSON

SECRETARY

STUDENT

BOY

SPEAKER

PRESIDENT SYWGERT

GRAYBAR

WALINSKY

SHABAZZ

PART 4:

HARARI

POWELL

BLACK SECURITY GUARD

PICKETER

SHABAZZ

FELDERE

LOUIS FARRAKHAN

TWO JEWISH MEN

HUGE BLACK CROWD

POLICEMEN

BLACKS

11-YEAR-OLD BLACK GIRL

GROUP OF HASIDIC BOYS

RABBI SPIELMAN

REVEREND DEL SHIELDS

MAN IN WHEELCHAIR

WOMAN

RABBI

MAN

MRS. SCHARF

MRS. ROSEN

POLICEMAN

LADY IN BLACK

MAYOR LINDSAY

MARIO CUOMO (WHEN HE WAS LAWYER)

POLICEMAN

MAYOR GUILIANI

BLACK MEN

JEWISH MEN

POLICE CHIEF

NEIGHBOR

HASIDS

LATINOS

KHALLID MUHAMMED

HASIDIC WOMAN

HUSBAND

MS. PECK

PECK'S ASSISTANT

LATIN WOMAN

NURSE

MAN

SOCIAL WORKER

HASID

VOLUNTEER

MR. STEIN

REPORTER

MRS. SELDOWITZ

CHILDREN

DEREK WILLIAMS

SHLOME SELDOWITZ

POLICEMAN

HASIDIC RABBI

BLACK TEENAGERS

JEWISH BOY, AGE 8

HASID JEWISH MOTHER

BLACK TEENAGER

JEWISH MAN

CLERK

NURSE

SERGEANT

POLICEMAN

RABBI BRIENDA

POLICEMAN

DETECTIVE

BLACK MUGGER

BLACK TEENAGERS

JEWISH OLD LADIES

DOCTOR

ERIC BRIENDEL

KHALLID MUHAMMED

RABBI

SISTER WARRIOR WOMAN

BROTHER ODEH

MALIK SHABAZZ

TV REPORTER

JEWISH DEFENSE ORGANIZATION STUDENT

DR. SPRINGER

STUDENT

DR. RUTH WISSE

BLACK MEN

BLACK WOMAN

JEWISH MAN

ELLIOT ABRAMS

ANNE ROLPHE

JEWISH MAN

CROWD

CONRAD MUHAMMED

FARRAKHAN

NURSE

DOCTOR

RAV HOROWITZ

MRS. HOROWITZ

HEAD NURSE

11-YEAR-OLD CHILD

HASIDIC MAN

HASIDIC WOMAN

RABBI

ANOTHER HASIDIC MAN

LITTLE BOY

ANTHONY BURTON

NEIGHBOR

BENJAMIN

SISKEL

AUDIENCE MEMBERS

HASID

SARAH NACHSON

ISRAELI SOLDIERS

BEGIN

SECRETARY

RABBI LEVINGER

BOY (AGE 10)

MOTHER

SOLDIER AT GATE

CABINET MEMBERS

PREGNANT WOMAN

ANOTHER WOMAN
YESHIVA STUDENTS (6)
TV REPORTER
MENACHIM BEGIN
ISRAELI SOLDIER
ISRAELI SETTLER
RABIN
ARAFAT
YOSSI SARID
IDF SOLDIERS
ISRAELI CIVILIANS
IDF COMMANDER
JUDGE
TWO WOMEN
FRIEND
PALESTINIAN
ISRAELI SOLDIER
RELIGIOUS WOMAN
SON (AGE 17)
MAN
ARAB KNESSET MEMBER
PRESIDENT WEIZMANN
SETTLERS
ARAB
SOLDIER
NAOMI HAZAN
ORTHODOX MAN
MILITARY OFFICER
SETTLER

HAIM
SOLDIER
MAN
TV REPORTER
ISRAELI POLICE OFFICERS
JEWISH PROTESTORS
JUDGE
STEN
AUDIENCE MEMBERS
HASIDIC MAN
MASTER OF CEREMONIES
JUDGE
CROWD OF YOUNG HIPSTERS

Bibliography

BOOKS

Begin, Menachim. <u>The Revolt</u>. New York: Nash Publishing, 1977.

Ben Ami, Yitshaq. <u>Years Of Wrath, Days of Glory</u>. New York: Shengold, 1983.

Kahane, Rabbi Meir. <u>Never Again</u>. New York: Nash Publishing Co., 1971.

Kahane, Rabbi Meir. <u>The Story of the Jewish Defense League.</u> Chilton Book Co., 1975.

Kahane, Rabbi Meir. <u>Time To Go Home</u>. New York: Nash Publishing Co., 1972.

Kahane, Rabbi Meir. <u>Uncomfortable Questions for Comfortable Jews</u>. Lyle Stuart, 1987.

Peters, Joan. <u>From Time Immemorial</u>. New York: Harper & Row, 1984.

PAMPHLETS

Kahane, Rabbi Meir. "Writings." Jerusalem: Jewish Identity Center, 1971-1972.

Kahane, Rabbi Meir. "Letters from Prison." Jerusalem: Jewish Identity Center, 1974.

Kahane, Rabbi Meir. Jerusalem: "Numbers 23:9." Jerusalem: Jewish Identity Center, 1974.

Kahane, Rabbi Meir. "The Arabs of Israel." JDL, 1974.

Kahane, Rabbi Meir. "Excerpts from the Book <u>Revolution or Referendum</u>." <u>Magazine of the Authentic Jewish Idea</u>, 1989.

ARTICLES - PART 1:

Allen, Julian. "Picture of Newton."

Blauner, Bob. "The Outlaw Huey Newton." <u>New York Times</u>, 1984.

Breindel, Eric. "If Jews Need Dialogue, It's Not with Farrakhan." <u>New York Post</u>.

Hammer, Robert. "Nightmare Revisited." <u>Jewish Press</u>, 1991.

Hochschild, Adam. "His Life As a Panther." <u>New York Times</u>, 1993.

Horowitz, David. "Hollywood Outrage." <u>New York Post</u>, 1995.

Kahane, Rabbi Meir. "Camp Meir, Jewish Defense." <u>Jewish Press</u>.

Kahane, Rabbi Meir. "On Racism in Schools and on Jewish Merchants in Troubled Areas." <u>Jewish Press</u>, 1968-1970.

Kashepava, Yan. "A Great Believer." <u>Jewish Press</u>, 1992.

Kelly, Michael. "Panther Whitewash." <u>New York Post.</u>

Lewin, Avrohom. "Kahane Assassination." <u>Jewish Press</u>, 1990.

Schwartz, Sender. "Kahane Funeral." <u>Jewish Press</u>, 1990.

Torah, Dvar. "A Life Sanctifying God's Name." <u>Judean Voice</u>.

Whyte, George. "Who Owns Dreyfus?" <u>New York Times</u>, 1996.

ARTICLES - PART 2:

Adelson, Prof. Howard L. "Outrage is Not Enough." <u>Jewish Press</u>. 1998.

Adelson, Prof. Howard L. "The SUNY Albany Disgrace." <u>Jewish Press</u>. Date unknown.

Adelson, Prof. Howard L. "Trouble from the Radical Left." <u>Jewish Press</u>. 1998.

Blitzer, Chaya. "Crown Heights Pogrom." <u>Jewish Press</u>. 1991.

Breindel, Eric. "Behind the Crown Heights Verdict." New York Post. 1992.

Breindel, Eric. "The Mayor's Speech." New York Post. 1992.

Breindel, Eric. "Must U.S. Jewry Vanish? New York Post. Date unknown.

Breindel, Eric. "New Outrage in Crown Heights." New York Post. 1995.

Breindel, Eric. "Once Again, a Tired Warning to Jews, 'Don't Overreact'." New York Post. 1994.

Breindel, Eric. "Pointless Dialogue." New York Post. 1992.

Breindel, Eric. "Why Do Farrakhan and Co. Target Jews for Calumny." New York Post. 1992.

Broderick, Don, Kranes, Marsha, Nolan, Jim and Phillips, Karen. "Crown Heights Slaying." New York Post. October 30, 1992.

Cohen, Richard. "Hate Night at Howard U." New York Post. 1994.

Cohen, Richard. "Rabbi Brevda Beaten and Robbed." Jewish Press. Date Unknown.

Deinzer, Annette and Myles, Gordon. "Fear in Forest Hills Again" (picture) Western Queens Tribune. 1995.

Fettman, Eric. "Black Anti-Semitism: It's Real." New York Post. 1999.

Freeman, Alan. "Farrakhan Spokesman Stirs Anti-Semitism: It's Real." New York Post. 1999.

Garber, Dr. Howard. "Black Anti-Semitism" New York Post. 1991.

Girgenti Report. "The Days of Rioting in Crown Heights." Jewish Press, 1991.

Hinds, Lester. "Flatbush: Where Fear Rules the Streets." New York Post. 1994.

Hoffman, Shifra. "Excusing the Holocaust." Jewish Press. 1993.

Horowitz, Craig. "The New Anti-Semitism." New York Times. 1992.

Horowitz, Craig. "The Sharpton Generation." New York Magazine. 1994.

Kahane, Rabbi Meir. "Life in These Jewish United States." Jewish Press. 1990.

Landesman, Mark and Potasnik, Rabbi Joseph. "Letters to the Editor." New York Post. 1992.

Mason, Jackie. "The Easiest Victim of Any Oppressor." New York Post. 1994.

Peyser, Andrea. "A Short Trip from '91 Crown Heights to World War 2 Warsaw." New York Post. Date unknown.

Southgate, Minoo and Koch, Edward. "A Rally to Intimidate and Silence." New York Post. Date unknown.

Southgate, Minoo. "Hate Back in Crown Heights." New York Post.

Southgate, Minoo. "The World According to Radio Station WLIB." New York Post. 1992.

Stein, Andrew. "Dialogue No Answer to Lynching." New York Post. Date unknown.

Steinherz, Joseph. "With God's Help." Jewish Press, 1995.

Stern, Moshe. "More Fights in Crown Heights." Jewish Press, 1991.

Tarzik, Jack I. and Stern, Moshe. "Letters to the Editor." Jewish Press. December 11, 1992.

Walinsky, Adam. "Defending Our Own." New York Post. 1994.

ARTICLES - PART 3:

Adelson, Prof. Howard L. "An Incident at the Glenwood Houses." Jewish Press, 1995.

Amsterdam, Diana. "Letters." New York Magazine, 1998.

Arutz Seven News Agency. "Soldiers Allow Attackers to Escape, Rather than Face Trial." Jewish Press, 1999.

Author Unknown. "A Young Tzadik from Our Midst." Jewish Press, September 25, 1998.

Author Unknown. "Firestorm of Violence Rings Hebron's Jews." Jewish Press, March 22, 1997.

Author Unknown. "Massacre of Freddy's in Harlem." Jewish Post of New York, On-Line Edition, 1997.

Author Unknown. "Post Opinion: 'Why did Violence Break Out: What They Said at the March'." New York Post, 1998.

Beres, Louis Rene. "Jewish Self-Hate in the Israeli Left." Jewish Press, 1998.

Benveniste, Shelley. "South Florida (POVERTY)." Jewish Press, January 9, 1998.

Cedar, Joseph. "Why People Run from Neighborhoods." Jewish Press, 1995.

Deinzer, Annette and Gorgon, Myles. "Were They Right? (PICTURE)." Western Queens Tribune, 1995.

Editor. "Anti-Semitism at New Paltz." Source unknown.

Editor. "Kahane Chai Outlawed." Jewish Press, 1995.

Greenberg, Eric J. "No Atoning for Farrakhan (PICTURE)." New York Magazine, 1996.

HaCohen, Meir. "Disappointment in Hebron." Jewish Press, 1997.

Horowitz, Craig. "A Tale of Two Cities (PICTURES)." New York Magazine, 1997.

Kessler, E.J. "Reform Set to Turn Towards Jewish Tradition." Forward, 1998.

Kramer, Hilton. "Times turn a Blind Eye to Black Anti-Semitism (PICTURES)." New York Post, 1995.

Leogrande, Dorine. "Siskel Gives Thumbs Down." Jewish Sentinel, 1997.

Levin, Avrohom. "IDF Officers: We Are Being Turned Into Cannon Fodder." Jewish Press, 1997.

Lewin, Avrohom. "Israelis Worried About Terrorism from It's Arab Citizens." Jewish Press, 1999.

Liebb, Julius. "For Many Jews in Williamsburg, Space for the Children is a Distant Dream." Jewish Press, 1996.

Liebb, Julius. "When Justice Did Not Go Away." Jewish Press, 1992.

Lieberman, Hillel. "Shlomo Liebman and Harel Bin-Nun Murdered at Yitzhar." Jewish Press, 1998.

Lipman, Steve and Levine, Richard. "Daddy's Home (PICTURE)." Jewish Press, 1996.

McConnell, Scott. "Crime: Some Radical Solutions." New York Post, 1992.

McConnell, Scott. "The Conspiracy of Silence." New York Post, 1992.

Miller, Laura. "They Keep a Vigil for a Ride to the Store." New York Post, 1995.

Murtha, Kerry. "Militant Group Furious over Jefferies Visit." Staten Island Advance, 1998.

Narrett, Eugene. "Who's Guarding the Promised Land?" Outpost, 1998.

Noel, Peter. "Blood Brother." New York Magazine, 1998.

Peil, Michael. "Long Island Railroad Murder." Internet: source unknown, December 21, 1997.

Porush, Menachem. "As I See It." Jewish Press, February, 1999.

Porush, Menachem. "A Letter to Bielin." Jewish Press, 1999.

Rapfogel, William E. "Jewish Poverty." Jewish Press, date unknown.

Reich, Aaron. "Israeli Far-Right Ex-MK Meir Kahane Assassinated in NYC 31 Years Ago."

The Jerusalem Post | JPost.com, 5 Nov. 2021

Rosenblum, Johnathan. "Orthodox Bashing Yossi Sarid...and Secular Hypocrites." Jewish Press, date unknown.

Shifren, Nachum. "Letter of the Month (Kahane)." Judean Voice, 1968.

Shulman, Chava N. "Leah Cohen: A Portrait of Compassion." Jewish Press, 1999.

Southgate, Minoo. "Al Sharpton Caught Playing with Matches." Jewish Press, 1995.

Southgate, Minoo. "Diversion, Denial as Threats Escalate." New York Post, 1994.

Stone-Katz, Adam. "Jews are Divided on Issue of Gun Ownership." Jewish Sentinel, 1998.

Thomas, Cal. "The Legacy of Labor's Secret Diplomacy (PICTURE)." Los Angeles Times Syndicate and Zionism Today, 1996.

Torossian, Ronn D. and Maoz, Moshe. "First Person Report on Million Man March." Jewish Press, 1995.

Weinberg, David. "Dancing Into Oblivion." Jewish Press, 1999.

Wilder, David. "Hebron, Past, Present and Forever." Jewish Press, 2000.

Winston, Emanuel A. "Land for Terror." Jewish Press, 1997.

SONGS
(IN ORDER OF APPEARANCE)

"Bashana Haba'ah." 1990, The Very Best of Israel NMC Music, Ltd. Mailing Address: P.O. Box 14, Holon 58100, Israel.

"Afn Pripitchuk." Workmen's Circle Song Book: Mir Trogen a Gesang.

"Hebrew Liberation Songs." Betar.

"Hatikvah (Israeli National Anthem)." 1990, The Very Best of Israel NMC Music, Ltd. Mailing Address: P.O. Box 14, Holon 58100, Israel.

"Yiskor." 1990, The Very Best of Israel NMC Music, Ltd. Mailing Address: P.O. Box 14, Holon 58100, Israel. Telephone: 035337730.

"A Special Man." 1993, Ya'didit Productions Hyperstudio, West Hempstead, New York. Telephone (212) 360-7477.

SPECIAL ACKNOWLEDGEMENTS:

"Rabbi Meir Kahane: His Life and Thoughts – 2 Volumes" – Mrs. Rabbi Kahane

Those Who Cannot Remember The Past Are Condemned To Repeat It.

— George Satayana

Part 1

ETHNIC CLEANSING

SCHOOLS

Scene 1

1968: RABBI KAHANE APPEARS.

KAHANE:

I'm sure you've all heard of me, the notorious rabbi, and head of the outrageous Jewish Defense League. Of course, you're asking, "Why, in America, of all places, the land of the free, do Jews or anyone else, need their own defense?" And the answer? That I am either out of control or quite mad. Our story begins in 1967, when I became editor of the Jewish Press, a large Anglo-Jewish newspaper with 160,000 readers, telling me about incidents I never read about in the general press.

WOMAN'S VOICE READING A LETTER HE IS HOLDING.

WOMAN:

My daughter attends junior high school in the Bronx where Black hoodlums are bused in and abuse her daily. I have had to protect her personally. Busing may benefit them, but what's in it for us?

KAHANE:

I can barely believe this. A racist, perhaps.

HE OPENS ANOTHER LETTER. A LEAFLET FALLS OUT. A VOICE OF A BLACK IS HEARD READING THE LEAFLET.

VOICE:

It is impossible for Middle East murderers of colored people to undo the years of brainwashing and self-hatred that has been taught to our black children by these bloodsucking exploiters and murderers, our Jewish teachers.

KAHANE:

Well, there's always a nut in every group.

A FLOOD OF LETTERS IS PLUNKED ON HIS DESK BY HIS SECRETARY. HE READS THROUGHOUT THE NIGHT. IN THE MORNING, HE SHOWS THE SECRETARY SOME OF THE LETTERS.

SECRETARY:

I'll call our major Jewish organizations.

MAN:
(ON PHONE WITH KAHANE)

The position of the American Jewish Congress is that these things have a tendency to die out.

KAHANE:
(ON PHONE TO ANOTHER MAN)

The American Jewish Committee is to be informed that I'm putting an ad in the paper calling for activism. We can no longer sit on our hands. Your members are welcome to attend the meeting.

MAN:

Alarmist! Anybody who thinks like that is crazy!

KAHANE OPENS ANOTHER LETTER. A LEAFLET FALLS OUT.

VOICE OF A BLACK:
(SAYING WORDS IN LEAFLET)

The only persons who can teach our children are African American brothers and sisters, not our so-called liberal Jewish friends.

KAHANE:
(TO SECRETARY)

Take an ad. All capitals. MEETING: WE NEED MILITANT JEWS TO CONFRONT MILITANT BLACKS.

(HE CHECKS THE CALENDAR.)

Eh...next Sunday.

SECRETARY:

A little strong, I'm thinking.

KAHANE:

I want the <u>crazies</u>.

SECRETARY WALKS AWAY, STUNNED.

REPORTER:
(ON TV)

A huge audience filled the auditorium at PS 19 today; teachers, principals and parents came to air their complaints.

A MEETING IS IN PROGRESS IN THE AUDITORIUM.

WHITE MAN:
(RISING)

I'm a school teacher and I've been beaten and threatened by militant blacks because I'm a Jew.

BLACK MAN:

He lies! A few harmless leaflets handed out, that's all.

KAHANE:

Like, for instance, this one put out by the Society for Liberation of the Black Man in America...

BLACK MAN:

"...We know now from your tricky, deceitful maneuvers that the Jew is our real enemy, and he is responsible for the serious educational retardation of the black children."

WHITE MAN:

We are all here, Jews and Negroes, to find a way to heal wounds. This man may not be all wrong. We should be willing to hear the other point of view.

ANOTHER WHITE MAN:

I'm here representing the Teacher's Union and I tell you we struggled hard to get where we are, took hard exams to get a job no one else wanted, low pay and miserable conditions cause no one else wanted us...not even the phone company. And, if I say so myself, we did a fantastic job.

BLACK MAN WHO HAS BEEN SHOUTING "GET OUT AND SHUT UP!" THROUGHOUT THE ABOVE SPEECH RISES.

BLACK MAN:

Stay off! Stay out! Stop teaching Negro children or continue to do so at risk for your lives! The Black community is enraged, you hear?

WHITE MAN:
(POINTING TO BLACK MAN)

I want that man arrested!

BLACK MAN:

Get off our backs or your relatives in the Middle East will find themselves giving benefits to raise money to help you!

(TO OTHER BLACKS)

Those with me?

ALL BLACKS RAISE THEIR HANDS.

KAHANE:

You must learn to defend yourselves. Those with me!

SILENCE IN THE HALL. SOME RAISE THEIR HANDS. OTHERS LEAVE. SOME TAKE NO SIDE.

JOHN LINDSAY:

If I am elected mayor, I promise I will work towards giving you, the parents, the power to control your neighborhood school and give your children the education they deserve. The Central

Board in it's ivory tower, miles away from all of you, must be decentralized, it's power given to you, who know best what is happening in your school on your street.

AUDIENCE MEMBER:

Don't listen to him. He's a liar! Democrat mayors never did nuthin', so you expect sumthin' from a Republican?

ONE MONTH LATER.

NEWSPAPER HEADLINE:

> "BLACKS CROSS PARTY LINES TO ELECT REPUBLICAN. LINDSAY WAS FIRST CANDIDATE TO ATTACK THE POWER OF THE BOARD OF EDUCATION, BLAMING THEM FOR THE PROBLEMS BLACK CHILDREN FACE IN SCHOOLS."

KAHANE:
(NARRATING)

Like the story of the blind men and the elephant. Each one touched him in a different place and thought that one spot was what he looked like. Maybe, as Mayor, he'll see the whole elephant.

(AUDIENCE APPLAUDS AND CHEERS.)

Scene 2

HOST ON A RADIO PROGRAM.

HOST:

With us today are Mr. Hatchett, public school teacher, Mr. Bundy, Chairman of the Ford Foundation Committee studying the quality of education we are offering our Negro children, and Rabbi Kahane.

HATCHETT:
(A BLACK TEACHER)

Our schools are colonies and Negro children are slaves in that colony, enduring genocide in white schools. They have full dictatorial control, with no regard for our sensibilities.

BUNDY:

The tyranny of the central Board of Education must be broken. We have a plan to decentralize: put educational power in your communities, Mr. Hatchett. The media and legislators are already supporting us. The local board will have complete control over curriculum, policy, and teachers. JHS 271, in Ocean Hill, Brownsville, Brooklyn, will serve as an experiment. Equitable treatment for white teachers and Negro children will be our goal.

KAHANE:
(TO BUNDY)

The racists in the Black Power movement can hardly wait. Where now, Hatchett can be fired for anti-Semitism. With your plan, Mr. Bundy, he would escape criticism, and be approved for a racist school program by an anti-Semite on his local school board.

BUNDY:
(TO KAHANE)

I understand now what Mr. Hatchett means by Negro people being completely misunderstood by us and worse, a callous indifference to their plight. Their concern for their people Rabbi, is not necessarily an assault on yours...or mine.

KAHANE:

I quote from Herman Ferguson, a potential Board member.

VOICE OF FERGUSON:

A black survival curriculum for Negro children: Math problems focus on mathematical considerations involved in firing, repairing, and making weapons. The Black student will know exactly where his battlefield is.

(BACK TO KAHANE)

KAHANE:

Indeed, he will. The front line will be the white taxpayer. The enemy will be you, Mr. Bundy, who created the plan, our Mayor Lindsay, who backs it, and the liberal, white middle class, who so righteously push it, in mad disregard of any sense of self-preservation. Have they ever thought how many of them would be hired by Ferguson?

BUNDY:

A few ravings are not typical utterances of our Negro community. Our first experiment in decentralization is the district known as Ocean Hill, Brownsville in Brooklyn, consisting of eight schools, six elementary and two junior highs. The governing board elected by the parents consisted of nine parents, a priest, a minister, and a teenage youth.

KAHANE:

The question that leaps to mind is when had Bundy ever spent one moment in a classroom or put foot in a school, centralized or not? The first act of the Governing Board was the appointment of Rhody McCoy, notorious racist and Jew hater, as superintendent of the District. He was Assistant Principal for eighteen years in a special school for disruptive students, a category he fought bitterly, claiming it was racist and the teacher's fault that they were destroying education in a regular school.

Scene 3

FIVE MONTHS LATER.

REPORTER:
(ON TV)

A public hearing will be held tomorrow at the Board of Education to discuss removing the powers of that Board.

FOLLOWING DAY:

OUTSIDE THE BUILDING MARKED "BOARD OF EDUCATION," A BLACK WOMAN IS DISTRIBUTING HANDBILLS IN THE STREET, WHICH READ: "AMERICAN TAX MONEY IS BEING DIRECTED FROM BLACK COMMUNITIES TO AID ISRAEL." IN THE HALL, A GROUP IS SITTING AT THE PODIUM.

A MAN GOES TO THE MICROPHONE. HE IS TALKING TO A LARGE AUDIENCE OF BLACKS.

MAN:

We all know why we're here, so I just want to introduce those on the podium, seven members from the Board of Education. On my right, Mr. Shanker, president of the Teacher's Union. On my left (BOOS & APPLAUSE) Superintendent of Schools Bernard Donovan.

HE RISES TO BOOS AND APPLAUSE.

SHANKER:

I'm here representing the Jewish teachers and I must begin by saying (HOLDS UP HANDBILL) this has no place...

BLACKS IN AUDIENCE:
(SHOUTING)

Get outta here!

JEERS AND DERIVISE HANDCLAPPING.

SHANKER:

I can't get a fair hearing in here.

HE STORMS OFF THE STAGE. BERNARD DONOVAN TAKES THE MICROPHONE. AUDIENCE TAUNTING AND JEERING.

BLACK MAN:
(JUMPING ON THE PODIUM)

The community, you out there, has just been declared in control of the schools. Come up here and give us your vote, whether you want this honky in or out!

DONOVAN:

This is anarchy and chaos. No educational system will survive this!

JEERING AND DERISIVE CLAPPING FROM THE AUDIENCE. PEOPLE STEP UP TO THE PODIUM AND ARE GIVEN PAPERS WHILE DONOVAN IS STILL TRYING TO TALK. BLACK MAN ON THE PODIUM IS HANDED A NOTE.

BLACK MAN:

200 people have voted for your dismissal. Out!!!

DONOVAN LOOKS TO BOARD MEMBERS WHO SIT SILENT. HE WALKS OUT, TALKING TO THEM.

You can fire me if you want, but they can't. I won't take this abuse. You're being led by mob rule. Not me.

(TO SHANKER)

Good luck, Mr. Shanker. Watch your back.

(DONOVAN LEAVES)

SHANKER:
(TO AUDIENCE)

Decentralization in Ocean Hill, Brownsville has already resulted in chaos, corruption, and political patronage.

AUDIENCE MEMBER:

Shut up!

SHANKER:

Nineteen Jewish teachers were illegally fired by the local board, and I urge the City Board to return these teachers.

AUDIENCE MEMBER:

Your time is up!

SHANKER:

The case against them was never publicly aired. Charges were also leveled against non-Jewish and Black teachers but dropped.

RISING ROAR THROUGHOUT HIS SPEECH TO DROWN HIM OUT. HE SHOUTS LOUDER.

Though the Jewish teachers have been cleared of all charges by an examiner, the local Board has refused to allow them to return to work.

AUDIENCE MEMBER:

Send the pigs to the slaughterhouse!

KAHANE:
(NARRATING)

And the media is silent.

MAYOR LINDSAY:
(NARRATING)

As your mayor, I can assure you I have pushed the plan to centralize the schools. Teachers will be protected. The name Lindsay will go down in the history of this city as one of correcting injustices, harmony, peace and understanding between us.

THE SIGN ON THE SCHOOL BUILDING READS "CLARA BARTON HIGH SCHOOL." A BLACK MOB RUNNING IN THE HALL STOPS AT THE DOOR MARKED "PRINCIPAL'S OFFICE." THEY STORM IN, ASSAULTING HER AND TWO TEACHERS. POLICE ARRIVE AND THEY FIGHT THE POLICE.

FOLLOWING DAY:

ON SCREEN:

> "BLACK JUVENILES INVADE A CLASSROOM, BEAT TEACHERS AND LOCK ONE IN A CLOSET."
>
> "LOWER EAST SIDE: MOBS ROAM THIS LARGELY RELIGIOUS, JEWISH AREA, KNOCKED DOWN BEARDED JEWS AND STEALING FROM STORES WITH BEARDED JEWS."

                    KAHANE:
                  (NARRATING)

The media is silent.

"A HIGH SCHOOL IN LAURELTON, QUEENS. A DOOR MARKED "MR GOLDSTEIN, PRINCIPAL." A LETTER IS SLIPPED UNDER HIS DOOR BY A BLACK JUVENILE WHO FLEES AND DISAPPEARS IN A CROWD OF STUDENTS IN THE HALL."

                    PRINCIPAL:
          (OPENS LETTER AND READS IT.)

Do you know what it feels like to have your daughter raped?

THE PRINCIPAL DROPS THE LETTER IN TERROR.

THE FOLLOWING DAY: A BOMB EXPLODES IN THE SCHOOL AND BLACK STUDENTS HANG A SWATISKA IN THE SCHOOL HALL.

                    SHANKER:
                  (NARRATING)

The Teacher's Union will strike if the nineteen teachers are not <u>reinstated.</u>

BLACK MAN:
(NARRATING)

Rap Brown sayin' the Panther's strikin' if they are. Get your guns, brothers, stop smokin' your reefers and use your money to buy guns.

FOLLOWING DAY: BOARD OF EDUCATION MEETING.

CHAIRMAN:
(ADDRESSING BOARD)

The Mayor feels our resistance to decentralization in increasing tensions. He asks for our approval of his plan citywide. Those opposed?

(NO HANDS RAISED EXCEPT ONE.)

OPPOSING BOARD MEMBER:

The Jewish teachers should strike back and demand our protection, defend themselves: the JDL, the police, the Army, the National Guard, if necessary... not be in the hands of local assassins masquerading as "Educators."

CHAIRMAN:

We are still a city under the rule of law.

OPPOSING BOARD MEMBER:

Which one of you would volunteer to stand in a classroom under protection of that law...the mayor's law? Terrorists running the schools. Teachers, principals, and students cowed. A deafening silence from him. It pays to avoid showdowns when you have one thought in mind...1600 Pennsylvania Avenue. He knows what the Jew-hating racists want...not decentralization at all...but a complete takeover. To quote one of their spokesmen: "I have a dream...that all Whitey textbooks be burned."

NO HANDS RAISED.

ANOTHER BOARD MEMBER:

Lindsay has prevented more bloodshed.

OPPOSING BOARD MEMBER:

His silence has meant to them an agreement with their obscenities, so, of course, they grow bolder and more menacing. Besides, we all know Jews can't win against Blacks, because they don't even know there's a battle going on, afraid to know, don't want to know...what every Black knows now. Decentralization in...Jews out.

CHAIRMAN:

Like the mayor says, this is not a Black-Jewish problem.

OPPOSING BOARD MEMBER:

Tell that to the Jewish teacher who was in the hospital with twenty stitches on her face, after a promising Black student uttered such wisdoms as "Get the Jew" and smashed it in.

CHAIRMAN:

She may have provoked him.

OPPOSING MEMBER:

You know, Mr. Goldfarb, the mayor makes more sense when he's silent. You might follow his example. Mostly Jews here. I ask now for another vote on the mayor's plan.

CHAIRMAN:

Those opposed?

ALL HANDS RAISED.

A WEEK LATER: IN COURT. TEACHERS, BLACK PRINCIPAL, BLACK JUDGE AND CHAIRMAN OF BOARD OF EDUCATION.

JUDGE:

After careful study, I find the defendants not guilty and see no objection to their return to work.

BLACK PRINCIPAL:

As principal of the school, I want a record to show that I protest this decision!

TEACHERS REJOICE. BLACK PRINCIPAL STORMS OUT.

A WEEK LATER:

KAHANE:

Mayor Lindsay appoints five new members to the Board of Education, including Reverend

Galamison, racist and Jew Hater. And lo and behold, the Board changed overnight in favor of decentralization, sharing its powers, approving its own demise and perhaps the school system along with it.

FOLLOWING DAY. UFT HALL. MAYOR, SHANKER, REV. OLIVER (BLACK) AND CROWD OF BLACKS AND WHITES IN HALL.

SHANKER:

Teacher's Union strikes Ocean Hill. Until the legitimate rights of its members are restored, and the experiment is over, I'm pulling 500 teachers out of the District.

BLACK IN AUDIENCE:
(SHOUTING)

You are a racist Zionist! We will not stand with you while you ruthless Zionist bandits and your puppets, the police, control our schools!

SHANKER:

How dare you! I came out fighting in the Army to fight for you, beginning with Illinois 1946! I fought to integrate restaurants and movie theatres by staging sit-ins and demonstrations. In New York, I fought to integrate pools on my summer vacations from college, and organized marches in Montgomery and Selma. Thousands of Union teachers joined a Civil Rights march on Washington in 1963 and contributed $40,000 to Dr. King's campaign in 1965. The time for action is now! A teacher in Brownsville endured a common experience...

FLASHBACK: A MALE TEACHER IS SEEN TRYING TO CLOCK IN. HE SEARCHES FOR HIS CARD AND IS SURROUNDED BY BLACK TEACHERS.

BLACK TEACHER:
(TO WHITE TEACHER)

We non-union. Teach as good as you or better. We sayin' the United Jew Union gotta go! Ya hear me loud and clear, Grossman?

HE RUNS AWAY SHAKEN. BACK TO PRESENT.

>SHANKER:

He hasn't taught a class yet this year.

>BLACK AUDIENCE MEMBER:
>(SHOUTING)

And he ain't gonna!

FLASHBACK: SCHOOL. A BLACK TEACHER BECKONS TO A GROUP OF BLACK STUDENTS IN HALL.

>BLACK TEACHER:

You goin' into Mr. Grossman's class. Whatever he tells you, do something else, y'hear?

STUDENTS ENTER GROSSMAN'S CLASS AND CREATE BEDLAM WHILE HE IS DESPERATELY TRYING TO TEACH.

BACK TO PRESENT IN THE HALL.

>BLACK AUDIENCE MEMBER:
>(SHOUTING)

Reverend Oliver! You should be ashamed, sitting there agreeing with them racists!

>REVEREND OLIVER:
>(JUMPING IN)

Lies! All lies! He knows a beautiful educational program has been established at Ocean Hill!

>SHANKER:

Teachers fearing for their lives, inexperienced ones in front of classrooms with half the student body absent. Beautiful?!

>MAYOR:

We must understand that the damage we've inflicted...well...there are consequences to be borne.

SHANKER:

Sociological pap! When will you begin to act like a mayor?! Sworn to uphold the law!

MAYOR:

The quality of mercy is not strained.

SHANKER:

But your credibility is. Under normal school conditions, the tormentors of Mr. Grossman would have been charged with conduct unbecoming a teacher and dismissed from the school system, not still at work and continuing their obnoxious activities. A full account by Board of Ed. Observers of disruption and terrorism by outsiders and non-union teachers at Ocean Hill is still being withheld by them. Doesn't the public have a right to know what happened at that school?!

KAHANE:
(NARRATING)

The media is silent.

MAYOR:

Teachers have sworn a committee to their students and have a responsibility to serve as an example to the young law and order.

SHANKER:

Herman Ferguson, the Black Anti-Semite will be principal of Ocean Hill, Brownsville, as soon as he escapes the annoyance of a conviction for conspiracy to murder...an excellent moral example our young. Your sudden passion for law and order seems to have found...me.

MAYOR:

You'll be arrested and jailed.

. . .

A WEEK LATER: CONEY ISLAND SECTION OF BROOKLYN...PS 288. GROUP BREAKS INTO THE SCHOOL AND REFUSES TO LEAVE. POLICE ARRIVE.

>WHITE PRINCIPAL:
>(TO COPS)

These people have to be removed.

>POLICEMAN:

We have to call the Central Board for permission.

HE CALLS AND HANDS THE PHONE TO THE PRINCIPAL.

>BOARD MEMBER:
>(TO PRINCIPAL)

We've advised the police they have to use their own judgment.

>POLICEMAN:
>(TO OTHER POLICEMEN)

That's it, men.

>(TO PRINCIPAL)

Sorry.

THEY LEAVE.

HEADLINE: "SHANKER JAILED."

Scene 4

MAYOR RECEIVES A GROUP OF RABBIS IN HIS OFFICE.

RABBI:

You must do something to relieve this tension and restore peace and dignity.

MAYOR:

Rabbi Hecht, I called this meeting to ask you to control Albert Shanker and the UFT.

RABBI:

Do you ask Cardinal Spellman to control heads of unions who are Catholic? Many Blacks are paid with city funds working for so-called "anti-poverty" agencies and use our tax money to buy guns to kill our merchants. Ask Reverend Oliver to control them. We're being robbed, assaulted, and murdered.

MAYOR:

You Jews have made me use up all my Negro credit cards. You're destroying my administration.

(TO KAHANE)

I didn't invite you.

KAHANE:

Your invitation said "Rabbis" and that's what I am. Yesterday, I received a frantic phone call from Springfield Gardens High School in Queens.

FLASHBACK: SIGN ON THE DOOR IN SCHOOL, "OFFICE OF PRINCIPAL, MR. ROSENBLUM." A ROCK IS THROWN THROUGH THE GLASS WINDOW OF THE DOOR. HE OPENS THE DOOR IN SHOCK. A BLACK JUVENILE AT THE DOOR.

BLACK JUVENILE:
(TO PRINCIPAL)

If you want to be alive, don't come to school tomorrow.

MAN COMES OUT OF ADJOINING DOOR MARKED "ASSISTANT PRINCIPAL." THE JUVENILE THROWS A LEAFLET IN HIS FACE.

ASSISTANT PRINCIPAL:
(READING LEAFLET)

"Dirty Jewish pig. You'll be sent home in a pine box."

BACK TO PRESENT.

LINDSAY:

Attacks against Jews are not anti-Semitic in essence, but anti-white.

KAHANE:

Do you admit Jews are victims of Black militants?

LINDSAY:

They are only reacting to the exploitation and suffering heaped onto them.

KAHANE:

You don't have to teach us about suffering, yet no one need fear us in the dead of night.

MAYOR:

A yellow truck, in addition to our fleet, has been assigned to Springfield Gardens High School to prevent violence be enabling the police to arrest more perpetrators.

BOMBS THROWN FROM THE ROOF OF THE HIGH SCHOOL HIT THE YELLOW TRUCK.

Scene 5

ON SCREEN: PS 20...LOCAL BOARD IS MEETING IN FRONT OF AN AUDIENCE ON THE LOWER EAST SIDE IN THE AUDITORIUM OF THE SCHOOL. BOARD MEMBERS ARE ON THE STAGE AROUND A TABLE...THEY ARE WHITE.

ONE MEMBER ADDRESSING ANOTHER (WHITE):

Miss Rakow, it's been suggested we should replace you as Superintendent with a Puerto Rican which reflects the majority of this community. I suggest Mr. Fuentes...

ANOTHER BOARD MEMBER:

I insist we consider him along with other candidates. It's only fair...

A GROUP OF BLACKS TAKE POSITIONS ON THE STAGE AND AROUND THE AISLES, TAKE THE MICROPHONES SHOUTING, "WHITE PIGS!"

WHITE BOARD MEMBER:

I think it would be beneficial...

BLACK MAN:

Up with black power!

WHITE BOARD MEMBER:

If you would only let us...

BLACK MAN:

...We'll kill you if you don't get out!

WHITE BOARD MEMBER:
(PLEADING)

We're only trying to...

BLACK MAN:

Get on outta here!

BOARD LEAVES.

FOLLOWING MORNING.

ON SCREEN: BOARD ATTEMPTS MEETING AT SEWARD PARK HIGH SCHOOL.

BOARD MEMBERS IN FRONT OF AN AUDIENCE. A GROUP OF BLACKS IN NATIONALIST GARB WALK UP AND DOWN THE AISLE, TALKING TO THE AUDIENCE.

BLACKS:
(SHOUTING)

You gonna let that white pig Rakow decide your child's life?

BLACKS & PUERTO RICANS IN AUDIENCE:
(SHOUTING)

No!

WHITES IN THE AUDIENCE:
(SHOUTING)

And who you calling pig?

BLACK:

(IN AUDIENCE)

Rakow is a white pig who stole money from the government. Nothing but a thief!

WHITES IN AUDIENCE:
(SHOUTING)

She is not!

BLACKS:
(SHOUTING)

She is so!

BOARD MEMBERS:
(TO OTHER MEMBERS)

Who do we want? Let's have a quiet vote.

EACH ONE SAYS "FUENTES" AS HE GOES FROM ONE TO THE OTHER.

BLACK MAN:
(JUMPS ON STAGE)

Fuentes...our new Superintendent!

CHEERS FROM AUDIENCE.

TWO DAYS LATER:

A BLACK MOB INVADES RAKOW'S OFFICE.

BLACK (IN MOB):
(SHOUTING)

You still here?!

RAKOW'S OFFICE IS DEMOLISHED. SHE AND THE OFFICE STAFF ARE TERRIFIED. THEY FLEE.

ON SCREEN: GROUP OF BLACKS INVADE OFFICE OF THE SUPERINTENDENT OF THE DISTRICT.

BLACK MAN IN GROUP:
(TO SUPERINTENDENT)

We want you to know, Superintendent Rosenberg, that we're sending you to the ovens.

FOLLOWING DAY. ROSENBERG AT HOME. HIS PHONE RINGS. A MESSAGE GIVEN ON THE PHONE. CALLER HANGS UP, CALLS AGAIN, REPEATS MESSAGE. GOES ON ALL DAY, EVERY MINUTE.

CALLER ON THE PHONE:
(THREATENING)

You're destroying the community. Get out or there'll be blood in the streets!

ROSENBERG CALLS POLICE. A FEW MOMENTS LATER, A KNOCK AT THE DOOR.

POLICEMAN:

The parent-teacher association is going through this every day. Some members have asked for and received police protection.

KAHANE:
(NARRATING)

And the media is silent.

AN OFFICE BUILDING IN MANHATTAN. BLACK GROUP MARCHES DOWN THE HALL AND ENTERS ONE OF THE CONFERENCE ROOMS.

ONE OF GROUP:
(TO OTHERS)

We're setting up our own school right here in this building and telling the Jew Principals they're fired.

THEY NAIL A FLYER ON THE WALL IN THE HALL.

FLYER: MEETING OF SCHOOL BOARD THIS MORNING. QUIET PLEASE.

Scene 6

KAHANE RECEIVES A LETTER.

          KAHANE:
          (READING)

The hush things going on around our school could make some startling headlines.

    FLASHBACK OF INCIDENTS LETTER IS DESCRIBING: A WHITE GROUP IN A ROOM AT A MEETING. A BLACK GROUP SUDDENLY ENTERS.

          LEADER OF BLACK GROUP:
          (TO WHITE GROUP)

Okay. The board meeting's over. Empty them chairs of your "you know what." We're taking them over. There's the door and be quick about it.

LEADER SNAPS HIS FINGERS. HE HURLS THEIR PAPERS OUT THE DOOR AND THEY SCRAMBLE FOR THEIR THINGS. ONE BOARD MEMBER PUTS HIS HAND IN HIS POCKET. BLACK MILITANT DRAWS HIS GUN AND BOARD MEMBER PULLS OUT A PENCIL TO MARK A PAPER HE TOOK FROM THE FLOOR.

          ANOTHER MILITANT:

That wimp ain't gonna fight back.

SECOND MILITANT KICKS HIM. PENCIL FLIES. BLACK CATCHES IT AND MOCKINGLY RETURNS THE PENCIL, WHICH BOARD MEMBER RECEIVES WITH A TREMBLING HAND.

OUTSIDE THE SCHOOL, AS BOARD MEMBER IS LEAVING, A BLACK JUVENILE APPROACHES.

JUVENILE:

You here again, Mr. Bernstein?

JUVENILE BEATS HIM WHILE POLICE STAND BY AND DO NOTHING. ON THE PICKET LINE, A TEACHER IS SPAT UPON. POLICE DO NOTHING.

BLACKS IN CROWD:
(SHOUTING AT TEACHERS)

Hitler didn't live long enough!

TEACHER BENDS HEAD CRYING.

BLACK:

There weren't enough gas chambers!

TEACHER:
(SHOUTING BACK)

You don't really mean that.

BLACK:
(SHOUTING)

UFT teachers hate Negro children. You'll never be back in here.

TEACHER:

You were an honor student thanks to me. How can you forget?

BACK TO PRESENT. KAHANE IS READING LETTER.

LETTER ON SCREEN:

"We need action. Show we're not running in fear." – Anonymous (An NYC teacher)

Scene 7

TEACHERS MEETING WITH SHANKER.

> TEACHER:
> (TO SHANKER)

The weapons used on us on the picket line is daily terrorism and it's taking it's toll. Fear, disgust and we're (PUTS HER HANDS UP) saying "Who needs this?"

> SHANKER:

It must be very evident the short-range benefits to be gained by their breaking the strike is nothing compared to the tragic loss that will be the fate of this city if the racist militants taste blood in the victory.

> MCCOY:
> (TO TEACHERS ON THE PICKET LINE)

I'm putting Mr. Shanker on notice that I'm hiring 500 new teachers to replace the strikers.

> TEACHER:
> (TO ANOTHER TEACHER)

How will we feed our children?

Scene 8

KAHANE:
(NARRATING)

Unfortunately, teachers will have to desert principle for pocketbook as time goes by. There must be a groundswell of indignation, but with the media looking the other way, who will know? Who will feel our pain, the danger that awaits us all?

HEADLINE:

SHANKER RELEASED FROM JAIL.

SHANKER AND THE MAYOR IN LINDSAY'S OFFICE.

LINDSAY:
(TO SHANKER)

I've found a solution. The strike, you can say, is over. Teachers will return to work, not as teachers, but as clerks.

SHANKER:

I'm going back to jail!

LINDSAY:

Your people are hurting. You are in no position to set conditions.

SHANKER:

I've arranged for help with other unions. And we ask for the same benefits as men who collect garbage...the privilege of being sick a few days a year without losing pay, an increase in our starvation wages, and the control and discipline of those who are putting our lives at risk...or else, the unions close the city down!

HE LEAVES.

A WEEK LATER: MAYOR AND SHANKER MEET AGAIN.

LINDSAY:

I agree to have teachers return as teachers with increased benefits, safety and dignity. Above all,

we want a united city. I've worked out an agreement: 19 teachers to be restored to their positions and all teachers will be assured of the protection of their legal rights.

SHANKER:

Not enough. I demand that several teachers and administrators, whose names I have here, be charged with harassment.

LINDSAY:

I'd rather not.

SHANKER GETS UP TO LEAVE.

LINDSAY:

Give me the list.

SHANKER HANDS LINDSAY THE LIST.

SHANKER:
(TO PRESS)

The strike is over. Teachers are returning to work.

20 MILITANT BLACKS LINE UP IN FRONT OF SCHOOL. ALL HAVE MILITANT NEGRO HAIRDOS. TEACHERS ARE GOING IN.

> BLACKS:
> (SHOUTING)

Get those dirty Jews out of school!

> ANOTHER BLACK:
> (SHOUTING)

Don't let those Jew bastards in the school to destroy our children!

RUMBLING THROUGHOUT THE CROWD.

Let's go get the Jews! Watch them run! We don't want Jews in our schools!

NEGRO DEPUTY INSPECTOR MOVES TO HELP TEACHERS, MILITANT BLOCKS THEM.

> MILITANT:
> (SHOUTING AT DEPUTY INSPECTOR)

You ain't nuthin' but a dirty Jew nigger!

THE INSPECTOR IGNORES THEM, GETS MILITANTS AWAY FROM TEACHERS. POLICE ESCORT TEACHERS INTO THE SCHOOL.

> BLACK MILITANTS:
> (SHOUTING)

We know where you live, Jew, and we're gonna get you!

> MAN:
> (NARRATING)

I am a non-Jew who was standing outside JHS 271 the day the strike ended. Teachers were returning from lunch and were handed a memo...

WE SEE THE MEMO.

"To all Jew teachers, from your employer, the community. We want you out. Make no mistake about that."

> MAN:
> (NARRATING)

I have never seen such vicious anti-Semitic hate, not much Black against White, as Black against Jew.

LATER: PRINCIPAL'S OFFICE. MILITANTS ARE MEETING WITH HIM. THE PRINCIPAL IS BLACK.

> PRINCIPAL:

Don't worry. We'll get rid of them. They'll soon be asking for a voluntary transfer.

> MILITANT:

We're gonna wait for them kikes to make up their minds. That's no control, man.

> PRINCIPAL:

Let me finish. I didn't say we wouldn't be helping them along. They'll be finding some nice notes under their lesson plans to put a shiver through their spines and that's only the beginning. A good dose of humiliation...and...with your help, plenty of terror, and those cowards will be running...Wherever they run, they'll find us.

> KAHANE:
> (NARRATING)

The media is silent, the UFT is silent, the Mayor...silent. "The new plans needed time," they said. And I knew...there was no time.

> NOTE ON SCREEN: THE JEWISH TEACHERS WERE ALL TRANSFERRED OUT, AND IT WAS INDICATED ON THEIR RECORD THAT, THE TRANSFERS WERE "VOLUNTARY."

Scene 9

MAYOR LINDSAY, BUNDY, KAHANE AND A BLACK ON TV.

LINDSAY:
(TO KAHANE)

I ask that the Jews help Blacks through a sense of justice. Help them get jobs and we'll all have peace and security...in tandem with my efforts.

KAHANE:

No Jew can condemn this appeal. However, we too, have a list of grievances. Your appeal is being made to a group that has helped more than any other... which you never mentioned, Black anti-Semitism, which you never mentioned, and an appeal to Black leadership to condemn Jew hate among their people, which you never made.

LINDSAY:

I will be discussing our plan to lessen tensions with them and their people as I'm doing with you and yours.

KAHANE:

Ask them to direct their sense of justice to school anti-Semitism, their sense of justice to the high rate if physical assaults, robbery, and murder visited on us by black hoodlums. We do not need you to teach us justice and charity. We practiced this before you and will do us after. We ask further that you direct this appeal to yourself on our behalf.

BLACK:

Since the Jews are out, Rabbi, educational genocide has come to an end. We now have a great learning climate at Ocean Hill schools.

KAHANE:

With the turmoil that reigns in JHS 271, I find this very doubtful. At any rate, you refer to a school that had above-average reading scores, honors for mathematical achievement, national medals for the school's various publications, a symphony orchestra, music scholarships and community leadership heaping praise on the school. You dare help yourselves to our horror! I protest the use of the word "genocide" for low reading scores...even if such was the case. You should be ashamed, Mr. Bundy, for what you have caused.

BUNDY:

How dare you! When we made our decentralization proposal, we were in liaison with a group at Ocean Hill who did not bring their plan for community control before us at all. Press, radio and TV were inundated by a small group saying the children had to be saved. We never knew the full story 'til now. It was never told. An educational system that took 200 years to build has crumbled. We've been duped.

Scene 10

KAHANE:
(NARRATING)

The peace and security for which we have all been yearning…well…let's see now…

FLASHBACK: BROOKLYN. BANDS OF HUNDREDS OF YOUTHS RACE THROUGH THE STREETS ENTERING VARIOUS SCHOOLS. THEY VANDALIZE, SMASH AND TERRORIZE. THEY TEAR THROUGH SUBWAY STATIONS AND CARS, RIPPING APART SEATS AND CAUSING DESTRUCTION OF SERVICES ON THE BMT BY PULLING EMERGENCY CORDS.

LEAFLET ON SCREEN:

"Jews are ruthless, racist Zionist bandits. Shanker is a racist Zionist, and we will not stand by while the ruthless Zionist bandits run us out of our communities. Zionists kill black people in their own land in the Middle East." – Jesse Grey

KAHANE:
(NARRATING)

Despite this, Jesse was placed on the city payroll, is connected with a community association that caters to the Lower East Side and was set up by none other than Sid Davidoff.

BLACK:
(NARRATING)

We, the Puerto Rican, and militant Black teachers will be in our schools. I tell you, if Black rhetoric were machine gun bullets, we would be free!

AMERICAN JEWISH CONGRESS SPOKESMAN:
(NARRATING)

The position of the American Jewish Congress is that the militant's views do not represent a significant number of Black people. It'll all go away in time.

KAHANE:
(TO ACJ SPOKESMAN)

A major myth leading to our destruction. For two painful years I have been scorned and vilified for disagreeing with this fantasy by the likes of you.

ACJ SPOKESMAN:

Peace is always a fantasy, and war a reality, to the likes of you.

KAHANE:

The young Black under 30, the Black intellectual on campus...these count the most, and these follow the anti-Semites...Jesse Gray, Les Campbell, Al Vann, Sonny Carson, and Herman Ferguson...militants who are far closer to the masses than the Whitney Youngs and Roy Wilkinses. Gray, Ferguson and 17 other militants were convicted of an attempt to assassinate both moderates. Ferguson to be a principal at Ocean Hill, Brownsville, if not guilty.

FLASHBACK: CAMPBELL TEACHING AN 8TH GRADE CLASS OF BLACK STUDENTS. STUDENT TIMMY JACKSON, AGE 14, IN FRONT OF CLASS.

CAMPBELL:
(TO CLASS)

Ask Timmy questions about our Afro-American heritage and Black power.

PUPIL:

We have leaders like Martin Luther King, and then we have leaders like Malcolm X and Rap Brown, and they tell us to use violence. Who is right?

TIMMY:

Well, I think Martin Luther King is not so good. Whitey don't want to give anything, so we have to fight for it.

FLASHBACK: JESSE GRAY.

GRAY:
(SPEAKING AT RALLY)

I'm calling for a hundred skilled Black revolutionaries ready to die. There is only one thing that can correct our situation and that is guerilla warfare!

ACJ SPOKESMAN:

The strike is over. That is not a myth. We are meeting with Black educators to talk unity. That is not a myth. The desire for peace and harmony between Blacks and Jews, I assure you, is now, as it has ever been, mutual.

KAHANE:

Mr. Orin Hatchett, a Black schoolteacher in the New York City school system, had this to say in an article in "Forum", a Black teacher's magazine.

HATCHETT:

The Black children are being educationally castrated by the Jews. They spell death to the minds and souls of our little ones.

THE FOLLOWING DAY:

HATCHETT ENTERS BUILDING TITLED, "BOARD OF EDUCATION HEADQUARTERS" AND WALKS TO A DOOR ON WHICH IT IS PRINTED, "OFFICE OF THE ADMINISTRATOR." HE ENTERS AND SHAKES THE HAND OF THE MAN BEHIND THE DESK. HE SITS DOWN.

SCENE SWITCHES TO THE SECRETARY IN THE ADJOINING ROOM.

SECRETARY:
(ANSWERING PHONE)

Board of Education, Administrator's office.

KAHANE:
(ON PHONE WITH SECRETARY)

This is Rabbi Kahane. I want to speak to the Administrator about Hatchett's article.

SECRETARY:

Just a moment.

SILENCE. ADMINISTRATOR PICKS UP PHONE.

ADMINISTRATOR:

Y-e-e-s?

KAHANE:

We expect Hatchett to be censured or discharged.

KAHANE HANGS UP.

ADMINISTRATOR:
(TO HATCHETT)

You are strongly advised to cease all racist activities!

HATCHETT:
(MOCKING)

May I go now? Sir?

HE GETS UP TO LEAVE WITHOUT WAITING FOR A REPLY, REACHES THE DOOR AND TURNS.

ADMINISTRATOR:

A memorial for Malcolm X. We hope a for a rational discourse.

HATCHETT:

I'm taking my class.

FLASHBACK:

KAHANE:
(NARRATING)

After Malcolm X's death, allegedly murdered by rivals, his sister offered the following:

MALCOLM X' SISTER:

It is the Jews who will raise money for the Blacks that they seldom get...just a lot of hot air. It's our troubles that pay their high-priced lawyers, and you're a damn fool if you expect justice in their courtroom. They stole Arab land and continue to kill these helpless people off. The Jew will find a new revolution... non-Jew against Jew.

A WEEK LATER: AT QUEENSBORO COMMUNITY COLLEGE, BAYSIDE QUEENS. IN THE LARGE HALL, LARGE PICTURES OF MALCOLM X ON THE WALLS, AND A HUGE SIGN SAYING, "AFRAM SOCIETY" IN FRONT OF THE HALL, WHICH IS FULL OF EIGHTH GRADERS, ALL BLACK.

BLACK ANNOUNCER:

And now, for our final speaker, last but not least...
HATCHETT APPEARS. LOUD APPLAUSE AND CHEERING.

HATCHETT:

What Malcolm say? He say, "Whitey been steppin' on us for too long, killin' us for too long, keepin' us down there for too long, and where we wanna be?"

CHILDREN:

Up there!

HATCHETT:

And who there now? Jew! That's who! We gotta turn things around. We...up there and...
STAMPS FOOT HARD ON GROUND.

Jew down there. Stamp him out like the vermin he is. Let me hear it now...everybody!

Scene 10   43

LOUD STAMPING IS HEARD WHILE HE STILL POUNDS AS THEY FOLLOW HIS BEAT.

> HATCHETT:
> (CHANTING)

MALCOLM! MALCOLM!

> CHILDREN:
> (SHOUTING WITH HATCHETT)

MALCOLM! MALCOLM!

> KAHANE:
> (NARRATING)

The following day, an article appeared in the paper that described the meeting as follows: "The purpose was to bring white and black students close to the issues of racial controversy." The reporter could not contain his shock, however, as he described the proceedings.

HATCHETT IS CALLED TO THE OFFICE OF THE ADMINISTRATOR OF THE BOARD OF EDUCATION.

> ADMINISTRATOR:
> (TO HATCHETT)

You've given us no choice but to order your dismissal.

HANDS HIM THE ARTICLE IN THE WASTEBASKET.

> HATCHETT:

Now, I have something to show you...heh-heh-heh.

ADMINISTRATOR READING. LETTER IS SHOWN ON SCREEN.

> We are happy to advise you that NYU has appointed you as Director of their school's new Martin Luther King, Jr. Afro-American Student Center.

THE ADMINISTRATOR IS STUNNED.

NEWSPAPER ARTICLE ON SCREEN:

> "Some Jewish groups protest the appointment of Hatchett."

KAHANE:
(BITTERLY)

The ACLU, two Jewish professors from NYU, and Victor Solomon, from the Black militant organization CORE, defended Hatchett. I decided to visit NYU's President, James M. Hester.

HESTER:
(TO KAHANE)

Black students and the Jewish radical Left are threatening violence if we rescind the appointment of Hatchett...so we've asked Arthur Goldberg, the best arbiter in the country to decide. After all, a Supreme Court judge, our representative at the UN...what more...

KAHANE:

...So, Goldberg, the court Jew was chosen. He'll find a way to keep Hatchett and you can spare yourself the trouble from any of us by having a Jew suggest the plan.

HESTER:

To quote the Bard, "He'll strut and fret his hour upon the stage and be heard no more."

KAHANE:

To quote Spinoza, "Any fool can find followers."

HESTER:

We will invite disaster, like Columbia University did, if we are not careful.

KAHANE:

A university that flees before racists for fear of being burned down doesn't really deserve to exist.

HESTER:

Jewish teachers are attacked because most of them are Jewish.

KAHANE:

Where is the correlation between one's faith and good or bad teaching? If teachers are good or bad, it's because they are good or bad, not because they are Jews, Irish, or Blacks.

SIX WEEKS LATER: HEADLINE IN PAPER: "NYU RETAINS ANTI-SEMITE."

HESTER:
(TO KAHANE)

Mr. Goldberg's report on the matter of Mr. Hatchett.

KAHANE READS LETTER ON SCREEN.

> Mr. Hatchett strongly denies he is anti-Semitic, though his expressions in his article may be so regarded. I strongly recommend he be retained.

KAHANE STORMS OUT.

HESTER:
(AS KAHANE IS LEAVING)

This ends the matter as far as I'm concerned!

KAHANE:
(NARRATING)

The following day, the Jewish Defense League was launched.

NEWSPAPER ARTICLE ON SCREEN:

> "15 MEMBERS OF JDL IN THE STREETS CARRYING POSTERS AND SHOUTING "FOR SHAME NYU" AND "NO MORE NAZIS AT NYU."

KAHANE:
(NARRATING)

At last, a newspaper article appeared about Jews in the streets protesting for themselves. We created a special group of fighters, which we named the "Chaya" squad. The word "Chaya" in Hebrew means "beast," and we wanted to develop Jewish "beasts" who would frighten the anti-Semite to the roots of his soul...and change the Jewish image in America.

. . .

46   Part 1

SIX MONTHS LATER. HATCHETT IS ON THE PODIUM AT NYU, ADDRESSING BLACK STUDENTS. HESTER IS SEATED AT THE PODIUM.

HATCHETT:
(IN MIDDLE OF SPEECH, SUDDENLY LASHING OUT)

We can't let these mother (BLEEP) whites control our police. The Jew, Albert Shanker, killin' our children, and Jews takin' our money. I say, kill 'em first, together with the guys nominated for President, who'll be controllin' all of us.

AUDIENCE CHEERS.

HESTER RUNS OUT OF THE AUDITORIUM INTO HIS OFFICE. HE IS VERY DISTRAUGHT. HE IS GREETED BY A COLLEAGUE.

HESTER:

700 Black kids in there and he's inflammatory!

COLLEAGUE:

I've already written a Notice of Dismissal.

HESTER:

No...I want the pleasure of telling him. You can send a copy of that letter to Goldberg.

KAHANE:
(NARRATING)

Last week, the Black students of Bernard Baruch branch of City College invited the Black Panthers to present a play that contained the line "Hitler did not burn enough Jews." The line was applauded and cheered. Bernard Baruch College, incidentally, was named after a Jew. Also, invited Sonny Carson as a guest speaker, who urged revolution. I decided to speak to the Provost of the College, Dr. Samuel Thomas. He told the press he would "investigate." I had some ideas of my own.

THOMAS:
(TO KAHANE)

We are still in the process.

KAHANE:

JDL did it's own investigation, ongoing and extensive...and would like to present our findings to the student body. I assume the students knew what type of program would be presented. And you have still not condemned them for inviting such types as these.

THOMAS:

I cannot say. I have no way of knowing that they knew the remarks would be made.

KAHANE:

And no shame, shock, or regret when they did know! You will prevent further occurrences of this kind, of course.

THOMAS:
(SHAKES HEAD NO)

An educational institution is a forum of all people.

KAHANE:

It would seem to me that you could have foreseen this disgraceful behavior from a group that calls itself "The Oppressed People's Theater," and takes pride in oppressing others.

THOMAS:

I could not say.

KAHANE:

Well then, since all the people includes me, I expect an invitation.

THOMAS:
(MOVING AWAY)

In the interest of moderation and avoidance of provocation, I think not.

KAHANE:

Well then, if this type of thing occurs again, I shall appear without invitation!

KAHANE STORMS OUT.

> ON SCREEN: SAN FRANCISCO STATE COLLEGE WRACKED BY BLACK MILITANTS.
>
> BLACK MILITANT TELLS HOWARD STUDENTS, A BLACK COLLEGE, TO ARM THEMSELVES WITH SHOTGUNS. THEY CHEER AND APPLAUD.

> KAHANE:
> (NARRATING)

The rash of college riots were buried in the New York Times and other papers, though property was smashed, opponents beaten, and buildings taken over.

Scene 11

BLACK PEOPLE IN LIVING ROOM LISTENING TO RADIO.

RADIO ANNOUNCER:

Good afternoon, ladies, and gentlemen. WBAI welcomes you to the Julius Lester program. Our guests today are Mr. Leslie Campbell, schoolteacher, and a young lady who is an honor student in his class.

APPLAUSE FROM AUDIENCE.

LESTER:

How old are you, Mary?

MARY:

That's my slave name.

LESTER:
(APOLOGETIC)

I'm sorry.

MARY:

I'm 15. And my name is Tashika. I'd like to read my poem.

LESTER:

Good girl! Cool, baby, cool!

APPLAUSE FROM AUDIENCE.

TASHIKA:
(READS POEM)

To Albert Shanker, head of the Teacher's Union

Hey, Jew boy, with that yarmulke on your head

You pale faced Jew boy, I wish you were dead.

I see you Jew boy,

Now you can't hide

I got a scope on you

Yeah, Jew boy, you gonna die.

PAUSE.

LESTER:

Beautiful!

BLACK PEOPLE IN LIVING ROOM APPLAUDING AND SMILING AND BLACK STUDIO AUDIENCE HEARD ENTHUSIASTICALLY APPLAUDING.

KAHANE:
(NARRATING)

Lester is a white hating militant who once cheered the news that the police has been shot in St. Louis. One of the directors of WBAI is the father of Andrew Goodman who was killed together with another young Jew, Michael Schwerner, and a Black, as they fought for civil rights in Mississippi.

LESTER:

With us today are Mr. Marson, a student at Samuel Tilden High School and Mr. Woods...

WOODS:

...I'm a student at NYU.

LESTER:

I'll begin with a discussion of Tashika's poem.

MARSON:

I'd say it discusses most of the student's feelings.

LESTER:

Mr. Woods.

WOODS:

What Hitler did to 6 million Jews is nothing compared to what's been done to Black people. As far as I'm concerned, more power to Hitler. He didn't make enough lampshades out of them. He didn't make enough belts out of them.

KAHANE:
(NARRATING SARCASTICALLY)

And our spokesman, rising to the occasion...Dore Shary, Chairman of the Anti-Defamation League.

DORE SHARY:

I caution the American people not the exaggerated fears of Negro anti-Semitism. Let us be crystal clear, the statements of a few must not be attributed to an entire people. Negro anti-Semitism presents none other than the dangers of fascism.

KAHANE:
(NARRATING SARCASTICALLY)

Mr. Albert Vorspan, director of Reform Jewish Movement's Commission on Social Action...has this gem of an offer...

VORSPAN:

I decry an inflammatory reaction by Jews that will bring us to the brink of hysteria.

KAHANE:
(NARRATING)

All this tolerance taking place against a background of threats to carry Jews out of their classroom's dead. In the face of this kind of reaction the JDL, being most incapable of such "understanding" takes a different approach to the situation.

LESTER AND CAMPBELL ON STAGE WITH BODYGUARDS, TALKING ON RADIO TO STUDIO AUDIENCE.

CAMPBELL:

What the Jews got we need? Power! Never mind handouts, handshakes, and platitudes.

AUDIENCE SHOUTS.

Power!!!

KAHANE AND FIVE OF HIS BOYS RUSH ON STAGE AND CHASE CAMPBELL AND HIS BODYGUARDS FROM STAGE. KAHANE GRABS MIC.

KAHANE:

We will march in front of your African American Association in Brooklyn and demand that you...

HE POINTS TO CAMPBELL.

Be thrown off the school system.

THEY MARCH OUT AND PROCEED TO THE BUILDING MARKED WBAI AND STORM INTO THE OFFICE WITH A DOOR MARKED "STATION MANAGER."

STATION MANAGER:

How dare you come barging in here like this! I'll call the police!

STATION MANAGER PICKS UP PHONE.

KAHANE:

Call them. Tell them JDL is here demanding the WBAI to apologize to it's listeners and pledge no hate like the Lester program be broadcast again.

STATION MANAGER PUTS DOWN PHONE.

We'll look into it.

FOLLOWING DAY:

> MAN ON PHONE:
> (TO KAHANE)

Rabbi Milpaugh here...and I must tell you that your actions are not entirely acceptable to the congregation or me. While anti-Semitism is deeply repugnant, the First Amendment cannot be betrayed.

> KAHANE:

The time has come to redefine free speech as not applying to haters and people who call the death of other people.

KAHANE HANGS UP.

BRONX SCHOOL: IS 48. SWATISKAS AND THE WORDS "JEW BASTARD" ARE PRINTED ON THE WALLS. ABOVE THEM IS PRINTED "WELCOME TO THE NEW JEW PRINCIPAL." PRINCIPAL ENTERS, SEES WALLS AND RUSHES OUT. LATER HE CALLS KAHANE.

> PRINCIPAL:

The board yielded to a few agitators and removed me.

> KAHANE:

We'll be right over.

LATER: JDL BOYS AND KAHANE APPEAR AT SCHOOL CARRYING PAINT CANS AND BRUSHES. TEACHER CONFRONTS THEM IN HALL.

> TEACHER:

Get over here!

> KAHANE:

We swore "Never Again" such filth on a wall. You get your class to scrub this off the wall or we slather it off ourselves with white paint and throw the rest around so the Nazis in here can break a leg or two. Oh...and Mr. Schwartz will be here tomorrow to assume his duties as Principal, or we'll be back.

LATER: CLASS SEEN SCRUBBING WALLS WHILE JDL WATCHES.

FOLLOWING DAY: SECRETARY OPENS DOOR MARKED "PRINCIPAL'S OFFICE." MR. SCHWARTZ IS SITTING AT THE DESK.

Scene 12

A MONTH LATER: A COLD WET NIGHT. TV AND PRESS REPORTERS ARE IN THE STREET.

> REPORTER:
> (TO AUDIENCE)

Hundreds of Jews are gathered in front of station WBAI. The JDL is carrying posters saying, "Lester must go!" A group of Jewish Leftists are shouting, "JDL must go!" and calling them Fascists.

ANOTHER JDL GROUP ON THE ROOF OF THE WBAI BUILDING.

> JDL BOY:
> (TO ANOTHER BOY)

We'll wait for Lester to begin his program, then we crash into the station and stop him cold.

POLICE SEARCH THE ROOF, FIND THE JDL BOYS AND ARREST THEM.

> TV REPORTER:

Mr. Lester has just arrived!

A RIOT BREAKS OUT BETWEEN JDL AND JEWISH LEFTISTS AND A FRIGHTENED LESTER IS LED BY THE POLICE INTO THE BUILDING.

A WEEK LATER: JDL BOYS RUN UP TO KAHANE, WAVING A NEWSPAPER HAPPILY.

>   BOY:
>   (READS FROM PAPER)

WBAI has ordered an end to all hate talk.

KAHANE AND THE BOYS HUG.

FOLLOWING WEEK:

>   KAHANE:
>   (NARRATING)

At IS 258, in a 7th grade class in Brooklyn, the teacher Paul Anthony is writing the assignment for the day on the board.

THERE ARE WHITE AND BLACK CHILDREN IN THE CLASS.

>   PAUL ANTHONY:

A poem by a student, Tashika. Repeat after me as you write:

To Albert Shanker, head of the Teacher's Union

Hey, Jew boy, with that yarmulke on your head

You pale-faced Jew boy, I wish you were dead.

I see you Jew boy,

Now you can't hide

I got a scope on you

Yeah, Jew boy, you gonna die.

CHILDREN RECITE POEM TO ALBERT SHANKER AS THEY WRITE. A WHITE LITTLE GIRL RUSHES HOME WHEN CLASS IS OVER AND SHOWS POEM TO HER MOTHER, WHO GASPS AND RUNS TO THE PHONE.

                    MOTHER:
                    (ON PHONE)

Rabbi!

LATER: KAHANE OPENS DOOR MARKED "MARY MCCASSEY, PRINCIPAL."

                  MARY MCCASSEY:

We expect Paul Anthony to be suspended.

KAHANE LEAVES. SHE PUTS POEM ON BOTTOM OF INCOMING MAIL BASKET.

                      TEACHER:
                     (ON PHONE)

Rabbi Kahane, this is Teacher's Union Chapter Chairman of school district 15. Black militants led by Gloria Oliver are threatening to disrupt our scheduled meeting to win community control of the school, which means throwing Jewish teachers out. Stein, the Board president, chairman the meeting, is a wimp. We need help!

LATER: AT SCHOOL BOARD MEETING, BLACKS AND WHITES SHOUTING. KAHANE AND HIS BOYS ENTER. OLIVER SMASHES WHITE TEACHER ON THE HEAD WITH A BOTTLE.

                   BOARD PRESIDENT:
                 (TERRIFIED, SCREAMING)

The meeting is adjourned!

OLIVER BRANDISHES A BOTTLE.

                       OLIVER:
                     (SHOUTING)

Anyone else want to tangle with Oliver???

                       KAHANE:
                (TO BOARD PRESIDENT)

Stein!! Don't you dare end the meeting...'till I have my say!

SHOUTING CONTINUES. JDL BOYS BANG ON TABLE, RAISE LEAD PIPES. ALL QUIET DOWN WHEN PIPES BANGED ON THE TABLE, THEN ERUPTS AGAIN. JDL BOY THROWS SPINET PIANO FROM THE STAGE AND ALL IS QUIET NOW.

KAHANE:
(TO OLIVER)

Black militants seized the main office of the Board of Education yesterday demanding community control (YOU) and an end of merit (US.) This time we'll show you we can play the same game.

KAHANE TURNS TO LEAVE AND HIS BOYS FOLLOW.

FOLLOWING DAY. SIGN ON DOOR SAYS, "BOARD OF EDUCATION MEETING IN PROGRESS." KAHANE AND HIS GROUP COME BURSTING IN. SOME FRIGHTENED MEMBERS FLEE THE ROOM.

KAHANE SITS DOWN AT CHAIRMAN'S DESK.

KAHANE:

Now, I'll chair the meeting. You ought to be ashamed of yourselves for your indifference to the use of our schools by racists, white haters, Jew haters, and the destruction of the schools as well.

(LOOKS AT WATCH)

The meeting is adjourned. Time for *Mincha.

KAHANE AND THE BOYS OPEN THEIR PRAYER BOOKS.

BOARD MEMBER:

We want you to leave.

KAHANE AND THE BOYS SIT DOWN, STILL PRAYING. A BOARD MEMBER GETS UP AND LEAVES THE ROOM. A SHORT TIME LATER, POLICE ARRIVE AND ARREST KAHANE AND SEVERAL OF HIS BOYS.

. . .

A WEEK LATER: THOMAS JEFFERSON HIGH SCHOOL. A BLACK PRINCIPAL IS SPEAKING TO CHILDREN IN THE AUDITORIUM.

PRINCIPAL:

Mr. Ogden Van, one of our teachers, will be our first speaker this morning.

MR VAN STEPS TO THE MICROPHONE.

VAN:

I'm going to read this poem and I want my Black sisters and brothers to memorize every word of it…especially two of them…hate and love. (PAUSE) Hate them. Love me.

Them…is white

Me is Black

Them is Jew

Me is you.

GASPS HEARD IN THE AUDIENCE. WHITE TEACHERS RUN UP TO THE PRINCIPAL.

TEACHER:
(TO PRINCIPAL)

Do something!

PRINCIPAL SHRUGS SHOULDERS.

VOICE:

I'm leaving. Any other Jewish teachers want to join me?

JEWISH TEACHERS FLEE IN PANIC.

A WEEK LATER:

> ON SCREEN: EASTERN DISTRICT HIGH SCHOOL, BROOKLYN. 200 STUDENTS RAMPAGING THROUGH THE SCHOOL. A DOOR HAS PRINTED ON IT "DIDEON GOLDBERG, PRINCIPAL." THE OFFICE IS SMASHED AND A SIGN IS PUT ON THE DOOR OVER HIS NAME. THE SIGN SAYS, "GET OUT GOLDBERG!"

KAHANE:
(NARRATING)

Obscene, violent literature was distributed against him and...for the first time...

THE PHONE RINGS. KAHANE ANSWERS.

KAHANE:

JDL.

VOICE ON PHONE:
(FRIGHTENED)

This is Dideon Goldberg.

KAHANE LISTENS, THEN HANGS UP.

KAHANE:
(NARRATES)

Not the police...the establishment...no one...but JDL. This was a turning point for us.

(TO JDL BOYS)

We're taking a drive to Goldberg's house.

KAHANE AND JDL BOYS ARRIVE AT GOLDBERG'S HOUSE.

KAHANE'S BOY:

We're taking you to school!

AT THIS SCHOOL, 30 JDL BOYS ARE WAITING. NOT ONE COP. GOLDBERG, PALE AND TREMBLING, BEING HELD UP BY THE JDL BOYS IS MARCHED INTO BUILDING. 100 BLACK STUDENTS ARE WAITING. NO ONE SAYS A WORD. GOLDBERG IS MARCHED INTO THE PRINCIPAL'S OFFICE. A BLACK MAN IS AT THE DESK.

MAN:

I'm Frank Stewart, the new principal.

(TO GOLDBERG)

Report to the main office of the Board. You'll be paid your salary.

KAHANE:

And a man with the only qualification being he is Black will take his job. If you think you'll sell out Goldberg, we'll wreck the school! We're going to settle this, and in the meantime, we're leaving Goldberg in the case of Chaim Bieber.

KAHANE POINTS TOWARD CHAIM BIEBER, A HUGE, POWERFUL MAN.

KAHANE:
(TO BIEBER)

Take him home.

BIEBER LEAVES WITH GOLDBERG.

IN GOLDBERG'S HOUSE, AN HOUR LATER. THE PHONE RINGS. BIEBER ANSWERS.

BIEBER:

Goldberg, you're keeping your job.

Scene 13

KAHANE:
(NARRATING)

Blacks, Puerto Ricans, and Jewish Leftists in New York are allied, demanding a quota system for accepting students based on the number of people in their ethnic group. This means <u>adding</u> thousands of Blacks and <u>dropping</u> thousands of Jews who had. We saw this as a potential disaster for Jew in America. If the merit system were scraped, it would be not only in schools but in every area of life. The Jew, with three percent of the total population of the United States, would be in the same situation he faced once before, in Europe and America. Quotas. Brooklyn College became the next battleground.

COLLEGE AUDITORIUM. BLACK MILITANT STUDENT TALKING TO A CROWD OF BLACK STUDENTS.

BLACK MILITANT STUDENT:

75 percent Jews here...25 percent...us! We want 25 percent of them...if they're lucky...and the rest go to...

BLACK STUDENTS IN CROWD:
(SHOUTING)

Third World!

BLACK MILITANT STUDENT:

Jew outta our world! Now, we're marching to President Peck's office! Brother's with me, come on!

BLACK MILITANT STUDENT MARCHES AND OTHERS FOLLOW. THEY KICK THE DOOR OPEN TO PRESIDENT PECK'S OFFICE. LEADER PUTS PAPER IN PRESIDENT PECK'S FACE.

LEADER:

18 demands on that list. Make sure you leave none of 'em out, you hear...or... we take this place over and you're out!

THEY STORM OUT, FISTS IN AIR.

THE FOLLOWING DAY, KAHANE AND 15 JDL BOYS ARRIVE AT THE COLLEGE. A BLACK STUDENT ATTACKS A JDL BOY AND IS FLOORED BY A KARATE PUNCH. ANOTHER 35 NON-JDL BOYS JOIN JDL. THEY PASS THE DEAN'S OFFICE. A MAN COMES OUT.

KAHANE:

I want to see the president.

DEAN:

President Peck is busy.

KAHANE:

Since he saw 50 of the other side, he'll see fifty of us immediately!

DEAN:

Well...perhaps the President can spare a few moments for you...

THEY MARCH TO PECK'S OFFICE, GO IN AND SURROUND HIS DESK.

KAHANE:

We are enraged Jews, which means we are prepared to burn the college down if your administration collapses before Black militants and pays them off in Jewish rights! If Third World students seize your office and you don't call the police, we'll be waiting in <u>this</u> world to drag them out ourselves!

KAHANE AND JDL BOYS LEAVE.

FOLLOWING DAY: BLACK MILITANTS DRAG THE PRINCIPAL OUT AND SEIZE HIS OFFICE.

AT POLICE HEADQUARTERS, PHONE RINGS. POLICEMAN LISTENS ON PHONE, THEN TURNS TO SERGEANT.

> POLICEMAN:

Sergeant, it's the JDL again. Shall I get the cuffs ready? I think he's due for another collar.

SERGEANT TAKES THE PHONE.

> SERGEANT:
> (TO KAHANE ON PHONE)

I've got a jail full now. Wait 'till next week to cause trouble, will you? Besides, the men want to get home on time for a change.

> KAHANE:
> (TO SERGEANT)

Brooklyn College is city property. If the law is not upheld, we'll be down there at 9pm.

KAHANE HANGS UP.

CLOCK ON WALL STRIKES 5PM. POLICE ARRIVE AT COLLEGE AND FORCIBLY CLEAR THE PRESIDENT'S OFFICE.

Scene 14

KAHANE:
(NARRATING)

I received an invitation from the 30,000-man Jewish Teacher's Association to be the guest speaker at their annual luncheon.

PHONE RINGS. KAHANE ANSWERS.

MAN:
(TO KAHANE)

I'm sorry to say this, but we contacted all the major Jewish organizations and they've bitterly denounced our invitation. Just want to let you know not to expect them. However, Israeli Consul General David Rivlin will be there to speak.

KAHANE:

I'll call Shanker. He'll come.

(ON PHONE WITH SHANKER)

Hope you can come to the teacher's celebration planned for me. I'm extending a personal invitation from me to you.

SHANKER:

I'm immediately cancelling my plans to purchase 10 tickets to the luncheon in the light of the invitation to a racist!

KAHANE:

For years your members have been under attack for hardcore anti-Semites pushing to end the merit system and destroy you all, yet you're still a hardcore Socialist more interested in civil rights than the Jewish ones.

SHANKER HANGS UP. PHONE RINGS. KAHANE ANSWERS.

WOMAN'S VOICE:
(ON PHONE)

Rabbi Kahane, this is the office of the Consul General. He regrets he has to cancel his appearance at the luncheon because of matters of state.

NEWSPAPER ARTICLE IN NEW YORK TIMES ON SCREEN:

"1200 TEACHERS GAVE RABBI KAHANE A ROUSING OVATION AT THEIR LUNCHEON."

Scene 15

KAHANE:
(NARRATING)

The steady erosion of the merit system created a student body that was more than 20 percent Black, Puerto Rican and patently anti-Semitic. The so-called Third World paper put out by Black and Puerto Rican students, with college funds, carried hate of Israel and Zionism regularly. The incidence of beatings and robbing on campus had skyrocketed at Brooklyn College.

IN THE STUDENT CAFETERIA, BLACKS ROPE OFF AN AREA AND PUT A SIGN UP, "WHITEYS OUT. THIS PART'S OUT."

STUDENT UNION ROOM. BLACKS ROPE OFF AN AREA, PUT UP SIGN SAME AS ABOVE.

A MONTH LATER. A JEWISH STUDENT PUTS A RECORD ON THE JUKEBOX IN STUDENT UNION ROOM CALLED, "BASHANA HABA'AH," THE ONLY HEBREW SONG IN THE JUKEBOX, WHICH CONTAINED A LARGE NUMBER OF BLACK "SOUL" SONGS.

A NUMBER OF BLACKS COME OVER. ONE SAYS:

BLACK:

This stuff gotta go. It's annoyin' us.

HE OPENS THE JUKEBOX AND BREAKS THE RECORD. TWO JEWS RUN UP TO THEM.

ONE JEW:

Hey, whatta think you're doing? This box is full of your soul songs. We have just this one. And we have souls too.

BLACKS PULL A GUN OUT AND TWO JEWS PUSHED AROUND.

AN HOUR LATER: KAHANE AND ONE HUNDRED JDL BOYS ON CAMPUS MARCH INTO STUDENT UNION'S FORBIDDEN AREA AND SING AND DANCE TO "BASHANA HABA'AH." A MAJOR BATTLE ERUPTS BETWEEN JDL AND BLACKS. POLICE FINALLY SEPARATE PARTIES.

3AM IN THE MORNING. POLICE WAKE KAHANE AT HOME.

POLICEMAN:

You are being served with a temporary restraining order forbidding you to appear on campus.

KAHANE:

I won't be here tomorrow. I'm flying to Florida to get help for one of our heroes rotting in jail.

POLICEMAN LEAVES.

LATER: JDL SHOWS UP AT BROOKLYN COLLEGE WITH 100 BOYS CARRYING HELMETS AND CLUBS AND MARCH TO THE PRESIDENT'S OFFICE.

JDL BOY:

Jewish rights will be respected by your administration, or we will take this college apart brick by brick.

KAHANE:
(NARRATING)

Incidents dropped dramatically; haters were more cautious about translating hate into action.

. . .

Scene 15

3 MONTHS LATER:

TV REPORTER ON TV:
(TO KAHANE)

City College is now the third month of a takeover by Black students, and we understand much of the difficulty is due to pressure by white groups resisting their justifiable demands to right wrongs.

KAHANE:

The President has totally capitulated by doing nothing. This timid man did not utter a word when a riot erupted in which a number of Jewish students were beaten over the head with lead pipes.

TV REPORTER:
(TO MAYOR LINDSAY)

Mr. Mayor, is it true you are thinking of running for President and therefore do not want to get involved in all these confrontations...sort of "backing away," so to speak?

LINDSAY:

I have a reputation to maintain: one who keeps the city "cool."

LATER:

BACK IN HIS OFFICE, KAHANE GOES TO HIS PHONE. IN THE PRECINCT POLICEMAN PICKS UP PHONE.

POLICEMAN:

Sergeant Holloran...Now listen here. Rabbi, we can't go to City College. We just don't have enough men.

POLICEMAN HANGS UP.

KAHANE:
(TO BOYS)

Well, where there are not enough men, we have to be men. Does anyone know the quickest way to City College?

BOYS NODS "YES."

Let's go.

> BOY:

They like lead pipes. Well, why not?

THEY PICK UP LEAD PIPES AND FOLLOW HIM OUT THE DOOR.

HEADLINE IN PAPERS THE FOLLOWING DAY ON SCREEN:

> "JDL ROUTS BLACKS FROM THEIR CITY COLLEGE TAKEOVER. POLICE QUELL RIOT, BUT BLACKS STRUCK ON HEAD WITH LEAD PIPES BEFORE THEY ARRIVED.

Scene 16

          KAHANE:
         (NARRATING)

A taste of what life would be like under the Black Power regime is being given to us in a rash of college riots that have been buried by the New York Times and other papers.

   FLASHBACK:

   ON SCREEN: NORTHWESTERN UNIVERSITY

          PROFESSOR:
     (LECTURING STUDENTS IN AUDITORIUM)

The Agency for International Development...

SUDDENLY THE LIGHTS GO OUT.

       GROUP OUTSIDE THE HALL:
      (SHOUTING TO PROFESSOR)

Up against the wall, mother (BLEEP.)

HE IS STRUCK FROM THE WINGS WITH TWO PIE PANS FULL OF WHIPPED CREAM.

ON SCREEN: OSHKOSH UNIVERSITY IN WISCONSIN. BLACK STUDENTS MARCH INTO THE SCHOOL PRESIDENT'S OFFICE, SMASH FURNITURE, BREAK WINDOWS AND DAMAGE EQUIPMENT.

STUDENTS:
(SHOUTING)

He is nothing but baloney and hogwash!

KAHANE:
(NARRATING)

Teachers were only the beginning. The only protection against bias the Jews had was Civil Service...where competitive ability counted...not race or religion. It took more than 100 years to establish a Civil Service here in New York, and in less than one it has been severely crippled.

Scene 17

KAHANE, ARTHUR GOLDBERG AND A MRS. BURTON LANE FROM STAMFORD, CONNECTICUT, ARE BEING INTERVIEWED AT DIFFERENT PLACES SO THEY APPEAR IN A BOX ON THE SCREEN WHEN IT IS THEIR TURN TO SPEAK.

ANNOUNCER:

Tonight, we have with us Arthur Goldberg, Mrs. Burton Lane, a housewife from Stamford, Connecticut, and the Militant Rabbi Meir Kahane. Mr. Goldberg, at present you are involved in a matter involving the Black Panthers, a militant organization parading weapons, scaring Americans, having armed confrontations with the police, and being anti-Semitic.

ARTHUR GOLDBERG:

I plan to lead a committee to investigate the persecution of the Panthers.

KAHANE:

JDL urgently suggests you take more time to investigate the persecution of Panther victims in inner cities.

GOLDBERG:
(TO INTERVIEWER)

You see how he proves my point...conviction without a shred of evidence...a Fascist.

KAHANE:

They threaten and assault Jewish merchants in the ghettoes, Jewish children in the schools for years. Liberal Jews like you paid no attention.

MRS LANE:
(TO KAHANE)

Don't be so concerned with Black anti-Semitism. It is white anti-Semitism that has the power to hurt us. Blacks are so relatively powerless.

KAHANE:

Mrs. Lane, you are as ignorant as you are hard-hearted.

GOLDBERG:
(TO KAHANE)

And you are living up to your reputation as a violent and unreasonable man...

KAHANE:

In Mrs. Lane's magnificent home in Stamford, where the nearest Black is not very near, you have no Black anti-Semitism problem.

(TURNING TO GOLDBERG)

Neither you nor she care about the tens of thousands of Jewish families who live in terror, to whom the Panthers are a daily nightmare; masses of poor, struggling, frightened little people.

MRS. LANE:

You're simply o-v-e-r-r-e-a-c-t-i-n-g. We were all friends once. We can be again.

KAHANE:

Thank you, Mrs. Lane for the opportunity to show the poetic side of my nature. Are you listening...Mr. Campbell and Tashika? And listen well!

Exiled and banned

Hundreds of years
Land after land

Tortured, starved
Betrayed
Ridiculed and enslaved

Made us wear
Caps of a dunce
And we were all friends once.

So much for friendship.

MRS. LANE:

I'm an English teacher and I can tell you that's bad poetry.

GOLDBERG:

What does JDL want? The past clouds our present and give us an ominous view of the future if we don't riot, attack, and move from one outrage to another.

KAHANE:

You have a very picky taste for violence. It's offended only by ours. When you were a delegate at the UN, Sonny Carson, a Jew hater and his bunch invaded a South African Embassy to protest their White Racism, and you never uttered a sound. However, when JDL staged a sit-in at the Syrian Embassy for vicious crimes against our people like hanging innocents...

FLASHBACK:

GOLDBERG:
(TO PRESS)

I deplore the actions of JDL and will personally sign the police complaint against the boys.

KAHANE:

We want to change the Jewish image, show that he is not always a victim. Protect Jewish property and lives by letting the Jew-hater know he is in danger of losing his. We want to instill self-respect and self-pride in a Jew who is ashamed of himself for running away. Teach the Jew that the pain of every Jew is his own pain, and that it's his obligation to do all that is necessary, even violence, to protect another Jew. To teach the Goldbergs and the Lanes that they are the first and last Jews, and fated to struggle for, or fall with, other Jews.

GOLDBERG:
(TO MODERATOR)

I'm being honored at a UJA dinner. Have to leave now.

MRS. LANE:

And I have to leave now. I must run to catch my train back to Connecticut.

KAHANE:

And I have to leave now. I'm going to hear a talk by a local Panther, who speaks on the block, revving up his people to commit mayhem with such topics as, "The only good Jews are dead ones." If he thinks to continue with this kind of talk, we plan to disabuse him of that idea. Care to join me? Mrs. Lane? Mr. Goldberg?

THEY SCURRY OUT. KAHANE SMILES SARCASTICALLY.

MODERATOR:

Now, for calls in the audience.

MAN:
(ON PHONE)

Rabbi, we'll be calling you at your office and you'll tell us where you'll be on the block. A hundred of us coming down from Connecticut to join you. Never again!

MAN HANGS UP. KAHANE SMILES.

ETHNIC CLEANSING

MERCHANTS

NEIGHBORHOODS

CITIES

Scene 18

FLATBUSH AVENUE, BROOKLYN. IT IS NIGHTTIME. THERE IS A SIGN ON THE STORE WINDOW. IT READS, "SPEIVAK'S LUCHEONNETTE." TWO BLACK MEN ARE SEEN ENTERING THE STORE. THEY SIT DOWN. MR SPEIVAK APPROACHES THEM TO TAKE THEIR ORDERS. THE TWO BLACK MEN ARE DRESSED AS AND LOOK LIKE TOUGHS.

BLACK MAN:

We want some apple pa-a, don't we, Joe?

JOE:

Yeah...we wants apples.

SPEIVAK:
(WITH HEAVY JEWISH ACCENT)

I'm sorry we don't hev apple. I can maybe give you...

BLACK MAN PULLS OUT GUN AND SHOOTS SPIEVAK. KAHANE RUSHES TO THE SCENE AS SOON AS HE HEARS ABOUT THE SHOOTING.

KAHANE:
(TALKING TO CROWD GATHERED AT SCENE)

Enough already! How many more merchants, old, young, children, grandmas, will be robbed and killed here before we defend ourselves?

Put a foot in your circle,

Your street

Your store

Your shule

To slay you,

Slay them first

That must be our way!

JEWISH MAN IN CROWD:

Troublemaker! Don't listen to him!

KAHANE:

Never again!

Not on my street

My shule

My store

Not sit home

And wait for death

To break in the door!

POLICEMAN:

You should be satisfied you don't have snipers.

MAN:

We'll have to take matters in our own hands.

POLICEMAN:
(FURIOUS)

Then I warn you that you will fall into ours.

MAN:

Just last week, a young man from a prominent rabbinical family was dragged in an alleyway and stomped on and punched.

POLICEMAN:

Compared to what's happening in other cities, New York is a paradise.

GROUP LEAVES.

> ON SCREEN: BLACK PANTHER MENACE SPREADS TO INTIMIDATION OF JEWISH MERCHANTS.
>
> BLACK PANTHER WALKS INTO GROCERY STORE, WEARING A JACKET, A BERET AND A BULLET AROUND HIS NECK.

PANTHER:
(TO MERCHANT)

Get outta here by tomorrow!

MERCHANT, TERRIFIED, NODS HIS HEAD "YES." THE PANTHER LEAVES. THE MERCHANT BREAKS DOWN, SOBBING.

> ON SCREEN: NEGRO RACISTS IN WASHINGTON D.C. ARE FORCING OUT JEWISH MERCHANTS.
>
> A MEETING IS IN PROGRESS. HUGE SIGNS SAYING, "PRIDE" AND "BUILD BACK" HANG ON THE WALL BEHIND THE SPEAKER. THE AUDIENCE IS BLACK, AS IS THE SPEAKER.

MAN:

We all know that no one puts the touch on the Black man like the Jews. Their businesses will be burned again and again. Enemies of Black people are Zionist Jews.

SECOND BLACK:

All that power you say they got, we gonna end up in jail, and they gonna get disaster loans from the government to set their selves up again.

THIRD BLACK:

We keep burning and demanding no loans be given to Jew businesses until Black control of stores is guaranteed!

FOURTH BLACK:

You dreamin.'

KAHANE:
(NARRATING)

The local government in Washington D.C. bowed to Pride's demands to turn over all Jewish businesses in Negro areas to Black control. Fear of riots forced the government's hand to suspend loans to Jewish merchants. Though the "Presidential Committee on the Administration of Justice" said that rioting occurred because of high prices in the ghettoes, studies found this to be untrue. Prices were fair.

BLACK MAN:

Liar!

ON SCREEN: GOVERNMENT REFUSES TO AID TO WASHINGTON D.C JEWISH STORES. REPRESENTATIVE BROYHILL APPEALS THE DECISION.

REPRESENTATIVE BROYHILL:

I appeal to the Justice Department, on behalf of Jewish merchants, who are subject to steady anti-Semitism, including arson, looting, boycotts, violence and threats to life and property, to reconsider its decision to withhold any and all financial assistance.

KAHANE:
(NARRATING)

In contrast to the above, a Jew, Stephen Pollack, assistant to the Attorney General, had this to say:

POLLACK:

The matter that Broyhill describes does not violate any laws administered by this department.

ON SCREEN: "BUILD BLACK," AN ORGANIZATION SUPPORTED BY FEDERAL FUNDS, IS PICKETING A STORE OWNED BY A RUSSIAN REFUGEE.

PICKETS ARE SEEN CARRYING POSTERS SAYING, "JEW OUT."

> PROTESTORS:
> (SHOUTING)

Blacks in!

> BLACK:
> (ENTERING STORE)

So, give us a moving date...like tomorrow.

> STORE OWNER:

I told you to bring me a buyer.

> BLACK:

I didn't say I was going to buy it. I want you to give it to me!

FOLLOWING DAY. SIGN ON DOOR SAYS, "CLOSED." BLACK ENTERS AND PUTS ON AN APRON BEHIND THE COUNTER. OTHER PICKETERS COME IN AND HELP THEMSELVES TO GROCERIES. THE SIGN IS CHANGED FROM "WALCZAK" TO "BROWN."

THAT EVENING: PICKETERS ENTER LIQUOR STORE WITH A SIGN THAT SAYS, "GOLDSTEIN'S."

> BLACK:
> (TO STORE OWNER)

You gave us two bad bottles, man. They done explode. I have to watch the store.

OWNER GIVES THEM TWO NEW BOTTLES.

LATERS: GOLDSTEIN AT HOME.

> GOLDSTEIN:
> (TO WIFE)

I'm worried they'll do something. I have to watch the store.

WIFE:
(GRABBING HIS ARM)

I won't let you go. It's too late! Dangerous out there.

HE DASHES OUT. GOLDSTEIN ARRIVES NEAR THE STORE. IT IS ON FIRE. HE STANDS THERE, NUMBED. THEN, HE TURNS TOWARD HOME.

GOLDSTEIN:
(TO WIFE)

I watched the store...burn.

BLACK:

Burn, baby, burn.

BROYHILL:
(TO POLLACK)

The Federal government is protecting the civil rights of Negroes and ignoring those of the Hebrews. I reject the double standards.

POLLACK:

A few incidents cannot set policy for the Department.

Scene 19

ON SCREEN: 1969: OCTOBER 23: BROOKLYN YESHIVA SET AFIRE BY ARSONISTS.

OCTOBER 30: YESHIVA FIRE IN EASTERN PARKWAY, BROOKLYN. THE REMAINS OF SEVEN TORAH SCROLLS WERE BURIED IN A PLAIN PINE BOX AS AN ELDERLY SCHOLAR KISSED THE COFFIN.

10 SYNAGOGUES DESTROYED BY FIRE IN NEW YORK CITY AREA. CULPRITS NOT APPREHENDED.

HOODLUMS SCRIBBLE SWATISKAS ON WALLS. BIBLES AND HOLY TORAHS USED AS KINDLING TO BURN DOWN BUILDINGS.

BLACK:
(WATCHING FIRE, SMILING)

Burn, baby, burn.

ON SCREEN: BRONX, NEW YORK: SUSPICIOUS FIRES STRIKE BRONX SYNAGOGUES. HEBREW INSTITUTE IN BRONX STRUCK BY ARSONISTS. RELIGIOUS BOOKS WERE USED TO START THE FIRE.

KAHANE:
(NARRATING)

Media...silent.

FEARS GRIPS JEWISH MERCHANTS IN BOSTON. ANTI-DEFAMATION LEAGUES MAKE STUDY OF SITUATION.

ADL SPOKESMAN:

We in the ADL found that the Jewish merchants in the black communities of Boston are gripped by desperation and fear, as are tens of other Jewish urban areas in the country, are being looted, vandalized, robbed, and people killed. Many fled, but those who couldn't face financial ruin. No one will buy in terror-ridden neighborhoods, insurance companies cancelling out, and trades fall as people are afraid to walk the streets. ADL suggests Jews move out and community leaders help Blacks buy stores, then help them to manage their own financial affairs.

KAHANE:

This is nothing but a capitulation to terror. We need a crash program to protect merchants against terrorists. To the school of ADL Masochists, we add another shining example, Jewish lawyers. Eldridge Cleaver, a Black Panther, spoke to 75 of them in California, who honored him as their guest.

FLASHBACK:

CLEAVER:
(TO LAWYERS)

We want to provoke a situation so the enemies of America will come in and pick the gold from the teeth of you Babylonian pigs. If I could get two machine guns out of this crowd, I wouldn't care if you applauded me or threw glasses at me. I'd get my Black (bleep) out of here. I mean all my insults. You people can take your credit cards and cut your mother (bleep) necks. People on my side, I hope you take your guns and shoot judges and police.

THE LAWYERS APPLAUD POLITELY WITH OBSEQUEOUS SMILES ON THEIR FACES.

ADL SPOKESMAN:

I say education is the answer.

KAHANE:

And I say, (SHOWS PICTURES FROM JDL ADVERTISEMENT) this is the answer. Create a Jew who will teach the world that "Jew" is not a synonym for "victim."

A BARREN FIELD. A SIGN SAYING, "CAMP MEIR." TWO LINES OF BOYS STANDING BEFORE A MAN IDLY, POOR POSTURE, WEARY, SWEATY, GRIMY.

MAN:

I know it's 90 degrees and so humid you can drink the air and barely breathe, but a Jew doesn't stand like you. Attention!

THE BOYS SNAP IN RIGID POSTURE. THE MAN WALKS DOWN THE TWO LINES OF 34 BOYS, KICKING EVERY FOURTH ONE HARD IN THE SOLAR PLEXUS. BOYS DOUBLE OVER MOMENTARILY IN PAIN; THEY STRAIGHTEN UP PROUDLY. FOR THE NEXT THREE HOURS, THEY'RE PUNCHING, KICKING, PARRYING, PRACTICING KARATE. FOR THE NEXT TWO HOURS, THEY ARE LEARNING TO FIRE WEAPONS.

CLOCK ON SCREEN SHOWS THE PASSAGE OF TIME.

BOY:
(NARRATING)

We come from some of the meanest streets in New York City. When this 8-week training is over, we go back to those streets, only this time we learn to give (PUNCHES AIR, KICKS, PULLS OUT GUN) as well as take.

MUSIC OF "AFN PRIPITCHUK" IS HEARD.

KAHANE:

"Afn Pripitchuk." We all know this lullaby, the old familiar words lulling us to sleep: "A rabbi teaches a child/If he can learn Torah,/What more does he need? In the '30s, with a catastrophe descending on us, Jabotinsky's rabbi goes on to answer what more he needs… "Learn to shoot." They didn't. And the darkness came. He was roundly condemned, as we are. And is now revered as a man of vision. We are in a fight for survival …now…again…still. In the Soviet Gulag and the Warsaw Ghetto, they sang this song (WE HEAR THE SONG, NOW WITH A GRIM, MILITARY BEAT) with these words:

The fire is burning

Surveillance is keen

Even should they beat you

Be ever alert

Fight on.

Scene 20

FOLLOWING WEEK: A NEWS REPORTER ON TV.

                  REPORTER:

Rabbi Kahane was arrested last week when he rushed to the scene of a murder of a concentration camp survivor and incited a riot. He's been released and is on his way now to Mattapan-Dorchester in Boston.

SCENE MOVES TO KAHANE BEING INTERVIEWED BY A TV REPORTER.

                  KAHANE:
                 (TO REPORTER)

A beautiful neighborhood there once...temples, stores, trees, peaceful streets, and now...muggings, burglaries, arson, murders, people fleeing, moving vans lining the streets to Brookline and Newton, while the old are left behind, barring doors in terror; the whole area like bombed-out Vietnam. We must do what we can to help them.

SHIFT ON SCENE TO REPORTER INTERVIEWING MAYOR LINDSAY.

                  REPORTER:

Do you and the police agree with Kahane's plan to help people help themselves in any way they can?

LINDSAY:

The Commissioner and I are appalled by the vigilante tactics of a madman. The solution is to ban guns, not to spread them!

SHIFTS BACK TO THE REPORTER AND KAHANE.

KAHANE:

You, Mr. Mayor and the police department ought to be ashamed! You've been doing what Jews have been doing for so long and so well...running! You must stop backing off when you are pushed and stand up for your people's rights, which means...when you have persuaded the hoodlums to give up their weapons, JDL will give up theirs.

ON SCREEN:

ONE MONTH LATER: MATTAPAN-DORCHESTER, BOSTON.

AN OLD MAN IS TALKING TO THE RABBI IN A BROKEN-DOWN SYNAGOGUE.

OLD MAN:

Nu, Rabbi, tell me...the synagogue, you'll keep it open?

HE RUBS CHAIR.

Twenty years, I'm in his chair. It knows me well. Has only one arm...like me... so we fit perfectly.

RABBI:

As long as you're alive and come.

THE FOLLOWING MORNING: POLICE SIREN IS HEARD IN FRONT OF THE TEMPLE. A BODY IS LYING ON THE FLOOR. A POLICEMAN EXAMINES THE BODY.

POLICEMAN:

Poor guy couldn't even defend himself. He only has one arm.

A WEEK LATER: KAHANE IS SPEAKING AT A BROKEN-DOWN SYNAGOGUE.

KAHANE:

> (TO RABBI)

It's too late—nothing we can do except help to move you all out.

RABBI NODS HIS HEAD "YES" SADLY, THEN GOES TO DOOR, KAHANE BEHIND HIM. THE RABBI PUTS A LOCK ON DOOR AND HANGS A SIGN THAT SAYS, "CLOSED."

A LIGHT FOCUSES ON THE OLD MAN'S CHAIR.

Scene 21

KAHANE:
(NARRATING)

A week before I came to Boston, there was a meeting of the Jewish Council, Mr. Hofstader, the New England Hebrew Academy, Mr. Stein, and a Black extremist, Elma Lewis.

MEETING IN PROGRESS. STEIN, HOFSTADERM AND MS. LEWIS ARE TALKING.

STEIN:
(TO MS LEWIS)

Mr. Hofstader, the Board, and I have discussed this at length, and we've concluded we cannot sell the building.

MR. HOFSTADER:

A magnificent place like this is an everlasting monument to our presence here. It's been an integral part of our lives.

LEWIS:

Gentlemen, you must be practical. I can no longer control the feelings of my people, who've suffered discrimination and exploitation at your hands.

STEIN:

And we have suffered murder and mayhem at yours. Yours is a false charge. Ours is not, as you can tell the ashes around us.

LEWIS:

Either you relinquish this place to me or it, too, will be reduced to rubble.

HOFSTADER:

Scar one stone and it would be like cutting into me. How much will you pay for the building? It's worth a million, at least.

LEWIS:

One dollar.

HOFSTADER LOOKS AT STEIN, STUNNED. STEIN NODS.

STEIN:
(DESOLATE)

Sold.

Scene 22

NEW YORK, ONE MONTH LATER: AN AUDITORIUM WITH A HUGE SIGN ON THE WALL, "CONFERENCE OF OPPRESSED JEWISH NEIGHBORHOODS." KAHANE IS AT THE PODIUM. A SPRINKLING OF PEOPLE IS IN THE AUDITORIUM. A POLICEMAN STANDS IN THE BACK OF THE HALL.

          KAHANE:

It's getting late. I want to sum up and then ask for volunteers to start the program. We have people here from Bronx Concourse areas, southeast Queens (Rochdale-Laurelton), Coney Island, Borough Park, Crown Heights, Williamsburg, East Flatbush, east New York, Upper Manhattan, and the Lower East Side. We'll have to Kaddish for all these areas if we don't take matters into our own hands, and expose the frauds that pass for politicians, their Jewish lackeys and our do-nothing Jewish organizations.

          MAN:
          (SHOUTING)

Vigilantes, we should be?!

          KAHANE:

When police do nothing, it's criminal not to act. If <u>we</u> do, <u>they</u> will. At least, let's start with the nice things. Put alarm systems on synagogues, insist schools be honest about the hoodlums and crimes they're busing covering up, picket blockbusters and take the elderly poor by the hand to safer places. The more courageous among us will set up defense patrols and those licensed to carry guns will do. We need a delegate from each area to get money and men.

POLICEMAN:

We can't allow groups of people to go haywire, deciding for themselves when to shoot somebody.

WOMAN IN AUDIENCE:

Officer, my child has learned to control his kidneys because his life is in danger if he goes to the bathroom in school!

POLICEMAN:

So, send your kid to Jew school!

WOMAN:

You pay for it?! Nobody pays. We only little people. You know we won't riot and do something.

POLICEMAN:

Plenty Jews with plenty money. Don't kid me!

KAHANE:

They give us nothing. Just tell me what good friends we have in those who let us die. The Jew is raped, and no one hears his scream.

A MAN RISES IN THE AUDIENCE.

MAN:

Rabbi, I work 14 hours a day in a tailor shop to earn for my wife and 5 children. I have no time and no money to spend on foolishness.

HE LEAVES. ANOTHER MAN RISES.

MAN:

I've lived here the way it is for years. Now you want me to go out and be a soldier? I'm 90 years old. I have nobody. If I go, nu?

HE SHRUGS HIS SHOULDERS. HE LEAVES AND SEVERAL FOLLOW. ANOTHER MAN RISES.

MAN:

If I tell a Jew to help himself, I'm the enemy. I tell you the truth, I have enough enemies.

HE LEAVES. OTHERS WALK OUT QUIETLY BEHIND HIM. ONE MAN REMAINS.

MAN:

I volunteer!

HE TAKES OUT 4 QUARTERS AND DROPS THEM IN JAR, WHICH IS THERE FOR THE PURPOSE. KAHANE WARMLY SHAKES HIS HAND.

POLICEMAN:

You'll never get this thing off the ground.

FOLLOWING DAY: KAHANE, HIS BOYS AND THE VOLUNTEER SIT AROUND A TABLE.

VOLUNTEER:

I have an idea, but please don't attack me all at once. Here, I think the main trouble is the people have no money. So, why don't we go to them that has. The big marchers, the main organizations.

ONE OF THE BOYS:

They'll spit on us.

VOLUNTEER:

It depends how you talk. We call our program "Operation Haganah" ...and we'll say we need 100,000 dollars, a small amount of money for the protection of small neighborhoods that are dying.

KAHANE:

Boys?

THE BOYS RAISE THEIR HANDS IN AGREEMENT.

> KAHANE:
> (WRITING AND TALKING LOUD)

Dear Mr. Maslow, a month ago I wrote to you requesting your help to save Jews and their neighborhoods. The problem grows more acute every day. Can we hope for help?

> MR. MASLOW:
> (WRITING LETTER BACK AND READING ALOUD)

Rabbi, I never received your request. If I did, I would have thrown it in the wastebasket.

> KAHANE:
> (WRITING BACK)

Your response is typical of the arrogant, unfeeling Jewish establishment functionary. You are the worst example of this curse. How many of the disgusting models of indifference who pass for Jewish leaders, live in these horror neighborhoods, and know their agony waiting for children, every minute of tardiness and anguish, where shadows and hallways mean danger?

> ARNOLD FOSTER:
> (ON PHONE)

Rabbi, this is Arnold Foster, Anti-Defamation League. Your request is brazen. We have always worked successfully with legitimate law enforcement agencies.

> KAHANE:

We are not trying to protect ADL, and our people have very different experiences with law enforcement agencies, or we would not be pleading with you or ending up in Mr. Maslow's wastebasket.

> FOSTER:

Racist!

> KAHANE:

I was a rabbi in Rochdale Village, a huge cooperative that was built in the heart of Jamaica's Black Ghetto. It was fully integrated, old Jewish pensioners, struggling civil servants, and me in a new temple built without windows. The elderly Jews were regularly mugged and a 25-year old Vietnam veteran, Barry Epstein, was murdered in the parking lot near his building.

FOSTER HANGS UP. WE HEAR THE DIAL TONE, BUT KAHANE KEEPS TALKING THOUGH NO ONE IS LISTENING. KAHANE'S VOICE KEEPS RISING IN RAGE.

KAHANE:

I, the racist, lived where liberals never ventured or gave a Jewish damn about those of us who did!

HE HANGS UP, FURIOUS.

Scene 23

ON SCREEN: REVERSE DISCRIMINATION.

JANUARY 1969:

VOICE:
(ON RADIO)

The mayor is proud to announce that Franklin E. White has been appointed as General Counsel of the Human Rights Commission. Mr. White...

MR WHITE:

First, let me get right to the heart of my administration, I believe the treatment of Negroes should not be <u>equal</u>, it should be <u>preferential</u>. The white society owes us that. Further, I feel Black campus disruptions are absolutely justified, and I will support them wherever they may be. I plan to abolish warren and oral examinations in schools, wherever they may be, in favor of quotas, and let the chips fall where they may.

KAHANE:

The chips fell on Jewish teachers who lost promotions. Jewish leaders did nothing or supported this trend to show their liberalism.

TV REPORTER:
(ON TV)

More than one city employee has admitted that officials close to Mayor Lindsay have shown them how to falsify applications, so they could be appointed to jobs for which they did not have legitimate qualifications.

1969:

>ON SCREEN: SAN FRANCISCO BOARD OF EDUCATION. MEETING ROOM.

>MAN:

The Board has decided to fire a number of administrators, with the exception of non-whites.

>ANOTHER MAN:

Do Jews, with a history of persecution and disadvantage as serious as or more so than others, fall into an ethnic category also exempt from firing?

>FIRST MAN:

We have no category for you as a Jew. The usual headings are White, Black, Puerto Rican, Oriental, American Indian, Other Spanish Origin, and Others. Jews are Others.

>KAHANE:
>(NARRATING)

the assault on merit in the schools was a particularly grievous one, since tens of supervisors were Jews who struggled all their lives to attain their positions on merit, and now faced a calamity. Protests were futile. As long as they remained respectable and turned the other cheek, they were doomed.

>ON SCREEN: NEW YORK CITY. LINCOLN HOSPITAL.

>THE MAYOR IS ADDRESSING THE STAFF.

>MAYOR:

After World War Two, Yeshiva University, the most famous Jewish school in the country, decided to create a medical school for young Jews, wishing to become doctors, to escape the quotas and restrictions on them in medical schools at the time. This hospital owned by the city, was the only one in poverty-stricken Black, Puerto Rican and Jewish poor area in the South Bronx. We needed staff, and fortunately, Yeshiva agreed to provide us with doctors and administrators. Five hospitals have a more dedicated and warm staff, working under terribly difficult budgetary working conditions, bringing superb care to the neighborhood. Today we honor, Dr. Arnold Einhorn for his superb leadership in the Pediatric Division.

AS HE STEPS US TO RECEIVE HIS AWARD, A GROUP OF YOUNG DOCTORS AND HEALTH CARE WORKERS GET UP AND WALK OUT DOWN THE HALL TO AN OFFICE AND SIT AROUND A TABLE. A MAN RISES TO SPEAK.

MAN:

I've drawn up the following list of demands: We, the Puerto Rican militants known as the Young

Lords and Blacks, known as the New Left, who represent the majority now in our community, demand control of the hospital on the ground of racial neglect of our needs...

HE PUTS DOWN THE PAPER, SMILING.

...which means...we want Black and Puerto Rican doctors and other health care workers to take this place over, and kikes, Koreans, and Filipinos out.

APPLAUSE FROM GROUP.

LATER: GROUP DISRUPTS CLASSES AND TAKES OVER OFFICES. THEY ENTER A DOOR MARKED "DR JOSEPH SMITH, OBSTETRICS AND GYNECOLOGY." DR SMITH JUMPS TO HIS FEET AND DASHES TO THE DOOR, AS THEY LOOK MENACING.

ONE OF THE GROUP:
(TO SMITH)

You're not going anywhere.

THE GROUP MEMBER PUSHES SMITH ROUGHLY BACK INTO HIS CHAIR AND TALKS TO ANOTHER MAN IN THE GROUP.

ONE OF THE GROUP:

Tell the director of this hospital we're holding Smith hostage 'til we get word that he is to be removed!

SIX HOURS LATER: PHONE RINGS IN SMITH'S OFFICE. MAN ANSWERS AND SMILES.

ONE OF THE GROUP:
(HANGING UP PHONE)

He's out.

FOLLOWING DAY. DOOR MARKED "DIRECTOR, LINCOLN HOSPITAL." SECRETARY ENTERS AND HANDS DIRECTOR A LETTER. HE READS IT.

DIRECTOR:
(TO SECRETARY)

Twelve doctors, eleven Filipinos, and one Korean, are asking to be relieved of their jobs because of harassment and intimidation.

PHONE RINGS. SECRETARY PICKS UP PHONE AND HANDS IT THE DIRECTOR. HE LISTENS AND HANGS UP.

DIRECTOR:

The city is appointing a Puerto Rican, Dr. Antero Lacot, as Administrator. Last week, we removed a few Jewish doctors working here at Lincoln. Blacks and Puerto Ricans took their place. They knew there'd be no trouble and, of course, there wasn't. such an abysmal lack of spine on the part of the city, and the school, in the failure to back up their staff. A shame. They're pushed and no one pushes back.

THE PHONE RINGS AGAIN. THE DIRECTOR'S SECRETARY ANSWERS.

SECRETARY:
(TO DIRECTOR)

Henry Schwartzchild, member of the Commission of Social Justice of the Synagogue Council of America.

DIRECTOR:

At last, maybe now we'll have some action to protest future things of this kind occurring. We need some respect for our staff, or everyone is vulnerable to the whims of one group or another.

HENRY SCHWARTZCHILD:
(TO DIRECTOR)

I feel, under certain conditions, it's proper for a community to assert its prerogative. Jewish rage here is totally uncalled for.

THE DIRECTOR HANGS UP.

A WEEK LATER: DOCTOR EINHORN IS BEHIND A DESK AND SURROUNDED BY YOUNG LORDS.

> YOUNG LORD:
> (TO EINHORN)

We're asking politely that you resign, and we've sent a demand to Yeshiva University that you will be removed from your post here if you refuse to go willingly. Time for the Jew Director of Pediatrics to pack up and make room for his assistant, Dr. Helen Rodriguez, or else.

A WEEK LATER:

> ON SCREEN: MEMO FROM DEAN LABEL C. SCHEINBERG, EINSTEIN MEDICAL COLLEGE OF YESHIVA UNIVERSITY, TO DR. ARNOLD EINHORN: YOU HAVE BEEN A SUPERB DIRECTOR OF PEDIATRIC SERVICES, BUT I REGRET THAT THE PEDIATRICS DEPARTMENT, FINDS IT ESSENTIAL AT THIS TIME, TO HAVE A DIRCTOR OF A DIFFERENT ETHNIC BACKGROUND.

> KAHANE:
> (MUSING)

Yeshiva taketh away under threat, and under threat, Yeshiva giveth back.

THE FOLLOWING DAY: A GROUP OF JDL PEOPLE APPEAR AT THE OFFICE OF YESHIVA UNIVERSITY PRESIDENT SAMUEL BELKIN.

> KAHANE:
> (TO PEOPLE IN OFFICE)

All of you are to leave this office in 15 minutes.

THEY RUN OUT. KAHANE LOCKS THE DOORS, PICKS UP PHONE AND DIALS.

> OPERATOR:

Yeshiva University.

KAHANE:
(TO OPERATOR)

Belkin is in the hall. Send somebody up here to tell him we want a clear statement that Einhorn will be kept in his post. This office will be in shambles, and a valuable bust of Einstein smashed, if police are called in.

ALL NIGHT KAHANE AND HIS GROUP ARE IN THE OFFICE. THE PRESS OUTSIDE AND SOME MEDICAL STUDENTS ARE ALLOWED IN.

STUDENTS:
(CHANTING)

We're with you.

LATE AT NIGHT: PHONE RINGS FOR KAHANE. HE ANSWERS, HEARS MESSAGE AND HANGS UP.

KAHANE:
(TO GROUP)

Einhorn stays.

KAHANE AND GROUP REJOICE.

MAN:
(ON PHONE)

Rabbi, this is Einhorn. I thank you for your efforts, but I must ask you to leave since I feel this is not the proper way.

KAHANE:
(TO EINHORN)

I tell you something that most Jews helped by the JDL do not understand. We are not doing this for you and we are not interested in what you think. We are doing this because Jewish rights are being trampled on, and we intend to see that those rights are protected, whether you like it or not.

SEVERAL MONTHS LATER: KAHANE RECEIVES A LETTER.

EINHORN:
(READING LETTER)

Dear Rabbi Kahane,

My best wishes for Rosh Hashanah, and I'm extending my deepest appreciation for your past interest in my cause and my deepest apologies for my past ingratitude which I deplore and for which I paid dearly.

Arnold Einhorn

Scene 24

OCTOBER 1969: AN ADVERTISEMENT BY JDL.

                JDL MEMBER:
           (READING ADVERTISEMENT)

John Lindsay must not be elected again as mayor of this city. He is a disaster for the Jews of New York. JDL blames the mayor for tolerating a violent outpouring of Jewish hate. For not acting against the presence of anti-Semites on the payroll. We want Jews to stop thinking as liberals or conservatives. We want a Jewish vote, just as Black leaders have a Black vote.

ARTHUR GOLDBERG IS SEEN STANDING ON A PODIUM.

                GOLDBERG:
                (TO AUDIENCE)

I was immediately contacted by major Jewish organizations in response to this ad. I am proud to see so many of you here (HE POUNDS AD.) it is once again outrageous, once again un-Jewish, once again...the Jewish Defense League!

AUDIENCE MURMURS IN AGREEMENT.

Three hundred of us, all heads of organizations, will give a loud protest to this kind of nonsense.

                KAHANE:
                (NARRATING)

I can't remember a time when 300 leaders managed to agree on a single document. My call for a Jewish vote scared these pygmies to action.

GOLDBERG:

There is no such concept. We vote for the candidate of our choice, not our religion.

KAHANE:
(NARRATING)

If there is no such concept, there should be one.

WOMAN:

The governing Board of B'nai Brith views with disfavor any specific Jewish backing of a particular candidate.

KAHANE:
(NARRATING)

Our problem is our Jewish leaders are a dichotomy: they are both meat and milk, Jewish and other "ism" takes precedence over what is good for Jews.

MAN:

ADL has made efforts to counter the JDL. We are opposed to them, as all Jewish organizations are.

Scene 25

AD IN NEWSPAPER ON SCREEN:

"ZIONISM IS RACISM! WE, THEREFORE, IN NO UNCERTAIN TERMS, CALL FOR THE IMMEDIATE CESSATION OF UNITED STATES SUPPORT OF THE ZIONIST GOVERNMENT OF ISRAEL."

KAHANE:
(NARRATING)

The ad is not shocking, merely echoing the views of the Black extremists that we already know. But the Jewish leadership, well…Sol Liebman of the National Jewish Advisory Council, which encompasses the "usual suspects," so to speak, B'nai Brith, AJ Congress, AJ Committee etc. etc. has this to say:

LIEBMAN:

It is imperative that you know that Council is satisfied that the signers of the ad are a tiny fringe of the black community and in no way are representative of it.

KAHANE:
(NARRATING)

Voila! We've been given our tranquilizer. There is no threat…Another rod and staff who daily comforts us…Will Maslow, Chairman of Negro-Jewish relations in a major organization, adds his contribution to "What, me worry?"

MASLOW:
(LOFTILY)

The signers of the ad are virtually unknown to the general public, white and black, and have no consequence or influence in the black community.

KAHANE:
(NARRATING)

So, back to your football games and mah jong parties. Unless we take a glance at the signers of the ad: Paul Boutelle, Socialist Worker's Party, whose youth group has exploded in high schools and colleges. Vince Benson represents Black intellectuals. Rev. Albert Cleague, an outspoken extremist recently elected to one of the highest posts in the National Council of Churches. Ella Collins, Malcolm X's sister. John Hawkins, editor of Wayne state U's student paper, who puts out dozens of anti-Israel and anti-Semitic articles, Les Campbell, notorious anti-Semite, leader of Afro-American Teachers Association; all totally backed by Arabs...and the new heroes of Black youth. To dismiss them as a "tiny fringe" or "without consequence or influence" is both irresponsible and insane.

Scene 26

BLACK:
(TO GROUP)

Well, the Feds finally realize we're alive, which means we need feedin', clothin', a decent place to live...but there's one hitch.

MAN:

Ain't there always?

BLACK:

This here anti-poverty program is giving money to Jews like they ain't got enough of what they took from our backs. But to get their hands on any money, they have to elect a delegate, and this guy apportions the bucks. You see what I'm sayin, don't ya? They don't vote, they get (HE GESTURES "NOTHING.")

MAN:

They vote for anything.

ANOTHER MAN:

Blackmail, man. They're afraid we'll make trouble. Politicians don't like us, shall we say, misbehavin'. This so-called poverty program is blackmail to keep us quiet by paying us off. With our Puerto Rican friends we'll make the payments easy...Just keep the Jews from voting...and we know how don't we?

ONE MONTH LATER:

> KAHANE:
> (NARRATING)

Every poverty area in the city has it's share of Third World representation, while the Jews, the third largest poverty group in the city, are represented by delegates in only two neighborhoods, and even these two are shaky. For months, black militants in Crown Heights are trying to intimidate the Jewish anti-poverty office and the Crown Heights Jewish Community Council. The neighborhood is a jungle, violent crime commonplace, and the Jew, as usual, terrified.

> MAN:
> (ON PHONE WITH KAHANE)

Rabbi, Sonny Carson us going to take over our office. Hurry up!

> KAHANE:
> (TO HIS BOYS)

Get on the phone! Crown Heights Jewish Council in trouble. Sonny Carson won't share any poverty money with them. We must let him know he'll have to!

TIMES ARTICLE APPEARS ON SCREEN:

> "JDL CAN GET 50 PEOPLE INSTANTLY WORKING VERY EFFICIENTLY ON THE PHONE."

30 MINUTES LATER: COMMUNITY COUNCIL OFFICE IS FULL OF JDL BOYS. ONE IS AT THE DESK. A PERCOLATOR IS NEAR HIM. THE PERCOLATOR IF FULL OF COFFEE. CARSON AND HIS BOYS COME IN.

> JDL BOY:
> (TO CARSON)

Sonny Carson, ain't ya?

CARSON NODS YES.

ONE OF CARSON'S BOYS:
(TO JDL BOY)

Better get movin' on outta here. Last night I told a Jewish teacher who was talkin' about them six million Jews to sit down or there'd be six million and one.

JDL BOY PUTS HIS HAND ON THE PERCOLATOR.

JDL BOY:

If you said that me, I'd cut you up in pieces.

BLACKS SITS DOWN FRIGHTENED.

KAHANE ANSWERS.

JDL BOY:
(LIFTING PERCOLATOR)

Now, who wants a taste of this coffee, fresh, straight from the pot. Sorry, no cup. Or, would you prefer to get on outta here with no refreshments served?

BLACK BOY:
(RISING FROM HIS SEAT)

You talkin' to Carson, man.

KAHANE:
(RISING FROM SEAT)

And you're talking to Kahane.

(TO HIS BOYS)

We're through talking.

CARSON'S GROUP ATTACKS. FIGHTS ERUPT AND JDL ROUTS CARSON'S GROUP.

ONE MONTH LATER.

MAN ON PHONE:
(VERY DISTRAUGHT)

Rabbi, Crown Heights Council here. We've been threatened. An election coming up for director of poverty funds and any of us found voting will be killed!

FOLLOWING DAY: CROWN HEIGHTS. CARS IN STREET WITH BULL HORNS.

MAN:
(SHOUTING ON BULL HORN)

Come out to vote! JDL is here!

KAHANE:

There was no trouble. We took 16 of 24 seats, including that of director.

THE FOLLOWING EVENING. AN INTERVIEW ON TV. INTERVIEWER REFERRING TO A GROUP AROUND THE TABLE.

INTERVIEWER:

Tonight, we'll be discussing Jewish Poverty. Yes, there is such a thing. Anti-Semites believe that Jews are Rothschilds, while Jews, on the other hand, pretend there are no Jewish poor. We hope to gain some perspective on this issue, and with us are Sonny Carson, Meir Kahane, Phillip Bernstein of the Council of Jewish Federations. We'll start with you, Mr. Carson.

CARSON:

The Crown Heights Poverty Council is recently in complete control of Jews, even though Black people make up 90 percent of the community.

KAHANE:

A lie. One out of every four is hardly 90 percent. The anti-poverty agencies who sit upon hundreds of millions of dollars (and more) arrogantly deny the Jewish poor their proper share of the funds. Black anti-Semitism within these agencies is blatant and Black militants who are employed by them have been guilty of physical attacks on Jews within these poor neighborhoods.

FLASHBACK: BLACK MAN TALKING TO FIVE PEOPLE IN OFFICE. TWO OTHER BLACK MEN WORKING WITH HIM BEHIND THE DESK.

BLACK MAN:

Those who are here to cast their vote for delegates to the Crown Heights Council and get their share of whatever is coming to them, form a line here.

THE BLACKS FORM A LINE. A MAN WITH A PAD TAKES THEIR NAMES. AT THE END OF THE LINE, A HASIDIC MAN APPEARS WITH LONG CURLS. BLACK MAN CONTINUES TO TAKE NAMES UNTIL HE COMES TO THE HASID.

BLACK MAN:
(TO HASID)

Sorry, the list is closed for today.

HASID:

But I was here yesterday, and the day before, and you told me the same thing.

HASID POUNDS PAD.

I want you to put my name right here...Shlomo Rubenstein...I spell for you...Shlomo...S-h-l...

BLACK MAN SHOVES HASID'S HAND AWAY.

Git off me pad!

HASID:
(POUNDING ON PAD AGAIN)

Shlo...Shlo...mo...

BLACK MAN STRIKES HASID WITH FIST WHILE HASID SPEAKS. TWO OTHERS KICK AND PUNCH HASID. HE SINKS TO THE GROUND. ONE BLACK MANS GRABS SCISSORS AND SNIPS HASID'S CURLS WHILE HE'S HELD DOWN.

> HASID'S FLASHBACK: SHLOMO IS A CHILD HIDING BEHIND A BAG IN POLAND, 1944. HIS FATHER IS ON THE GROUND, SURROUNDED BY NAZIS. THEY'VE CUT HIS FATHER'S CURLS AND THEY ARE LAUGHING. BOY SOBS.

RETURN TO PRESENT. BLACKS LAUGH UPROARIOUSLY, WHILE HASID GRABS EACH SIDE OF HIS HEAD, FEELING FOR CURLS HE KNOWS ARE GONE, AND SOBS.

(TO OTHERS)

THE HASID IS DRAGGED DOWN THE STAIRS AND IS FLUNG ON THE SIDEWALK. ANOTHER HASID PASSES BY AND PICKS UP THE INJURED MAN. THE SECOND HASID IS LISTENING WHILE THE FIRST TELLS THE STORY, THOUGH OTHERS DO NOT HEAR HIM.

TEN MINUTES LATER. THREE JDL BOYS ENTER, WEARING YARMULKES. THE BLACKS IN THE ROOM ARE LAUGHING, PUTTING THE HASID'S CURLS ON AND OFF EACH OTHER.

JDL BOY:
(TO BLACK IN VOTING OFFICER)

We came to vote.

BLACK BOY SLAMS YARMULKES FROM THE HEADS OF THE JDL BOYS.

BLACK BOY:
(TO JDL BOYS)

You just did.

BLACK BOY PUTS FOOT ON EACH YARMULKE.

BLACK BOY:

Number one...two...three.

JDL BOY:
(TO BLACK BOY)

Pick them up.

BLACK BOY LAUGHS. JDL BOY TAKES BLACK BOY BY THE NECK.

JDL BOY:

Pick them up!

BLACK BOYS SHOVES HIS HAND AWAY. JDL BOYS GRAB BLACK BOYS BY HAIR AND BEND THEIR HANDS BACK.

JDL BOYS:

Pick them up!

GROANING IN PAIN, THE BLACK BOYS PICK UP THE YARMULKES. JDL BOYS PUT THE YARMULKES ON. THEN, THE JDL BOYS GRAB EACH BLACK BOY AND CUT OFF HIS HAIR SO THAT THEY ARE ALMOST BALD. EACH BLACK BOYS FEELS FOR HIS HAIR LIKE THE HASID DID. JDL BOYS TAKE CURLS FROM THE BLACK BOYS HANDS. BLACK BOYS ARE BEATEN SENSELESS. JDL BOYS DRAG BLACK BOYS DOWN THE STAIRS, DUMP THEM IN THE STREET AND LEAVE LAUGHING.

JDL BOYS:
(TO BLACK BOY)

Next time you see one of these, (POINTS TO YARMULKE) you run for cover. And these, (SHOWS CURLS) are going back to Shlomo.

ACTION SHIFTS BACK TO THE PRESENT.

CARSON:

The Jew does not think like us, look like us, or give a damn, except to exploit us, and suck all our blood. The Jew kids have day camps, summer camps, bus trips, and much more. He can do it because he's in control of all the programs in the city.

KAHANE:

Again, you lie! Jews are not represented on 24 of the 26 poverty councils handing out money in the city.

CARSON:

Jews tanning themselves in Miami and gorging themselves on rich Jewish food.

KAHANE:

Ever though to look beyond the Fountainbleau and Eden Roc hotels to South Beach? Nearly 30,000 Jews, 80 percent of them are wallowing in the luxury of an annual income under 3,000 a year. In New York, the same, and 100,000 at the 4,500 level, making Jews the third largest poverty group in the city. Nationwide, 15 percent of all Jewish households have incomes of 3,000 dollars or less per year. And 15 percent of six million Jews adds up to a great many poor ones that no one is bothering with.

CARSON:

C'mon, y'all stickin' together.

KAHANE:

Brownsville, in Brooklyn, once a thriving Jewish neighborhood, is now a surrealistic thing with buildings that look bombed out and are now burned out with drugs, crime, welfare and violence. Elderly Jews have no temples, no centers. They have no life. The Jewish Federations of the major cities, their drive to gain more prestigious parts in the play of life, have forgotten the Jewish poor, if they ever knew they existed in the first place. So much for sticking together.

PHILLIP BERNSTEIN:

Rabbi, I'm getting tired of listening, and I'm sure I'm talking for the rest of us as well. Now, if I may interpose a few words. I'm proud to say I flew to Mississippi with Walter Reuther in 1965 to spend Jewish Communal funds on a Mississippi project for Negroes. And the New York Times mentioned my name, Phillip Bernstein.

KAHANE:

Poor Jews in South Beach and Brownsville are too parochial and provincial and do not make the Times so...

BERNSTEIN:

You want all of us to fit into those two categories?!

KAHANE:

Don't flatter yourself!

THE FOLLOWING DAY: HUMAN RESOURCES ADMINISTRATION BUILDING. A MAN IS SEEN ENTERING THE BUILDING AND GOING DOWN THE HALL TO A DOOR MARKED "ANTI POVERTY FUNDS ADMINISTRATION." THE PHONE RINGS. A SECRETARY PICKS IT UP.

SECRETARY:

I'll see if he's in.

MAN:

Him again?!

SHE NODS "YES." HE TAKES PHONE FROM THE SECRETARY.

MAN:

Sugarman.

SUGARMAN:

I've told you time and time again, if you have a complaint, put it in writing...You will? Good!

AN HOUR LATER: JDL BOYS ARRIVE WITH POSTERS READING, "JEWS ARE POOR, TOO."

KAHANE:
(SHOUTING AND POUNDING POSTER)

Here it is in writing, Mr. Sugarman.

KAHANE SITS DOWN WITH HIS GROUP ON THE FRONT STEPS OF THE BUILDING, BARRING PEOPLE FROM ENTERING.

KAHANE:
(SHOUTING AND POUNDING POSTER)

No, we won't go 'til you remember!

SUGARMAN COMES RUNNING OUT.

SUGARMAN:
(TO KAHANE)

I'm not to blame! When the anti-poverty progress began, Blacks and Puerto Ricans rushed forward with their demands, but no Jewish poverty representative came up to speak for the Jews.

KAHANE:

We're demanding funds now!

SUGARMAN GOES INSIDE AND BECKONS KAHANE TO FOLLOW HIM TO HIS OFFICE. SUGARMAN'S ASSISTANT IS ALSO PRESENT.

KAHANE:
(TO SUGARMAN)

We want pressure from your office to make sure we get our proper share of poverty money, business loans, employment without discrimination against us, rent subsidies for our poor, data gathered on: deserving students turned down by schools, teachers dismissed, quotas set in schools and civil servants denied promotions. We will try to obtain funds from communities for a battery of lawyers to defend our rights. Community control, which will find Jews thrown out of neighborhoods because they are not Black or Puerto Rican, will be met with legal and militant actions, lawsuit, demonstrations, and sit-ins.

SUGARMAN'S ASSISTANT:
(TO SUGARMAN)

Jewish lawyers, defending the likes of you? Never happen. Employment without bias? Never happen. Honest data from bureaucrats? Never happen. The Jew cowering behind the door...no threat. The Black in front of it with a gun...is. Thousands of cowering Jews against thousands of menacing Blacks... no contest.

KAHANE GOES TO WINDOW AND NODS. HIS BOYS COME IN. THEY ARE ALL GIANTS, POWERFUL LOOKING, THREATENING. SUGARMAN'S ASSISTANT LOOKS FRIGHTENED.

KAHANE:
(POINTING TO BOYS)

Thousands of these...no contest.

ASSISTANT:

We will contact the Police Department immediately to have a policeman on duty at election time, and all data will be scrutinized by us.

KAHANE:

And us!

KAHANE AND BOYS LEAVE.

Scene 27

JUNE 1971. IN A TV STUDIO AN INTERVIEWER HAS A GROUP AROUND THE TABLE.

INTERVIEWER:

We'll be discussing Jewish militancy. Our guests today, (EACH NODS AS HE IS INTRODUCED) are Mr. Eisenrath, Reform Temple, Mr. Pincus, Workmen's Circle, Rabbi Meir Kahane, Leader of JDL and Mr. Lichtenstein, Mr. Eisenradt, we'll begin with you.

EISENRADT:

Rabbi Kahane, you violate every ethic and tradition of Judaism.

MR PINCUS:
(TO KAHANE)

You are a self-appointed vigilante group that deserves the unified condemnation of the Jewish community.

RABBI LICHETENSTEIN:

This is a statement endorsed by the American Jewish Committee, B'nai Brith, the ADL, the American Jewish Congress, Jewish War Veterans, the National Council of Jewish Women. The Union of American Hebrew Congregations (REFORM), the Jewish Labor Committee, and the United Synagogue of

America (CONSERVATIVE): Jewish security does not lie in taking the law into one's hands. Unfortunately, the JDL has fallen victim to the very tactics it claims to oppose. We consider it's activities no less harmful and dangerous because it has called itself "Jewish."

KAHANE:

How dare you speak for poor Jews for whom you have done nothing!

EISENRADT:

Taking the law in your own hands and proud of it!

KAHANE:

You should be ashamed of the problems you wish to solve. Those who pass for Jews at the American Jewish Committee leaped to the aid of the poor little Jewish girl named Barbra Streisand who could not move into a $240,000, 20 room apartment on Park Avenue. On her behalf, they ran to court...while we... well, the best way is to tell you a story...

Scene 28

FLASHBACK:

ON SCREEN: SUMMER 1969, NEW JERSEY.

MAN:
(ON PHONE, SHOUTING)

Rabbi, send people with shotguns. There's a riot here! They're going to destroy our stores and us!

BLACKS:
(SHOUTING)

Get the Jew! Break the wall, damn it!

LATER: JDL BOYS IN FRONT OF STORE WITH SHOTGUNS, SPEAKING TO THE PRESS.

JDL BOY:

If rioters had entered, they would have been shot.

BACK TO PRESENT.

RABBI LICHTENSTEIN:

That's un-Jewish and you know it! It's unethical, immoral, and injuring our cause!

KAHANE:

Your ignorance of Judaism is exceeded only by the abysmal boorishness of your congregants. You might search Jewish history for the right response to evil and oppression. Joshua, David, Rabbi Abika, and more...examples of Jewish leadership that took an active and violent part in our struggles for freedom.

RABBI LICHTENSTEIN:

We need no one to tell us what the proper way for the Jew to behave is.

EISENRADT:

Jewish Panthers are what you are. No different. Every time I think of you, I cringe.

KAHANE:

We hear you call us that name and we smile. That reputation protects the poor and trembling. Yours doesn't. you sleek and contented ones that turn a deaf ear to the desperate cries of your own while marching for Black rights in Mississippi. How liberal, how universal, how hypocritical!

TV INTERVIEWER:

James Forman, a militant Black, shocked America by demanding half a billion dollars in reparations from Whites and threatened violence if it is not forthcoming. He has already been given money by churches, contacted the biggest and richest of the synagogues, Temple Emanuel, and informed them he would appear at their Friday evening service to make his demands to recompense for wrongs done to Blacks.

KAHANE:

I decided he would not.

EISENRADT:

I see merit in Forman's demands.

KAHANE:

It might very well be that you had Baptist slave owners for ancestors, but most Jews came here in galleys long after the slaves were freed. Blacks deserve nothing from us and that's what they're going to get no matter where they go. If anyone is talking about reparation, and if anyone deserves it, we Jews are first in line. The shadow of the inquisitions, the Crusades, and both the Catholic and Protestant massacres of Jews are difficult memories to erase.

EISENRADT:

Rabbi Perleman says his congregation was ready to capitulate. It was not your business to interfere.

KAHANE:

We didn't care whether Temple Emanu-el wanted us there or not. I'm not really worried about assimilated Jews whose kitchen costs more than Forman demands. We didn't go there to defend Temple Emanuel, but the synagogue. If this temple paid blackmail, then other temples would be targets.

FLASHBACK: JDL BOYS IN FRONT OF TEMPLE EMANU-EL, SOME WITH BASEBALL BATS, SOME WITH IRON PIPES, NONE SMILING, LOOKING LIKE TOUGH HOODLUMS, WAITING FOR FORMAN. THE PRESS IS THERE TOO.

JDL BOY:
(TO REPORTER)

We told Forman that if he shows up, we'll break both his legs, and they'll carry him home in a box.

MANY POLICE APPEAR.

POLICEMAN:
(TO KAHANE)

You'll have to move across the street.

JDL BOY:

We came to pray.

POLICEMAN STOPPED.

BACK TO PRESENT.

KAHANE:

Forman never showed up.

EISENRADT:

The JDL is spoiling to commit assault and battery. Jews carrying baseball bats and chains, standing like goon squads and led by a rabbi, are the same as ministers of the gospel standing in front of burning crosses.

KAHANE:

The Formans of the world have to learn that no synagogue or Jew will be threatened without reacting!

LICHTENSTEIN:

Speaking for the ADL National Chairman, Mr. Dalsimer, he accuses the JDL of imitating the mindless tactics of racial hoodlums, thereby increasing the danger of explosive riots. We find the group's paramilitary operations and sensationalist appeals to raw emotions and embarrassment. We advise them to stop this trend and concern themselves with what's happening to our fresh air.

KAHANE:
(NARRATING)

We laid aside the Jewish book, raised the ancient Jewish fist, and the calls came in as the week went by...

FLASHBACK:

MAN:
(ON PHONE)

Rabbi, we need help! Give it to us!

MR. PINCUS:

By no stretch of the imagination would I describe any of your actions as "help."

KAHANE:

My powers of description fail me when it comes to that comment. Last week, vandals attacked a Yeshiva. Its windows smashed, its body smeared with rotting vegetables, its pride...humbled. But the following day, when a small synagogue in Borough Park, Brooklyn was attacked on our holiest day, Yom Kippur, and its Jews beaten and terrorized, it was JDL that marched down the block telling the Puerto Rican residents we would smash heads. Fear of JDL galvanized the police into action, and arrests. Later, police had to close off the streets in Borough Park as 1500 people came to hear me speak. Vandals attack a synagogue. My answer was clear and bold. Let that synagogue attack the vandals. Should a gang bloody a Jew, let a Jewish group look for the gang.

INTERVIEWER:
(NARRATING)

Rabbi Kahane has written a play on the subject. We are going to present it now. It is based on a true incident. In the summer of 1969, the Philadelphia Board of Rabbis issued "guidelines" on how to behave if militants attempted to take over a synagogue. The spiritual leaders advised no violence and to allow the militants to have their say. The play is titled, "THE PHILADELPHIA STORY, A ONE ACT MELODRAMA, (A COMEDY)." The opening scene is the Board of director's room of Temple Shalom Shalom Shalom, the most prestigious congregation in the area. Rabbi, will you take over?

KAHANE:
(NARRATING)

James Forman has just finished addressing the congregation, after striding in with 10 machete-carrying aides, demanding to speak before the services have concluded. In conjunction with the guidelines issued by the Board of Rabbis and the Community Relations Council, Rabbi Merton Eisenkopp graciously allowed Foreman to take the pulpit. He proceeded to attack all the "pigs" and "bloodsuckers" of the temple and finished with a demand for $200,000 to be paid in cash. The directors have just finished congratulating Mr. Forman and are walking into a room led by Chairman J. B. Coleman.

BOARD MEMBER A:

Wow! Was that a speech! That guy has to have gall to come in here and insult us like that!

BOARD MEMBER B:

I'm still not sure we should have let him take over the pulpit.

BOARD MEMBER A:

What would you prefer? A fight in the synagogue?

BOARD MEMBER B:

Well, maybe that's the way...

COLEMAN:

Gentleman, gentleman, let's knock it off. We've got important business to talk about, and I want to deal with it before Rabbi comes in. he's busy exchanging theological views with Forman now, so let's hurry.

BOARD MEMBER A:

You're right J.B. We've got to decide what to do about this demand.

BOARD MEMBER C:

I say we have no choice. Who needs trouble from that guy? What the hell is $200,000? Costs us that to renovate last year. Give him his money, call up the newspapers and let's get the thing over with.

BOARD MEMBER B:

And what makes you sure he'll be satisfied with that? Besides, are you sure that the members are going to be willing to give away that kind of money to Forman?

BOARD MEMBER A:

That's no problem. We'll get the rabbi to give them a sermon in social justice, the guilt that must be in all our hearts, and the thing will be a breeze.

BOARD MEMBER B:

First of all, I don't want to give the guy that money; and secondly, I still think we won't get him off our back.

BOARD MEMBER C:

Money talks. That's the name of the game.

BOARD MEMBER D:

Not a penny from me, even if you cowards decide to.

BOARD MEMBER A:

Watch who you're calling a coward!

BOARD MEMBER D:

I'll say it again!

BOARD MEMBER A:

You say that once more...

COLEMAN:

We have enough problems...cut this out. If we don't give money, God knows what he'll do, and he may ask for more. The congregants may be very upset about this.

PAUSE.

I think I have a solution.

HE TAKES A DEEP BREATH AND PLUNGES IN.

The way to get Forman off our backs is to make him our rabbi.

STUNNED SILENCE.

BOARD MEMBER A:

I must be going crazy. You said, Forman our Rabbi?

COLEMAN:
(GLOOMILY)

That's what I said.

BEDLAM BREAKS OUT. ALL MEMBERS SHOUT "NEVER!" AT COLEMAN. BOARD MEMBER D TURNS PURPLE AND HAS TO BE RESTRAINED BY TWO OTHERS. COLEMAN LEAPS TO HIS FEET.

COLEMAN:
(SHOUTING)

Will you all shut up! And I'll explain. Forman is a good speaker. He has a deep voice. He's tall and broad shouldered...the women will love him. If we make him our rabbi at 40,000 a year, we can get him off our backs and help other temples, too. After all, no rabbi is going around threatening synagogues.

BOARD MEMBER A:

But J.B., he's not even JEWISH!

COLEMAN:

We can tell the press it's our contribution to interfaith harmony in the world.

BOARD MEMBER C:
(UNHAPPILY)

But he doesn't know anything about Judaism.

BOARD MEMBER D:
(SARCASTICALLY)

What's the difference?

BOARD MEMBER B:

Rabbi Eisenkopp. We have a contract with him, and he's such a nice guy.

COLEMAN:

We'll make him rabbi Emeritus and let him keep his membership in the golf club. He'll understand. He's made enough speeches on behalf of Forman.

THE BOARD SITS QUIETLY, THEN LOOKS UP AT EACH OTHER, NODDING GLOOMILY.

COLEMAN:

We'll inform Rabbi Forman of his appointment immediately.

EISENKOPP:

I think that Mr. Forman's...

BOARD MEMBER D:

(QUIETLY)

Rabbi Forman.

EISENKOPP:

I beg your pardon?

COLEMAN:

Uh sit down Rabbi. There's something we have to discuss with you...

Scene 28 Part A

                KAHANE:
                (TO GROUP)

Rabbi Eisenkopp, I might add, was all in favor of quotas, Jews dusting off their chairs behind their desks for a Black to take his place, as you all are. Well, now, if it came to you having to do what you're glibly telling others, they have to...

HE SMILES.

You'd have to be carried out on your chairs...now, wouldn't you?

SILENCE.

Anybody?

ALL THE GROUP MEMBERS STARE AHEAD.

                KAHANE:

I thought so.

              RABBI EISENRADT:
              (TO MODERATOR)

I will not sit in this man's presence another moment.

OTHERS RISE.

He will have to continue to entertain your audience without us.

THEY ALL LEAVE. THE MODERATOR APPEARS STUNNED AND CONCERNED.

KAHANE:
(TO MODERATOR)

No problem. Several years ago, 1965 to be exact, I remember another example of the inexplicable, masochistic drive that sends Liberal intellectuals sprawling at the feet of the assorted Black artists to be berated, spat upon, and insulted. In Greenwich Village, in New York, there was a discussion of art, politics, and Civil Rights. One of the panelists was Leroi Jones, another Archie Sheep, both Blacks, and another panelist was a Jew, Larry Rivers. Jones is an author of a play called "The Toilet," which is a good description of the origin of his works...sick, raving cesspools of hate and dirt. 123 Liberals were in the audience waiting for the strokes of the whip. Mr. Jones was happy to oblige.

FLASHBACK:

JONES:

This here is "revolutionary theater," one that hates whites. I want to clear that up right now. Fascist and "Fascism," both of these words have been made obsolete by the words "America" and "Americanism" (CHEERFULLY), and our enemy include all of you out there who are listening.

A PAUSE.

(TO LARRY RIVERS, ON PANEL)

You are also included in this group.

RIVERS CHUCKLES AT THIS WITTICISM.

MR. SHEEP:
(TO RIVERS)

I consider you a friend, an enemy.

(TO AUDIENCE ON STAGE)

We have been murdered, lynched, drawn and quartered by you white folk in Mississippi. Cheney, a Black man, and two white Jews, Schwerner and Goodman, were killed too by the rednecks, but I refuse to praise the white men because they went to Mississippi to assuage their consciences.

JONES:

I regard the two whites as artifacts, mere paintings on the wall.

RIVERS IS UNHAPPY. HE HAS BEEN SQUIRMING THROUGH THE EVENING.

RIVERS:
(SOFTLY)

The Jews also suffered; 6 million of my people were destroyed by the Nazis.

SHEPP:

I'm sick of you cats talkin' about the 6 million Jews. I'm talking about the 5 to 8 million Africans killed in the Congo.

A PAUSE.

This ends our presentation for tonight. Donations for our cause will be accepted at the door. In revolutionary theater, the audience bows to us. Black bowin' to whites is out (SHOUTING) ya hear?! And we ain't applauding you...no way!

AUDIENCE BOWS, THE APPLAUDS.

JONES ARROGANTLY WATCHES THE BOWS WITH SATISFACTION.

BACK TO THE PRESENT:

KAHANE:
(SARCASTICALLY, TO AUDIENCE)

Does the Panther sponsored tour of Harlem, during which the "white pig establishment landlords" were identified as "Jews," predominantly, trouble you? Or is the issue of "Panther News" showing a pig labeled "Zionist" upset you, or Eldridge Cleaver's comment, "Zionists are our enemies wherever they may be" cause you some discomfort? Do we question our support for Panthers merely because they attack our merchants? Let us not be oversensitive. Let us realize oppressed people do overdo their attacks and that we, as moral and suffering people, must learn to accept a little bit of anti-Semitism for the general good.

INTERVIEWER:

We are being barraged with calls. Would you take a few from the audience?

KAHANE NODS "YES."

CALLER:

Rabbi, I must say I am shocked that simple goodness, the attempt to understand the torment in the hearts of the unfortunate, is considered by you to be a degrading illness. What will happen to our world if we listen to such as you?

KAHANE:

You're Jewish of course.

SILENCE.

Of course. Then it's time for you to consider membership in the Jewish Association of Masochists, JAM. You just may pass the stringent requirements: smile when being berated, beaten and kicked while shouting happily, "Beat me again," and intensive hours of breast-beating.

ANOTHER CALLER:

I am proud to be an understanding and reasonable Jew and will do all I can to maintain that reputation of our people in spite of your efforts to defame us.

KAHANE:

As a start, you might demand that your local synagogue hold a fund-raising affair for the nearest Panther hoodlum being tried for murder and hold a mass picketing of some little Jewish-exploiting merchant. And you could throw in Kol Nidre appeals and Yizkor memorials for those Panthers who have met their Maker at the hands of their brothers. With those efforts, you will surely see a phenomenal rise in JAM membership shouting "Beat me, beat me, beat me again!"

ANOTHER CALLER:

Rabbi, thanks to you, I just tore up my membership card in JAM. Too much humbleness was my sin...not too much pride. That's wrong. A man must possess some pride in his being, or he's not a man...not a person...not the Jew he should be.

KAHANE:

You're Jewish?

CALLER:

Mind your own business!

KAHANE:

You're Jewish, the most dangerous kind...an incurable Leftist...a fatal disease. Those who hate us have no better allies than you do. Never a word of criticism about the viciousness of Black haters. On the contrary, you back them, excuse and echo their attacks, "Jewish landlords, Jewish 'gouging' and Jewish 'oppressors.' Blacks have more contempt for you than I do for aiding them against your own people. And the tragedy is, you are incapable of shame!

ANOTHER CALLER:

Rabbi, my name is Mrs. Rachel Goldstein...and I wish to point out that if we, the entire white community, went down on our hands and knees and begged for forgiveness for the damage and cruelty done to the Negroes, we'd never wipe out the shame.

KAHANE:

Unfortunately, that position Madam has resulted in our being kicked. I am ashamed you're <u>ashamed.</u> JDL is here to pull the Jew from degradation where he doesn't belong to pride in his being...where he does. A Jew on his knees is a desecration of God's name. It is the Black who should beg our forgiveness for the damage and cruelty he's done to us!

ANOTHER CALLER:

Rabbi, the Black Panther News has a cartoon of a pig carrying a twisted weapon with a Star of David on it. The cartoon's labeled "World Zionism."

KAHANE:

Would you make a call for me to the Daily News and tell them the JDL will be demonstrating against the Panthers in front of their own headquarters in the heart of Harlem? You may join if you call this...

CALLER HANGS UP.

ANOTHER CALLER:

Rabbi, this is the Police Department. We suggest you reconsider this decision.

Scene 28 Part A

KAHANE:

You are invited to be present tomorrow morning.

THE FOLLOWING MORNING: FIFTY UNIFORMED AND BERETED YOUNG MEN AND WOMEN JUMP OUT OF A VAN AND TAKE THEIR PLACES IN FRONT OF THE BLACK PANTHER BUILDING. THE BIGGEST AND TOUGHEST ARE STANDING GRIMLY, EYES STRAIGHT AHEAD, ARMS FOLDED IN FRONT OF THEIR CHESTS LOOKING LIKE PANTHERS, TOUGH AND DANGEROUS. UNBELIEVING SPECTATORS AND REPORTERS WATCH.

JDL PICKETS:
(SHOUTING)

Stay out of our streets! Panther pigs! Cowards! Where's your courage now?

POLICE STAND NERVOUSLY BETWEEN THE TWO CAMPS. A HUGE PANTHER SHOUTS WARNING TO THE JDL PICKETS OVER AND OVER.

PANTHER:
(SHOUTING)

Get the hell out of here, or you'll be sorry!

THE FOLLOWING DAY. KAHANE IN HIS OFFICE.

KAHANE:
(NARRATING)

That evening, television networks devoted an enormous amount of time to JDL, the first time anyone picketed the Panthers on their own turf. And what stunned them the most was that it was done by Jews.

PHONE RINGS. KAHANE ANSWERS IT.

CALLER:
(ON PHONE)

Rabbi, I am a law enforcement officer in West Virginia, and I must tell you what you did the other day was the greatest thing I've ever seen in my life!

HE HANGS UP. THE PHONE RINGS AGAIN.

> SECOND CALLER:

This is Hertz. We ask that you never use our trucks for such things again!

THE FOLLOWING WEEK
THE PHONE RINGS. KAHANE ANSWERS.

> CALLER:
> (ANGRY)

This is a Black Panther on the line. In our newspaper, we printed a full page exposing your attack on us and letting people know you're the most vicious and dangerous group in America!

> KAHANE:

Bless you. If you Panthers are afraid of JDL, the black hoodlums everywhere will think twice about acting against us. That is exactly our purpose, and we thank you for helping us out.

> PANTHER:

Question: What do you get for the conductor, celebrity, and very rich man in his Park Avenue duplex who has everything? In the case of Leonard Bernstein, the answer is: a Black Panther.

PANTHER LAUGHS.

KAHANE HANGS UP IN RAGE.

Scene 29

A REPORTER INTERVIEWS LEONARD BERNSTEIN AND HIS WIFE.

REPORTER:

Mr. Bernstein, I understand you're giving a party for the Panthers. Interesting.

BERNSTEIN:

We plan to raise dollars for the 21 Panthers who are languishing in jail.

REPORTER:

They're accused of rather serious crimes, plotting to kill policeman, and conspiring to dynamite department stores, police stations and railroad facilities.

MRS. BERNSTEIN:

This will not be a frivolous party, but a chance for all of us to hear what's been happening to the Panthers. They've really been treated very inhumanely. Everyone will be there, Mrs. Vincent Astor, Otto Preminger, art dealers and composers, a whole host of "beautiful" people, about 50 of them, I would say.

THE NIGHT OF THE PARTY. PANTHERS ENTER IN THEIR BATTLE OUTFITS. THE BERNSTEINS GREET THEM.

PANTHER:
(TO THE BERNSTEINS)

Donald Cox, Field Marshal in the Panthers.

BERNSTEIN EXTENDS HAND. COX WILL NOT TOUCH HIS.

PANTHER:

I just returned from a trip to Algeria with Eldridge Cleaver.

PANTHER LOOKS TO CLEAVER, WHO NODS. BERNSTEIN BEGINS TO EXTEND HIS HAND IN GREETING, THEN WITHDRAWS IT QUICKLY, AND NODS, TOO.

PANTHER:

We attacked Zionism and praised the Fatah terrorists.

BERNSTEIN AND GUESTS LISTEN POLITELY.

BERNSTEIN:
(TO PANTHERS)

Please sit down.

ANOTHER PANTHER:
(TO CLEAVER)

Hey man, haven't seen you since you back from Algeria. I heard you were treated like a king. Everything free. All you had to do was help yourself.

CLEAVER:

Yeah...to what?! No gettin' high, no touchin' the chicks...man...I sure missed a hamburger...all that slop they got there...

HE MAKES DANCING MOTIONS.

No jivin' music, no basketball. No one takin' pictures of me, invitin' me to talk and payin' me good money. I'd rather be in jail over here then what they call free over there. Here I'm Field Marshal Cleaver. Here, I'm important. That's fun. No damn fun over there, bein' nothin'. All you Panthers got me to thank. Me and Huey started you up. Made up somethin'. Made ya somebody. Bernstein...even though we agreed to be here, I want to make our position clear. America is the most oppressive country in the world, and if we had the chance, we would kill all the capitalists we could lay our hands on.

MRS. BERNSTEIN GASPS. SHE IS TERRIFIED.

COX:
(TO MRS. BERNSTEIN)

He didn't mean you, even though you are rich.

MRS. BERNSTEIN IS RELIEVED AND SMILES APPRECIATIVELY. BUTLERS COME IN WITH FOOD, MAIDS WITH DRINKS, AND MRS. BERNSTEIN LEADS GUESTS TO HUGE JAR ON TABLE. THEY PROCEED TO THROWS BILLS AND CHECKS IN.

LATER THAN NIGHT:

MR BERNSTEIN:
(ANNOUNCING TO GUESTS)

We've reached our goal, $10,000, thanks to all of you!

DISTINGUISHED WASP WHITE MAN:
(TO BERNSTEIN)

You know we Democrats are the party of minorities, and we are concerned when there are divisions between, so we deeply appreciate your attempt to maintain harmony. We'd have a problem accommodating both sides of our party if they have opposing goals.

A PANTHER HAS BEEN LISTENING TO THE CONVERSATION.

PANTHER:
(TO WASP)

Come, come...you know you're relieved that Black anger is being aimed at Bernstein...not the White Anglo-Saxon Wasp. That's why you give in to quotas and preferential treatment. Leaves you unharmed but cripples the Jew. Latins and Blacks have power now, so you politicians fear us more than the Jew. He's expendable. You can throw him to the alligators.

BERNSTEIN WALKS AWAY. HE DOES NOT WANT TO GET INVOLVED.

POLITICIAN:

(TO PANTHER)

You're an insult to our party!

PANTHER:
(SHAKING HEAD "NO")

Unload all your guilt on the Jew. We blame him for all your sins, and you're absolved. We make the Jew pay for his sins and you have just to sit quietly and let him.

WASP POLITICIAN:

You owe so much to the Jew, and you dare talk...like this?!

A WOMAN JOINS THEM.

PANTHER:

Control, man. That's all it is. Boss us around with the buck...but no more. The days of nice and polite NAACP and Urban League are over. We told them Jews get out, stay off, shut up...or your relatives in Israel will have to raise money to help you get out from an enraged Black community.

WASP ROLLS HIS EYES AT HER, WITH CONTEMPT FOR HER TOADYING. A POLITE, BLACK GUEST JOINS GROUP.

BLACK GUEST:

In my last speech at Brooklyn College, I told it like it is...it's the Jew, in particular, who has kept the Black man in chains. You should have heard the applause from our Black students, man!

BLACK GUEST PULLS OUT PAPER FROM POCKET.

BLACK GUEST:

My son wrote this article from the NYU Black newspaper, subsidized by the school, so you know it's a quality publication. (HE READS) Speaking of the Jews who feed us alcoholic beverages, narcotics, pornography and smut literature, it is clear they make a mockery of the family as a necessary institution of life. In every black ghetto, the owners of the roach and rat-infested tenements who gyp the Negro occupants are Jews! (HIS VOICE RISING) Those responsible from Negro degradation are Jews! (SHOUTING NOW, WITH LOUDEST EMPHASIS ON LAST WORD) The owners of the grinding sweatshops which cruelly exploit Negro workers are still more Jews! (PAUSE) That says it all. (HE PUTS PAPER BACK IN HIS POCKET WITH A SMILE OF SATISFACTION.) Brilliant boy, my son.

WOMAN:

As an artist, I can tell you that, as a class, we are not prone to such behavior, and I can only offer my apologies for those of us who are.

BLACK GUEST:
(LOOKING AT PAINTING ON WALL)

I understand that.

(WALKS TO PAINTING)

This is your contribution to our cause tonight.

(HE GRABS A PEN FROM A NEARBY DESK)

I think it needs some improvement. Make it easier to sell...

(HE DRAWS SEVERAL LINES ACROSS THE PAINTING WITH THE PEN, THEN TAKES A FEW STEPS BACK)

Now that's better.

WOMAN:
(GASPS AND MUTTERS)

You shouldn't have done that!

BLACK GUEST:

You never worry about us Goy artistic people. You simply blacklisted, mangled, bankrupted and trampled upon us. Stupid and incompetent Jewish artistic hacks reaped millions. We should sink the dagger to the hilt in the corpse of the Jewish artistic power system. I couldn't get a nickel for my paintings...but you...

WOMAN:
(GUSHING)

Oh, I'd love to see your work. I know so many people. Maybe they...

BLACK GUESTS STORMS AWAY AND WALKS INTO MRS. BERNSTEIN. HER ARMS ARE EXTENDED HANDING THE JAR

FULL OF MONEY TO THE PANTHER AND BROADLY SMILING. PANTHER HANDS THE JAR TO THE BLACK GUEST. HE ACCEPTS IT. ALL PANTHERS AND BLACK GUESTS LEAVE. BLACK GUEST RETURNS TO PICK UP PAINTING. WOMAN HELPS HIM OUT THE DOOR WITH MONEY AND PAINTING.

THE FOLLOWING DAY:

KAHANE:
(ON PHONE FROM BERNSTEIN)

Bernstein, now it's our turn for a party. The boys and I are coming to your house for a chat. No food 'cause it's not Kosher, so no cost out of pocket for you.

BERNSTEIN:

You'll be stopped at the door!

KAHANE:

We'll disrupt your next concert, denounce you as a traitor and murderer of your own. A dollar for a Panther is a bullet for us...(TO HIS BOYS) He'll see us.

LATER: KAHANE AND TWO JDL BOYS ENTER BERNSTEIN'S APARTMENT. THEY STAND. BERNSTEIN DOES NOT INVITE THEM TO SIT DOWN.

BERNSTEIN:

I know the Panthers are anti-Israel, but I find it necessary to defend the civil liberties of all people. I find it deplorable and painful that fellow Jews should place me in a defensive position when there are so many important issues on which we should be working together.

JDL BOY:

Would you have held a party for American Nazis when their civil liberties were threatened? Would you hold such a party for your own to protect their civil liberties...the right to peace on the street, in the stores, in their homes? The right to work and eat? The right to live?!

BERNSTEIN:

Panthers are idealists who care about everything concerning their people from police brutality to installing stop lights on busy street corners and giving out free breakfast to children.

KAHANE:

How gentle. How touching. How absurdly naïve! You're fortunate you missed some of <u>their</u> parties. What do you know of their world that you commit the abomination of aiding and abetting its atrocities? Nineteen of them killed in shoot-outs with one another, others jailed on charges like drug dealing and murder, running extortion rackets, gunning down those who get in their way. Huey Newton, a graduate from a street gang who is at various times calling himself "Minister of Defense...Supreme Commander...Supreme Servant" raising money for the Party by selling drugs...a Party that regularly bullwhips members with cat-o-nine tails for infractions of disciplines...a Party that tortures former members...had a stomping session where several attacked an errant Panther 'til his face disappeared. And more depravity of such gruesome nature that no one will talk about it! Types like this have an arsenal of guns to fit their agenda: killing cops, a militia to take over the country, and shoot to kill anyone that's in their way...Black or White.

BERNSTEIN:

I don't believe it.

KAHANE:
(TAKES OUT PICTURE)

Here is a picture of "Supreme Commander" Newton with a spear in one hand, a rifle in the other. That is in the rooms of Black students in Ivy League colleges as well as on the walls of slums...

HE PUTS PICTURE ON THE WALL, TAKES A HAMMER AND NAIL OUT OF HIS POCKET AND BANGS THE NAIL INTO THE PICTURE ON THE WALL.

Fits perfect.

BERNSTEIN:

You've ruined my wall!

KAHANE:

Only the beginning. Don't forget to invite him to your next concert. I don't think he has a subscription. We'll be there without an invitation. You're not convinced...

DROPS CARD ON TABLE.

Here's my phone number in case you want to make a contribution...see the light, so to speak.

KAHANE AND JDL BOYS LEAVE. BERNSTEIN STARES AT PICTURE, TAKES IT FROM THE WALL, CRUMPLES IT, AND THEN STRAIGHTENS IT OUT AGAIN. BERNSTEIN LOOKS HARD AT IT, STARES INTO SPACE, DEVASTATED, CRUMPLES IT AGAIN AND THROWS IT IN THE WASTEBASKET. BERNSTEIN PICKS UP CARD AND CALLS KAHANE.

> BERNSTEIN:
> (TO KAHANE)

Rabbi, I believe it.

> ON SCREEN: HUEY NEWTON WAS KILLED IN 1989, FOUND IN THE STREET SHOT TO DEATH FOR TAKING COCAINE FROM OTHER GANGS BY FORCE.

Scene 30

THE METROPOLITAN MUSEUM OF ART. A POSTER OUTSIDE THE MUSEUM SAYS, "HARLEM ON MY MIND."

A MAN WEARING A SKULLCAP ENTERS THE METROPOLITAN MUSEUM OF ART AND TAKES A CATALOGUE. WE SEE A PAGE ON THE SCREEN. IT REFERS TO THE HARLEM EXHIBIT.

WRITTEN ON PAGE:

> "Every hurdle that the Afro-American has yet to jump stands the Jew who has already cleared it, and the already badly exploited Black was allowed to be further exploited by the Jews."
>
> – Candice Van Ellison

THE FOLLOWING DAY OUTSIDE THE MUSEUM, 30 JDL PICKETS ARE SEEN PROTESTING THE EXHIBIT.

> JDL PROTESTERS:
> (SHOUTING)

Hoving must go! Heave-ho to Hoving!

> HOVING:

Her observations are anything but racist. I condemn the tenor of the times, which forces a young person who has lived in Harlem all her life, to have such opinions.

BERNSTEIN:

We do not consider it part of our function to censor the opinions of authors whose books we publish.

KAHANE:

Might I ask why you decided to publish the catalogue in the first place?

BERNSTEIN IGNORES THE QUESTION.

SCHOENER:

I believe the Jews must face the realities of the world in which we live. Miss Van Ellison has merely drawn attention to the facts.

KAHANE:
(TO HOVING)

Mr. Hoving, as long as that catalogue is there, we will be there.

TIMES ARTICLE: CONTROVERSIAL CATALOGUE WITHDRAWN DUE TO THE PRESSURE OF THE JDL. DIRECTOR SAYS THE DIGNITY OF THE MUSEUM DEMANDS THE RENEWAL OF DEMEANING INFLUENCES.

Scene 31

KAHANE:
(NARRATING)

In early 1971, an FBI office was broken into by Jewish Leftists and later, their files appeared in the papers, JDL among them.

ON SCREEN: FBI FILE...TOP SECRET:

Names of JDL members have been provided by Samuel Gaber, Regional Director ADL. The Source of this information must remain secret, as we do not wish it to become public knowledge.

KAHANE:
(NARRATING)

The ADL lists several possible ways the JDL and its leaders might be accused of violating the law. The question that remained unanswered was the exact role of the B'nai Brith, and its Anti-Defamation League in effecting arrests and imprisonment of members of the JDL. Anti-Defamation League is a particularly obnoxious group, whose zeal knows no bounds as it searches for JDL crimes.

TV INTERVIEWER:
(TO GROUP AROUND THE TABLE)

Today we have Mr. Benjamin Epstein, the National Director of ADL, Mel Ziegler of the New York Magazine, and Rabbi Meir Kahane...Mr. Epstein.

EPSTEIN:

The FBI calls us very frequently for information on our area of concern.

ZIEGLER:

When I visited ADL, I came away with the feeling that it does, indeed, know a lot about defamation.

EPSTEIN:

We cooperate with all government agencies. To put an invidious interpretation on such an action is mischievous and even slanderous.

KAHANE:

Gnomes who have no dignity and no self-respect cannot be expected to behave properly... for example, the Annual Salute to Israel Parade Committee, at which we, of course, marched.

> FLASHBACK: DAY OF PARADE. JDL MARCHING WITH A STAR OF DAVID FLAG. BEHIND THEM, THE NEO-NAZI NATIONAL RENAISSANCE PARTY WITH SWATISKAS AND POSTERS SAYING, "GAS THE JEWS." JDL TURNS AND ATTACKS NAZIS.
>
> MAN IN OFFICE TALKING TO KAHANE THE FOLLOWING DAY.

MAN:

Are you aware eight members of the Renaissance party were sent to the hospital after your unprovoked attack on them?? I give you my word, if I am Chairman of the Israeli parade next year, you and your hooligans will not be permitted to march!

KAHANE:

No one is going to carry such signs in this city!

CHAIRMAN:

As parade chairman, I am responsible for a peaceful and orderly program. They were a small, unimportant group of Nazis who we had to protect as they're guaranteed free speech by the First Amendment.

KAHANE:

Hitler had twelve people. There is no such thing as a little bit Nazi. We do not grant the Nazi the right to persuade people to put me in the oven.

BACK TO PRESENT:

EPSTEIN:
(TO INTERVIEWER)

You see what we have to deal with. The Rabbi and his bunch have no respect for the law.

KAHANE:

If that were your concern, you would be better served exposing the Nazi's files rather than ours. Stokely Carmichael, the fiery Black racist, now affiliated with the extremist Black Panther organization, spoke before Arab students at the University of Michigan and had this to say:

FLASHBACK:

CARMICHAEL:
(SPEAKING)

We intend to make it clear we will help the Arabs in any way we can, not only with materials, but also with their lives.

LOUD APPLAUSE.

There are many of us who are getting prepared to fight imperialism. We will fight for Egypt. The only solution to the Black problem in America is armed revolution. We will become the fifth column. They can't stop us.

BACK TO PRESENT.

ZIEGLER:

I should think this needs some looking into by our government...the ADL...

KAHANE:
(TO ZIEGLER)

...the Press...you.

NEWSPAPER HEADLINE: YMHA OPENS DOOR TO BLACK HATE GROUP.

KAHANE:
(NARRATING)

The Young Men's Hebrew Association is allowing a Black Nazi organization to use its facilities. We went to see the YMHA Director, Mr. Weiner.

FLASHBACK:

KAHANE:
(TO WEINER)

The Weusi group is viciously anti-Semitic. We ask that you don't let them in the door.

WEINER:

The city gave them 1 million dollars for economic advancement, so it's a recognized, legitimate group.

KAHANE:

You must have known our story concerning their hate-white agenda when you accepted their application.

WEINER:

Such information is privileged.

ON SCREEN:

NEWSPAPER ARTICLE:

"B'nai Brith gives 10,000-dollar gift to Militant Black Activist, Rev. Milton A. Galamison."

KAHANE:
(NARRATING)

Why not? A foe of Jewish teachers threatened to take over the schools if decentralization was not approved, which was unlawful, yet he was rewarded with the post of Vice President of the New York City Board of Education.

ON SCREEN:

ANOTHER ARTICLE:

"B'nai Brith Anti-Defamation League advocates preferential treatment be given to Negroes when a Jew and a Negro are equally qualified.

KAHANE:
(NARRATING)

A Jewish Anti-Defamation League, whose reason for being is to be vigilant for signs of discrimination against us, is not discriminating against itself!

ON SCREEN:

HEADLINE:

"A HARROWING WAVE OF BLACK ANTI-SEMITISM IN NEWARK SHOWS ARAB FINANCIAL BACKING."

KAHANE:
(NARRATING)

A Black Militant named Hassan, with a long criminal record, who served time in prisons in the District of Columbia, Virginia, and Pennsylvania, has suddenly gone from poverty to riches. He had distributed incendiary leaflets and was involved in a disastrous Newark riot. A sample of his literature in a Newark High School:

ON SCREEN:

LEAFLET:

"Take notice: This Black man you call "nigger" is Semitic Arab and the Arab world will protect it's kin! If black men are further abused in America, the Arab American will declare a war against the Zionist Jew in this America. Call our bluff. Signed, "The Arabs."

ETHNIC CLEANSING

IDENTITY

Scene 32

BLACK MILITANT:

Them Jews want to know why we with the Arabs and not then. I'll tell 'em why. You know the trees they got planted all over Israel from Jews over there? Well, they should have our names on them, not the Jew names. The money for them trees come out of my back, and out of the back of every Black brother in the ghetto.

JEW:

It's clear the Jew knows of your reality, but you know nothing of ours.

ON SCREEN:

NEWSPAPER HEADLINE:

"New York schools throughout the city flooded with blatantly anti-Semitic leaflets that betray signs of Arab financial support to Blacks. Sirhan Sirhan the Arab who assassinated Robert F. Kennedy was revealed to be a vicious hater of Jews."

BLACK:
(NARRATING FROM LEAFLET)

Middle East murderers of Colored people have brainwashed our children, and taught them self-hate. These bloodsucking exploiters must go. Their tricky, deceitful maneuvers are really our enemy and are responsible for the serious educational retardation of our Black children.

KAHANE:
(NARRATING)

Despite the fact that these leaflets appeared throughout the city, none of the New York newspapers even mentioned them. The inexplicable refusal of major Jewish organizations to cry out against Black racism, as they do against white, will ensure the growth of this horror. Decent non-Jews will turn to extremist groups in frustration and despair, seeking protection, as they will have no one else to turn to.

SCENE 33

NEWSPAPER HEADLINE ON SCREEN:

"31-YEAR-OLD YESHIVA IN BROOKLYN CLOSES ITS DOORS DUE TO LACK OF FUNDS."

                KAHANE:
              (NARRATING)

Some years ago, a symposium was held, in the course of which a number of young, Jewish intellectuals were asked to give their ideas on JUDAISM AND THE JEWISH PEOPLE. Arnold Shine:

                SHINE:

It is folly to concern oneself solely with Jewish affairs. As for my children, the possibility they may convert does not concern me.

              KAHANE:
            (NARRATING)

Ned Polsky:

              NED POLSKY:

I see no virtues unique to the Jewish tradition and some evils. I am an anti-Zionist. Jewish chauvinism is no less despicable than any kind.

KAHANE:
(NARRATING)

These are the voices of self-haters. Their children follow every bizarre ideal and pathetically ask who I am? Can you tell me? While the American Jewish Committee, the B'nai Brith, the ADL, the Federations fought to open country clubs and against Jewish education, their children cheered on Black Panthers, even as they spouted their obscenities against "Zionists." They joined the Arabs calling for the dismantling of Israel and leaped into a nihilist world of drugs. After performing their nod to instant Judaism, which was quickly done as quickly forgotten (the hideous horror, the obscene ostentatiousness of the Bar Mitzvah), they go to search for "meaning" in Zen or Jesus. JDL was determined to tell them who they are.

MAN:

I fear the Jewish community may be propelled into isolationism from America, toward group separatism, by focusing on Jewish education in Yeshivas, and I would find this profoundly disheartening.

KAHANE:

Mr. Arent, as a member of a farce called the National Jewish Community Relations Advisory Council, an organization whose title far exceeds its wisdom, I can only say that your crass insensitivity is exceeded only by the Norwalk Jewish Community Center. They held a carnival on Tisha B'av, the saddest day of our history, when throughout centuries, oceans of tears were shed. It was then that we lost our land and wandered into centuries of exiled torment.

ARENT:

Thanks to secular Jewish groups such as ours, the Supreme Court dealt a death blow to public funds going to help support Yeshivas.

KAHANE:

I will speak to youth on campuses about Judaism, its history, its tragedy and its dignity, starting with their clubs.

ARENT:

Hillels are supported by the ADL. You can forget about appearing there.

KAHANE:

I've already been accepted by Rabbi Eliezer to speak at a Hillel on a campus in Canada.

MAN:
(PICKING UP RINGING PHONE)

Rabbi Eliezer.

WE SEE ANOTHER MAN TALKING TO HIM ON THE PHONE.

OTHER MAN:
(TO RABBI ELIEZER)

Rabbi Wald of the Reform Temple here. I understand Kahane is to speak at Hillel. We demand you cancel his visit.

RABBI ELIEZER:

I will not!

HANGS UP. THE PHONE RINGS AGAIN. RABBI ELIEZER ANSWERS. WE SEE A WOMAN TALKING ON THE PHONE WITH HIM.

WOMAN:

This is B'nai Brith. There will not be another penny from us for Hillel unless you cancel the appearance of that racist scoundrel. And we may start looking for another Rabbi.

ELIEZER:

You can start now or wait til after his speech.

KAHANE:
(NARRATING)

A week before my arrival, the Canadian Jewish Congress, the "Holy See" of Canadian Jewry, called in the Hillel student leader who was involved in scheduling my appearance.

MAN AND STUDENT IN OFFICE.

MAN:
(TO STUDENT)

I'll be brief. Your defiance is unacceptable. We will not have a fascist addressing the student body.

STUDENT:

If you'll excuse me, the Rabbi has never forbidden the use of free speech at any of his appearances.

MAN:

If you proceed with this, there'll be consequences. Your grades have not been up to par as it is.

STUDENT SHRUGS SHOULDERS AND LEAVES. WOMAN TALKING TO RABBI ELIEZER. ON PHONE.

WOMAN:

Rabbi, you will be unable to find a placement anywhere. Get rid of that man or else!

ELIEZER:

I'm willing to let the students decide...unless, of course, you are willing to face a full-scale rebellion on campus. Young people, as you know, love protesting, and defending him, and I will be most welcome to their passionate spirits.

WOMAN ON PODIUM ADDRESSES STUDENTS.

WOMAN:

The B'nai Brith is asking that each of you look into your hearts and ask yourselves whether you want to encourage a man who is a disgrace to our people to spread his poison to impressionable minds.

STUDENTS STOMP THEIR FEET AND SHOUT "KA-HA-NE!" WOMAN TRIES TO OUTSHOOT THEM BUT FAILS. SHE BANGS ON THE DESK, AND SHOUTS "BE QUIET OR WE'LL CLOSE THESE CLUBS. REMEMBER WHO'S PAYING THE BILLS HERE!" THE STUDENTS SHOUT EVEN LOUDER "KA-HA-NE!" UNTIL SHE LEAVES THE PODIUM. A STUDENT JUMPS TO THE PODIUM. HE IS

SCENE 33

THE STUDENT LEADER WHO HELPED SCHEDULE KAHANE'S APPEARANCE.

STUDENT:

Are we going to give in to tolerationism that can't bear to hear a difference of opinion?

STUDENTS ROAR NO!

KAHANE:
(NARRATING)

This was the beginning. I went on to appear on campus after campus, all over the United States, to packed auditoriums.

(SPEAKING TO STUDENTS)

There are many religions in the world. What makes us different from the rest, unique, set apart? The study of Torah. Throw yourself in its waters. It envelops you, captures your heart, your mind, your consciousness, your being. The outside world fades into forgetfulness, the petty, foolish, mundane world of materialism. Deeper and deeper your plunge. Torah is a garment. Wrap it around you. Torah is a new world. Discover it. Torah guides you in every act of your life. Boorishness, immaturity, grossness, and lowness are cleansed from your being as the waters of Torah wash across your soul.

THE STUDENTS ARE MESMERIZED DURING HIS SPEECH. AT THE END, THEY RISE, WILDLY APPLAUSE AND SHOUT "BRAVO!"

A WEEK LATER:

KAHANE IS BACKSTAGE ABOUT TO GO OUT ON THE PODIUM OF AN AUDITORIUM TO ADDRESS STUDENTS WHO ARE SCREAMING AND SHOUTING, "KAHANE, FASCIST!"

BOY:

Two hundred Leftists out there, mostly Jews and Arabs, all anti-Israel and anti-JDL. You really think you should go out there?

KAHANE GOES OUT THERE. THE SCREAMING CONTINUES.

KAHANE:
(SHOUTING)

I will stand here all night, but you will never get me to cancel this speech!

KAHANE'S GROUP OF VERY STRONG, POWERFUL BOYS GOES THROUGH THE CROWD SHOUTING, "LET HIM SPEAK." ALL QUIET DOWN.

KAHANE:

You came here to the university and contrasted the farcical Judaism you learned with the depth taught by agnostic professors, leftist movements, and radical causes...

STUDENT:

Orthodoxy is nonsense. Forget temples. You can pray at home. Forget being Kosher for clean food, when we have the Pure Food and Drug Act, and why be forbidden to light a lamp on the Sabbath when it's no longer work. Orthodoxy is dying and there's no reason to grieve old, bearded men who have nothing in common with us at all!

KAHANE:

Wrong! Judaism is not a travesty dreamed up by status-seeking parents and glittering but vapid temples. Your image of Orthodoxy is a product of ignorance. We have a select and unique group of Orthodox young men who have deep knowledge of Torah, and can discuss Plato, Keynes, Faraday, and Marx, who can win your admiration and make it possible for you to say, "I can be an Orthodox Jew, now."

A SHOUT FROM A MAN IN THE AUDIENCE.

MAN:

I'm Rabbi Stein, a Reform Rabbi, and with me is Rabbi Meyer, a Conservative Rabbi, and we protest your obvious prejudice against our forms of Judaism that rejects all the outdated rituals of Orthodoxy, and are legitimate, if not more so, than yours!

KAHANE SMILES.

KAHANE:

Imagine, if you can, a Passover that never quite manages to survive the Seder, usually in the grandparents' home in Brooklyn, which is a hodgepodge of

Manischewitz matzoh and getting it over as quickly as possible to get the food. But Hanukkah sees an upsurge in piety...because it's an easy holiday to keep. No fasting, no scrubbing the house, no sitting a makeshift room in the cold, no inconveniences as other holidays demand...just gifts and celebration. What foolishness! What should a man who loves bacon and eggs think of the one who died rather than have the flesh of the swine cross his lips. Or what should one like you, who desecrates the Sabbath riding in his fancy car, think of the fool who died, rather than violate it? What should a spiritual leader like you, who looks upon the Torah as pagan myth and rabbinical fraud think of those men who died thinking this is really the word of God? Those old Jews suffered tyranny under the Greeks without a murmur. It was only when these religious beliefs were trampled, the ones you have no use for, that they rose up. Now, it appears to those like you, that they died needlessly...that Hanukkah is one great mistake. And so, if I were a Reform or Conservative Rabbi, I would try to bury this ghost...to flee from the tormenting question, "how do Jews who are sophisticated and modern reject the laws of the Maccabees died for, yet celebrate their martyrdom?" in other words, to the non-Orthodox Jew, what in the world is Hanukkah?

RABBI STEIN:
(JUMPING TO HIS FEET SHOUTING)

Imagine the Sea of Torah he's talking about. A whole auditorium of beards, black hats, not daring to glance at a woman who's hidden behind a curtain with the rest of her sex...oops...I shouldn't have mentioned the word.

KAHANE:
(TO STUDENTS)

I can always depend on such as him to prove my point...a crying need for Jewish education. The pipe-smoking plutocrats at the Federation of Jewish Philanthropies hand out millions, but not a cent for Jewish education. We want to Judaize the Federation, starting with picketing at the homes of their leaders. Those with us?

A ROAR ERUPTS FROM THE AUDIENCE. STUDENTS ARE CLAPPING AND SHOUTING AND RUNNING TO THE PODIUM TO VOLUNTEER.

A WEEK LATER:

EXCLUSIVE NEIGHBORHOOD WITH BEARDED, UNKEMPT, LONG HAIR HIPPY TYPES PARADING IN FRONT OF THE FEDERATION LEADER'S HOME NAMED "HEYMAN" AND

CARRYING POSTERS, "FEDERATION MONEY FOR JEWISH CAUSES" AND "HEYMAN IS UNJEWISH."

HEYMAN COMES RUSHING OUT OF HIS HOUSE.

> HEYMAN:

I'll see you in court.

> JDL BOY:

We'll be picketing all your nonsense, synagogue breakfasts, dinners, banquets...

HEYMAN STORMS BACK TO HIS HOUSE S SHOUTING GOES ON OUTSIDE.

A WEEK LATER:

A COURTROOM. KAHANE, HEYMAN AND NEW YORK STATE SUPREME COURT JUDGE GREENFIELD ARE INSIDE.

> JUDGE:
> (TO KAHANE)

You understand the Federation issued an injunction against you. The law forbids you, therefore, from interfering with the home lives of officers and trustees of the Federation.

HEYMAN, DELIGHTED, TURNS TO GO.

> JUDGE:
> (TO HEYMAN)

One moment, Mr. Heyman. JDL disagrees vehemently with the way in which you distribute Federation funds, serving others and not your own. May I remind you of the rabbinical law, "As between the poor of another community and one's own, the poor of one's own community comes first."

A MONTH LATER:

MR. HEYMAN ADDRESSES A GROUP.

> HEYMAN:

Gentlemen, the Federation has received thousands of letters to increase funds for Jewish education. Those in favor of 100,000 dollars, raise their hands.

ALL RAISE THEIR HANDS.

KAHANE:
(ANSWERING A REPORTER'S QUESTION)

A disgraceful pittance. We will be uninvited guests at their next dinner.

SEVERAL WEEKS LATER:

A FLYER IS CIRCULATED BY JDL BOYS AT FEDERATION DINNER. IT READS: "NOT ONE PENNY SHOULD BE GIVEN THEM. THROW THE RASCALS OUT."

JDL BOY:
(SHOUTING)

From their fashionable eastside offices, these leaders, in their gray flannel suits, and ever-present pipes in their mouths raise tens of millions of dollars each year. Money for hospitals whose clientele is not Jewish, for unwed mothers, 90 percent of whom are not Jewish, but funds for Jewish education, the heart of Jewish survival, is forbidden.

WHILE HE IS SHOUTING, OTHERS ARE SHOUTING "GET OUT OF HERE, WE'LL THE POLICE." THE POLICE ARRIVE AND TAKE HIM OUT WHILE THE SHOUTING MATCH GOES ON. AFTER THEY LEAVE A MEMBER RISES.

MEMBER:

If you don't mind, I'd like to say something...about my shame and ignorance that I passed onto my son...a youngster who, like most Jewish boys, needed sacrifice and a cause. And he found it. If not Jewish, then non-Jewish, anti-Jewish, even the Viet Cong and Fatah. Thanks to me, his school, and his temple, he never heard of other heroes who fought for Jewish freedom, and who are at least as precious as the Vietnamese. His heroes were Fidel, Che and Ho.

FLASHBACK:

MAN IS TALKING TO HIS SON, AGE 13.

SON:

Today the Rabbi talked to me about the Sabbath and Kosher food...why we have these rituals. Interesting.

MAN:

This is not the purpose of the Bar Mitzvah, that you learn such nonsense. You must understand that.

BACK TO THE PRESENT:

He understood so well that in college he went to school on Yom Kippur after I and his mother spent two hours worrying about what to wear. That night, he informed us he was planning to join the New Left...anti-Semitic, anti-Israel, anti-himself and us, most of all. Then, a miracle happened.

FLASHBACK:

JDL BOYS PUTTING UP POSTERS WITH PICTURES OF THEM AND WORDS BELOW. MAN'S SON APPROACHES...

SON:

Who he?

JDL BOY:
(POUNDING PICTURE)

Never again will a Jew wonder who is Dov Gruner, young or old! He was never a man, your age, of a Jewish National Liberation movement who was hanged fighting for the cause of Jewish freedom...

(SEE PICTURE ON FOLLOWING PAGE)

JDL BOYS PUTS UP ANOTHER POSTER AND ANOTHER, NAMING PEOPLE ON EACH.

Shlomo Ben Yosef, another hero to whom we should be like and to whom we should be grateful. He was also hanged...so you could be free in your land. And so many others killed, jailed, tortured...young men like you who had enough pride and love to fight for their own...and die for them.

(SEE PICTURES ON FOLLOWING PAGE)

BACK TO PRESENT:

MEMBER:
(TO AUDIENCE)

Shall I go on?

MURMURS OF ASSENT.

The following week Kahane appeared speaking on campus. My son came to me that night...

FLASHBACK:

SON:

For the first time after hearing Kahane, I felt I was a Jew. He made so many of us feel more Jewish in one hour that all the fat cat rabbis and brotherhood meetings have in all our years. My Judaism came alive, and I don't think it will ever die. I'm going to organize a chapter of the Jewish Defense League on campus. So many of us feel now that he gave us the greatest gift of all, the gift of our heritage.

BACK TO PRESENT:

MEMBER:

I thought I'd be furious, but strangely, I felt as grateful as he did. I had my song back and myself...as well.

MEMBER IS APPLAUDED

HEADLINE ON SCREEN:

"FEDERATION TO GIVE $200,000 TO VANDALIZED YESHIVAS."

KAHANE:
(NARRATING)

The federation of Jewish Philanthropies has never, in its 51 years given a penny for Jewish Orthodox Hebrew schools. The total damage is $750,000...and the Federation has millions, which it distributes liberally to anyone, but Jews... especially types like us. I think, at last, we've put them to shame. They'll never give us credit. No matter.

END OF PART ONE

Fifty Years Since The Hanging Of Dov Gruener

SHMUEL BEN ELIEZER
Staff Reporter

This week marks the fiftieth yahrzeit (anniversary) of the hanging of four Irgun operatives in pre-state Israel by the British.

The four, Dov Gruener, Mordechai Alkashi, Yechiel Dov Dresner and Eliezer Kashani, were secretly executed at four in the morning without prior warning to either their families or the prison rabbi.

The four Olei Ha-gardom (hanged prisoners), as they are known, refused to ask for a pardon, insisting on their being treated as prisoners of war.

Dov Gruener had been captured during a raid by the Irgun on the British Police station in Ramat Gan. During his trial he became famous for standing up to his captors. He became the symbol of the Yishuv's fight for independence from the yoke of British rule. Dov Gruener, whose nickname was 'the little lion', was immortalized in the symbol of the city of Ramat Gan, which depicts a lion cub fighting a full grown lion (the British Empire).

In retaliation for the hanging of the four Irgun freedom fighters, the Irgun staged a spectacular raid on Acre Prison, 20 days later, made famous in the movie "Exodus" starring Paul Newman.

This week, veterans of the Irgun and former prisoners of the Acre Prison gathered to remember their fallen comrades. A monument is being erected in their memory.

More News on Pages 18, 42, 60, 72

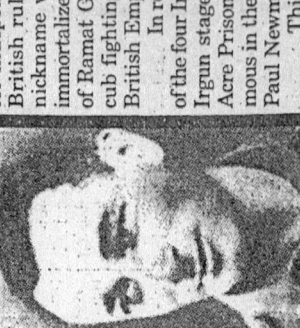

Dov Gruener z"l
Irgun freedom fighter hung by the British 26 Nisan

Part 2

ETHNIC CLEANSING

RUSSIA

Scene 1

KAHANE:
(NARRATING)

And now the JDL must take on another problem. In 1953, the Russian government, under the rule of the tyrannical dictator Josef Stalin, prepared to continue the physical extermination of the Jewish people, which began in 1936, when Yiddish artists and writers were liquidated. In 1948, the reign of terror continued against Jewish intellectuals when Shlomo Mikhoels was found decapitated on a street in Minsk...1952, a secret trial and execution of 24 of the leading intellectuals, and a huge number of others were sent to prison camps. This was followed by the accusation of a plot by Jewish doctors to "poison the entire Russian leadership." Russian press and radio hammered away at this so-called "scheme" relentlessly. And this was followed by final preparations being made for mass deportations to Asia, which were to be a prelude to...mass genocide...then, Stalin died. And so, for 18 years, there's been a divided and weakened Moscow needing friendship from the West, making it unable to simply sweep people up without the benefit of trials. All this could change tomorrow. A new Stalin could emerge. The intense hatred for Jews, traditional in Russian society, would again find an outlet. Despite all of this, for 50 years, the silence of the American Jew is deafening. We sit in our hotels and bungalow colonies, take European and Israeli tours and hikes, downing our falafel and pizza, our frankfurters and chopped liver, and will not rush into the street or pick up the phone to help. JDL determined that there would not be the same lack of reaction to Jewish disaster as there was by Jews in World War 2. So, the battle for Soviet Jewry begins. And there is little time. Never Again!

A CHORUS OF VOICES IS HEARD BEHIND KAHANE, REPEATING THIS SLOGAN IN A STACCATO CADENCE.

A WEEK LATER:

JANUARY 1970. AN ARTICLE APPEARS IN THE PAPER.

ARTICLE ON SCREEN:

> "The Moscow Philharmonic Orchestra appeared at Brooklyn College for a concert. It was part of the growing American-Soviet cultural exchange program for which both governments had such high hopes. Music lovers filled the auditorium for a night of culture."

KAHANE:

So did JDL.

FLASHBACK:

IN THE CONCERT HALL, THE FIRST NOTES BURST UPON THE AUDIENCE. FROM A BACK DOOR, AT THE SAME TIME, A BAND OF JDL YOUNGSTERS RUSH ON STAGE, SHOUTING "LET MY PEOPLE GO." THE SOVIETS FLEE THE STAGE, AND TWO JDL BOYS STARTING HEBREW LIBERATION SONGS AND WAVING ISRAELI FLAGS. THE AUDIENCE IS BOOING AND SHOUTING TO JDL BOYS, "YOU GET OUTTA HERE. WE DIDN'T COME HERE TO SEE THE LIKES OF YOU! WE'RE CALLING THE POLICE!" SEVERAL OF THE AUDIENCE CLIMB TO EJECT JDL. THEY ARE THROWN BACK. AS FIGHTS BREAK OUT, PEOPLE FLEE THE HALL. POLICE ARRIVE AND RESTORE ORDER.

KAHANE:
(NARRATING)

The Brussels conference on Soviet Jews will soon convene in Belgium. I plan to attend and share my vision with them.

HE STARES OFF INTO SPACE.

Jewish leaders in every capital in the world led a march of 25,000 of us, sitting down and refusing to move until they promised to save our brothers and sisters. The theme of the march was: NO FREEDOM...NO TALKS...NO BENEFITS FOR THE SOVIETS...In other words, *Nyet to them, as they say to us. Nyet...to trade talks, disarmament talks, cultural talks, space talks, tourism talks...and "yes" to legal harassment of Soviet officials, embargo and boycott, non-violent civil disobedience, non-stop demonstrations at Soviet embassies, compulsory courses on the Soviet-Jewish question in all Jewish schools.

A WEEK LATER:

KAHANE IS IN COURT. 4PM.

JUDGE:

You have been charged with obstructing governmental operations time and time again.

KAHANE:
(CYNICALLY)

In which Jewish leaders never took part.

JUDGE:

In light of your brazen, brazen defiance of the law, I have no alternative but to find you guilty. The case is adjourned for sentencing. Next case.

KAHANE:
(NARRATING)

Within minutes after the verdict was delivered, I was on my way to Brussels. In my pocket was a refusal to be recognized as a delegate, courtesy of the American Conference on Soviet Jewry and hoped that my appearance would prompt those delegates who believed in free speech to insist on my appearance.

SEVERAL HOURS LATER, KAHANE ARRIVES IN BELGIUM AND IS GREETED BY THE PRESS.

REPORTER:
(TO KAHANE)

It is to our understanding that you are barred from the conference.

KAHANE:

Then they are behaving like the Russians they're allegedly fighting. I will proceed to the hall. We shall see if they are capable of such tyranny.

AT THE ENTRANCE TO THE HALL, A GUARD HANDS KAHANE A NOTE. THE PRESS IS WITH HIM. HE READS.

KAHANE:
(TO PRESS)

Rabbi Schachter's reply. He's the conference chairman. They've decided to bar me.

A PAUSE.

Spilled our blood on the barricades, and now this...while playwrights, producers, authors and architects who have done nothing are allowed entry.

PRESS:

You'll force your way in and make demands, of course, as you always have.

KAHANE:

I'm leaving because I did not come to disrupt the conference, and I will unveil my program to the press later in my hotel room.

KAHANE LEAVES THE HALL AND IS NEAR HIS CAR WHEN HE IS SEIZED BY THREE MEN. ONE OF THEM SAYS, "POLICE." KAHANE STRUGGLES WITH THEM.

KAHANE:

I demand to see your credentials!

THEY SHOW CARDS SAYING THEY ARE "SURETE ETAT," STATE SECURITY (OFFICIAL TRANSLATES TO KAHANE.) KAHANE IS TAKEN AWAY TO THE POLICE STATION, AND THE OFFICE OF A TOP OFFICIAL, A. REUSS, A GENIAL MAN.

AT THE CONFERENCE HALL.

MAN:

The chairman calls Otto Preminger, the famous Hollywood Producer, to favor us with his thoughts on how we can help our benighted brothers in the Soviet Union.

OTTO PREMINGER:

I vehemently protest the exclusion from the conference of JDL, the exclusion of Dov Sperling, a Soviet Jewish hero who spent two years in a prison camp.

BOOS FROM THE AUDIENCE.

I demand the right to finish my speech!

BOOS CONTINUE. PREMINGER LEAVES THE STAGE.

CHAIRMAN:

We now have with us today Mr. Menachim Begin, who will address us now.

BEGIN:

I'll start by saying I, too, had the same attacks made by me as on Rabbi Kahane. As you know, if not for me, there would not have been an Israel. If not for him, there would not be the exodus we hope for from the Soviet Union.

JEERS FROM THE AUDIENCE. ONE MAN LEAVES HIS SEAT AND APPROACHES THE PODIUM.

MAN:

Mr. Chairman, William Wexler here from B'nai Brith. I want it on record that this man is a liar! And with me is Rose Halpern, Jewish Agency executive....

BEGIN DOES NOT ANSWER WEXLER. ROSE HALPERN, WEARING A FANCY HAT, BEGINS SCREAMING AT BEGIN.

ROSE HALPERN:

Fascist!

KAHANE:
(NARRATING)

And Begin, who led the radical, militant Jewish national liberation force, the Irgun Zvei Leumi, into the pages of Jewish history, the man who risked his life every minute for so many years, the man who hid from the British and whose family lived in constant fear, while Wexler and Halpern lived the good life in America and tormented him the way they're tormenting me now.

BEGIN:

(TO HALPERN)

Madam, you have a hat on your head. I had a price on mine.

MEANWHILE, AT THE POLICE STATION.

OFFICER REUSS:
(TO KAHANE)

I apologize for this, but this was not my doing. My government has been under great pressure from the Conference. They refer to you as "undesirable." We have endured tremendous pressure from the Soviets as well, who have also labeled you as "undesirable." However, we would still let you go free if the conference says they will allow you to enter the hall. I am waiting for word from them now.

THE PHONE RINGS. REUSS ANSWERS, LISTENS, THEN HANGS UP. REUSS SHAKES HIS HEAD "NO."

OFFICER REUSS:
(APOLOGETICALLY)

The Minister of Justice says you're to be expelled.

KAHANE:
(NARRATING)

The irony of a Christian apologizing to a Jew for the actions of his fellow Jews.

MEANWHILE, BACK AT THE HALL, A STORM BREAKS OUT AS SOME DELEGATES ARE FURIOUS AT KAHANE'S TREATMENT.

MAN:
(JUMPING ON THE PLATFORM)

I demand to know what happened! Why Kahane was not allowed...

HE IS PUSHED OFF THE PLATFORM. OTHERS RISE DEMANDING EXPLANATIONS, SHOUTING, "YOU HAVE NO RIGHT...YOU SHOULD BE ASHAMED," ETC.

AT THE AIRPORT, KAHANE AND POLICE IN A CAR PULL UP TO A BRITISH AIRWAYS PLANE. REPORTERS AND CAMERAMEN SURROUND THEM. A BRIEF SHOVING MATCH BETWEEN THE PRESS AND POLICE ERUPTS AS THE PRESS TRIES TO GET NEAR

TO KAHANE, THE POLICE PREVENTING THEM FROM DOING SO AND MANAGING TO GET KAHANE ON THE PLANE.

AT THE CONFERENCE:

CHAIRMAN:

Rabbi Kahane is now talking in the air where he belongs. His plane is gone, and we can all breathe easier. Now we can peacefully proceed with our agenda.

OTTO PREMINGER:
(SHOUTING)

JDL was excluded because little people fear its power to sway Jews, and fear its power to shake them from their do-nothingness. It was fear that led them to the shameful expulsion of the Jew.

CHAIRMAN BECKONS AND POLICE ENTER THE HALL. PREMINGER IS EXPELLED.

CHAIRMAN:

And more will be expelled if they cannot behave in a proper manner.

SILENCE IN HALL.

MAN:
(ON PODIUM)

We are proud to say we have arranged for the following conferences to be held with heads of state for further discussion.

HE DRONES ON BUT IS NOT HEARD.

KAHANE:
(NARRATING)

Because concrete plans were barred from the agenda and the usual platitudes droned on, the Jews in Russia were doomed to disappointment, high hopes dashed, and the little time they had left continues to run out.

Scene 2

A WEEK LATER:

ON SCREEN: CONCERT HALL IN ROSLYN, LONG ISLAND

MAN:
(TO AUDIENCE)

I'm Robert Bernstein, Director here, and I want to welcome you all to our presentation today, none other than the great Russian violinist, Valery Klimovrthy. Enjoy!

MR. KLIMOV APPEARS ON STAGE AND STARTS PLAYING. BERNSTEIN SITS DOWN, AND HIS SMILE TURNS TO HORROR AS JDL MEMBERS RACE PAST TWO POLICEMEN AND STORM THE STAGE. THE VIOLINIST AND HIS ACCOMPANIST AT THE PIANO ARE HERDED BACKSTAGE. SOME PEOPLE IN THE AUDIENCE FLEE. THE POLICE ARRIVE.

BERNSTEIN:
(TO AUDIENCE)

I've never seen a more blatant example of hooliganism in my life! The actions of this group are doing nothing but embarrassing the Jews of America.

KAHANE, WHO IS IN CUSTODY WITH OTHER JDL MEMBERS, SHOUTS TO BERNSTEIN.

KAHANE:

The American Jewish concert lover like yourself, who laces love of art over his people, gets nothing but our contempt!

BERNSTEIN:

We're building bridges of friendship. I can't expect the likes of you to understand that!

KAHANE:

Feel good at a concert, and the cries of the victims aren't heard. I can't expect <u>you</u> to understand <u>that!</u>

KAHANE IS LED AWAY.

A WEEK LATER: KAHANE AND 200 OF HIS FOLLOWERS ARE SEEN IN THE COLD AND DRIZZLE MARCHING TO THE SOVIET EMBASSY AT 67TH STREET AND THIRD AVENUE, WHERE ANOTHER HUNDRED FOLLOWERS ARE WAITING. LINES OF HELMETED, CLUB-CARRYING POLICEMEN WAIT BEHIND BARRIERS TO PREVENT ANY ATTEMPT TO REACH THE SOVIET MISSION DIRECTLY BEHIND THEM.

POLICEMAN:
(TO KAHANE)

Rabbi, I'm a Jew and I ask you, from one to the other, to behave as one.

KAHANE:

I will.

POLICE INSPECTOR:

You'll have to move to the State Armory, just a block away from here. You cannot stand at the intersection.

KAHANE:

We intend to enter this block and stand in front of the Park East Synagogue. Though it's across the street from the Soviets, we want to pray in front of the synagogue.

POLICEMAN:
(BARELY HOLDING BACK A SMILE)

Come on Rabbi. You don't really want to pray.

KAHANE:

But I do. I intend to exercise my freedom immediately.

VOICE ON BULLHORN:
(BELLOWING)

Kahane, if you take one step further, I'm coming for you.

POLICE INSPECTOR:

No one is permitted on this block. You must move immediately...captain's orders!

KAHANE:
(TO POLICE INSPECTOR)

I will.

PROTESTORS WITH KAHANE START CHANTING "FREE SHARANSKY. LET MY PEOPLE GO." KAHANE PUSHES HIS WAY INTO A BARRIER AND INTO THE POLICE BEHIND IT. A CROWD OF JDL SURGES FORWARD. CLUBS BEGIN TO FLY AND FISTS IN RETURN. A 75-YEAR-OLD SPECTATOR FALLS TO THE GROUND FROM A POLICE BLOW ON THE HEAD. KAHANE IS BRUTALLY BEATEN AND BLOODIED ON THE HEAD AND BODY BY POLICE.

SOME DEMONSTRATORS TRY TO INTERVENE, AND THEY ARE BEATEN MERCILESSLY. DESPITE THE BLOWS, THE CHANTS CONTINUE, "FREE SOVIET JEWS. FREE SHARANSKY!" THEY KEEP CHANTING UNTIL THE LAST PROTESTOR IS DRAGGED OFF IN A PADDY WAGON.

KAHANE:
(NARRATING)

For the second time in 24 hours, I spent several hours in jail, this time charged with felonious assault, riot, harassment, and disorderly conduct. No matter. Until the Soviets capitulate, they will have no peace. The media responds only to actions and arrests. Millions of Jews depend upon my appearance on page one in Russia. So, I must turn a deaf ear and a blind eye to police warnings.

POLICE INSPECTOR:
(TO PRESS)

From now on, demonstrators will be allowed to picket on the block of the Soviet Mission itself, where they can be seen and heard.

TEN DAYS LATER:

NEWSPAPER ARTICLE ON SCREEN:

"JDL IN 100-HOUR VIGIL OUTSIDE SOVIET MISSION IN SNOW AND BITING COLD."

KAHANE:
(TO HIS GROUP)

Now, an attack on Russian tourism. Communists they may be, but they still have the Capitalist love for money. So, then of us to TASS, their press agency, four to INTOURIST, their travel agency, and ten to AEROFLOT, the airline office...now!

FOUR JDL BOYS ENTER THE OFFICE MARKED "TASS" AND TAKE OVER THE OFFICE. FOUR RUSSIANS IN THE OFFICE ARE ORDERED TO BE QUIET. JDL BOYS CARRYING LEAD PIPES AND SPRAY PAINT. THEY SPRAY THE WALLS WITH "*AM YISROEL CHAI" (THE PEOPLE OF ISRAEL LIVES) AND "LET MY PEOPLE GO."

ANOTHER GROUP OF JDL BOYS ENTER THE OFFICE MARKED "INTOURIST."

JDL BOY:
(TO RUSSIANS)

Those who want to leave, get out now.

THEY ALL LEAVE. BOY TAKES THE KEYS AND LOCKS THEM OUT.

AT KENNEDY AIRPORT, A PASSENGER PLANE ARRIVES FROM MOSCOW.

>> JDL BOY:
>> (TO OTHERS)

I just arrived from Moscow. Let's give them a nice welcome.

FRIGHTENED STEWARDESSES WATCH AS TWO JDL BOYS CHAIN THEMSELVES TO THE FRONT WHEEL OF THE PLANE SHOUTING, "AM YISROEL CHAI!"

FOLLOWING DAY:

KAHANE OPENS NEWSPAPERS. THE HEADLINE SAYS, "JDL OUTRAGES SOVIETS."

>> KAHANE:
>> (TO HIS BOYS)

In the headlines, at last! If the public knows, we have a chance. Silence was our graveyard in World War 2 and has been in Russia.

>> JDL BOY:

We vow Never Again...to be quiet, respectable, and dead.

FOLLOWING DAY:

TIMES EDITORIAL PAGE ON SCREEN:

> "JDL enters the premises of the Communist Newspaper in New York and threatened the staff because they failed to report the plight of Soviet Jews."

KAHANE READS AND SMILES

>> KAHANE:
>> (TO HIS GROUP)

Only noise and gimmickry, the bombs, the guns, the violence, not our educational programs that attracts the media.

>> JDL BOY:

Forgive me, Rabbi, but...sometimes we don't think anyone over there takes us seriously.

KAHANE:

The Soviets are stupid enough to play in our hands. Their newspapers, radio, and TV report everything we do in detail, boosting the morale of Jewish activists. To know that someone outside cares enough to risk himself is the sweetest news a prisoner can hear.

RUSSIA, ONE MONTH LATER. WE SEE PEOPLE BEING ARRESTED EN MASSE. IN COURT, THE JUDGE, WITH 12 PEOPLE BEFORE HIM (DEFENDANTS), IS LOOKING AT THEIR PAPERS.

JUDGE:
(AS HE PUTS EACH PAPER DOWN)

Jew, Jew, Jew.

HE THEN SPEAKS TO PRISONERS IN RUSSIAN. WHAT HE SAYS CANNOT BE HEARD BUT IS ON SCREEN IN ENGLISH.

JUDGE:

You are charged with attempting to hijack a Soviet airliner at the Leningrad Smolny airport and fly it to Sweden. How do you plead?

EACH ONE SAYS, "NOT GUILTY."

NEW YORK: TV NEWS REPORTER IS SEEN TALKING TO KAHANE.

TV NEWS REPORTER:

Major Jewish groups are denouncing these accusations as lies, calling the plot a frame-up.

KAHANE:
(TO PRESS)

Once again, the establishment has taken the wrong line. What would the establishment say if the Jews really meant to hijack the plane? What matters is that, under tyranny, they had every right to try to escape.

Scene 3

AN OFFICE BUILDING IN MANHATTAN. TWENTY-SEVEN JDL MEMBERS ARE IN AN ELEVATOR GOING TO THE 19TH AND 20TH FLOORS. THEY GO TO DOORS MARKED "AMTORG TRADING CORPORATION, SOVIET TRADE MISSION." THEY JAM THE ELEVATORS AND ORDER THE SOVIETS TO WALK DOWN. ONE PUTS UP A STIFF FIGHT AND SLIDES DOWN A FLIGHT OF STAIRS.

TV NEWS REPORTER:

Within minutes of the occupation of the offices, which lasted more than two hours, the area swarmed with newsmen and police. Soviet diplomats were flying on their way from Washington to New York.

WIRE SERVICES CARRYING STORY ON SCREEN:

"Unbelievable! 15,000 Russian Jews leaving, 10 to 15 times more than the yearly average until now, with the daily averages skyrocketing to 34 per day."

NEWSPAPER ARTICLE ON SCREEN:

ADL says, "The reason is simple for this thaw in relations. They're leaning toward democracy in all fields. What better proof of our diplomacy and quiet pressure than this? JDL had nothing whatsoever to do with it."

KAHANE:
(TO HIS GROUP)

Not nearly enough is getting out. Passover is coming...

HE LOOKS HARD AT THE GROUP.

If you know what I mean.

FOLLOWING DAY: JDL ENTERS AMTORG AGAIN.

JDL MEMBER:
(TO SOVIETS)

We are here to visit plagues on our modern Pharaohs. You have the honor of receiving the first.

HE PULLS OUT A FROG AND SHOWS IT AROUND.

There are 50 more of the same family that will be visiting today.

THE FROGS ARE RELEASED. PEOPLE SCAMPER, SCREAMING, AND JUMPING ABOUT AS THE FROGS ARE ALSO JUMPING ABOUT. THEY THEN PROCEED TO AMTGORG OFFICE LABELED "RECEPTION AREA."

SECOND JDL MEMBER:

Gentlemen, our holiday of Passover is coming. Since your Biblical knowledge is non-existent, a brief summary is in order. Thousands of years ago, a tyrant called "Pharaoh" held us in bondage, and God, a strange word here as well, in his mercy, visited plagues on our tormentors so we could escape freedom. It's your turn now.

HE TAKES OUT A WHITE MOUSE.

SECOND JDL MEMBER:
(TO THE OTHERS)

Let them go!

50 MORE MICE SCAMPER OUT OF BOXES. MORE JUMPING AND SCREAMING BY STAFF.

LATER: POLICEMAN INTERVIEWED BY REPORTER.

POLICEMAN:

The mice were not recovered.

KAHANE:

The news was flashed all over the world, and people were roaring with laughter.

FOLLOWING DAY:

JDL GROUP IS SEEN PUTTING A BIG GARBAGE PAIL IN THEIR CAR. THEY DRIVE TO THE SOVIET MISSION.

JDL MEMBERS:
(TO OTHER MEMBERS)

Get ready. We're passing the Soviet mission any minute now.

OTHER MEMBERS TIGHTEN THEIR GRIP ON THE PAIL.

JDL MEMBER:

Now!

THE SECOND BOY HEAVES A PAIL OF GARBAGE THROUGH THE SOVIET MISSION'S WINDOW. JDL MEMBERS FLEE.

INTERVIEWER:
(ON TV)

Our guest today is Rabbi Wolfe Kelman of a Conservative synagogue to comment on JDL.

RABBI KELMAN:
(ARROGANTLY AND RIGHTEOUSLY)

Jews do not rejoice in the torment of their oppressors.

A WEEK LATER: A POLICEMAN RUSHES OUT OF THE PRECINCT.

SERGEANT:
(ON PHONE)

Captain, we have to evacuate the Amtorg offices. We've got calls the place is going to be bombed.

THE SERGEANT RUSHES OUT.

AN HOUR LATER: A MAN PICKS UP THE PHONE IN HIS OFFICE.

MAN:

United Press International.

VOICE:
(ON THE OTHER END OF THE PHONE)

Free all Jewish prisoners. Let my people go! Never Again!

THE PERSON ON THE OTHER END OF THE PHONE HANGS UP. A BOMB IS HEARD EXPLODING.

PRESS HEADLINE:

"Amtorg offices of Soviets heavily damaged by a bomb."

REPORTER:
(TO KAHANE)

You claim responsibility, of course.

KAHANE:
(TO REPORTER)

We know nothing of the incident.

MAYOR LINDSAY:
(TO REPORTER)

The incident is an outrage to every New Yorker!

TV REPORTER:

U.S. Ambassador to the United Nations, George Bush, called on Soviet Ambassador Yakov Malik to express his regrets.

REPORTER:
(TO BUSH)

Ambassador Bush, it seems like the JDL is making some inroads on the situation. People are being let go over there more than ever.

188   Part 2

BUSH:

I'm damned upset. This kind of outrageous action must stop!

A WEEK LATER:

TV NEWS REPORTER:

A heavy explosion rocked the Soviet trade delegation building in Amsterdam, Holland, injuring four Soviet officials and causing an estimated $140,000 in damage. Once again, a message was found, "Never again! Let my people go!...A call is coming from one of our listeners.

WE HEAR THE LISTENER.

LISTENER:

Mr. Weller, I am a survivor. I can tell you that Rabbi Kahane sparked a flame of strength and self-respect blazing in the Jewish heart from New York to Amsterdam. How many of us wish that he was around when 6 million died?

LISTENER HANGS UP.

RUSSIA. OFFICE OF FOREIGN MINISTER.

FOREIGN MINISTER:
(TALKING TO SECRETARY, WHO IS TAKING NOTES AS HE DICTATES)

Vasily V. Zugnetzov, First Deputy Foreign Minister of the Soviet Union, is demanding the presence of the United States Ambassador Jacob D. Beame to personally receive a warning of the serious deterioration of relations between the two countries. International law obligates the protection of foreign missions. Failure on your part to do so raises doubts that you wish to maintain normal relations.

HE FURIOUSLY SIGNS THE NOTE.

THE FOLLOWING DAY: PEOPLE ARE LINED UP AT A MOVIE IN RUSSIA. ON THE MARQUEE IS THE TITLE OF THE MOVIE (TRANSLATED ON SCREEN TO ENGLISH) "THE CRIMINAL COURSE OF THE ZIONIST JDL."

. . .

THREE HOURS LATER: PEOPLE SOLEMNLY LEFT THE THEATRE. WE SEE SEVERAL ENTERING THEIR HOMES, FLINGING OFF THEIR CLOTHING, AND DANCING FOR JOY. ONE MAN HUGS HIS SICK OLD MOTHER IN BED. THE MAN SPEAKS TO A WOMAN. HE IS NOT HEARD, BUT THE ENGLISH WORDS ARE ON THE SCREEN.

MAN:
(TO WOMAN)

We saw newsreels of JDL giving to them and giving to them!

HE PUNCHES THE AIR JOYOUSLY.

Our criminals are smashing the Russians!

AMERICA:

INTERVIEWER:
(ON TV)

Today, we'll be discussing JDL tactics. Our guests are Rabbi Kahane and Mr. Finkel from the Board of Jewish Relations.

(TO MR FINKEL)

At first, you refused to sit in the same room with Kahane...

MR FINKEL:

If we silence the voice of reason, he wins.

KAHANE:

I should hope so.

FINKEL:

You are destroying all the work we've done throughout the years to lessen suspicions. William Cole, the CBS correspondent in Moscow, was just ousted because of you and your...

KAHANE:
(INTERRUPTING)

What would happen if a fanatical Jew shot the Soviet Ambassador? The Russians don't care two pins about him. It's what he represents, prestige and honor. There is a limit to what Russia will take without destroying the détente both they and Washington want so badly. After all, they need what we're selling, and we need them to buy. And this is the political logic of JDL violence.

FINKEL:
(TO INTERVIEWER)

Can't you see he's just using you to spread his vile propaganda? He's a killer, and no one in his right mind should give him an audience. You see how he talks. He's probably capable of doing just that.

KAHANE:
(TO FINKEL)

The Russian Ambassador Yost has requested to see me at the earliest possible moment. I gather he's less suspicious of me than you. I can't blame him. Despite all your efforts, he sees that you are a fool and a liar, and I am not.

FOLLOWING DAY:

KAHANE ENTERS OFFICE OF AMBASSADOR YOST.

YOST:
(TO KAHANE)

Please be seated.

THEY BOTH SIT DOWN.

YOST:

We are not a religious country. Only the Zionist traitors are unhappy. The rest of your people are not. We will encourage the Zionists to leave if you discontinue your provocation.

KAHANE:

It is in your hands to put an end to JDL violence, and the price is Soviet Jews. There will be no end to threats to détente until that price is paid…which is… any and all who want to go…atheists, agnostics, happy or not happy!

YOST:

Not only will this be transmitted to Washington and my government, but you have sealed the fates of the Leningrad hijackers. They will be sentenced to death!

KAHANE STORMS OUT.

LATER: AT JDL OFFICE.

> JDL BOY:
> (TO KAHANE)

The respectable are, at last, holding a rally across the street from the Soviet Mission.

> KAHANE:

That is far away. Let's get the car.

A SHORT TIME LATER: PEOPLE ARE SEEN DEMONSTRATING ON THE ON THE SYNAGOGUE STEPS ACROSS THE STREET FROM THE SOVIET MISSION. A CAR COMES DRIVING DOWN THE STREET AND ONTO THE SIDEWALK, CRASHING DOWN POLICE BARRIERS AND BARRELLING INTO THE SOVIET IRON FENCE. AT THE SAME TIME, A PIPE BOMB EXPLODES AT THE OFFICES OF AEROFLOT AND INTOURIST. TEN MINUTES LATER, WIRE SERVICES REPORT THEY RECEIVED CALLS THAT THE BLAST WAS SET OFF TO PROTEST THE FORTHCOMING LENINGRAD TRIALS AND ENDED WITH THE MESSAGE: "LET THE WORLD KNOW THAT, WHILE THE JEWS ARE ON TRIAL IN RUSSIA, THE SOVIET UNION WILL BE ON TRIAL. NEVER AGAIN!"

THE FOLLOWING DAY: KAHANE TALKS TO REPORTERS IN HIS OFFICE.

> KAHANE:

First, let me say the Jewish Defense League has no idea who bombed the Soviet offices, but it applauds those who did. There will probably be similar acts of violence by those distraught over Soviet Jews.

. . .

LATER:

TV INTERVIEWER:

Our guests today: Yuri M. Vorontzov, of the Soviet Embassy, Dmitri Kolesnik, UN Representative of the Soviet Union, John King, U.S. State Department, B'nai Brith President, William A. Wexler, Eleazer Lipsky of the American Jewish Congress, Joseph Hefner, NY Daily News reporter, Rabbi Kahane, Dore Schary, Anti-Defamation League, and the NYC Cultural Affairs Committee.

VORONTZOV:
(TO INTERVIEWER)

I have handed a stiff note to your State Department, warning of the consequences of the actions of the Jewish Defense League.

KAHANE:

When the U.S. government is shaken by a small group of militants who have the attention of its whole population, the grand design for détente is, the say the least, threatened.

KOLESNIK:

This act was committed by bandits from Zionist circles. The Soviet Union expects the government of the United States to take appropriate measures to prevent any such acts from occurring.

JOHN KING:

The Nixon administration condemns the senseless, criminal bombing of the Soviet airline office. The FBI is busily at work on the case and more men have been assigned to guard Soviet offices.

KAHANE:

All you have to do is "Let my people go," and all this gnashing of teeth will be unnecessary.

WEXLER:

A <u>mindless</u> act of terrorism badly serves the Jews of the Soviet Union.

Scene 3   193

KAHANE:

You can easily repair the situation by sending another memo. That's been your area of expertise. I'm sure they're brilliant, to the point, and worthless.

LIPSKY:

Such violence plays into the hands of Russian propagandists and hurts our cause.

TV INTERVIEWER:

I didn't think I'd be defending a Jew against Jews, but all the Russians have to do is treat your people with decency. If not, they deserve what they get.

DORE SCHARY:

I learned today that the Bolshoi had been cancelled, and I'm terribly disappointed.

KAHANE:

Tell that to Maria Kishnikov, whose Visa was cancelled as she stood on the dock about to leave. She hadn't seen her children in years.

TV INTERVIEWER:
(HAPPILY GRINNING AT RUSSIAN)

Tomorrow's headline will read, "Bye-Bye Bolshoi."

KAHANE:

Hardly an American now who does not know the Leningrad trial is coming up. Take a memo, Mr. Wexler: "JDL will continue to dramatize our plight in any way we can." That is <u>mind</u> at it's <u>best</u>.

FOLLOWING DAY: JDL BOYS LISTENING TO THE RADIO IN JDL OFFICE.

NEWS REPORTER:
(ON RADIO)

It is now an open secret that the Leningrad trial will open soon, and the death penalty will be asked for some of them. The mayor had ordered that no demonstrations are to be held at the Soviet mission. The date for the trial is near.

AN HOUR LATER: JDL OCCUPIES THE PARK EAST SYNAGOGUE ACROSS THE STREET FROM THE MISSION. NO ONE CAN COME IN OR GO OUT. THEY DRAPE BANNERS ON THE BALCONY FACING THE MISSION SAYING, "LET MY PEOPLE GO." THEY SING HEBREW SONGS OR CURSE RUSSIANS, SAYING "BI TI SDEKH" AND "EDK DEVIL" AS THEY LEAVE THEIR BUILDING. THE CURSING TURNS THE SOVIETS PURPLE WITH RAGE.

JDL MEMBER:
(TO POLICE ATTEMPTING TO COME UP)

If you try to eject us forcibly, blood will flow in the synagogue.

RABBI SCHNEIER:
(TO POLICE)

Please, I beg you to leave.

NEWS REPORTER:
(ON RADIO)

For the second day, JDL is occupying the synagogue, defying pleas, threats, Russian protesting, and shouting curses in Russian: "Drop dead! Go to hell!"

SCHNEIER:
(TO PRESS)

This kind of tactic is harmful and counterproductive.

REPORTER:
(ON RADIO)

Thousands of Jews and non-Jews are in the streets, cheering JDL on.

JDL BOYS PICKETING THE U.S. MISSION TO THE UN: POSTERS SAYING THE FOLLOWING: "END TRADE WITH RUSSIANS, END DISARMAMENT TALKS WITH RUSSIANS, END SPACE AND

CULTURAL TALKS WITH RUSSIANS," ...AND THEY ARE SHOUTING WHAT IS WRITTEN ON POSTERS AS WELL.

AT THE BUILDING MARKED "UNITED FEDERATION OF TEACHERS," THEY ARE SITTING IN FRONT OF THE BUILDING SHOUTING, "NO UFT-SPONSORED TOURS TO THE USSR." AT A BUILDING MARKED "COLUMBIA ARTISTS MANAGEMENT CORPORATION," THEY TAKE OVER OFFICES SHOUTING, "THIS IS FOR SPONSORING SOVIET CULTURAL TROUPES."

NEWSPAPER ARTICLE ON SCREEN:

> "In the trial held on camera, the Soviet court in Leningrad sentenced ten to stiff prison terms ranging from four to fifteen years, but Mark Dinchitz and Edward Kuznetsov were sentenced to death."

KAHANE:
(TO REPORTER)

The phones at JDL never stopped ringing. The public and news media turned on us. No one cared about the other groups because they were all impotent, helpless, and hapless. The question was asked over and over, "What do you plan to do?" And on the spot came the answer, "Two Russians for every Jew." And it was flashed all over the world by the United Press.

FOLLOWING DAY:

RADIO ANNOUNCER:

JDL again occupies Park East Synagogue. Kahane left and went to Hunter College, a block away.

HUNTER COLLEGE AUDITORIUM IS PACKED WITH HUMANITY WAVING ISRAELI FLAGS. TV AND RADIO CORPS IN FRONT OF THE PLATFORM.

REPORTER:
(TO KAHANE)

You'll be careful now, Rabbi, of course, not the worsen the situation.

KAHANE:

Two Russians for every Jew!

THE HUGE AUDIENCE STARTS CHANTING OVER AND OVER, "TWO RUSSIANS FOR EVERY JEW!" MAN RISES TO INTRODUCE KAHANE.

> MAN:
> (IN AUDIENCE)

The man we've been waiting for is here. Rabbi Kahane!

AS HE RISES, A THUNDEROUS ROAR GREETS HIM.

> KAHANE:

I am proud to see young angry Jews instead of the apathetic ones I saw two years ago when we began our campaign. Three million Jews are being ripped from us now, and it is our obligation to break ant and every law now to save them! We Jews have a hang-up called respectability. It's time to bury respectability before it buries us!

PANDEMONIUM ERUPTS IN THE HALL. A VAST SEA OF CLENCHED FISTS AND ISRAELI FLAGS AND CHANTING AGAIN AND AGAIN, "NEVER AGAIN," "FREEDOM NOW," AND "AM YISROEL CHAI!"

> TV REPORTER:

More than 2,400 people burst into the street and are marching down Third Avenue, where hundreds of helmeted police with horses and barricades are waiting between the Jews and the Soviet Mission.

> KAHANE:
> (SPEAKING TO THE CROWD)

There were rabbis arrested in Selma, Alabama, for civil rights for Blacks. We want the same arrested for Soviet Jews. We want people to sit in the streets. We have come to demonstrate physically, "Two Russians for every Jew murdered in Russia!"

> POLICE INSPECTOR:
> (ON BULLHORN)

You're ordered to disperse...now!

> KAHANE:
> (SHOUTING)

Scene 3 197

Push forward! Past the barriers guarding this horrible Mission!

HELMETED COPS ARE PUSHING, SHOVING, AND SCREAMING AT THE CROWD. SOME POLICE AND DEMONSTRATORS SMASH THROUGH TWO WINDOWS OF THE MISSION. A CAN OF PAINT IS THROWN FROM THE SYNAGOGUE AND SMASHES THROUGH A RUSSIAN WINDOW.

ON-SCREEN: HEADLINE IN PAPER THE FOLLOWING DAY:

> DAILY NEWS HEADLINE: "RABBI, SIX SEIZED, AS JEWS, COPS CLASH."

TV REPORTER:

More on the JDL. Yesterday, 100 hours dragged by the Russians livid with anger, as Jews standing in sub-zero weather insulted every Russian that left the building. We understand the frustrating Soviets have filed another protest with the U.S. and the UN. By now, we've lost count.

THE FOLLOWING DAY: KAHANE FLIES INTO HIS OFFICE.

KAHANE:
(TO HIS GROUP)

The Soviets have backed down! The death sentences were commuted!

THEY HUG, SING AND DANCE.

FOLLOWING DAY:

FRONT PAGE STORY IN NEW YORK TIMES ON SCREEN:

> "The Soviets warn that the United States cannot expect protection for its premises since it has not provided security for the Soviets."

KAHANE:
(TO REPORTERS)

The Soviet Union is threatening to retaliate against the United States in the USSR!

SOVIET AMBASSADOR:
(DICTATING TO SECRETARY)

To state Department, Robert J. McCloskey. This is to advise that we are well aware that JDL actions have been committed in connivance with and full knowledge of the United States government.

MCCLOSKEY:
(TO HIS SECRETARY)

Ambassador Dobrynin, the State Department strongly rejects your implication that the United States government officially inspires retaliation and that we have even done so, as well. We find such talk and threats serious and most disturbing.

KAHANE:
(TO REPORTER)

Both Americans and Russians are being pushed by us into positions they don't want...a threat to détente.

REPORTER:
(TO KAHANE)

Anti-Defamation League says, and I quote, "Your rampaging activities in connection with the Leningrad trials, and sensationalist appeals to raw emotions, are an embarrassment, a potential danger and completely outside Jewish tradition, which is a responsible, heartfelt, and prayerful response to our problems."

KAHANE:
(TO REPORTERS)

Since it was the "responsible, heartfelt, and prayerful response" of the ADL, B'nai Brith etc., that had helped six million Jews to an early grave when there was no "embarrassing," "dangerous JDL, and since those who run the Jewish establishment would not know Jewish tradition if they fell over it, I give the statement the <u>no reaction</u> it deserves.

DAILY NEWS EDITORIAL ON SCREEN:

> "The Jewish Defense League is swearing vengeance on the Russian tyrants. If they have any sense, they will view these developments with alarm. This might even mark the death warrant of the Soviet Union. Let us devoutly hope so. We encourage every Jewish warrior against the damnable Red despotism.

KAHANE:

(NARRATING)

It's editorials like this from a non-Jewish paper, when placed in juxtaposition with the inanities of Jewish leadership, that makes Strong men weep.

NEWSPAPER ARTICLE ON SCREEN:

> "A United States Secretary at the American Embassy in Moscow was threatened, and his car smashed. Soviets are carrying out their threats."

KAHANE:

From this article, from the Russians themselves, an idea was born…mass harassment of Soviet diplomats by none other than…

FOLLOWING DAY:

NEWS HEADLINE ON SCREEN:

> "American officials' cars vandalized, and embassy officials accosted with Moscow."

KAHANE:

(NARRATING ON BLOCK OF SOVIET MISSION WITH SEVERAL JDL MEMBERS)

Teams are being formed to harass Soviet diplomats. Our purpose is to provoke a crisis in Soviet-American relations that would stop the two countries from building bridges over Jewish bodies.

FOLLOWING DAY:

TIMES HEADLINE ON SCREEN:

> "JDL PLANS TO HARASS RUSSIANS. SOVIET CARS ARE SEEN LEAVING THE MISSION. A JDL CAR IS FOLLOWING WITH A SIGN. THE SIGN READS, "WE ARE FOLLOWING RUSSIAN SWINE WHO OPPRESS JEWS."

DOBRYNIN:
(TO SECRETARY)

To State Department: We demand something be done. This is disgraceful. We are being called the foulest of names by JDL: "pigs" and the dirtiest four-letter word in the English language.

TIMES HEADLINE ON SCREEN:

"JDL IS PLAYING A GRIM GAME WITH THE RUSSIANS."

TV INTERVIEWER:

Today we have the wife of Ambassador Dorbynin, who has complained bitterly about the JDL.

MRS. DOBRYNIN:

The lives of our families have been changed. We're angry and frightened all the time, like we're living under enemy occupation. We don't dare go alone to the supermarket, and the children aren't allowed to go to Central Park on their bicycles. It's like being in jail. But my dentist, who is Jewish, says he disapproves of the JDL, and it does not represent the views of the Jews of New York.

NEWS ARTICLE ON SCREEN:

> Soviet retaliation escalates. More cards of American diplomats were vandalized. Averill Harriman, a troubleshooter, was sent to Moscow. He said he deplored JDL's actions, but retaliations by Russians would be counterproductive.

FOLLOWING DAY:

POST HEADLINE ON SCREEN:

> "SOVIET AMBASSADOR DOBRYNIN GOES HOME, AND ICE GETS THICKER."

KAHANE:
(NARRATING)

Through January 1971, the articles which appeared in the Soviet Press almost daily dealt with one subject only...the JDL and Meir Kahane...our sit-ins, raids, assaults, and bombs, were given detailed and nationwide coverage. There now begins a desperate effort to stop JDL.

JOHN KING:
(U.S STATE DEPARTMENT, TO PRESS)

Of course, we've taken note of what Kahane is saying, and the Justice Department will take all necessary steps to stop him.

MAYOR LINDSAY:
(TO PRESS)

The police department will be as alert and forceful as necessary to deal with this threat.

KAHANE:
(TO PRESS)

We hope he applies these standards to police fighting crime. So far, he has not. The ultimate in attacks against me was reached by three leading uncle Jakes of the Jewish world: Max M. Fisher, President Nixon's Court Jew, Rabbi Wexler, now Chairman of "Conference of Presidents of Major American Organizations," somewhat analogous to the "King of Kings" long on title, short on everything else Jewish. They shot off a telegram to President Nixon that read, and I'm summarizing, "we want to advise that the desperate and criminal tactics of the JDL win sympathy for the Soviet Union by their use of mindless violence that decent men abhor. We, of course, will continue to create a climate of opinion that will cause the release of millions of Soviet Jews."

Scene 4

NEWSPAPER HEADLINE ON SCREEN:

"NIXON MEETING AT WHITE HOUSE WITH PROMINENT JEWISH LEADERS."

WHITE HOUSE:

JEWISH LEADER:
(TO NIXON)

Mr. President, we want to assure you at the outset that we had nothing to do with JDL's outrage. We ask that you do what you can to stop these irresponsible and criminal actions.

NIXON:

All decent, law-abiding citizens share your feelings. However, I want to add at this time that I will join you in urging freedom of emigration for Soviet Jews and will make a public declaration of that effect.

JEWISH LEADER:
(OVERJOYED)

This is the first time an American president has said he backs freedom for Soviet Jews. A historic moment, indeed!

NEWS HEADLINE ON SCREEN:

"MAYOR LINDSAY ORDERS CRACKDOWN ON JDL. KAHANE ARRESTED.

COURTROOM: JUDGE ON BENCH D.A ROGERS AND KAHANE.

JUDGE:

The District Attorney will approach the bench.

ROGERS APPROACHES JUDGE.

JUDGE:
(TO ROGERS)

Mr. Rogers, there is a matter of bail for your consideration.

ROGERS:

Judge Marra, it may seem high, but we're requesting bail be set at 7,500 dollars; not the usual amount, I know, but these are not ordinary times, and the defendant must learn he has to change radically from the way he's conducting himself toward the court and the state.

ROGERS STEPS AWAY FROM THE BENCH.

JUDGE MARRA:

Rabbi Kahane, bail is set at 3,000 dollars. Now, I warn you to behave yourself.

ROGERS:

Your honor, the city is planning to bring two indictments before the Grand Jury. There's going to be a crackdown on him and his bunch.

THE JUDGE NODS WEARILY AND WAVES HIM OUT OF THE COURTROOM.

IMMEDIATELY ON HIS RELEASE FROM THE COURTROOM, KAHANE ADDRESSES THE PRESS.

KAHANE:
(TO PRESS)

I applaud the harassment and the bombings to save 3 million of my people. The international uproar is a good thing. Besides, the mayor's sudden zeal for law and order contrasts sharply with his failure to crack down on the Panthers and the Young Lords.

THE FOLLOWING WEEK:

DISTRICT ATTORNEY ROGERS:

The District Attorney's office is putting before the Grand Jury four criminal indictments involving the takeover and explosion at Amtorg.

THE FOLLOWING DAY: A HUGE PLATE GLASS WINDOW AT AEROFLOT OFFICE IS SMASHED BY TWO MEN WHO HURL A LARGE ROCK FROM A SPEEDING CAR THROUGH A WINDOW.

MAN:
(CALLING FROM PUBLIC PHONE)

Never Again!

HE HANGS UP.

MAYOR LINDSAY:
(TO POLICE)

Inspector, we're getting demands and bitter denunciations from the Soviets, and I can't blame them. Federal Protective Devices are being sent here to guard the Russians. Do what you can to help them.

INSPECTOR:

Looks like God's helping the Rabbi, Sir. But we'll try.

KAHANE:
(NARRATING)

UN Secretary U. Thant called an emergency meeting of the UN Committee on relations between countries. Russia bitterly attacked the U.S. for its failure to stop JDL. They reported nine incidents. As for JDL, we were pleased. We want to provoke a crisis so the U.S. will take a significant step to free Russian Jews.

. . .

FOLLOWING DAY:

NEWSPAPER HEADLINE ON SCREEN:

"KAHANE AND 7 OTHERS INDICTED ON ASSAULT, RIOTING, CRIMINAL MISCHIEF."

TV REPORTER:

If all the world's a stage, the JDL and the Soviet Jewish question stand at its center. There is no longer a farmer in Iowa who does not know there is a problem with Soviet Jewry, as the newspapers and television give it hours and pages of publicity. All condemn the JDL but are impressed by the phenomenon of the "New Jew" ...militant, tough, karate, and gun-wise Jew, whose slogan is "Never Again!" Mr. Robert Mayer of Newsday is here with us now."

MR. ROBERT MAYOR:

JDL, through its dumbbell actions, has partially succeeded. A month ago, few people were concerned. Now...the world. That is why survivors from the camps support JDL. That is why condemning JDL is right but not entirely satisfying.

KAHANE:
(NARRATING)

The January 20 issue of Newsday had a marvelous cartoon showing a Soviet diplomat and a Black militant cowering the alley, while a mob of angry Jews carrying weapons stormed past carrying a banner that read, "Jewish Defense League." The caption had the Black saying, "That's funny! They don't look Jewish!"

Scene 5

ORTHODOX RABBI:
(TO KAHANE)

I have a statement prepared by myself and other leading Orthodox rabbis.

HE READS.

Every manifestation concerning Russia that is provocative and arrogant is a highly dangerous act, which can harm many. I've already told you thousands have been exiled because of your activity.

KAHANE:
(TO RABBI)

With all due respect, Rabbi, with all our urgings, you've never produced one name of an exile. From the half-assimilated, fully ignorant men who pass for Jewish leadership in the secular Jewish establishment, one can never hope for courage, warm Jewishness, and told Judaism. But from scholars and committed Jews...like you? I recall a Sabbath morning when I stopped off to pray at a Yeshiva where I had studied for 13 years and been ordained. Following the service, I walked over to the Dean...

FLASHBACK:

KAHANE:
(TO DEAN)

*Gut Shabbos.

> DEAN:
> (TAKING KAHANE'S HAND)

You are murdering Russian Jews.

> KAHANE:

I have no desire to argue with you.

KAHANE ATTEMPTS TO MOVE AWAY. DEAN GRABS HIS HAND.

> DEAN:
> (HOLDING KAHANE'S HAND EVEN TIGHTER)

You are murdering Russian Jews.

> KAHANE:
> (LOOKING HARD AT HIM)

Let us say you are right. Let us agree that protests and public demonstrations are bad for Russian Jews. But in all the years I saw in this Yeshiva, I cannot recall even one Psalm said for Russian Jews. I do not recall one fast day for Russian Jews. I do not remember the subject even being mentioned. Surely, those things do not hurt Russian Jews.

DROPS KAHANE'S HAND WITHOUT SAYING A WORD. THEY PART. DEAN GOES TO THE HALL TO A CONFERENCE ROOM WHERE OTHER RABBIS ARE WAITING FOR HIM.

> OTHER RABBI:
> (TO DEAN)

More and more of our Yeshiva boys are joining JDL. We must think of some way to bring them back to their senses. I thought it was clearly understood by the boys that we are against any kind of protest, much less this...!

> ANOTHER RABBI:

Don't worry. It'll pass.

> ANOTHER RABBI:

We can no longer sit by and do nothing.

ANOTHER RABBI:

I have a letter here from my father, a leading Jewish scholar.

HE READS.

Not one Jew has been saved because of these demonstrations. On the contrary, they are harming very much.

DEAN:

I have a proposal. It would be very appropriate, I think, to have a prayer meeting. A sea of thousands of Yeshiva boys at Manhattan Center praying for our people…

THEY ALL NOD IN AGREEMENT.

ONE MONTH LATER: A NEWS REPORTER ON TV.

NEWS REPORTER:

Five thousand Yeshiva boys at Manhattan Center called a prayer meeting for Soviet Jews. JDL demonstrated with 40 of its members.

KAHANE:

Another letter was read at the prayer meeting from the leading Jewish scholar. He now says he never opposed demonstrations, per se, but simply wanted them to be "not anti-Soviet but pro-Jewish." No matter. We knew what caused the change. JDL had driven those who had been silent to a <u>public</u> meeting for the first time. <u>That</u> was a phenomenon. But there was a second one. The JDL demonstration received a headline in the Times that read, "JDL plans to Harass Russians." The prayer meeting received one paragraph at the bottom of the JDL story. So much for how to get press coverage.

Scene 6

A CONFERENCE IS IN PROGRESS.

>MAN:
>(TO GROUP)

Gentleman, here we are, the most important leaders of the top organizations in the Jewish world, and I can only say I'm ashamed of all of us! In spite of all our feverish backstage efforts in the last few months to stop the JDL from further harassment of the Soviets, we have abysmally failed!

>ANOTHER MAN:

Not true. We wanted Kahane arrested, and he was!

>ANOTHER MAN:

You think that means anything to him? Rubbish. It only feeds his purposes: another headline.

>ANOTHER MAN:

We'll let the police know we welcome them taking him in, and the courts know we want him kept there till he's forgotten about. Let him rot in jail forever, gentlemen. We have the government of Israel behind us. They've bowed to American pressure and declared that they vigorously oppose the acts of terrorism in the Soviet struggle that are being carried out in the US and elsewhere.

ISRAEL. MEETING IN PROGRESS.

BOY:
(RISING)

I wish to address the Knesset on the issue of the JDL. The Israel Student's Union supports the JDL.

SOUNDS OF PROTESTS ARE HEARD.

MAN:
(RISING)

Shmuel Tamir, Knesset member, wants the record to state that if JDL harries Soviets, there's no reason for us to disassociate from it.

ANOTHER MAN:
(RISING)

I have a statement from former Jewish prisoners in Russia supporting the JDL.

HE READS.

Dov Sperling, Rachel Getz, Anatoly Dekatov, Avraham Shifrin, Miriam Gerber, Aryeh Falkov, Yosef Schneider, Boris Shiayen and Mordechai Lapid.

PAUSE.

Years from now, will their names be forgotten like those before them?

KAHANE:
(NARRATING)

Above all, it was the little Jew who supported us. In a Letter to the Editor, he wrote:

MAN:
(SAYING WHAT HE WROTE)

If we could read the journals of the time of the Maccabees, they probably also said that many Jews believed they were dumb and increasing anti-Semitism.

Thank God there are so-called "dummies" willing to suffer scorn from the "polite" people to call attention to injustice.

KAHANE:
(NARRATING)

It was the sudden awakening of the dead that was JDL's greatest achievement... the dead all around us, dead Jewish leaders, the dead congregations, the dead Jews, suddenly coming to life. Seven affluent Long Island suburban synagogues announced that each would hold a prayer service in front of the Soviet estate to "accent our oneness with the Soviet Jewry." Mr. Heyman, president of a temple, went so far as to say the following:

HEYMAN:

We won't wave any banners or call any names, but rather accent the dignity of prayer. This is a

counterbalance to some of the wild things that have been going on at JDL. We feel it's not necessary to do that kind of thing. We don't want to do anything militant like Kahane, but we would like the opinion of world Jewry to be felt by the Soviet Union.

KAHANE:
(NARRATING)

Good, pure, dignified Mr. Heyman. How nice it would have been had his weight been felt ten years earlier or ten months or ten weeks earlier. But until that moment, no Russian Jew had heard of him because the Heymans of the world were dead and buried in mausoleums known as Temples.

CHICAGO: TEMPLE AFTER TEMPLE HAS A SIGN ON IT SAYING, "LET MY PEOPLE GO."

B'NAI BRITH BUILDING ON MADISON AVENUE, NEW YORK, HAS A SIGN IN ITS HEADQUARTERS SAYING, "SAVE SOVIET JEWRY."

KAHANE:
(NARRATING)

There is a passage in the daily prayer service that reads, "Blessed art thou, O Lord, who revives the dead." But we wanted the Jewish establishment to do what we couldn't do...if they had the wisdom and insight...to do what the Blacks did...go to Washington after every riot or outrage by Black militants and warn the government there would be more of the same, or worse, by <u>sane</u> and law-abiding groups, unless certain demands were met. And they were. We wanted the Jewish establishment to work the same with its militants. Condemn the act, then warn the government that the violence would continue if Russian concessions were not made with the government's help.

HEYMAN:
(NARRATING)

Kahane trying to drag us all down to his level...one that's destructive and fruitless!

NEWSDAY HEADLINE ON SCREEN:

"THREE SOVIET AUTOMOBILES ATTACKED IN MARYLAND AND ON SET AFIRE. GOVERNOR WARNS OF EXACERBATION OF SITUATION."

TV REPORTER:

The Soviet government has suddenly announced that a number of Soviet activists who have

been in jail for years, are granted exit visas that have been refused time after time by the government.

A WEEK LATER:

LOS ANGELES TIMES HEADLINE ON SCREEN:

"SOVIETS LETTING JEWS OUT AT RECORD RATE."

Scene 7

TV REPORTER:

Rabbi Kahane, Mr. Wexler, the American Jewish Committee, and Mr. Schachter from the Jewish Agency are with us today to discuss the unprecedented wave of immigration in the 53-year history of the Soviet Union. Last year, only 83 a month could leave, and now at the beginning of the year, it has already reached 188 per month!

KAHANE:

A grudging offer. We're not selling them peace at that price: far too cheap, far too low for 3 million.

MR. WEXLER:

Liberalization is only a temporary thing put into effect because the Communist Party Congress is scheduled to be held.

MR. SCHACTER:

Emigration will come to a halt when they get rid of their agitators.

KAHANE:
(TO SCHACTER AND WEXLER)

As usual, Jewish brilliance is piled on top of Jewish brilliance so that simple common sense does not win out and prove that JDL has been right all along. No matter, things will get more difficult for the intellectual nitpickers of your school of thoughtlessness.

A MONTH LATER:

AN ARTICLE IN JEWISH POST AND OPINION:

> MAN:
> (READING)

JDL making progress in building a militant Jewish organization, despite overwhelming opposition from the Jewish establishment: a continuous barrage of denunciations. In Montréal, a standing ovation of 1300 people. In Philadelphia, the same response from 500, mostly youngsters. Even a rabbi, at last, Barry Schwartz of New Jersey, said, "No other group comes close to JDL on focusing public attention on the current tragedy."

A WEEK LATER:

HEADLINE IN TIMES ON SCREEN:

> "HUNDREDS OF JDL DEMONSTRATORS BLOCKED TRAFFIC AT THE SOVIET MISSION BY SITTING IN STREETS. 27 ARRESTED."

KAHANE IS IN THE OFFICE READING A LETTER TO HIS BOYS.

> KAHANE:

A letter from the State Supreme Court Judge to JDL: You are ordered to cease and desist from any appearance in front of any Soviet property. Defiance of this order will lead to immediate arrest.

HE PUTS IT ON THE TABLE. THEY ALL LEAVE.

AN HOUR LATER:

> TV REPORTER:

Two hundred JDL members defied a State Supreme Court order and demonstrated at the Soviet Union's estate at Glen Cove. Kahane arrested.

KAHANE APPEARS BEFORE THE JUDGE.

JUDGE:

You are charged with conspiracy and possession of firearms.

MAN STEPS FORWARD.

(TO KAHANE)

The Italian Civil Rights League is behind you every inch of the way.

KAHANE LEAVES THE COURTROOM.

KAHANE:
(TO MARCONI)

I'm going to the Soviet mission. I think it's the best way we part here.

AN HOUR LATER:

ANNOUNCER:
(ON RADIO)

Kahane and 130 others were arrested at Soviet Mission.

STREET SIGN SAYS EAST 67TH STREET. A WEALTHY RESIDENT IS OUTSIDE HER BUILDING.

WOMAN:
(HAUGHTILY TO PRESS)

This is going on...every day. We're paying 600-900 a month to live here, and we're being driven to distraction. I don't know how much longer any of us can put up with it. We're going to court.

IN COURTROOM. WOMAN AND JUDGE.

WOMAN:

We want to keep JDL from our street.

KAHANE:
(NARRATING)

The Judge, an Italian American, threw out the case.

. . .

A WEEK LATER: ON RADIO

> RADIO ANNOUNCER:

JDL announced a week-long series of demonstrations in Washington to include homes of Soviet

diplomats and, for the first time, the Commerce Department approved the Mack Company's plan to build a truck factory in the Soviet Union.

OFFICE OF U.S AMBASSADOR.

> MIALIK:
> (ON PHONE)

This is the Russian Ambassador. A bomb was found at the base of the wall surrounding our estate in Glen Cove only a short time before it was scheduled to explode. We have no doubt the hysterical Zionist criminals placed the bomb. Another incident, and we will retaliate against you Americans.

POLICEMAN ARRESTING KAHANE AT THE SOVIET EMBASSY.

> POLICEMAN:
> (TO KAHANE)

You cannot even shout an insult at a foreign embassy here, much less demonstrate within 500 feet of the place.

> KAHANE:
> (NARRATING)

The continuing need of the USSR for American trade and dollars gives us a splendid opportunity to attack the Soviets at their jugular and draw concessions from them...but...it is summer. Our rabbis are away for the duration, and our Jewish offices are on short hours, with their Executive Directors on three-day weeks, if they can be found at all. I say these words looking forward to a summer-long romance with the following events: June 23...trial for protesting Iraqi persecution of Jews. June 28...third act of a farce entitled "JDL at the Soviet Tass Agency." Following two hung juries in this case, it would have normally been dropped by the State, but the city was determined to prosecute a hundred times, if necessary, no matter what the cost. July 6...Act One of a "Conspiracy" charge, starring government agents and informers. August 16... trial on riot charges at the Soviet Mission last December.

Scene 8

ISRAEL: MAN ON PHONE.

MAN:

Rabbi Kahane, this is Abraham Zaimonson, uncle of Sylvia Zaimonson, one of the 12 in the Leningrad trial. She didn't hijack nothing. For that they gave her 10 years in prison. She's suffering from TB and ulcers. Israel is doing nothing for her…Thank you, Rabbi. God bless you.

FOLLOWING DAY: KAHANE TALKING TO THE PRESS.

KAHANE:

If anything happens to Sylvia Zaimonson or another Jew, Soviet diplomats throughout the world will be open targets for Jewish militants. "Two Soviets for every Jew" will be put into practice, I assure you, if necessary. It is vital to get the name of Sylvia Zaimonson known to a world that knows all about Angela Davis, a Black militant, but never heard of a Jewish prisoner. Soviet Premier Alexei Kosygin is planning a trip to Canada. I plan to disrupt the visit.

THE FOLLOWING DAY, KAHANE ARRIVES IN CANADA. HE IS ARRESTED WITH 6 OTHER JDL MEMBERS AS HE LEAVES THE PLANE, HELD IN JAIL OVERNIGHT AND IS TAKEN TO A PLANE THE NEXT MORNING WITH REPORTERS THERE.

KAHANE:
(NARRATING)

I consider this a marvelous opportunity. Tomorrow, after I'm bailed…

(KAHANE SMILES WITH SATISFACTION)

THE FOLLOWING DAY: KAHANE WALKS TO THE SOVIET EMBASSY ALONE WITH REPORTERS BEHIND HIM.

REPORTER:
(TO KAHANE)

Police are coming up behind you. You're not heading from the Soviet Embassy?

KAHANE:

If the police are behind me, I'll be quick about it. They're busy fellows.

KAHANE STANDS IN FRONT OF THE SOVIET MISSION. A POLICEMAN STARTS PULLING HIM AWAY.

KAHANE:
(SHOUTING)

The Soviet Union is a tyranny, and the Soviet Union stinks.

HE PUTS HIS HANDS OUT TO THE POLICE TO BE HANDCUFFED. THEY ARREST HIM.

KAHANE:

I could think of nothing more elegant to say to get me arrested.

POLICEMAN:

You deliberately challenged a District of Columbia ordinance. No insults in front of a foreign mission.

KAHANE:
(NARRATING)

At a subsequent trial, the ordinance was struck down as unconstitutional.

. . .

A MONTH LATER: TWO POLICEMEN ARE LEADING KAHANE TO AN AIRPLANE.

> POLICEMAN:
> (TO KAHANE)

And don't come back.

KAHANE SMILES WITH SATISFACTION AND BOARDS A PLANE.

> SECOND POLICEMAN:
> (TO THE FIRST POLICEMAN)

He won. He knew we'd given him trouble, arrest him, not let him stay, and that would be a bigger story than if he did get in.

> FIRST POLICEMAN:

He's old news already. People are tired of his shenanigans. I know I am.

FOLLOWING DAY:

NEW YORK POST HEADLINE ON SCREEN:

"CANADA BARS KAHANE WHILE KOSY'S THERE."

NEW YORK POST HEADLINE ON SCREEN:

"JDL activity top topic in Moscow. It is the first and last subject of conversation. It has cut down on American tourism, cancelled cultural exchanges, and one is astonished to find the extent to which this tiny group has disturbed relations between the United States and the Soviet Union."

TV INTERVIEWER DAVID FROST WITH ISRAELI FOREIGN MINISTER ABBA EBAN.

> DAVID FROST:

Our guest tonight is Israeli Foreign Minister Abba Eden. Eh...about Sylvia Zalmonson...

> EBAN:

JDL hinders the cause of Jews seriously.

FROST:

But, for the first time, Sylvia Zalmonson's name is known worldwide.

EBAN:

JDL has corrupted and degraded her, and the yearnings of all Soviet Jewry. Just yesterday, a sniper fired four shots into the window of the Soviet mission. This degrades all of us.

FROST:

No one was hurt.

EBAN:

The Soviet Jews do not want to be blamed for a war between the two superpowers. That would certainly hurt our people very deeply.

ON SCREEN:

> A MEMO TO RUSSIAN TRAVEL AGENTS FROM THE RUSSIAN GOVERNMENT.
>
> Do not let our harassment of American journalists and diplomats disturb you; that does not apply to tourists.

Scene 9

THE UN. A SPEAKER IS BEING INTRODUCED.

CHAIRMAN:

The debate on the China question will proceed. Mr. Chow…

MALIK INTERRUPTS.

MALIK:

I must interrupt for a matter of immediate urgency. The JDL, Zionism, and the U.S. are bringing our two countries to a serious crisis, and I must condemn the U.S. for not stopping these attacks.

WHILE MALIK IS SPEAKING, JDL GROUPS ARE SHOWN TRYING TO TAKE DOWN THE SOVIET FLAG AT THE UN, OTHERS THROWING PAINT OVER A SOVIET DIPLOMAT AT THE SOVIET MISSION, SPILLING BLOOD OVER A DIPLOMAT SPEAKING AT A UNIVERSITY, AND SMASHING GLASS DOORS AND FURNITURE.

NEWS HEADLINE ON SCREEN:

> MOSCOW BOILS OVER NEW YORK SNIPER. HINTS AT RUPTURE IN RELATIONS. POLICE ARREST 18-YEAR-OLD ISAAC JAROLSLAWICZ, A JDL ACTIVIST.

MAYOR LINDSAY:

I must praise the police for a brilliant, swift, and superb job.

> KAHANE:
> (NARRATING)

Liberal Jews condemn JDL and assume the boy is guilty. U.S. attorney in the case is Robert Morse, a Jew. The police, under political pressure to arrest someone, hastily picked up this youngster.

IN THE COURTROOM:

> ROBERT MORSE:
> (TO JUDGE)

I demand 100,000 dollars bail!

> JUDGE:
> (TO MORSE)

Incredible! Denied. 25,000.

TWO MONTHS LATER:

POST HEADLINE ON SCREEN:

> "JORALEWICZ CHARGES DROPPED. POLICE ADMIT HE IS NOT THE SNIPER."

AN ASSOCIATED PRESS DISPATCH FROM MOSCOW ON SCREEN:

> "Soviet authorities recently ordered medical treatment for labor camp inmate Sylvia Zalmonson after threats by militant Jews in the United States, that two Russians would be killed there if she died in the camp."

Scene 10

KAHANE:
(ADDRESSING AN AUDIENCE)

A little more than a week ago, they held the greatest mass arrest in Washington's history. 1300 Jews, mostly young, sat down on the President's street and made worldwide headlines as they were led away to jail.

FLASHBACK: YOUTHS ARRESTED AND SHOUTING "NEVER AGAIN" AND "AM YISROEL CHAI" (THE PEOPLE OF ISRAEL LIVE)

GIRL:
(AGE 16, NARRATING)

I made the trip because I saw a JDL poster of a Soviet cartoon showing a Jewish man being hanged on a Star of David, and the caption below said, "What to do with a Star of David."

BOYS WITH FACES SHINING AND SPARKLING EYES ARE SEEN BEING ARRESTED, PUT IN POLICE VANS, AND SHOUTING TO KAHANE, "BRING MORE BUSES!"

A GROUP OF NAZIS SUDDENLY APPEAR CARRYING SIGNS SAYING, "KILL THE JEW." JDL BOYS PUMMEL THEM AND KNOCK THEIR TEETH OUT. NAZIS WERE SAVED BY POLICE INTERVENTION.

BACK TO THE PRESENT:

> KAHANE:
> (NARRATING)

Here we are, Jews being arrested, not for Vietnam, Laos, Mozambique, or Antarctica, but at last, crying out for their own people...with us...because...we showed them the way up the mountain, walked there before them and they climbed with us to the heights of danger. We didn't offer...we demanded...real sacrifice and idealism... they gave it to us...we took it, and they understood...it is not Israel's enemies who would bury her, but her friends, by failing to understand the need to stand tough and strong anywhere in the world.

THE AUDIENCE APPLAUDS HEAVILY.

Scene 11

A WOMAN COMES TO VISIT RABBI KAHANE.

WOMAN:

Forgive me, Rabbi. I don't like to bother you, but my son was arrested in one of your demonstrations. Please don't misunderstand me. I'm proud of what he did, but I'm a religious woman, and I brought up my son to be Kosher. He won't eat what they give him, and I worry he should get sick. I have no money for bail. Can you help me?

KAHANE:

It is an honor to know you and your son. You are truly blessed to have each other. Yesterday, I went to plead your case at the Young Israel of Flatbush, asking them to plead for bail from the pulpit. "After all, the American Jewish Congress," I said, "had accepted an ad in its newspaper, a full page, Communist sponsored, calling for 'Bail for Angela Davis' titled, 'An appeal to the Jewish people.' And we abandon our own?"

> FLASHBACK: A RABBI AND THE PRESIDENT OF THE TEMPLE ARE ON THE PODIUM. KAHANE IS IN THE AUDIENCE.

RABBI:

The JDL has approached us for funds to release one of their members from jail.

(TO KAHANE)

We will have nothing to do with this criminal element in our midst, which will only encourage this unsavory behavior in other weak elements among our people. Sorry.

KAHANE JUMPS UP TO THE PODIUM AND SEIZES THE MICROPHONE.

KAHANE:

Three young Jews are in jail with no kosher food while you eat Sabbath meals in comfort?! Shame! You have long since forgotten what being Jewish means!

A MEMBER OF THE CONGREGATION RUSHES TO THE PODIUM AND ATTACKS KAHANE. SOME RUSH TO DEFEND HIM, AND A FIGHT BREAKS OUT IN THE TEMPLE, WHICH IS FINALLY STOPPED BY THOSE SEPARATING THE BATTLERS.

THE FOLLOWING DAY: KAHANE ADDRESSES STUDENTS IN AN AUDITORIUM.

KAHANE:
(ADDRESSING AN AUDIENCE)

All that we have fought for, and dreamed of through the centuries of our suffering, is despised and rejected... what will be our future? Do not despair. We have Avraham and Nancy, the unheralded, the far-from-famous, who take their place in history with true Jewish heroes.

> FLASHBACK: WHILE KAHANE IS RELATING THIS INCIDENT, A YOUNG WOMAN AND A YOUNG MAN ARE ABOUT TO BOARD AN EGYPTIAN AIRLINER AT KENNEDY AIRPORT BOUND FOR LONDON. THEY ARE ARRESTED, AND ON THEIR PERSONS ARE FOUND LOADED GUNS AND A LIVE GRENADE.

THE PRESENT:

KAHANE:
(NARRATING)

Avraham and Nancy Hershkowitz, ages 19, man and wife, both JDL members, are accused of planning to seize an Arab airliner...

A WOMAN IN THE AUDIENCE JUMPS TO HER FEET HYSTERICALLY.

WOMAN:

My son was arrested several times in your protests, and I'm furious. I have no control over your corrupting him!

KAHANE:

...allegedly in retaliation for continuous outrages by Arab murderers such as hijacking, blowing up airlines, and other heinous acts against our people that were greeted by pride and cheers in the Arab world. For this, they are in prison, though they are innocent, and the case will be dismissed.

WOMAN IN THE AUDIENCE:
(SHOUTING)

They could have killed somebody. I forbid my son to take a life for any reason!

MURMURS OF AGREEMENT IN THE AUDIENCE.

WOMAN:
(SHOUTING)

I'd disown him!

ANOTHER WOMAN:

What kind of girl does such a thing?! Not my Libby! I'd lock her in the house!

MURMURS OF AGREEMENT IN THE AUDIENCE.

KAHANE:
(TO WOMAN)

You watched a world do nothing about Arab terrorism, saw them go free, and commit more seizures and murders. A bail of 250,000 dollars was set from Avraham. Nancy was released. He's been in jail for five months now because he cannot raise bail. Panthers get Jewish money for bail, but Jewish leaders sit and watch a young Jew rot away.

WOMAN:
(RISING AND SHOUTING)

Not a penny! My son should follow his example...be influenced by such as him?! Never!

MURMURS OF APPROVAL.

KAHANE:

The charges against them are not true, not because they would not have done whatever they felt necessary to do for our people. In their labor of love for JDL, they knew no hours. If a thousand chores had to be done, they did it. They marched for Soviet Jews, struck back at Neo-Nazis, and preached Jewish self-respect. They believed in the right of our people to live in peace.

WOMAN:
(RISES, SHOUTING)

Then I demand to know what they were doing with guns and grenades!

KAHANE:

You should ask the Arabs what they are doing with guns and grenades. But you really don't have to, do you? Our corpses, orphans, and widows, speak for themselves.

SILENCE. THEN ANOTHER PRESENT PARENT RISES TO SPEAK.

WOMAN:
(QUIETLY AND RESPECTFULLY)

I agree with what you're doing, but I always feel, "Why does it have to be my child?"

KAHANE:

Without a doubt, the most difficult thing I have to face after every JDL demonstration that involves the arrest of young members is the inevitable call or visit from the parent of an arrested youth with that question. And the reason why it must be your child is that the market in dedicated children is not that glutted, and to find a youngster who is ready to feel the pain of someone else and do something about it, is to find a pearl. The cry of the Jew in Damascus or Leningrad is his cry, though he lives in Los Angeles, and the fear and poverty of the Jew in Brooklyn are his, though he resides in Great Neck. To find a youngster who is more afraid of not going to jail when the obligation exists...all this to find a gem. And blessed is the parent who has such a child.

ANOTHER WOMAN RISES.

> WOMAN:
> (QUIETLY SPEAKING)

My boy never even truanted from school. His career would be ruined, I'm afraid.

> KAHANE:

No divine decree ever ordained that the Jewish parent must bring forth into the world a doctor, lawyer, or engineer. But from the days of Abraham, the Jewish parent was commanded to create a child who knows that it is not life that is all important but how one lives that life.

> WOMAN:
> (RISING)

I'm proud of my daughter, Nancy, and her wonderful husband, Avraham. I want everyone here to know.

ANOTHER WOMAN RISES.

> WOMAN:

This morning, my son Avraham was sentenced to five years in prison.

GASPS FROM THE AUDIENCE.

I came to tell the Rabbi (HER VOICE BREAKING) I'm proud...of...him.

SOBS ARE HEARD.

> KAHANE:
> (TO THE TWO MOTHERS)

Avraham will soon be free, and all Jews who care and understand look you proudly in the face, jump to attention and salute you, for your children, Avraham and Nancy, have truly "made it."

KAHANE SALUTES THEM. THE AUDIENCE RISES AND SALUTES THEM TOO.

ETHNIC CLEANSING

IRAQ

Scene 12

HUNDREDS OF JEWS MASSED IN FRONT OF THE IRAQI U.N. MISSION ON EAST 79TH STREET, MANHATTAN, WITH SIGNS READING "FREEDOM FOR IRAQI JEWS" AND "THREE IRAQIS FOR EVERY JEW." KAHANE STANDS ON TOP OF AN AUTOMOBILE AND SPEAKS TO IRAQI DIPLOMATS LISTENING BEHIND DRAWN BLINDS.

> KAHANE:

Listen, Arabs! Your government hung twelve Jews in your country in the public square, and we know another show trial and more hangings are being planned around Passover. If one Jew is hung in Iraq, one Iraqi diplomat will hang in New York!

GROUPS OF JDL PEOPLE CHARGE ACROSS THE STREET, RESULTING IN A MASS RIOT. KAHANE AND OTHERS WERE ARRESTED.

AT PRECINCT:

> POLICEMAN:
> (TO KAHANE AND JDL BOYS)

We missed you, Rabbi.

A POLICEMAN LEADS HIM TO JAIL AND OPENS THE CELL DOOR.

Your suite awaits you.

THE POLICEMAN CLANGS THE CELL DOOR BEHIND KAHANE AND THE OTHERS.

A tough judge out there today. He is not amused or impressed by any one of your shenanigans. It'll be a long time "no see" if he's in one of his moods. You're charged with the usual: second-degree riot, disorderly conduct, and resisting arrest.

SCENE SHIFTS TO A SESSION IN THE UNITED NATIONS.

AMBASSADOR FROM IRAQ:

Iraq is making a formal demand on the United States Mission to the United Nations to prevent the new program of terror from being launched by the Jewish Defense League against Iraqi officials in New York.

KAHANE:
(NARRATING)

JDL attacks on Arabs were launched by their assaults on Jews in London and by sources claiming they would begin to attack Jews in America. We immediately fired off telegrams to the major Arab UN missions and embassies.

ARABS OPEN TELEGRAM. WORDS ON SCREEN.

> We are warning you that, should Arab terror occur, the offices and personnel of Arabs will be targeted for the punishment you'll deserve.

AT THE UN:

MAN:

The Minister from Jordan is appalled by the inability of the United States to deal with the violence of the Jewish Defense League.

MAN:

Ambassador from the Soviet Union...we are gravely concerned about this matter and ask the Secretary-General to confer with the U.S Ambassador to see what measures can be taken.

TWO MEN ENTER INTO KAHANE'S OFFICE.

MAN:

(SHOWING HIS BADGE)

FBI.

OTHER MAN:

Did you send these telegrams?

SHOWS KAHANE TELEGRAM TO ARABS.

KAHANE:

See my lawyer.

THEY LEAVE.

KAHANE:
(NARRATING)

A few days later, more than 3,000 people turned out for a JDL rally at the United Nations, at which Congressman Biaggi and I blasted Arab terror. To his credit, he was the first Congressman to take part in a JDL function, despite the objections of his Jewish advisors.

THAT EVENING: REPORTER ON TV.

REPORTER:

Rabbi Kahane and thousands of others marched from Arab mission to Arab mission while he read the text of his telegram to Arabs over a bullhorn.

A WEEK LATER:

TV REPORTER:

Arab guerillas near the Lebanese border attacked an Israeli school bus and murdered eight young Jewish children.

THE FOLLOWING DAY: ANOTHER TV REPORTER.

REPORTER:
(ON TV)

Two Arab offices in New York, one a front for terrorists, the other the office of chief Arab lobbyists, were attacked, and the occupants were savagely beaten.

> KAHANE:
> (READING PAPER TO HIS GROUP)

Seven Arab terrorists who hijacked planes will be released by the European government that jailed them.

PUTS THE PAPER DOWN.

They've been blackmailed.

LATER: A DOOR SAYING PALESTINIAN LIBERATION MOVEMENT SHATTERS. A BOMB RIPS THROUGH THE OFFICE.

> KAHANE:
> (NARRATING)

Invitations for me to speak are coming up from all over the country. I will be taking my first trip to California. I have never yet appeared there.

FOLLOWING DAY: KAHANE IN COURT.

> JUDGE:

For your attack on the Iraqi embassy, you are sentenced to a 90-day jail term or 500 dollars bail.

KAHANE PAYS BAIL.

> JUDGE:

You appear before me one more time, even from spitting on the sidewalk, and you will be our guest for a long, long time. You are seriously being admonished to change your ways.

> KAHANE:
> (NARRATING)

I'm flying out to the West Coast as a guest of our JDL chapter in Los Angeles.

. . .

A WEEK LATER: AN ARTICLE IN THE NEWSPAPER <u>POST AND OPINION</u>.

MAN:
(READING)

Rabbi Kahane received an overwhelming reception on a whirlwind visit to Los Angeles, where he spoke to all audiences, Reform, Conservative Orthodox, to <u>standing room only crowds</u>.

Scene 13

BROOKLYN JEWISH JOURNAL HEADLINE ON SCREEN:

"JOURNAL READERS SUPPORT JEWISH DEFENSE LEAGUE."

WOMAN:
(NARRATING)

What did the other organizations do? Nothing. Many of us admire him but will not talk about it.

NEW YORK DAILY NEWS ON SCREEN:

"The rush to hear JDL speak was so great that not even the bombing of the Jewish Center, where Kahane was to speak, stopped his appearance. It was rescheduled, and he spoke to a packed audience.

KAHANE:
(NARRATING)

Our goal was to act as a catalyst for the established organizations to follow. And we gave them no rest. They now feared...loss of membership, loss of funds, prestige, and leadership. Leading thinkers in Reformed Judaism were now saying, in language only they can understand, that Kahane is right...to preserve our neighborhoods, our merit system, and our lives.

TV INTERVIEWER WITH THEODORE BIKEL, DAVID BERGER, ADL, MRS. MICKEY GARELIK, ADL, SIMON BLOOM, EDITOR OF AMERICAN JEWISH LEDGER.

INTERVIEWER:
(TO THEODORE BIKEL)

While many Jews are now cheering Rabbi Kahane, I'd like to know, as a member of the American Jewish Congress, when you'll be joining the chorus of accolades, which, of course, I presume you will.

BIKEL:
(FUMING)

Where Kahane and his paramilitarists prey upon the fears, frustrations, and prejudices of our people, we will address ourselves to their hopes, their needs, and their reaction!

MRS. MICKEY GARELIK:

Our ADL chapter in Nebraska voted unanimously to condemn Kahane, but I am not sure where JDL activities fail. However, I am sure there will be millions of us who went to our deaths silently and nonviolently in the war.

DAVID BERGER:

The JDL is a barbaric bunch, and their protection is something we do not want here or abroad!

Scene 14

SIMON BLOOM HOLDS UP THE NEWSPAPER HEADLINE OF HIS PAPER, AMERICAN JEWISH LEDGER, WHICH READS,

"EXTRAORDINARY PHENOMENON OF AMERICA TODAY MEIR KAHANE OF JEWISH DEFENSE LEAGUE."

BLOOM:
(TO BERGER)

A huge audience line up against the wall, waiting and waiting for him to arrive. Can you say the same about the ADL? I should think not.

FLASHBACK: KAHANE JUST FINISHED HIS SPEECH. THE APPLAUSE IS IN WAVELENGTHS LIKE THE POUNDING SURF. BLOOM TALKS TO AN OLD COUPLE AS THEY'RE LEAVING.

OLD COUPLE:
(WOMAN)

When I came in, I hated him. Now that we've heard him, we love him.

BERGER:

B'nai Brith order's it's chapters not to give JDL speakers the right to appear.

BLOOM:

And the members are not ignoring you.

KAHANE IS ADDRESSING A GROUP OF YOUNG PEOPLE AND THEIR PARENTS. ON THE WALL IN THE AUDITORIUM IS A SIGN THAT READS "GET OUT OF VIETNAM," AND "DEAR PARENTS, WE'RE ASHAMED OF YOUR SILENCE." KAHANE LOOKS HARD AT THE SIGN. A PAUSE.

KAHANE:

I am looking at all you wealthy youngsters who have never known and never raised a voice on behalf of the Jewish poor, the oppressed Jewish neighborhoods, Soviet Jews, and I say, "I'm ashamed of your silence."

THE CLOCK TURNS TO SHOW KAHANE SPOKE FOR AN HOUR.

STUDENT:

(SHOUTING)

All you've done is make me feel guilty!

KAHANE:

Then we've succeeded. If you're ashamed to be a timid Jew, you'll be proud to be a brave one. That's what JDL is all about. Knowing it's glorious to defend our rights. We've succeeded in bringing thousands back to our heritage. We've succeeded in focusing attention on our poor, succeeded in giving pride to our people, to stand tall and firm as you will. And opened the door of Soviet prisons through the willingness of people to act in a gut manner as you will. Join us and we will teach you, if you're prepared to sacrifice, nothing cannot be overcome. If we are not, the battle is lost before it's fought.

STUDENT WALKS TOWARD THE STAGE AND JOINS KAHANE TO THE APPLAUSE OF THE CROWD AND BRAVOS. OTHER STUDENTS FOLLOW HIM.

APPLAUSE DIES DOWN.

MAN:
(SHOUTS)

Say what you will about the tactics of Rabbi Kahane. No one can deny he returned us to our people by the fist, not the book, and ignited the spark in the indifferent hearts of Jewish campus kids of self-worth...that Jewish is beautiful!

THE AUDIENCE APPLAUDS THIS MAN.

WOMAN:
(IN THE AUDIENCE, TO KAHANE WITH A THICK RUSSIAN ACCENT)

I come here from Russia. First, they are letting out nobody, then a few hundred, then thanks to you, Rabbi, 15,000, then 34,000, then 37,000, 40,000, and more, leaving a place where they would be in jail or in the grave. When I left the Soviet Union, my friends made me promise, if I ever saw you, to thank you, in their name, for all that you have done for us. Russian Jews have not heard of many of the Zionist organizations, but they have all heard of Kahane.

A LONG SILENCE, THEN PEOPLE HEARTILY APPLAUDING.

Are Jews Safe In America?

Neo-Nazis protesting the Holocaust Museum in Washington D.C.

Scene 15

SKINHEAD TALKING TO THE CROWD

SKINHEAD:

White man, awake! Your sons and daughters are being sacrificed on the altar of school race just so the treasonous Jews and liberals can appease their black supporters.

ANOTHER SKINHEAD:

Do you believe that law enforcement should be relaxed so blacks can murder, rape, loot and burn without fear of punishment? That Negro loafers and their illegitimate offspring are entitled to 80% of the welfare money...that arrogant Negroes should get the jobs of better-qualified whites? That white children should be forced to go to school where they are shaken down, molested and assaulted?

CROWD SHOUTS "NO!"

MAN IN CROWD:

Are we gonna go on being slaves under the Jew masters?! Let's get Blackie back to Africa. Boating! Not busing!

CROWD SHOUTS "YAY!"

SKINHEAD:

The military is getting full of Black officers. How many here want their sons trusting a dumb nigger?

MAN IN THE CROWD:
(SHOUTING)

Jews giving America to the Third World, and we lose ours! Once the Black plague takes over, there's no turning back.

MAN ASCENDS TO THE PODIUM.

MAN:

Black gangrene...destroying our cities. Washington, Cleveland, Newark, St. Louis...already dead and soon to follow Atlanta, Jacksonville, Richmond, Philadelphia, New York, Dallas, Nashville, Little Rock, Chicago, Detroit. Boston's Mayor Kevin White said, when he visited New York's devastated area of Brownsville, and I quote, "This could well be the first tangible sign of the destruction of our civilization." Unquote.

SKINHEAD:

Jews promote every type of filth in books and TV. Their leftist propaganda. Glorifies dope and promotes a generation gap among Gentile parents and children. The Jews want a world that's animalistic and stupid. The Jews are the greatest threat in the world!

ANOTHER SKINHEAD:

How 'bout public housing? For Negroes? People poor, aged, disabled forced out and the New York Jewish Senator pushin' for more...wants Negroes to live in the suburbs that we run to, or he says, the central cities will be destroyed. I say, destroy him first and the Jews who elected him!

ANOTHER SKINHEAD:

Young people in Nazi Germany. Fascist Italy, Communist Russia, or Red China can support their families without sending their wives to work or slaving endless hours of overtime to keep a roof over their heads. And we know who's to blame, don't we? Big rents from Jewish landlords and backbreaking taxes to keep their Black friends in the standard of luxury to which they've become accustomed. And big Jewish bureaucrats making sure Blacks hired and Whites fired!

KAHANE:
(NARRATING)

There is an unfortunate tendency that comes from liberal arrogance and a superficial understanding of what happens outside his intellectual ghetto that leads to a conception of the Nazis and Fascists as being devoid of intelligence and skill. That they are sick is beyond dispute, but this has nothing to do with their cunning, intelligence, or the danger they pose to the Jew. They may be sick, but they are not fools.

SKINHEAD:
(NARRATING)

The truth is we understand the mind of the masses all too well, the causes that make them angry, frustrated, bitter and filled with hate...and we know how to increase all of these emotions. Watch me.

(TO CROWD)

Well, what are you going to do about it, Whitey? Are you just going to sit there and let us all go down the drain?

HE SHOWS A POSTER WITH A SCENE OF BLACKS LOOTING, ROBBING, ATTACKING, WHILE A PATHETIC LOOKING WHITE MAN HOLDS UP HIS HANDS AND SAYS, "SO WHAT IF THEY LOOT, BURN, RIOT, MURDER, MAIM, ROB AND RAPE? NO ONE HAS BOTHERED ME YET!"

MAN IN THE CROWD:
(ENRAGED, SHOUTING)

We gotta do some KILLING! Cut 'em off root and branch, the devil Jew stirring up the niggers after us. What's integration but the slow mass murder of our race?

SKINHEAD:
(NARRATING)

You don't catch any of them living near the niggers. What's at the bottom of it? One four letter word: Jews!

KAHANE:
(NARRATING)

It is the Jew who is portrayed as the evil genius behind the scenes, using the Negro to destroy America so he can take it over. The lies, the foolishness, the ludicrousness, are not relevant. Forget them. All that's needed for them to be believed is crisis... anarchy, drugs, breakdown of family life, crime and sexual license, the desperation to flee the cities, open hate between Blacks and Whites, and the government is seen as favoring Blacks in jobs and housing, when they had to pull themselves up by their bootstraps. The fact was clear. Huge numbers of Whites do not wish to live with Blacks, white parents complaining and racial confrontations commonplace in schools that have degenerated into places of terror and hate. White parents, hardly neo-Fascist types, as some foolish politicians cry, violently react to the thought of their children being driven into neighborhoods they know that are filled with violence, crime, and drugs. The tragic truth is that large numbers of people who consider themselves liberals, highly educated, basically tolerant and decent, but because of their contact with Black violence in schools, neighborhoods and jobs, turned into people who openly fear and dislike Blacks. With the unsophisticated, the uneducated masses, the reaction is far more severe, and the Haters (with a truer perspective than Capitol Hill, an Ivy League University, or the National Conference of Christians and Jews) sense the hatred within tens of millions of them. They dislike Blacks and want to know how to get rid of them. The Haters, the Fascists, the Skinheads, and all varieties sense this, a sense a golden opportunity.

SKINHEAD:
(TO OTHER SKINHEADS AROUND THE TABLE)

The only real hope at this point in history is a revolution, and the masses are ripe for it. We're putting out a newspaper detailing how to make bombs and shoot guns and carrying a different quotation from Hitler's "Mein Kampf" in each issue. We are his heirs. Through us, he rises from the grave. This month marks the 25th anniversary of the infamous ritual murder of Nazis and their so-called crimes WW2.

HE LIGHTS A CRUCIBLE AND SLOWLY READS THE FOLLOWING NAMES: "HERMANN GORING, JOACHIM VON RIBBENTROP, WILHELM KEITEL, ALFRED ROSENBERG, HANS FRANCK, JULIUS STREICHER, ALFRED ARTUR VON SEYS-INQUART."

KAHANE:
(NARRATING)

Indeed, the most striking thing about the Hater's propaganda is their deep, furious, and obsessive hatred for the Jew. It's a hatred that never leaves them, that they express continuously and will accept no other solution but that of...

SKINHEAD:

If the white race is to survive, the monster must not be talked about...it must be KILLED! To kill it, we must ATTACK! The Jew-Communist Zionist race-mixing Marxist face...smash it! Crush it! Kill it!

KAHANE:
(NARRATING)

The bankruptcy of cities and their inability to care for the most basic needs of their predominantly Black citizens must eventually lead to rioting against whites, Blacks flocking in droves to Black racists, and whites capitulating to similar insanity.

SKINHEAD COMMANDER:
(NARRATING)

We're concentrating now on winning minds, and a huge number of our books and publications reaching millions of people. These are a few. There are hundreds more.

BOOKS ON SCREEN: PROTOCOLS OF THE LEARNED ELDERS OF ZION, JEWISH RITUAL MURDER, THE TALMUD UNMASKED, THE MYTH OF THE 6 MILLION, THE JEW COMES TO AMERICA, IRON CURTAIN OVER AMERICA, JUDAISM IN ACTION."

KAHANE AND COMMANDER ARE INTERVIEWED ON TV.

INTERVIEWER:
(TO COMMANDER)

Except for the Rabbi here, Jewish leaders, along with millions of ordinary Jews, scornfully and angrily dismiss you as worthy of mention and call the Rabbi here paranoid, overreacting, irresponsible and dangerous.

COMMANDER:

Well, we're getting television and radio coverage more and more every day; groups are springing up in cities where once we were thought to be out of the question. We Nazis are active in Detroit, Cleveland, Connecticut, Philadelphia, Trenton, Washington, Los Angeles, Chicago, Seattle, San Diego, and Northern California. We are not hiding a thing. Our storefronts boldly show swastikas, I've been interviewed many times on radio and TV to applauding and cheering audiences, and we have some groups in high schools.

(TO RABBI KAHANE)

As long as Jews make nothing out of you, Rabbi, we're ahead of the game. Any one of them can listen in to our White Power station all over the country and hear our message to the caller...the latest one being, "The Jew tells the Negro he don't have to burn cities anymore. With whites flying out, he'll have it in his hand anyhow. See, Rabbi, I saved you the price of a phone call.

KAHANE:

If an American Nazi party leader poses a danger to American Jews, then not to assassinate such a person would be one of the most immoral courses I could imagine...and he knows JDL is serious. In Los Angeles, we had running battles with your bunch, a bombing, and attacks at your so-called conference. Sent a number of you to the hospital from what I recall. Not enough, of course.

COMMANDER:
(RANTING NOW)

We, the National Socialist Party are part of the mighty invincible movement, which is continuing the heroic, earth shaking struggle begun by our Fuhrer, Adolph Hitler!

HE JUMPS UP AND MAKES A NAZI SALUTE. KAHANE ASSAULTS HIM. HE GOES DOWN AND OUT.

KAHANE:

I rest my case.

Scene 15   249

Scene 16

1971:

>JDL BOY:
>(TO HIS GROUP)

The rabbi is immigrating to Israel today. Let's surprise him.

EL AL LOUNGE AT KENNEDY AIRPORT. HUNDREDS OF JDL MEMBERS TURN OUT TO WISH HIM FAREWELL…SINGING AND DANCING, AND WHEN HE IS ABOUT TO LEAVE, A GREAT ISRAELI FLAG IS UNFURLED, HUNDREDS OF ARMS SHOOT UP IN THE AIR WITH FISTS CLENCHED, AND "HATIKVAH" IS SUNG. AS THE NOTES OF THE SONG DIE AWAY, THE ROAR OF NEVER AGAIN, NEVER AGAIN, NEVER AGAIN!" RINGS OUT.

KAHANE IS SEATED ON THE PLANE NEXT TO AN ELDERLY GENTLEMAN.

>ELDERLY MAN:

Where do you get youngsters like that?

>KAHANE:

They come to you if you're worthy of it.

OUTSIDE THE PLANE, A HUGE, POWERFUL MEMBER OF THE CHAYA SQUAD TURNS TO THE GROUP.

JDL BOY:
(SHOUTING)

What's the best going away present we can give Meir?

MOMENTS LATER: AT THE SOVIET UNION'S AEROFLOT AIRLINES COUNTER, HORRIFIED EMPLOYEES AND STARTLED BYSTANDERS WATCH AS THE JDL HORDE STORMS IN, RIPPING DOWN THE SOVIET FLAGS, TEARING UP THEIR AIRLINE RECORDS, AND SMASHING THEIR INSTALLATIONS.

KAHANE:
(NARRATING)

I'm going home. Israel is home, and home is sweet. "And thou shall settle in it." And so, says the Torah.

THE PLANE CARRYING KAHANE IS SEEN RISING INTO THE AIR.

ON SCREEN: THE DREAM

KAHANE:

For 190 years, the Jew had a dream. For each and every Jew who crawled the earth of exile, it was the same dream...the return to Zion. Driven from his land, Israel, by the Roman Legions, the Jews wandered the four corners of the earth, experiencing all the degradation and terrors, and horrors of exile. In Christian Europe, they were faced with the choice of forced conversion or death and rape. More than 1500 were murdered as they clung to their faith. In the Rhine valley, more than 1200 perished at the "hands of Christ." And more death and torture came to the Jews of Bohemia and France. In York, England, the entire Jewish community was massacred. In Paris, the Talmud was burned, and Martin Luther called for a similar fate for those who produced it. 166 Jews accused of poisoning wells were thrown alive into flames. Bavarian Jew killers in the Rhineland massacred thousands of Jews with pitchforks and axes. And during the Black Plague, when the filthy, unwashed mobs and noblemen were decimated by the disease, well over 200,000 Jews were hanged, burned, drowned, and hacked to death as an antidote to the Black Plague. And the blood libels. In Norwich, England, Jews accused of murdering a Christian child, and drinking his blood, died horribly. And the insane charge of "desecration of the host," when Jews were accused of beating and stabbing the wafer that made up the Christian Eucharist, more than 100,000 Jews died because of that madness that spread to Bavaria and Austria. Spain, Portugal, France, England...Jewish communities were made up of loyal, quiet, and above all, terrified Jews who were uprooted. The abominations were accompanied by murder, rape, and humiliation. And as he fled east, the havens in Poland and Russia turned into Slavic nightmares. From 1648 to 1649, a quarter million were massacred, and on and on to the Czar and Hitler. And during all those centuries, the Jew had a dream to return to Zion...a place where he and his children could walk tall and proud and free, and above all...unafraid. What yearning! The life cycle of the Jew was never free of the ever-present love of Zion. When he was born and circumcised at the joyous feast, the little infant hears the words...

A PARTY SCENE. RABBI IS SAYING WORDS.

RABBI:

May the All-Merciful bring consolation to a people dispersed among the nations.

KAHANE:
(NARRATING)

This child is already a Zionist. And when he reaches the age of spiritual manhood, the Bar Mitzvah, he intones:

BAR MITZVAH BOY:
(SPEAKING IN A TEMPLE)

Zion is the source of our life.

KAHANE:
(NARRATING)

And he is a firmer Zionist. When he marries, he smashes a glass under the canopy to remind him that as long as he remains in Exile, there can never be complete happiness for him with Zion in the hands of strangers. And under the canopy, he hears the blessing proclaim:

COUPLE UNDER A CANOPY, AND THE RABBI IS BLESSING:

RABBI:

May Zion exult at the joyful reunion of her children in Jerusalem. May there soon be heard in the cities of Judah and the streets of Jerusalem the sound of joy and gladness, of happy weddings, and young people feasting and singing...

KAHANE:
(NARRATING)

And a Zionist couple was joined.

A DYING MAN IS TALKING TO THE RABBI.

MAN:

I couldn't go to the earth of Zion, without...

HE PULLS A LITTLE BAG FROM UNDER HIS BED.

...this little bit of it that slept with me.

HE KISSES IT AND DIES.

KAHANE:
(NARRATING)

He died a Zionist...to return to Zion...to no more horror, no more fear...no more terror...no more humiliation. Only...tranquility and pride, security and sovereignty. A Jewish state. The Dream.

Scene 17

THE NIGHTMARE:

THREE YEARS LATER: KAHANE IS ON TRIAL IN AN ISRAELI COURT. PROSECUTOR IS ADDRESSING THE COURT.

PROSECUTOR:

Since the Rabbi came here and formed JDL, he has been a serious problem. He is before the court now charged with the crime of having plotted to wreck the visit in Washington of Soviet Communist party chief Leonid Brezhnev when he left Israel to visit the US a year ago. It is a crime to plot to commit a crime in a foreign land ...and we are only asking that this law be enforced...

KAHANE:
(BURSTING IN INTERRUPTING)

The flow of Soviet Jews into Israel must go on. The moment that the Russians feel détente is secure, our major leverage is gone.

JUDGE:

If this continues, you will be remanded.

PROSECUTOR:

We ask that Rabbi Kahane be deported to the United States immediately to be punished for his crime.

JUDGE:
(TO KAHANE)

You may now speak...but no rabble-rousing or propaganda.

KAHANE:

In the 1967 war, we crushed four attacking Arab armies and liberated Gaza, the Sinai, Sharm-el Sheikh, the old city of Jerusalem, the West Bank of the Jordan, and the Golan Heights in Syria, did we not? And yet, we refuse to declare the sacred Jewish soil in these areas. Hebron, Schechm, Judea, Samaria, and Gaza are Jewish! We refuse to allow Jews to purchase their <u>own</u> land on their <u>own</u> soil. <u>This</u> is a crime!

JUDGE:

The prisoner will be remanded and is to return to the United States for sentencing.

KAHANE:
(NARRATING IN JAIL)

A Jewish court in a Jewish state hears a Jewish prosecutor demanding the punishment of a Rabbi to be handed over to the Gentiles. A crime against our tradition as well as me. Israel will do anything to stop what she conceives to be harmful to her vital interests in Washington...and Soviet and Iraqi Jews are not as important as good relations with Mr. Nixon.

POLICE COMMISSIONER:
(VISITING KAHANE IN JAIL)

Don't you realize you're harming our friendly relations with the United States?

KAHANE:

Not a word about the murder of five Iraqi Jews yesterday, members of the same family...and I'm committing a crime?

POLICE COMMISSIONER:

I'll even help you pack.

HE LEAVES.

ONE MONTH LATER: KAHANE IS AT KENNEDY AIRPORT BEING GREETED BY THE PRESS.

KAHANE:

Henry Kissinger, the Jewish Secretary of State, who makes the American Jews burst with pride, Is a danger to the survival of Israel. Two days before the Yom Kippur War in 1973, Kissinger pressured not to strike first despite Israel knowing that it would be attacked...on its holiest day when we were innocently praying in our temples. Later, as we stood on the verge of destroying the military might of our attacker, the Egyptians, he forced a cease-fire on Israel, then pressured us into insane territorial concessions. He had us commit ourselves to total withdrawal from the territories we liberated with the blood of our sons in 1967...land for which we dreamed and cried for millenniums.

REPORTER:

On the contrary, he's regarded as a statesman who wants, above all, peace in the area for Arabs and Jews.

KAHANE:

You must be a reporter for the New York Times. Kissinger is a monumental egoist who is blind to Jewish reality, as is the Times. He wants to escape an oil embargo by Arabs, capture a special place in the Arab heart, avoid a confrontation with the Soviets, and above all, assure his place in history. The price is his own people.

JANUARY 15, 1999:

NEWSPAPER ARTICLE ON SCREEN:

> "Kissinger returns to Israel to form a 60-million-dollar fund to finance joint Israeli-Palestinian technology projects."

REPORTER:
(NARRATING)

Kahane was right.

Scene 18

1975:

NEWSPAPER HEADLINE USA ON SCREEN:

"JDL OPERATIONS OFFICER DECLARES PALESTINE LIBERATION ORGANIZATION CHAIRMAN ARAFAT WILL NOT LEAVE NEW YORK ALIVE TODAY (SHOWS PICTURE OF OPERATIONS OFFICER.) THE OPERATIONS OFFICER CITED ARAFAT'S THREAT TO TAKE ALL OF ISRAEL AND THROW THE JEWS INTO THE SEA, AND ARAFAT'S TERRORIST OPERATION, WHICH KILLED SCORES OF ISRAELI MEN, WOMEN, AND CHILDREN BRUTALLY, AND WILL CONTINUE TO DO SO...IF..."

LATER: ARMED JDL MEN ARE LINING A ROOM. ON THE TABLE IS THE REVOLVER. FBI ENTERS AND ARRESTS OPERATIONS OFFICER.

FOLLOWING DAY:

NEWSPAPER ARTICLE ON SCREEN:

"ARAFAT SNEAKED INTO NEW YORK AND FLED OUT. HE WAS HERE LESS THAN ONE DAY. JDL OPERATIONS OFFICER HELD ON TO A STAGGERING 100,000 DOLLARS BAIL.. JDL MUTED."

KAHANE:
(ADDRESSING A JEWISH AUDIENCE IN AMERICA)

I've returned to America to demand that American Jewish leadership follow a program of "Not One Inch." The Arabs killed Jews and refused to accept a Jewish state in 1967, when Sinai, Gaza, Judea, and Samaria, what they call the "West Bank," and the Golan Heights were in their hands. Arabs refused to accept an Israel in 1947 when it was a tiny grotesque joke of a state. They killed the Jews in 1920, '29, '36, and '39. The Arabs will never accept a Jewish state of any size. They will always try to eliminate Israel and Israelis. Therefore, no concessions dare be made. Not one inch!

AUDIENCE MEMBER:
(SHOUTING)

We have no right to tell the Israelis what to do!

KAHANE:

The present Israeli government is a vassal of Kissinger, who stands for giving up the Sinai for nothing in return. The present Israeli government must be replaced by one that insists on no territorial concessions, and the lead must come from you...whose influence over the Israeli government is greater than its own people.

AUDIENCE MEMBER:
(SHOUTING)

Freedom for the Palestinians!

ANOTHER AUDIENCE MEMBER:
(SHOUTING)

There is no Palestine! Today is officially launched as "There is No Palestine Day." JDL is marching to the various Arab Consulates, as well as the Israeli and U.S. missions to the UN, and pledging, at each stop, to fight retreat. Those with us! (A ROAR OF APPROVAL) Follow me!

THE AUDIENCE FOLLOWS HIM OUT.

AN HOUR LATER: A HUGE RIOT AT THE SOVIET MISSION. KAHANE AND 50 OTHER JDL PEOPLE ARE ARRESTED. AN UNKNOWN PERSON FIRES SHOTS INTO THE MISSION.

. . .

A WEEK LATER: KAHANE AND JOACHIM PRINZ OF THE WORLD JEWISH CONGRESS ARE BEING INTERVIEWED ON TV.

KAHANE:

Israel should have unrestricted Jewish settlements in every part of our country under our rule. This is historic Jewish land, not occupied territory. American Jewish leaders should lead a takeover of Israeli consulates to dramatize the problem, and funds should be raised for those parties opposite the policy of retreat in Israel.

PRINZ:

On the contrary, we must call for flexibility. An Israeli victory of that kind, stealing another's land, would be even worse for Jews than defeat.

A WEEK LATER: 20 JDL BOYS PITCHING TENTS ON A LAWN UNDER A SIGN SAYING, "JOACHIM PRINZ." PRINZ COMES OUT ENRAGED.

A JDL BOY:
(TO PRINZ)

We're just putting up some "Refugee Tents." A reminder of what would happen to the Jews of Israel if they listened to men like you. Besides, you should be consistent and not complain if your land is stolen.

FOLLOWING DAY:

MAN ON THE PHONE:
(TO POLICE)

Officer, JDL is staging a sit-in at our temple again! ...Emanuel, of course. Now he's demanding we change the Israeli government! We want him arrested! And throw away the key!

HE HANGS UP.

THE FOLLOWING DAY: KAHANE IS ARRESTED WITH SEVERAL OTHERS.

NEWSPAPER HEADLINE ON SCREEN:

"JDL SITS AT THE ISRAELI CONSULATE IN NEW YORK. JDL CHAIN THEMSELVES TO ISRAELI EMBASSY IN WASHINGTON."

A WEEK LATER: KAHANE IS IN COURT IN NEW YORK.

COURT CLERK:

Court is in session. Judge Jack Weinstein presiding.

JUDGE:
(TO KAHANE)

You have twice willingly and intentionally violated the terms of a 5-year probation imposed in July 1971. You are therefore sentenced to one year in prison.

KAHANE:

I violated probation. You did what you had to do with a clear conscience. I did what I had to do with a clear conscience.

Scene 19

ISRAEL 1983:

KAHANE IS RUNNING FOR ELECTION TO THE KNESSET AND IS ADDRESSING AN AUDIENCE. PEOPLE ARE CARRYING POSTERS SAYING "ELECT KAHANE." THE AUDIENCE IS JEWISH.

KAHANE:

You're asking about my program for the Arab problem, and it's as follows: First, the free use of weapons against stone throwers and other attackers of Israelis, civilians as well as soldiers.

AUDIENCE MEMBER:
(SHOUTING)

A dangerous man. Don't listen to him. He'll make us killers!

KAHANE:

Secondly, offering the Arabs the choice of remaining in Israel, with full individual rights (social, cultural, religious, economic), but they cannot vote or sit in the Knesset, as they must recognize Israel is the State of the Jewish people.

AUDIENCE MEMBER:
(SHOUTING)

Dictator! Czar!

KAHANE:

Third, leaving the country willingly, with compensation for property, or refusing both and being removed from the land.

AUDIENCE MEMBER:
(SHOUTING)

We should <u>give</u> them their land. <u>What we took</u>!

KAHANE:

We must declare Jewish sovereignty over all the liberated lands...what they took. We took back what's ours, and they have the nerve to call it occupied! The Temple Mount is <u>occupied</u>? Hebron is <u>occupied</u>? The Land God gave us is <u>occupied</u>?

AUDIENCE MEMBER:
(SHOUTING)

What happened to one person, one vote...the core of democracy?

KAHANE:

And we must keep in mind the huge Arab birth rate and the pitiful Jewish one threatens the existence of Israel as a Jewish state. That which Arab rocks and bullets have not succeeded in doing, Arab babies can.

AUDIENCE MEMBER:
(SHOUTING)

We'll be treating the Palestinians like the Germans treated us...Judenrein (JEW FREE). If Israel becomes like you want, it will be Arabrein...Arab free!

KAHANE:

You dare compare another Jew to Hitler, of cursed memory? A Jew who never called for any harm to Arabs. It is written, "The stranger within your midst shall climb higher and you shall descend lower and lower."

AUDIENCE MEMBER:
(SHOUTING)

The German Jew can be considered in the same category as the Palestinian!

> KAHANE:

Did German Jews dream of eliminating the German state? On the contrary, they had a groveling need to be accepted and loved by that state!

> AUDIENCE MEMBER:
> (SHOUTING)

Racist!

> KAHANE:

You know that any Arab who converts to Torah Law is acceptable to Kahane and is at least as good as Shimon Peres, a man high in government and low in Torah Judaism. You know the Kahane is bound by Judaism that is color blind and ethnic blind, but not blind to the obscenities of these accusations! The leftist establishment entrenched in this government since its founding fears, above all, my "Return to Judaism" movement. You are more willing to let the Arabs take the future than the religious Jew. You hate him more than the Arab.

FOLLOWING DAY: NEWSPAPER EDITOR ADDRESSING HIS STAFF IN THE NEWSROOM.

> EDITOR:

We're losing thousands of our young Leftists to this fanatical, ultra-Orthodox menace. I want daily pressure on the Kahane guy in the press, on TV and radio stations, to wit: He's a dangerous Fascist, and we don't want a country of Black hats standing over us. Make that very clear!

Scene 20

1984:

RADIO ANNOUNCEMENT: "KAHANE AND HIS KACH MOVEMENT HAVE ONE SEAT IN THE KNESSET."

RADIO INTERVIEWER:

We will continue to inform the public this man is a gangster, an abomination, a disease. Shulamit Aloni has a few words for us.

ALONI:

I can't even bring myself to mention his name.

KAHANE:
(NARRATING)

So much for the liberal defender of, and I quote, "The conquered and oppressed Arab," unquote. Aloni...who wants to rewrite history in such a fashion that even the Holocaust is to be discounted, lest our youth get a realistic knowledge of what happened to European Jewry and develop a passion for our land. Aloni...who opposes the visits of Israeli youth to the sites of the extermination camps to keep them from the truth of Jewish suffering and our history, telling our young that their ancestors were guilty of acting immorally so that now they must pay the bill.

RADIO INTERVIEWER:

And finally, with us today, Luba Eliav, a prominent intellectual and Leftist who, we're sorry to say, lost the election.

ELIAV:

That doesn't bother me so much as the fact that Kahane, a murderous psychopath, is in the Knesset.

KAHANE:
(NARRATING)

Editorials, television programs, radio debates...a veritable Niagara Falls of hysteria over the election of Kahane, despite the election of two members of the pro-PLO party and four communists whose loyalties are equal with Arabs.

SHIMON PERES:
(PRIME MINISTER)

Kahanism is a sword of Damocles hanging over Israel.

DOOR MARKER "MINISTER OF POLICE."

POLICE MINISTER:
(IN OFFICE, TO POLICEMAN)

Since there are no legal means to prevent rallies by Kahane, we will refuse permits anyway. If he wins on appeal, we'll allow rallies, but not where he wants them and without loudspeakers. Or we'll ban rallies on the grounds it might lead to violence. And Parliament has just decided to remove his right to travel freely. He'll need my permission.

KAHANE:
(BARGING INTO POLICE MINISTER'S OFFICE)

Because others commit violence against us, we can't hold a rally? You're deliberately holding up our permits, delaying them as long as you can, so we can't hang posters announcing a rally until it's too late, but you permit counter rallies in front of ours. They have loudspeakers to abuse us, eggs and rocks were thrown at us, and we're Fascist?

POLICE MINISTER:

I have a communication on my desk from the Minister of Education. You are banned from speaking at schools, so don't try it.

KAHANE:
(BITTERLY)

Anti-Zionist Arabs and Leftists can spread their poison freely? Or do they need a permit?

POLICE MINISTER:

They're given compulsory material to be taught to all children on the dangers of Kahane, I'm happy to say.

FOLLOWING DAY:

KAHANE IS READING A LETTER FROM A SOLDIER.

SOLDIER:
(READING LETTER)

The army is supposed to be totally non-political, yet it forces us to sit and listen to lectures by leftists against you. I protested to the Public Relations Officer of the Israel Defense Force, and he replied that you threaten the existence of the State of Israel. I think he does.

Scene 21

RADIO COMMENTATOR:

President Chaim Herzog, following the custom of a newly elected government, was to meet with all the representatives of all political parties to discuss the new government.

HERZOG IS AT KNESSET MEETING. KAHANE IS PRESENT.

HERZOG:

I will be the first president of Israel to honor the Communist party's convention with my presence.

KAHANE:
(JUMPING TO HIS FEET)

You should be ashamed! A party used by the Arabs to express their Anti-Zionism, and you're…

KNESSET MEMBERS WALK OUT ON KAHANE, RIGHTEOUSLY INDIGNANT.

HERZOG COOLLY WAVES HIM AWAY.

HERZOG:
(DECLARING LOFTILY)

I am the President of all the people.

A WEEK LATER: AN AUDITORIUM WITH AN AUDIENCE AND A HUGE BANNER READING: CONVENTION OF THE COMMUNIST PARTY.

HERZOG:
(ON PODIUM)

I have in my hand a message of greeting from Yassir Arafat.

CHEERS FROM THE DELEGATES.

VOICE OF ARAFAT:

I am delighted, in the name of the PLO, to turn to comrades in battle with appreciation and respect...for your support in defense of the inalienable rights of the Palestinian people against the colonialist Zionist aggression of your people.

THE FOLLOWING DAY, IN HERZOG'S OFFICE. SECRETARY APPROACHES WITH A LETTER:

SECRETARY:

Meir Kahane is inviting you to a convention of his Kach Party.

HERZOG TAKES THE LETTER AND THROWS IT IN THE WASTEBASKET.

KAHANE:
(NARRATING)

Army radio set aside an entire day to harangue against Kahanism:

ARMY RADIO:

The army is issuing a major warning: Kahane wishes to establish a Torah state. We are glad to announce that State television and radio will not allow Kahane to appear on programs, or talk shows, or be interviewed. They refuse to attend any of his press conferences. They do not cover events organized by Kahane. Newspapers refuse to allow him to respond to attacks on him.

A NEWSPAPER, "THE JEWISH CHRONICLE OF GREAT BRITAIN," PUBLISHES A LETTER FROM A READER.

LETTER ON SCREEN:

> Why, in view of your hysterical obsession with Kahane, do you not give him the right to reply?

EDITOR'S REPLY ON SCREEN:

> Sir: Not only is Kahane a neo-Nazi, but so are all those who, like him, use hate propaganda against the Arabs of Israel, as Hitler and Goebbels used against the Jews. It would be better for both of us if you read a New York paper and stopped reading ours.

KAHANE:
(READING A LETTER, HE IS WRITING)

To Mr. Martin F. Stein, UJA: I would like to meet with you to discuss issues that, unfortunately, cannot be resolved with a check. I shall be in the U.S. for a brief time shortly.

A WEEK LATER: STEIN IS READING HIS REPLY.

STEIN:
(READING HIS REPLY)

Unfortunately, Rabbi Kahane, I will not be able to meet with you due to the substantial differences in our viewpoints.

KAHANE:
(READING HIS REPLY)

For years, the Arabs have refused to meet with Israelis due to differences in their viewpoints. Can it be that an Arab has infiltrated the UJA? You'd probably meet with Louis Farrakhan to discuss your difference in views, but not Kahane.

Scene 22

UNITED STATES, 1986:

TV INTERVIEWER:

Rabbi Kahane's startling election to the Knesset in Israel has provoked some interesting reactions. Arthur Hertzberg, a well-known intellectual in the Jewish establishment...

HERTZBERG:

When I heard the news, I sat down to read Psalms as a balm to my troubled soul.

INTERVIEWER:

Mr. Bookbinder...

KAHANE:

...Hyman Bookbinder, the aging Liberal of the American Jewish Committee, whose greatest contribution to the American Jewish life was his retirement...

BOOKBINDER:

The election of Kahane is a disgrace...

KAHANE:

...Any other reaction by you would lead to an immediate assessment by us where we went astray.

WOMAN:

I have here a statement signed by the American Jewish Committee, the American Jewish Congress, B'nai Brith, the Anti-Defamation League, Hadassah, the Jewish Labor Committee, the National Council of Jewish Women, the Union of American Hebrew Congregations (REFORM), the United Synagogue of America (CONSERVATIVE), Women's American ORT, and the Women's League for Conservative Judaism.

SHE READS A STATEMENT.

"We abhor Kahane's goals and practices. We reject this affront to our history, our traditions, and beliefs."

KAHANE:

Your knowledge of Judaism, its traditions, and beliefs would fill a thimble, and the arrogance of your ignorance is overwhelming. Your fear what I'm saying, not because it is false, but because it is true. Not one of you has ever dared to consent to a debate with me...because none of you can. So...you defame. Every time I was to appear on the media, that list of organizations sent them frantic letters full of smear material asking them not to permit me to speak...and how vicious were these accusations. A veritable spy network follows me around to prevent all news of my appearance.

WOMAN:

Zionism, according to our definition, is the effort to create a society that tries to implement the highest ideals of democracy for all the inhabitants of Israel, regardless of religious beliefs. By definition, Kahane's vision of a society that denies such rights cannot be a Jewish state, even if Jews are in the majority. Zionism is a Hebrew-speaking social democratic country; simply and clearly put...an ethical nation.

KAHANE:

Fraud! As if all Arabs, despite their learning to speak Hebrew and being socially democratic, should be a majority of Israel and call this Zionism. A <u>Jewish</u> state is a <u>Jewish</u> majority. Without it, there is no Jewish state, no matter how ethical!

TV INTERVIEWER:

And now we hear from Rabbi Harold S. Silver, who spent a month in Israel and wrote an article titled "Kahane's Demagogy: A Perversion of Zionism, Judaism, and Democracy." It deals with the issues Kahane has raised: Democracy equalizing Arab and Jew so the Arab can peacefully take over the country with a majority vote, and Kahane rejecting that possibility...non-Jews ruling Israel.

SILVER:

We must work harmoniously with Arabs.

KAHANE:

Do the Arabs have the right to work for us harmoniously inside Israel for a majority of the Jewish state?

SILVER:

It is important that Jewish leaders do not get involved in public debate with Arabs, since the Arabs would intellectually destroy them. But the Jewish majority control would be imperiled by an influx of Arabs, and higher Arab fertility. That would affect the unique quality of Jewish life in Israel. Still, I have every confidence that Israel will make decisions inspired by a minority-respecting democracy.

KAHANE:

Had you been in Israel longer than a month, you would have met some 700,000 Arab citizens who share the same dream, a minority respecting the majority, a democracy with Silver as part of the <u>Jewish</u> minority.

WOMAN:
(TO KAHANE)

My committee is in the process of petitioning the President to withdraw your American citizenship.

KAHANE:
(TO WOMAN)

In these days of equality of the sexes, I think I owe you a story about a rabbi's spouse from my collection of Jewish leaders. The truth is, they are not making

Rebbetzins the way they used to. For example, Rebbetzin Nelly. The Rebbetzin is married to Marty, the Rabbi of the prestigious Hillel group at the University of California in Berkeley.

FLASHBACK: MAN IS ON THE TELEPHONE.

MAN:

Rabbi Ballonoff, we have a serious problem. Kahane is coming to lecture at Hillel tomorrow.

RABBI HANGS UP, RUSHES TO HILLEL, AND FRANTICALLY SHUTS THE DOORS. A STUDENT TRIES TO ENTER. HE BARES THE WAY.

RABBI:
(TO STUDENT)

No one goes in or out till that maniac Kahane leaves this town!

THE RABBI GOES HOME. NELLIE GREETS HIM.

NELLIE:
(TO RABBI)

I'm furious!

A BABY CRIES.

I'm filing a lawsuit against Dr. Lahr for the outrageous performing of an operation on an 8-day-old child.

SHE PICKS UP THE CHILD.

NELLIE:
(TO CHILD)

You haven't been well since that day, now, have you?

IN COURT.

PROSECUTING ATTORNEY:
(TO JUDGE)

The Rebbitzin is the guardian, and her 8-day-old infant is the plaintiff, Your Honor. This action is against Dr. Lahr, who, without consent of the plaintiff (BABY), forcibly removed the foreskin from the plaintiff's penis, and, by reason of this, the plaintiff has suffered extreme and severe mental anguish and physical pain. He does now and will, in the future, suffer permanent mutilation. He does now and will, in the future, will suffer cosmetically, as he will be abnormal in appearance when compared with persons who have not had their sexual organs altered. The inhumane act was done with the defendant knowing full well that the removal of the foreskin had no medical basis and was done for traditional, cultural, and religious reasons. For that reason, the plaintiff asks for punitive damages.

KAHANE:

Reform and Conservative rabbis reject all the rituals of traditional Judaism, so why shouldn't

Nelly abolish circumcision? In short, why can a Rabbi stamp on Torah and not a Rebbetzin? Are they not equal? Of course, they are. Nelly is not a Rebbetzin, nor are the "rabbis" Rabbis.

TV INTERVIEWER:
(PICKS UP PHONE)

A call from one of our listeners, Dan Ben Amotz, for Rabbi Kahane.

KAHANE:

I can't imagine what he can possibly say to me. He's one of the new Israelis to whom Jewishness means less than nothing since he sees so much in it that his decadent soul despises. But, he's neither a cool and proper middle class, nor an artist, so perhaps I can, at least, listen to him without resisting the impulse to offend.

AMOTZ:
(TO KAHANE)

I also love to tweak the nose of the hypocritical and terrified Israeli Jewish establishment and that's why I'm going to be honest about you...the only one to expressly openly the secret yearnings of so many of us. You, at least, say the truth. "The Jewish State can allow itself to be democratic as long as the Arab is in the minority."

KAHANE:
(TO AMOTZ)

But you would not hesitate, if forced, to choose to give up the Jewish character of Israel for democracy.

AMOTZ:

I would not.

KAHANE:
(STARTING OFF)

Remember when the tears flowed unashamedly from men of steel? Their hearts were broken. If such an abomination could be conceived by man, there was no longer hope. If such evil was in his breast, there was no longer light. If from civilization this could emerge, there was no longer purpose. Such an era is guilty of the greatest of all crimes, the destruction of God's dream. All the nations were as guilty as Eichmann. The appeasers, the closers of gates to the desperate. Those who came upon the camps and met the horror face to face remember that moment when their hearts went cold, the sun stood still, the wind was silent, and their tears were buried with their bodies in the cold, damp earth. And then, when a people reborn took a land that was desert and waste and made it green with Jewish grass, sparkling with Jewish life, that was a miracle! And now you want to betray God and the dead.

ARAB:
(CALLS)

Israel has no right to exist, it took our land and made us refugees. There should be a separate Palestinian State!

KAHANE:

Israeli youth echo these sentiments. The Arab propagandist teaches us our history. And we need another miracle…. schools brimming with youngsters who know our history, who are not disastrously bankrupt of Jewishness. Clean our films of "Hate Judaism" films, and let them teach this:

ON SCREEN: 135 C.E., THE ROMAN CONQUEROR IS SPEAKING TO HIS TROOPS.

ROMAN:

The temple is destroyed. Judah is conquered…even in name. it is now…Palestina. The name Judea and the Jew were abolished…for all time.

HIS TROOPS CHEER HIM.

BACK TO THE PRESENT:

> MAN:
> (CALLING IN)

So, you admit we've been outta there all this time. Other people moving in, and we just throw them out, take the key and move in...just like they did to us in Poland?! Put us in camps and went to sleep in our bedrooms?! And we do the same?!

> KAHANE:

Three million remained in scattered villages and became the only state that bears the same name, speaks the same tongue, upholds the same faith, and inhabits the same land as it did 3,000 years ago. There never was an Arab state in Palestine, and there never was a Palestine Arab nation. No state has such an impressive international birth certificate...the promise of the Bible.

> MAN:
> (CALLING IN)

I'd rather live with Arabs than your kind of Jew. I say kill the Orthodox before they kill us.

> KAHANE:

Ah...a good American Liberal Leftist who will vote Democrat even if they nominate the Black Jew Hater Farrakhan. There is no word that is referred to with greater contempt in Israel than "*galut," exile. It is blamed for the Jewish inferiority complex, physical fear and mental abnormality. Unfortunately, it is also true that the Israeli is beset with the complexes of the Jew in "galut"; a problem with such magnitude, and such a potential for explosion, that is threatens the very existence of the state. The "Galut" has crept into Israel and brought with it inferiority and shame to the Sabra, the native-born Israeli. That is at the root of their desire to escape their Jewishness, their opposition to their own religion. He looks down upon the religious, consciously avoids them, and prefers non-Jews. He is embarrassed at being Jewish and fervently hates them, as you do.

> MAN:

A classic case of the pot calling the kettle. You shocked not only Israel but the world, when you set up your killer bunch, the JDL, in, of all places, Israel!

KAHANE:

The JDL is here because we have to be reminded Zionism is "*Ahavat Yisroel" ...love for the Jewish people. We must be reminded Zionism does not separate religion from nationality...they are one. We have to be reminded the core of Zionism is not the Communist Manifesto but the Holy Torah. And this is why JDL is in the Land of Israel.

Scene 23

FLASHBACK:

ON SCREEN: UNITED NATIONS, 1947.

SECRETARY:

A Palestinian state is proposed. Those in favor of creating two separate states out of what is now called Palestine? Those opposed will now cast their votes.

ARAB DIPLOMATS RISE AND PROCLAIM, EACH IN TURN:

ARAB DIPLOMATS:

No partition, no Jewish immigration, no Jewish state.

THEY WALK OUT.

NEWSPAPER HEADLINE ON SCREEN:

"PARTITION PLAN DOOMED BY ARAB OPPOSITION."

KAHANE:
(NARRATING)

So-called displaced Arabs were nowhere to be found before Israel inhabited the land, contradicting their claim that they had been there since the beginning of time. Mark Twain and others had this to say:

ON SCREEN: 1867

MARK TWAIN:

On our visit to Palestine, we never saw a human being the whole route. Nazareth is forlorn, Jericho in ruins, Bethlehem, Bethany...desolate. The Galilee, the land of milk and honey where angels sand, is now inhabited by birds of prey, sulking foxes, the hush of solitude. Palestine sits in sackcloth and ashes.

ANOTHER MAN:

The Sharon plain, once a thing of exquisite fertility and beauty, is in wretched desolation, the city and palaces returned to dust.

ANOTHER MAN:

The melancholy of abandonment weighs on the Holy Land. It has been given over to Bedouins and marauders who wandered over it.

KAHANE:

Dr. Carl Herman Voss, Chairman of the American Christian Palestine Committee, has this to say:

VOSS:

The Arab population of Palestine was small until Jewish resettlement restored the barren lands and drew to it Arabs from neighboring lands, many of whom usurped Jewish homes. The British never checked Arab credentials. They were allowed unlimited entry; their papers signed that they belonged in Israel. British wanted peace with the Arabs, no Jews, and no trouble. Few Arab individuals died where they were born. Families were continually moving to where they heard there were better conditions.

ARAB:
(TO KAHANE)

We have family ties for thousands of years to the land you're occupying.

KAHANE:

Nonsense. You invented that lie long after we brought the land to life again, and you came in droves to take advantage of the opportunity to settle down and prosper. Bedouins wandering landless and starving, exploited, abused by your absentee landlords, you rushed to find a haven with us.

ARAB:

Jewish atrocities caused the Arabs to become refugees.

KAHANE:
(NARRATING)

May 14, 1948, on Israeli's Day of Independence, she issued the following proclamation while being attacked by Arab armies and Israeli Arabs were fleeing:

FLASHBACK:

ISRAELI MAN:
(ON THE RADIO)

In the midst of wanton Arab aggression, we have yet to call upon the Arabs of Israel to return to the ways of peace and help develop the state with full representation.

APRIL 23, 1948. UN SECURITY COUNCIL:

SECRETARY GENERAL:

Jamal Husseini, of the Arab Higher Committee...

HUSSEINI:

The Arabs would not submit to a truce but preferred to leave, which they did.

ON SCREEN: HAIFA

BRITISH POLICE:

Every effort is being made by the Jews to persuade the Arab populace to stay, that their lives will be safe.

KAHANE:
(NARRATING)

In his book, "The Secret Behind the Disaster," Nimr al-Hawari, a former commander of the Arab Youth paramilitary organization in Palestine, has this to say:

AL-HAWARI:

The Palestinian Arabs were led by gangster leadership, which herded them like docile sheep. They blinded the Arabs' eyes and clogged their brains, filling them with rattling sabres and delivering fiery speeches, so they fled.

KAHANE:
(NARRATING)

Iraq's Prime Minister thundered:

PRIME MINISTER OF IRAQ:

We shall smash Israel with our guns and destroy and obliterate every place the Jew will seek shelter in.

ON SCREEN: 1949. ISRAELI STATESMAN

ISRAELI:

Israel will accept 100,000 refugees in a general settlement of the refugee problem, and we hope each Arab state will make a similar contribution.

ARAB:

Absolutely not! And it's further resolved that Arabs are forbidden to negotiate with Israel.

ON SCREEN: 1950

EGYPTIAN AND LEBANESE NEWSPAPERS:

"The solution of the refugee problem is the dissolution of Israel. In demanding the restoration of the refugees in Palestine, the Arabs intend to return as masters. A large Arab majority will form a fifth column for the day of revenge and reckoning.

ON SCREEN: 1951. AT THE UN.

MAN REPORTING:

The Palestine Commission has concluded, after extensive investigation, that Israel cannot make commitments to solve the refugee problem unless she is assured of her security by her Arab neighbors...which, to date, they have not.

ARAB:

There are 2 million refugees.

KAHANE:
(NARRATING)

Myth! More like 30,000. The padding of rolls has been notorious.

ON SCREEN: 1957. AT THE UN. THE SYRIAN PRIME MINISTER IS SPEAKING.

PRIME MINISTER:

The Palestine refugees have the right to annihilate Israel. Any other solution is a desecration of the Arab people and an act of treason.

ANOTHER MAN STEPS TO THE PODIUM.

MAN:

Our agency, the United Nations Relief and Works agency, has fed, trained, housed and educated them at a cost of more than one-half billion dollars...and it's been a hard and thankless task.

MAN:
(NARRATING)

The Palestine Commission was created to negotiate a resolution to the refugee problem in Palestine. The World Council of Churches sent its advisor on refugee affairs to the Commission, and he had this to say, "After World War 2, there were some 40 million refugees throughout the world. They were resettled in other countries, and adjusted well, and the international community did not have to support them. The U.S Senate Foreign Relations Committee joins us in urging that the refugees are being used as political hostages, with nothing done to help them by the Arab leaders, who fear their political leverage will then be lost."

SECRETARY-GENERAL:

The delegate from Syria...

SYRIAN DELEGATE:

The Jew is a perfidious liar. He blames the Nazis...who only took back what the Jews took from them...and is doing the same to us. Blaming us for wanting to reclaim what's ours...and you believe them.

SECRETARY-GENERAL:

The delegate from Israel...

ISRAELI DELEGATE:

Arabs have conceded they have the room. Syria...millions of acres needing labor for cultivation. Iraq...underpopulated and needing labor to develop its tremendous wealth in oil, water and land. Both nations can absorb 950,000 refugees, a higher number than there legitimately are, probably.

U.S DELEGATE:

Our secretary of State indicates the United States is willing to lend Israel funds to enable her to compensate the Arabs and thus facilitate resettlement in Arab lands.

ON SCREEN: A PALESTINE CHRISTIAN COMMITTEE MEMBER IS SPEAKING.

PCC MAN:

We have made a study of Arab property claims inside Israel and arrived at a figure of 300 million.

ISRAELI DELEGATE:

These figures are wildly exaggerated. Even so, we offer to pay compensation for Arab property without even waiting for a peace settlement. Hundreds of thousands of Israelis were forced to abandon property in Arab lands without a penny compensation for their losses, whereas we have already released 10 million blocked bank accounts of the refugees.

KAHANE:
(NARRATING)

In 1967, Israel offered to negotiate a five-year plan for the rehabilitation of the refugees and contribute technical and economic assistance. A year later, the offer was renewed.

ARAB:

You cannot buy our people with new plumbing!

ON SCREEN: A REPRESENTATIVE FROM THE UN RELIEF AND WORKS COMMITTEE (UNRWA) IS SPEAKING.

UNRWA REPRESENTATIVE:

No group of refugees was ever treated with so much solicitude and concern by an international agency as ours, but the Arab governments obstructed us at every turn. Their contributions were minimal, their restrictive regulations overwhelming. The U.S. provided most of the money. Even Israel made a substantial contribution. The Russians, nothing. And yet, the Arabs made pronouncements like President Nassar of Egypt.

NASSER:

If the Arabs return to Israel, Israel will cease to exist.

UNRWA MAN:

Nassar's rule in Gaza was devoid of concern or compassion. In that congested purgatory, the refugees were virtual prisoners. Very few were allowed to emigrate; they were barred from Egypt, they suffered discrimination and repression.

A VOICE IS HEARD.

MAN:

The Egyptian delegate accuses the UNRWA of conspiring with Israel to solve the refugee problem.

HE GETS UP FROM HIS SEAT AND WALKS OUT. ANOTHER MAN'S VOICE FOLLOWS HIM.

MAN:

The delegate from Saudi Arabia likens Nasser's regime in Gaza to Hitler's regime in the countries he occupied in World War 2!

UNRWA MAN:

Many refugees have their own homes, and jobs, and are well educated due to our efforts, I'm glad to say. As a class, they live far better, and longer and learn more than many Arabs who live in squalor in Egypt, Syria, and Iraq.

Scene 24

> KAHANE:
> (NARRATING)

Peggy Tishman, the wife of a hugely wealthy businessman, and past president of the UJA, visits Israel.

ON SCREEN:

FLASHBACK: JORDAN.

TISHMAN IS SITTING AT A TABLE WITH A GROUP OF ARABS AT A DINNER IN JORDAN.

> PEGGY:

My friends. Stateless people! Palestinians who have no Palestine. My love for Israel is so great that I can only mourn for them.

> ARAB:

Well, the question is, "Do the Israelis really want peace?"

> PEGGY:

At every dinner party I've attended here, this is the one invariably asked.

SHE PONDERS THE QUESTION.

KAHANE:
(NARRATING)

Try to imagine this scene: Mrs. Tishman and I ate at a dinner table...

KAHANE AND MRS. TISHMAN AT A TABLE.

KAHANE:
(TO TISHMAN)

Jordan...a country that twice tried to wipe out Israel, destroyed every Jewish synagogue but one, barred Jews from praying at the Wall for nineteen years, and you don't question <u>their</u> question...do we want peace? Which brings <u>me</u> to a question, "Why do Jews support the UJA Federation, which opposes their religion and their homeland?" And another question, "Is mourning the answer for Arabs who plot our annihilation?"

SHE FLEES IN PANIC.

Scene 25

ON SCREEN:

1989: THE INTIFADA...ARABS RIOTING TO TERRORIZE SETTLERS INTO LEAVING THEIR LAND, WHICH ARABS CALLED "OCCUPIED."

KAHANE:
(NARRATING)

The Jew is afraid of his own land. Professor Menachim Stern, an internationally known Hebrew University historian was walking to work. A teacher and students find him.

FLASHBACK: A BODY LIES ON THE GROUND.

TEACHER:
(BENDING OVER HIM)

He was stabbed five times.

LATER: ISRAELI POLICE ARRIVE.

POLICEMAN:

This was a revolutionary act on the part of the Arabs.

KAHANE:
(TO POLICEMAN)

An obscene term you now use rather than what it is...the usual Arab terror.

LATER: AT THE FUNERAL.

RABBI:

Professor Stein was an expert on the Second Temple, our Second State, whose destruction lead to the horrors of exile.

KAHANE:
(NARRATING)

He was murdered in the third Jewish state. And more, in the heart of The Dream...the state was created so that Jews would never again be murdered because of their Jewishness.

A BUS IS SEEN DRIVING ON THE ROAD. AN ARAB GETS ON IN TEL AVIV, SUDDENLY SEIZES THE WHEEL, AND TURNS THE BUS SHARPLY TO THE RIGHT. THE BUS GOES OVER A CLIFF AND INTO A DEEP CHASM.

LATER: ARAB IN CUSTODY.

POLICEMAN:
(TO ARAB)

You're charged with multiple murders...14 Jews died immediately, and two others in the hospital.

ARAB:
(STARING OFF)

To sanctify in the name of Allah.

ARAB PUTS DOWN A LITTLE PRAYER RUG, BENDS OVER AND PRAYS.

KAHANE:
(NARRATING)

And day after day...It was a few minutes before 11 AM on Jerusalem's main street. There is a bus stop, the main post office, and main police station. Jerusalem, the capital of Israel, the center of the Dream...

AN ARAB WALKS TOWARD THE BUS STOP, SHOUTS "*ALLAH AKHBAR" (GOD IS GREAT), AND STABS FIVE JEWS. TWO DIE IMMEDIATELY. THE ARAB IS CAUGHT. THE ISRAELI CROWD ATTACKS HIM. THE ISRAELI POLICE CHARGE IN WITH HORSES AND TEAR GAS THE JEWS.

IN THE COURTROOM: THE ARAB IS BEFORE THE JUDGE.

JUDGE:

You murdered two old men, ages 91 and 76!

HE SHAKES HIS HEAD IN DISAPPROVAL.

You must have some remorse for such an act.

ARAB:

After praying the *Al Kadar prayer, I planned the act. My purpose was to kill Jews.

JUDGE:

You are hereby sentenced to spend the rest of your life in jail.

KAHANE:
(NARRATING)

It would be nice to think the police saved the Arab's life so he might receive such a prison sentence. But no, he'll soon be freed.

Scene 26

A WEEK LATER:

               POLICE CAPTAIN:
                 (TO KAHANE)

We are bringing 3,500 of our men to Jerusalem to prevent acts of vengeance against Arabs. You are warned not to make trouble.

                  KAHANE:

The cost will, of course, be borne by Jews.

FOLLOWING DAY: KAHANE AND HIS KACH PARTY ARE PROTESTING, CARRYING POSTERS SAYING, "ARABS OUT! STOP THE KILLINGS!" POLICE ARRIVE ON HORSES, TEAR-GASSING THEM. THEY ARE ARRESTED AND THROWN INTO JAIL WITH AN ARAB.

                   ARAB:
                 (TO KAHANE)

I've already murdered two Jews. Watch yourself.

FOLLOWING DAY: WOMAN COMES TO POLICE PRECINCT.

                  WOMAN:

My name is Mrs. Barahami. My boy has been missing for two months. He is only 13.

POLICEMAN:
(NOT TOO INTERESTED)

He probably ran away from home.

WOMAN:

We loved him. Why would he do that? Maybe Arabs...

POLICEMAN:

Nonsense.

TURNS TO PAPER ON DESK.

We'll let you know.

SAME DAY: ONE ISRAELI IS WHISPERING TO ANOTHER.

FIRST ISRAELI:

The body of a 13-year-old Oran Barahami was found in Jaffa. He had been brutally slain but first sexually mutilated and raped. The body was mutilated so badly that, at first, the pathologist had difficulty determining the sex. Two Arabs from Gaza were caught and confessed.

OTHER ISRAELI:

I could kill them!

HE TURNS AROUND TO SEE IF ANYONE HEARD.

FIRST ISRAELI:

Sh-sh...me, too.

Scene 27

A POLICE PRECINCT. A WOMAN ENTERS.

WOMAN:
(TO POLICEMAN)

My brother is missing. My brain tells me he could be alive, but my heart says something horrible has happened. If he was kidnapped, my mother will die. He was...sorry, he is her favorite son.

KAHANE:

Avi Sasportas, a nineteen-year-old whose brother was a paratrooper, was finally found after weeks of searching by thousands of soldiers and civilians...He was well within The Dream...his body found in a shallow grave...shot in the head and his body cut to pieces.

A COMMITTEE MEETING. MEMBERS ARE SEATED AROUND THE TABLE.

MAN:

Members of the Cabinet, in the matter of Avi Sasportas, it has been decided that we must call for restrictions on hitchhiking by soldiers. Those opposed?

SILENCE.

Passed.

MAN PICKS UP PAPERS.

We have petitions here for Kahane's idea of removing Arabs from Israel who are against our state. Those who are not can remain but not vote. Others who leave will be helped by our government to find jobs where they resettle and be given ample funds until they are independent.

MEMBER:

The majority of us in Tel Aviv, I can tell you, are adamantly opposed, and I mean...adamantly! And the German Jews in Naharia are horrified at any thought of removing Arabs.

THE PETITION ARE DISCARDED.

ON SCREEN: A WEEK LATER:

NEWSPAPER ARTICLE:

"Body of young man Brurya Rotman is found. Police arrest Israeli Arabs.

A SHECHEM POLICEMAN IS ON PATROL. A STONE COMES CRASHING DOWN FROM A BUILDING. HE IS KILLED.

KAHANE:
(NARRATING)

And they say stones do not kill. Sergeant Meisner was a sportsman, a member of the polo team and the Nature Society. His circles are shocked by any suggestion of the removal of Arabs.

TV INTERVIEWER:
(TO ARAB)

Israeli Chief of Staff Don Shomron is in the area.

ARAB IS UNCONCERNED.

SHOMRON:
(TO INTERVIEWER)

The Arab residents shielding the perpetrators will pay a heavy price. They will not repeat their acts. They will be terrified.

TWO DAYS LATER: THE ARMY BLOWS UP THE UPPER FLOOR OF THE BUILDING FROM WHERE THE STONE SLAB WAS DROPPED. THE FLOOR THAT WAS DESTROYED WAS UNOCCUPIED. AS THE PART OF THE BUILDING EXPLODED, SHOUTS OF "ALLAH AKHBAR" ARE HEARD FROM THE ADJOINING BUILDING."

TV INTERVIEWER:
(TO ARAB OWNER OF ADJOINING BUILDING)

This will have an impact on future incidents. As the owner of this building, are you planning to evacuate?

OWNER:

This is no deterrent whatsoever. We build and build again.

ISRAELI POLICEMAN:

Ibraham Tahtuk, you are under arrest for the murder of Benjamin Meisner.

LATER: POLICE ARREST AN ARAB IN HIS HOUSE.

HE IS TAKEN OUT, AND HIS HOUSE IS DEMOLISHED. GRAFFITI ON THE ADJOINING BUILDING READS, "SALUTE THE HERO, IBRAHAM TAHTUK."

THE FOLLOWING DAY: AT THE ISRAELI CIVIL ADMINISTRATION BUILDING.

THE HEAD OF OFFICE IS ON THE PHONE LISTENING. HE HANGS UP AND TALKS TO AN AIDE.

HEAD OF OFFICE:
(TO AIDE)

The roof of a nearby building to Tahtuk's home was also damaged.

THE AIDE WAVES HIS HANDS TO INDICATE, "FORGET IT."

HEAD OF OFFICE:
(ON PHONE)

We promise to pay for the damages.

Scene 28

KAHANE:
(NARRATING)

On the Sabbath, Shlomo Cohen was on his way to prayers at the Western Wall, inside the old city of Jerusalem.

SHLOMO AND FRIEND ARE WALKING.

FRIEND:
(DREAMILY)

You know, Shlomo, I'm the happiest man just to be walking in this little alley on my way to our Holy Wall.

SHLOMO HUGS HIM.

FRIEND:

Just to stand here, where my grandfather prayed…the same words in the same place, and now we'll both be together in spirit…and in joy, 'cause what he asked for came true, "This year in Jerusalem!"

THEY ARE AMBUSHED BY FIVE ARABS WHO STAB SHLOMO COHEN TO DEATH.

KAHANE:
(NARRATING)

In response to the murder, Mayor Teddy Kollek of Jerusalem, a supporter of coexistence in Jerusalem between Jews and Arabs:

MAYOR KOLLEK:

Even the best plans can't prevent an individual crime like this.

KAHANE:
(NARRATING)

As for Shlomo's father...

FATHER:
(AS HIS SON'S BODY IS BEING LOWERED TO THE GRAVE)

Put me in your place. Don't leave me here.

KAHANE:
(NARRATING SADLY)

The Dream. And before the outbreak of Arab rioting known as the intifada by so-called Palestinians, our soldiers were in an ongoing, undeclared war. Their crime? Hitching rides.

1987: A Dutch convert to Judaism, going back to a base. Two Arabs gave him a lift and murdered him with an ax.

1985: Another soldier, returning on leave, is strangled, and hacked to death. He was also given a lift.

1984: A woman soldier...gang raped and murdered. She hitched a ride...

And the body of a civilian, a cab driver, was also found. He was shot to death and fought bitterly before dying.

POLICE:
(TO PRESS)

He might have been the victim of a criminal act under circumstances we cannot spell out at this time, except to say the victim is also under suspicion.

WOMAN:
(TO POLICE)

I'm his mother. We will never forgive the stain on his honor, and I demand an apology!

REPORTER:
(TO MOTHER)

Where is your evidence that the police are wrong?

MOTHER:
(TO POLICEMAN)

I know my son! Where is yours that you are right?!

KAHANE:
(NARRATING)

1,150 Arab murderers were later freed in exchange for six Israeli soldiers.

1988: A SETTLER (MAN) IS GIVING IS A SPEECH.

SETTLER:

First of all, we must remember we are not <u>settlers</u> on <u>someone else's land</u>. This land is <u>ours</u>. What we took back from the Arabs in a war that <u>they</u> started was <u>our</u> land...not <u>temporarily</u> taken, so they have an excuse to call us settlers, and finally, the government asked us to put our lives here so that we can protect our borders. Yet, they still call us "settlers." We tell our government and the Arab murderers that we will continue to build and live as usual...intifada or no intifada.

ONE WEEK LATER: AN ISRAELI MAN IS ATTACKED BY AN ARAB WHO SHATTERS HIS HEAD WITH A ROCK AND THEN SHOOTS HIM TWICE IN THE HEAD. AN ARMY COMMAND CAR PASSES BY. ARAB OPENS FIRE ON THE CAR, KILLING ONE AND WOUNDING TWO OTHERS.

ISRAELI MAN:
(TALKING TO SETTLERS)

We have with us today the Commander of the army's Central Command, General Mitzna.

GENERAL:

I can only say the incident was an isolated one that does not indicate anything.

SETTLER:

With all due respect, General, you spoke the same way, with no particular interest in us, <u>condemnation</u> when Arabs attacked my wife on a bus. She was a pregnant woman, and we were attacked by the Arabs in retaliation.

GENERAL:

I'd never seen such an abomination.

SETTLER:

You refer, of course, to the Jewish reaction, not the attack on my wife.

GENERAL:

Our bus driver was armed and might have used his weapon, following your example. We can't have that!

SETTLER:

You know that's a lie! He was afraid you'd arrest him if he dared to defend himself. Even the army didn't defend itself. You can't prevent anything anymore. They know it...and we're lost.

KAHANE:
(SPEAKING TO AN AUDIENCE)

And one day, the heavens opened and wept in Jericho. There, in the city that was the first to fall before the invading Children of Israel more than 3,000 years ago, there in the city near which Elijah rose to Heaven, where a mother and her three children went up in flames in a bus hit by firebombs. She was age 27. The children were aged one to three. She, trying to save them, watched them as they were consumed, and then she lost her life as the bus exploded. A soldier who tried to rescue them also later died. Rachel Weiss is buried in a cemetery regularly smashed or desecrated by Arabs...She is asleep forever with her children...Netanel, 3, Rafael, 2, Ephraim, 1.

ISRAELI LEFTIST:
(IN AUDIENCE)

Racist!

KAHANE:

Leftist! The real haters! The Fascists of Israel are so poisoned with jealousy at the satisfaction of the religious life that you would make me the object of a public lynching!

KAHANE:
(NARRATING)

Three teenagers wrote to a newspaper from a settlement:

FIRST GIRL:
(RECITING HER LETTER)

Life for Jews here is a daily terror. We are twelve miles from the sea and Tel Aviv but we feel as if we live in a country that is not ours.

SECOND GIRL:

Husbands, wives, and children leaving settlements in cars never know whether a rock or firebomb, or bullet with snuff out a life, looking at every orchard, hunch over a wheel, and fear walking outside the fence that surrounds us. Is there one Arab town surrounded by barbed wire like ours?

THIRD GIRL:

Our home is a veteran of tragedy. A firebomb was thrown into a car driven by the Moses family. The pregnant mother was burned alive; her five-year-old son lingered for three months before passing away. He joined an 8-year-old from a nearby settlement, whose body was found near his home, his face smashed to pieces by a rock. Two months later, another firebomb attack. Tens of attacks in our settlement every month, and hundreds in other settlements. The army is impotent. It fails to report even half of the attacks and gives us little or no protection.

KAHANE:
(NARRATING)

And they say, "STONES DO NOT KILL." A 20-year-old soldier was struck on the head by a rock and died. Countless others have remained vegetables or brain damaged because of stones...and "stones do not kill?" A month later, Vardi Bemberger is seriously injured by a rock. Later, she is to tell the press...

BEMBERGER:

I am happy that my husband did not fire. Had he done so, he would have undoubtedly been arrested. Our friends prefer to hand back their weapons or not use them, even in clear cases of self-defense.

KAHANE:
(NARRATING)

The Dream. The Nightmare! The abomination!

A WATER CARRIER IS SURROUNDED BY ARABS SAYING, "SLAUGHTER HIM." HE SAYS TO THEM IN ARABIC, "GET AWAY FROM HERE," AND RUNS. THEY JUMP ON HIM WITH AXES AND KNIVES AND STAB HIM IN THE BACK AND NECK.

WATER CARRIER:
(IN HOSPITAL, TO PRESS)

I felt I was immersed in blood.

REPORTER:

You had a revolver. Why didn't you use it?

WATER CARRIER:

You know the answer.

Scene 29

ON SCREEN: KNESSET.

KAHANE:
(TO THE KNESSET)

Not only is the Army in the hands of officers who, because of their Leftist orientation and un-Jewish education, feel guilty about the plight of the so-called Palestinians, but you, the Left at the political level, have made it your own personal "Jihad" to defend the so-called, "oppressed Palestinians." The soldiers' hands are tied, their morale is lowered, and the morale of the Arabs is raised. The self-hating and guilt-ridden Left among us opened Pandora's box of masochism and gave a major push to the destruction of the Israel Defense Force.

MEMBERS OF THE KNESSET ARE WALKING OUT WHILE HE IS TALKING.

SETTLER:
(ON PHONE)

I am a settler in Kiryat Arba. You tell your commander the Arabs are waiting for us outside the gate with bombs. We can't even send our children to school. Help us!

SOLDIER:

This section is not in our area of operations.

THE SOLDIER HANGS UP.

FOUR SOLDIERS ARE CONFRONTING A CAPTAIN.

> ONE SOLDIER:
> (FRUSTRATED AND ANGRY)

Weeks of attacks by stones and firebombs, and we can't even shoot a plastic bullet?!

> COMMANDER:

You are members of the elite Givati unit, chosen for the honor because you exercise good judgment and self-control. Dis-missed!

THE FOLLOWING DAY: ARABS PURSUE THE SOLDIERS WITH ROCKS. THEY LOSE CONTROL, APPREHEND ONE OF THEM, AND BEAT HIM UNTIL HE DIES.

MONTHS LATER, THEY'RE ALL IN JAIL.

> ONE SOLDIER:

Nine months in here, our women and children out there, and we're punished for being normal, trying to protect them, trying to be men, to be Jews, to be human.

HE PUTS HIS HEAD IN HIS HANDS, ANGUISHED.

What have I done?

> ANOTHER SOLDIER:

Mad orders are meant to be violated.

Scene 30

KAHANE:
(NARRATING)

The Arab village of Nahalin has had a long and bloody record of murdering Jews since our state was born. In 1948, they captured 35 students and slaughtered them in cold blood one by one. In 1989, the Border Police were sent to Nahalin to make arrests for taking more Jewish lives. They were known to be a tough, no-nonsense unit.

1989:

ARAB:
(TO HIS MEN)

They'll be met with a well-planned ambush and attacked with heavy rocks and firebombs.

BORDER POLICE RESPOND WITH FIRE AND KILL FOUR ARABS.

ISRAELI PRESS HEADLINE:

"KNESSET IS OUTRAGED BY EXCESSES OF BORDER POLICE!"

ON SCREEN: U.N.

SECRETARY-GENERAL:

The world is outraged by the atrocities committed by the Israelis. The record will record our displeasure.

KAHANE:
(NARRATING)

The Leftist-dominated news media in Israel went on a literary orgy of hate and condemnation of the raid and the border police that was equaled only by the Arab attacks on them.

MEMBER OF KNESSET:
(TO KNESSET)

A Board of Inquiry had condemned the Border Police and called for the removal of a Colonel and the reprimand of a Lieutenant Colonel. The Border Police will no longer participate in operational activities involving settlers.

KAHANE:
(NARRATING)

The Border Police were never again the kind of deterrent it was before. A year ago...the intifada in full swing, Prime Minister Shamir...

ON SCREEN: 1988:

SHAMIR:

I do not recall people being in such a happy mood as these days. The intifada is dying.

KAHANE:
(NARRATING)

1989. Note that date. What can one say?

ON SCREEN: 1988:

PRESS HEADLINE:

"CHIEF OF STAFF SAYS INTIFADA US DYING."

KAHANE:
(NARRATING)

And Defense Minister Yitzhak Rabin...

ON SCREEN: 1988:

RABIN:

We can begin to sense a measure of weariness in the Arab part of the population as a result of the activities of our security forces.

KAHANE:
(NARRATING)

Note the date...What can one say?
PRIME MINISTER SHAMIR MEETING WITH SETTLERS.

SETTLER:

Why is there no action against the intifada, which has now gone down in the Guinness Book of Records as the longest dying phenomenon in history?

SHAMIR:

Rest assured we are close to bringing the intifada to an end.

MAN:

My name is Rafi Levi. My job is to protect a bus in case of attack...

FLASHBACK: A BUS IS RIDING WHEN TENS OF ARABS DASH OUT SCREAMING, CURSING AND THROWING ROCKS AT IT. ONE ARAB TRIES TO HIT LEVI WITH A STONE. HE STOPS HIM WITH BOTH HANDS WHEN ANOTHER ARAB FROM BEHIND GRABS HIS THROAT WITH BOTH HANDS. WITH THE BUTT OF HIS WEAPON, LEVI HITS THE ARAB IN THE STOMACH AND FREES HIMSELF. THE ARAB WITH THREE STONES HITS LEVI ABOVE THE EYES, GRABS HIS GUN BELT AND PULLS ON IT. LEVI COCKS THE WEAPON. ANOTHER BUS ARRIVES.

OTHER BUS DRIVER:
(YELLING)

I'm coming to help!

LEVI UNCOCKS THE WEAPON.

> PRIME MINISTER SHAMIR:
> (TO LEVI)

I understand your suffering, but the Arabs minded that you were armed and that your job was to protect the bus.

> ANOTHER SETTLER:

How does he allow Arabs to reach him and injure him and not shoot? The answer is he was afraid to be arrested and jailed.

> SETTLER:
> (WARNING)

Something new will be happening in Israel. And this time...<u>our</u> orders!

A SETTLER IS DRIVING HIS CAR. IT IS PELTED WITH STONES. HE LEAPS OUT AND CHASES TWO YOUTHS AND SHOOTS THEM, KILLING ONE. HE IS JAILED.

JEWS ARE ATTACKED AT THE WESTERN WALL BY THOUSANDS OF ROCK-THROWING ARABS. FOUR SHOT AND ONE KILLED.

PRESS HEADLINE ON SCREEN:

> "JEWS FROM KIRYST ARBA AND HEBRON, AFTER YEARS OF ARAB ATTACKS, DECIDED THEY WOULD SHOOT ANY ARAB WHO THREW STONES AT THEM.

ON RADIO:

"Angry Jews from Kiryat smashed Arab cars and houses. The police plan to deal more strictly with settlers who commit acts of vengeance against Arabs. Three Jews were remanded to jail for retaliating against an attempted murder of one of them by Arabs. 12,000 cases of Arab assaults and murders have been committed. The Left is raging against the Jews. In two days, we'll be celebrating Jerusalem Day, the liberation of the Old City in the 1967 War. A police captain is with us and has a few words to say:"

> POLICE CAPTAIN:

There will be no rallies in the city, no groups larger than 50 allowed in, and no Israeli flags to be flown. Flyers have been distributed to that effect.

RADIO ANNOUNCER:

Kahane's party, Kach, has challenged your orders, I understand. They announced they will demonstrate.

POLICE CAPTAIN:

They will be arrested.

Scene 31

KAHANE:
(NARRATING)

Frederick Rosenfeld, an American Jew, is hiking with a friend.

FRIEND:

You know, Fred, I'm beginning to think we ought to throw these Arabs outta here after what's been happening.

ROSENFELD:

Don't you dare say a thing like that! I'm shocked!

HE STORMS AWAY AND WALKS ON ALONE. HE SEES ARABS COMING AND HAILS THEM IN A FRIENDLY FASHION. ARABS HAIL HIM, SMILING AND FRIENDLY.

ROSENFELD:
(TO ARAB)

Haven't seen you in a while. How've you been?

HE SHOWS THEM HIS CAMERA.

My new one. Easy to work it.

HE SHOWS HOW. THEY TAKE PICTURES TOGETHER, AND EAT FRUIT TOGETHER, THEN ONE ARAB NODS TO THE OTHER, WHO GOES BEHIND ROSENFELD AND STABS HIM IN THE BACK. THEN ALL ARABS LEAVE.

ROSENFELD IS BLEEDING WHILE OTHER ARABS ARE PASSING BY.

ROSENFELD:

Help me.

NO ONE COMES TO HIS AID. HE DIES AFTER BLEEDING THE WHOLE DAY.

AT THE FUNERAL, HUNDREDS OF SETTLERS SURROUND THE OPEN GRAVE. PRIME MINISTER SHAMIR IS PRESENT.

MAN:
(OFFERING SHAMIR THE SHOVEL)

You fill the grave yourself. Maybe you'll have a little compassion.

ANOTHER MAN:
(TO SHAMIR)

Traitor!

ANOTHER MAN:

Quiet! We should show respect for the dead.

HE IS BOOED.

SHAMIR:
(ADDRESSING THE GROUP)

Every funeral is a difficult experience for me...

MAN:

Resign!

SHAMIR:

Your behavior is disgraceful, but I am immune...

SETTLER:

Prime Minister of the Intifada!

SHAMIR:

...to such things. It is regrettable we suffer from dissension...it only...

MAN:

Get him outta here!

A HEAVY FORCE OF POLICE HASTILY MOVES HIM OUT AND INTO HIS CAR.

SHAMIR:
(SHOUTING)

Kahane is to blame for this!

THE SETTLERS SURROUND THE CAR.

SETTLERS:
(SHOUTING)

Traitor! Resign! And take our Defense Minister, Yitzhak Rabin with you! Who is he defending, us?

KAHANE:
(NARRATING)

Something new and revolutionary occurring in Israel!

Scene 32

RADIO ANNOUNCER:

Ten settlers were on their way to the grave of the prophet Nathan when Arabs attacked them from all directions. Kahane plans a demonstration at the site.

KAHANE AND HIS FOLLOWERS ARE MARCHING IN THE AREA AND CRYING OUT "VENGEANCE! VENGEANCE!" THEY CLASH WITH POLICE WHO CHARGE WITH HORSES INTO THE CROWD, TEAR-GASSING THEM.

TV REPORTER:

Though we are, as you know, an openly hostile opponent of Kahane, we must admit that the crowd that marched on the Arabs with him and clashed with police were men carrying attaché cases and elderly women. This is, however, a momentary reaction that will soon subside, despite Kahane's incendiary provocation.

ON SCREEN: KNESSET.

KNESSET MEMBER:

It is our moral and civic duty to condemn acts of revenge. Nothing will be accomplished by such actions.

ANOTHER MEMBER:

Attacks on Arabs are inhuman, un-Jewish, and criminal. We will not do unto others what was done to us. The test of Israel's strength is whether we can uphold the values we demand of others.

KAHANE:

Either by ignorance or intention, you corrupt Jewish values. Judaism demands we act in every way against an enemy that wants to wipe us out. Pious words of absurd humanism will have no effect while we remain the targets of Arab hatred.

THE FOLLOWING WEEK:

ON SCREEN: TERRORISM DAY AFTER DAY.

NEWSPAPER ARTICLE:

"Sixteen Jews murdered on Tel Aviv bus. Settler killed by a stone."

SETTLER:

Jewish anger and fear are bursting its boundaries. We protest and are met by army roadblocks and threats to arrest. One more incident, and we will "die or conquer the hill."

FOLLOWING DAY:

HEADLINE:

"SETTLER IS STRUCK WITH A STONE IN THE FACE WHILE DRIVING. CONDITIONAL IS CRITICAL."

LEAFLETS ARE BEING DISTRIBUTED ON THE STREET. THEY ARE TITLED "GIDEON'S SWORD." A MAN PICKS ONE UP.

MAN:
(READS)

We've had enough of all the terror employed day after day against innocent people. The day of vengeance has come. With our own hands, we shall behead the PLO terror, beat them in the streets, beat them wherever they live and sleep. If you have done something for us, may Heaven bless you. Can you in the government say you did everything to save our lives? No, you cannot. You are partners in the murders of Jews.

THE FOLLOWING DAY: JEWS THROW STONES AT ARAB CARS, BREAK SEVERAL WINDOWS AND SHOUT, "DEATH TO ARABS!" A CONSTRUCTION TRUCK PASSES BY DRIVEN BY AN ARAB. THEY TRY TO ATTACK THE ARAB BUT ARE STOPPED BY ISRAELI POLICE FIRING TEAR GAS.

FOLLOWING DAY: KAHANE LEADS HIS GROUP.

KAHANE:
(SPEAKING PASSIONATELY)

Because I urged we expel the Arabs, my party which is clearly supported by hundreds of thousands was banned. Because I urged the expulsion of Arabs I, a Knesset member, have been banned from appearing on State television and radio for four years, banned from speaking in schools, banned from appearing on campuses, my bills not debated in Knesset...because I am right.

FOLLOWING DAY:

NEWSPAPER HEADLINE ON SCREEN:

"VIOLENCE ERUPTS AFTER A SPEECH BY KAHANE."

LATER:

JEWS BEATING AN ARAB AND SHOUTING "DEATH TO ARABS!" POLICE USE TEAR GAS TO DISPERSE THE CROWD.

A JEWISH FUNERAL IS IN PROGRESS. SHIMON PERES ARRIVES TO PARTICIPATE IN THE FUNERAL. HE IS BOOED AND CURSED AS HE ARRIVES. POLICE HAVE TO ENCIRCLE HIM TO PROTECT HIM FROM ANGRY MOURNERS WHO TRY TO ATTACK HIM.

NEWSPAPER HEADLINE ON SCREEN:

"VIOLENCE IN JERUSALEM FOR THREE DAYS. POLICE ARREST 21 PEOPLE FOR RIOTING AND STONE THROWING AGAINST ARABS WHO ARE SEEKING REVENGE."

KNESSET MEETING:
(WITH PRESS)

We deplore irresponsible acts committed by Jews filled with bitterness.

KAHANE:

Shamir appearing on <u>Arabic</u> television...

SHAMIR:

Jewish attacks on Arabs introduce anarchy into our lives and sap our strength. They are negative and very dangerous.

KAHANE:
(NARRATING)

And Peres, on a visit to an Arab town, where he was warmly welcomed...

PERES:

I am ashamed every time that someone tries to attack a man because he is an Arab. All people are worthy of living in peace and security.

KAHANE:

No one is attacking Arabs because they are Arabs, and <u>Arabs</u> do not let <u>us</u> live in peace and security. Yesterday, an Arab forced an Israeli bus down a steep ravine. It exploded in flames. Fourteen people died but not the terrorist. For a while, he is placed in the Hadassah hospital, the same one as the Jews he attempted to murder. I blame the bus tragedy on those who refuse to accept my demands for an Israel free of death-dealing enemies, the Arabs in the midst who we educate, feed, clothe, house...and hate us.

PERES:

I am convinced the average Palestinian wants peace and goodwill...what every man wants...everywhere.

KAHANE:
(NARRATING)

Arabs claim they are anti-Israel, not anti-Jewish. In A.D. 867, it was an Arab Caliph who invented the yellow badge that Jews were ordered to wear. After World War 2, 30,000 Jews were compelled to leave the Arab countries because of the anti-Jewish policies of their governments. As for the "average Arab," there were savage eruptions against the hapless Jews among them. In Libya, a pogrom against their 4,500 Jews. Many burned in their shops and cars, hurled from rooftops and balconies, others were beaten to death. In Iraq, Jews were hanged publicly. In Egypt, they were imprisoned and tortured. The numbers dwindled from 80,000 Jews to 1,000. In Syria now, 4,000 Jews are terrorized by night arrests, interrogations, imprisonment, and torture. They are subject to humiliation, threats, and curfews. All synagogues have been burned and ransacked. The UN has been impotent in this problem and rejected all appeals to inquire into our plight. And yet, our youth is taught that <u>we</u> are the oppressors, and <u>we</u> must feel guilty about our Arab tormentors. We have indeed gone made.

TV REPORTER:

For the first time, crowds of Jews turn on the Israeli police, stoning them. Arab cars are stoned and burned as crowds shout, "Death to Arabs!" Rage has spread throughout the country. Police hasten to protect Arabs and arrest many Jews, but the rioting continues!

Scene 33

ON SCREEN: NOVEMBER 5, 1990: KAHANE IS IN THE UNITED STATES ON A LECTURE TOUR, ADDRESSING AN AUDIENCE IN MANHATTAN, NEW YORK.

KAHANE:

In the last five years, we've seen Jewish neighborhoods turned into cesspools. Radical Right anti-Jewish hatred side by side with militant Black fascist ravings, our children beaten for their bicycles, their lunch money, or simply because they're Jews...and the lack of reaction to all of this is frightening. The government is paralyzed, school boards are afraid to take action, police fail to uphold the law, and we see liberals raising money for extremists. We see a nation going mad. It's for you to understand that for us, there can only be a respite from slaughter in our own land. Minutemen, Nazis, and National States Righters proposing nothing less than our extermination have come out from under the rocks.

AUDIENCE MEMBER:

Why should we go to a place that you have described in less than glowing terms? You were barred from the Knesset and face a 10-year jail term there, I understand.

KAHANE:

The rabbis tell us that the Almighty appointed Moses and Aaron as leaders of the Jews on condition that they accepted being pelted with stones. Things have not changed. But I will run. There is a loophole, and I have amassed a huge number of votes. The Land remains eternal, and the government of weak and frightened men can be changed when we are rid of Leftist judges who sentence me. No government will be able to be formed without us. And that will be the beginning of a historical change in Israel and the creation of a truly Jewish state made in the image of the God of Israel.

AUDIENCE MEMBER:

JDL is abandoning us here, so we're forced to go to Israel?

KAHANE:

It is one thing to fight a local neighborhood battle against hoodlums and quite another to face an impossible array of national enemies. We sit on a potential powder keg.

AUDIENCE MEMBER:

Exaggerating!

KAHANE:

Just as I returned to New York, an incident involving Nazis erupted at Long Island's Hofstra University. The school, with a large Jewish enrollment, was shocked by the placing of an advertisement in the school paper that began with the words, "Hitler was right," placed by the American Nazi Party. A student member placed a large Nazi swastika flag in his dormitory window. JDL insisted I speak. The school authorities typically facilitated. I spoke...and made clear my position that the student should have been physically beaten. Had the Jews in Germany done that to such as him, there would not have been the disaster that spread from our early passivity. And I urged the Jewish students to make Aliyah to Israel after I held up pictures of the concentration camps and made clear my view that it could happen here.

WOMAN:
(AUDIENCE MEMBER)

Anti-Semitism is on the wane in Brooklyn, which has the nation's largest Jewish population.

KAHANE:

I recognize you, Ms. Adelman. You're a writer for the Brooklyn Jewish Journal. I'm glad you spoke up. You're a perfect example of the little, myopic, insecure people who write this way to assure themselves they're safe from harm, who want to be loved so much they rather die than face hatred. I have this week's article, which says, and I quote, "New anti-Semitism in Williamsburg," written by, of all people, Sylvia Adelman.

ADELMAN:

One area does not speak for a whole borough.

KAHANE:

One area and 12 Nazis...spoke for a whole country now, didn't they?

ADELMAN:

I am an American first!

KAHANE:

I quote from the philosopher Santayana, "Those who cannot remember the past are condemned to repeat it." It is time to go home. It is time to go because there is so little time left. A dark cloud moves in over the horizon slowly, gathering in the blackness and shutting out the light of reason. The chain of pogroms, persecution, hissing hate, exile, and extermination will not be broken here. It's a time...

SEVERAL SHOTS RING OUT. KAHANE FALLS, STRUCK IN THE NECK AND THE HEAD. THE ASSASSIN RUNS. AN OLD MAN STANDING NEXT TO HIM, IRVING FRANKLI, TRIES TO STOP HIM AND IS SHOT IN THE LEG. THE ASSASSIN RUNS DOWN THE STAIRS INTO THE HOTEL LOBBY AND INTO THE STREET WHERE HE TRIES TO HIJACK A CAB, POINTING HIS GUN AT THE TAXI. SUPPORTERS OF KAHANE IN THE STREET POINT TO THE ASSASSIN AND SHOUT, "THAT'S THE MAN WHO SHOT KAHANE!" A POSTAL SERVICE POLICE OFFICER SEES THE ASSASSIN WITH HIS GUN DRAWN AND SHOUTS AT HIM TO HALT. THE ASSASSIN CONTINUES RUNNING. THE OFFICER FIRES AT HIM. A GUNFIGHT ENSUES, AND THR ASSASSIN IS HIT IN THE NECK. THE OFFICER IS WOUNDED IN THE SHOULDER, TAKEN TO BELLEVUE AND RECOVERS. HE HAD A BULLETPROOF VEST.

. . .

Scene 33

FOLLOWING DAY:

NEWS HEADLINE ON SCREEN:

"RABBI KAHANE ASSASSINATED. AN ARAB EL SAYYID A' NOSAIR, CHARGED WITH HIS MURDER. MORE THAN 25,000 ATTEND HIS FUNERAL."

CANTOR SINGS YISKOR.

RABBI:
(GIVING EULOGY)

A giant walked among us, and we were blind to his greatness. Though he was forced to give up his American citizenship and his Kach party was disenfranchised in Israel, he left an indelible mark on Jewish history in both countries. In our innermost souls, we knew he was right, but we lacked the courage and shuddered at the thought of admitting it. God ordained that justice must be the basis for the continued existence of the world. On this was based Rabbi Kahane's plea: "Until when will you judge lawlessly and favor the presence of the wicked?"

ISRAEL:

PERES:

I'm shocked. We should never let the gun replace reason.

PRIME MINISTER:

We deplore the assassination, but we must do our utmost now to show restraint and responsibility so that there is no further outbreak of violence.

NEWSPAPER ARTICLE ON SCREEN:

"Shortly after the news broke, a man shot two Arabs to death. A Kach spokesman said it was in revenge for the murder of Rabbi Kahane and predicts more like acts like this would follow. The IDF is conducting an intensive search for him. An unknown Arab group calling itself "The Light Rays of the West" claims responsibility for Kahane's murder. The Knesset will honor Kahane's memory with a moment of silence.

KNESSET IN SESSION. WE SEE A MASS OF EMPTY SEATS IN KNESSET HALL.

MAN:

The Rabbi was a member of the Knesset from 1984 to 1988. Those four years didn't make a difference. Of 120 members, there are only 20 of us here. The atmosphere is similar now to what it always was when he was a member...that of isolation. Left-wing parties have only one member present. Couldn't spare the time for a one-moment memorial? The government is represented by one person and no one else?! They boycotted him during his life, and they're boycotting him in his death! I can see why the two Arab members of the Knesset stayed far away from Jerusalem today. Kach threatened to take revenge for the killing...but...the rest...for shame!

TV REPORTER:

The Islamic Jihad some time ago offered a twenty-thousand-dollar reward to anyone who would kill Kahane. Last week, there was a decision taken in Baghdad among various terror groups to draw up a list of Jewish leaders to be murdered. Is Kahane's murder the first one on the hit list? The police have decided to extend protection to PLO leaders who have received threats on their lives. No such protection was ever offered to the Rabbi, though he knew he was a target for assassination.

RABBI:
(NARRATING)

Never once during his lifetime did Rabbi Kahane even physically hurt a fly. He was a truly kind soul who supported many orphans and widows. His funeral in Jerusalem lasted over 6 ½ hours. 200,000 walked three hours to his final resting place. He was known and loved by millions throughout the world. Who will lead us now? Kahane, of course, if he would only listen...it is so many of us who are dead. Not him. Kahane *Chai (lives)!

Scene 34

MAY 1991...THE TRIAL.

ARABS ARE IN THE COURTROOM SITTING ON OPPOSITE SIDES FROM THE JEWS. NOSAIR'S LAWYERS, WILLIAM KUNSTLER, A JEW, AND MICHAEL WARREN, A BLACK, ARE EMBRACING NOSAIR AND LAUGHING WITH HIM. KAHANE'S SON LUNGES AT NOSAIR. HE IS REMOVED. IN THE HALLWAY, ARABS AND JEWS ARE WAITING TO ENTER THE COURTROOM. BOTH GROUPS START FIGHTING EACH OTHER. A RIOT ERUPTS. FOUR OFFICERS ARE INJURED TRYING TO SEPARATE GROUPS.

FOUR JDL BOYS ARE HANDCUFFED BY POLICEMEN.

POLICEMAN:
(TO JDL BOYS)

We're taking you in for incitement to riot and assault.

BOY:
(POINTING TO ARABS)

And what have they been doing? Playin' potsy? One of them killed one of us, and they came after more of us right here.

THEY ARE DRAGGED AWAY BY FURIOUS POLICEMEN. MANY OTHER JEWS FIGHTING ARABS ARE INJURED.

COURT OFFICERS STANDING IN HALLWAY KNOCK ONE JDL BOY UNCONSCIOUS. A POLICEMAN RUSHES TO HIS SIDE AND SAYS, "CALL AN AMBULANCE! HE NEEDS TO BE HOSPITALIZED!"

LATER AT THE POLICE PRECINCT, FOUR JDL BOYS ARE BEATEN IN POLICE CUSTODY.

FOLLOWING DAY:

NEWSPAPER HEADLINE ON SCREEN:

"KAHANE'S SON ATTEMPTS TO ASSAULT NOSAIR."

                JDL SPOKESMAN:
                  (TO PRESS)

Among the jurors chosen, there was not one Jew! Nosair did not act alone. This case is international terror right here in the United States, and if not thoroughly investigated, there will be more. This case is too big for a 9 – 5 Prosecutor up against a big lawyer like Kunstler...an abomination. What Arab has ever defended a Jew?

DECEMBER 1991: THE JURY IS FILING INTO THE COURTROOM. THEY ARE MOSTLY BLACK. THE FOREMAN HANGS A NOTE TO THE JUDGE. THE NUMBER OF COURT OFFICERS IS DOUBLED FROM 20 TO 40. JEWS AND ARABS ARE SITTING ON SEPARATE SIDES. COURT OFFICERS STARE AT JEWS WITH UNDISGUISED HATRED.

                FOREMAN OF JURY:
                (ANNOUNCING VERDICT)

Of Rabbi Kahane's murder, we find the defendant "not guilty." Of shooting Mr. Irving Franklin, we find the defendant "not guilty." Of shooting the postal officer Carlos Acosta, we find the defendant "not guilty." For gun possession, assault, and coercion, we find the defendant "guilty."

ARAB AND BLACK SUPPORTERS OF NOSAIR SHOUT, "ALLAH IS GREAT!" COURT OFFICERS ARE SILENT. JEWS RESPOND WITH, "DEATH TO NOSAIR," AND COURT OFFICERS GO INTO ACTION. ONE JEW IS BRUTALLY EXPELLED FROM THE COURTROOM. OTHERS ARE PUSHED AND SHOVED AS THEY'RE LEAVING

PEACEABLY. AN ELDERLY MAN IS ROUGHED UP AS HE IS LEAVING.

> JDL MAN:
> (TO COURT OFFICER)

This man has a heart problem. I will not stand by and allow another Jew to be murdered!

A DOZEN COURT OFFICERS ATTEMPT TO ARREST THE JDL MAN. ANOTHER, KNOWN TO THE OFFICERS, PREVENT HIS ARREST. LATER, IN THE LOBBY OF THE COURT BUILDING, AN ARAB SHOUTS, "DEATH TO THE JEWS!" JDL MAN RESPONDS WITH "NEKHAMA!" A DOZEN COURT OFFICERS THROW HIM AGAINST THE WALL, THEN THROUGH THE REVOLVING DOORS AND INTO THE STREET.

> JDL MAN:
> (TO AUDIENCE)

The Rabbi's killer may yet get a jail sentence, but only if we are heard. Please write and express your outrage to Judge Schlesinger and request that the maximum jail term be handed down. May God avenge Rabbi Kahane's blood! From now on, JDL will be called "Kahane Chai," Kahane lives!

JANUARY 1992: ARABS PICKET THE JUDGE'S HOME CARRYING POSTERS AND SHOUTING, "FREE NOSAIR" AND "SLAUGHTER THE JEWS!" JDL PICKETING JUDGE'S HOME CARRYING POSTERS AND SHOUTING, "DEATH TO NOSAIR!"

> ON SCREEN: SCENES OF KAHANE CHAI PROTEST IN FRONT OF THE STATUE OF LIBERTY.

> TV REPORTER:

300 JDL demonstrators fought Arab protestors outside Judge Schlesinger.

NEWSPAPER ARTICLE ON SCREEN:

> "Nosair was sentenced to 7 to 21 years. His lawyers are proud and pleased with the verdict. JDL enraged with Jewish judge."

> JDL MAN:

He will be eligible for parole in 6 years with that obscene sentence. He should have received the maximum...at least that...31 years...no parole.

TV REPORTER:

JDL is giving the Judge and Nosair's lawyers no rest. They are picketing their homes, accusing them of crimes...indifference and callousness. They also protested at the Statue of Liberty.

THREE PROTESTORS ARE ARRESTED WHILE UNFURLING A FLAG THAT SAYS, "JEW, IT'S TIME TO GO HOME" (SEE PICTURE ON FOLLOWING PAGE.)

ONE PROTESTOR:
(SHOUTING)

When they betrayed our Rabbi in a travesty of justice, they betrayed this statue...the justice for which it stands! Jews must leave America. They can longer expect justice here.

HE IS LED AWAY.

ON SCREEN: SCENES OF PROTESTORS BEING LED AWAY FROM THE STATUE OF LIBERTY.

NOTE ON SCREEN:

"As JDL suspected, Nosair was involved with international terrorists who later bombed the World Trade Center in New York City, killing and injuring scores of people. He was convicted of conspiracy and is serving a life sentence.

Scene 35

KAHANE IS ALONE, READING ALOUD A LETTER TO HIS FOUR CHILDREN.

                KAHANE:
                (READING)

My children, I look out the window of the world and see the abominations that go on, the savages that pass for men, the heartaches that none can escape. I see the tragedies that shake to the core, the hurts that cannot be healed, the sighs that pierce the soul, the questions that cannot be answered, and the weariness that knows no relief. Know and understand this, my children. Man was not created to strive for laughter, but duty, not joy, but goodness, not security, but holiness. The Almighty created our world to bring the perfect ideals of Love, Goodness, and Justice. To living actual reality through Man. It is the task of the Jew especially to pursue this mission. And it is a fearsome yoke. It attracts sacrifice and martyrdom, hatred, and tragedies. It is a life of loneliness and non-conformity, of facing the mass and daring to be different. It is a solitary traveler caught in a storm that whips him, lashes him, drenches him, and seeks to destroy him. But it is the one life worth living, and so we bless God and thank Him for allowing us to live such a life. Love all, the frail flower, the desperate man, and let his love lift you to the heights of holiness. Seek out those who need you and aid them. Seek out those who are oppressed and fight their battles. Seek out those who are desperate and shelter them. Be like unto Him. As He is tender and merciful, so shall you be tender and merciful. As He is loving, so shall you be loving.

WOMAN:

His handshake was strong, and his gray beard and the eyes of a prophet were full of attention and understanding. In a soft voice, so contrasting with his previous fiery speech, he said:

KAHANE:

I have to save my people.

END OF PART TWO

Part 3

WAS HE RIGHT?

Scene 1

THE MORE THINGS CHANGE...

    FLASHBACK: 1987

                    KAHANE:
                    (NARRATING)

Crown Heights is a Brooklyn neighborhood populated by about 207,000 people, Jews and Blacks living side by side. The fact that the Jews are also very poor, how many children, obligations, and pressures, yet...do not take drugs or break up homes, but study, have real values and happiness, causes seething jealousy and resentment. Jews are regularly mugged, robbed, and terrorized. A Black explosion against them is inevitable.

                    WOMAN:

I am a social worker here, and I tell you that you grossly misunderstand the situation.

                    KAHANE:

The usual nonsense repeated ad infinitum by sociologists, Community Relations people and manicured Establishment types, before you go running back to your gilded ghettoes in Long Island and Westchester, where the only Blacks you are seeing are wearing white uniforms, waiting and serving and being nice.

HASIDIC MAN:

As a leader in this community, Moses Mendel by name, I feel you're nothing but an incitement to violence.

KAHANE:

A strong defense patrol or get out! Not to another Heights or depths in Exile, but Home to Israel.

SOCIAL WORKER:

We don't need types like you in either place...here or there.

A WEEK LATER: THREE FUNERALS ARE IN PROGRESS. THERE ARE THREE CASKETS, TWO ADULTS AND ONE CHILD.

KAHANE:

As we see here, the result of self-delusion is tragedy. Myopic leaders, taking no precautions, and we have...this. Israel Rosen and Shlomo Fishman, two young victims of Black hatred, both murdered, are being buried here today. A young Hasidic child, the victim of a drunk Black driver (and there are many such accidents), is also being buried here today.

WE SEE THREE SETS OF MOURNERS AND THREE RABBIS INTONING THE KADDISH. THE SOBS OF THE MOURNERS ARE HEARD AS ALL THREE VICTIMS ARE LOWERED TO THE GROUND.

HASIDIC LEADER WHO SCORNED KAHANE IS IGNORED BY EVERYONE HE TRIES TO APPROACH.

KAHANE:

The media, turning its head, is silent, bored, indifferent, and uncaring. The Establishment, even more so. But we are not.

JDL SETS UP A TABLE IN THE STREET WITH POSTERS SAYING, "STOP THE KILLING. JOIN US." THE HASIDIC COMMUNITY LEADER WHO SCORNED KAHANE IS THE FIRST ON LINE.

Scene 2

1990. RADIO PROGRAM IN PROGRESS.

BYRD:

Ladies and gentlemen, this is Talk radio 1190, WLIB, your host Gary Byrd with Eric Muhammed of the Nation of Islam, live from the Apollo Theater. We're taking calls from the audience now.

PHONE RINGS, A MALE CALLER, HIS VOICE FILLED WITH HATE, HOSTILITY AND THREAT, AS ARE ALL VOICES OF THE BLACK CALLERS COMING AFTER THIS ONE.

MALE CALLER:

I say the Jews lie.

BYRD:

Well, brother, I'm glad to see you agree with us, the biggest lie being the Holocaust they claimed happened. Pictures and all, a damned lie!

CALLER:

JDL. Never again!

THE CALLER HANGS UP.

MALE CALLER:

I got statements that the Rothschilds, the Vanderburg's...all of them were Jewish people in the slave trade.

BYRD:

Brother, listen quickly. There's a book, "The Secret Relationship Between Blacks and Jews," outlining all this history you're talking about. Brother Muhammed, of the Black African Holocaust Council, has done extensive research on the topic...

MUHAMMED:

...when we say "Holocaust," we are not trying to piggyback on the so-called Jewish community. But, to allow them to utilize a term that does not apply to them is unacceptable when we have so many concerns and traumas in our community that we need to address.

MALE CALLER:

They'll soon be having another one if they keep this up!

BYRD:

It's like they own it. It's like it's their word.

FEMALE CALLER:

The Jews are the true devil with their trickery and deceit, trying to deceive people.

BYRD:

Sister, thank you for your attitude. And now, let us welcome Minister Conrad Muhammed of Temple Number 7 in the Nation of Islam. "Hotep, my brother, good afternoon."

MUHAMMED:

Who has the power? Jews!!! Controlling us in Crown Heights! Too many of our children are being beaten up by gangs of them Hasidim!

Scene 3

AUGUST 1ST TO 18TH, 1991. GARY BYRD, HOST ON WLIB.
THE PHONE RINGS, HOST PICKS UP THE PHONE.

FEMALE CALLER:

The Jews want to own everything!

ANOTHER FEMALE CALLER:

They're insulting the Black community!

MALE CALLER:

How long we gonna take their stuff?

GARY BYRD:

The most prominent of the Jewish Pilgrim fathers used to kidnap Black Africans disproportionately more than any other ethnic or religious group in New World History and participated in every aspect of the international slave trade. The immense wealth of Jews was acquired by the brutal subjugation of Black Africans. Minister Louis Farrakhan agrees that Jews had a significant role in enslaving us. What better authority than our brother?

CALLER:

Hotep, Gary. This is Shaheeb from "Creation Underground." We understand the Jewish international banking dynasty controls this planet and has everybody on payroll.

MALE CALLER:

Farrakhan is definitely a prophet. And the thing about Jews is that they see that better than we see it, and they're scared of it. Just goes to show how vain they are. They expect everybody to apologize just because they speak the truth about them. It just shows up how weak they are as a people and they getting me sick. We here at crown Heights want to thank WLIB for waking us up and I can tell you we're mad, most of us boilin' overhearin' these truths from your mouth. I say, "Let's go!"

Scene 4

MONDAY AUGUST 19, 1991. ON SCREEN: 8:20PM.

A HASIDIC DRIVER KILLED A 7-YEAR-OLD BOY, GAVIN CATO, AT PRESIDENT AND UTICA AVENUE IN CROWN HEIGHTS, BROOKLYN, AND INJURED HIS COUSIN AS WELL. THE POLICE, CITY AND HASIDIC AMBULANCES RESPOND. BLACKS ON THE STREET ATTACK THE DRIVER OF THE CAR THAT STRUCK CATO, AND OTHER HASIDIC CARS AND DRIVERS AS WELL.

POLICE:
(TO HASIDIC AMBULANCE)

Take the Hasidic driver out of here. Their lives are in danger.

HASIDIC AMUBLANCE TAKES HASIDIM. CITY AMBULANCE TAKES THE CHILDREN, BLACK LEADER, REV. AL SHARPTON, SHOUTS TO BLACK CROWD.

SHARPTON:

They don't care what happens to our children!

HATZOLOH DRIVER:

A Hasid ambulance, must, by law, follow the instructions of the police.

BLACK:

(IN CROWD)

Jews helping themselves and leaving us to die!

VIOLENCE ERUPTS IMMEDIATELY.

9PM. A FEW POLICE OFFICERS ARRIVE, ABOUT 15 OR 20. BOTTLES ARE THROWN AT THEM.

A VOICE ON A BULLHORN IS HEARD SHOUTING AT POLICEMEN.

VOICE:

This is the Captain speaking. You are ordered to withdraw! Forthwith! And I mean now!

POLICE WITHDRAW.

AT THE SCENE OF THE ACCIDENT, PRESIDENT AND UTICA, A CROWD OF ABOUT 500, SOME FIRING WEAPONS.

A WOMAN, EIGHT MONTHS PREGNANT, IS RUSHING DOWN THE STREET. A GROUP OF BLACK YOUTHS IS RUNNING AFTER HER. SHE IS TERRIFIED. SHE TRIPS AND COLLAPSES. THEY RUSH BY HER, LAUGHING, AND PASS ANOTHER WOMAN WITH A 5-YEAR-OLD CHILD. THE BLACK YOUTHS APPROACH AND YELL, "KILL THE JEWISH KID! KILL JEWS! HEIL HITLER!" POLICE OFFICERS, ABOUT 5 FEET AWAY, JUST STAND BY AND DO NOTHING. THEY TURN THEIR EYES AWAY TO AVOID CONFRONTATION WITH THE BLACKS.

LATER: PREGNANT WOMAN IN HOSPITAL. DOCTOR AT HER BEDSIDE. SHE LOOKS AT HIM QUESTIONINGLY. HE SADLY SHAKES HIS HEAD, "NO." THE WOMAN PUTS HER HEAD IN HER PILLOW AND SOBS.

DOCTOR:

We couldn't save him.

ON SCREEN: THREE OTHER JEWS STABBED DURING RIOT. THEY SURVIVE.

SCENE: A WOMAN IS LOOKING OUT HER WINDOW. SHE SEES A BLACK MOB RUNNING DOWN THE STREET, SCREAMING "GET THE JEW!" THE MOB IS PULLING PEOPLE OUT OF CARS AND STABBING THEM.

THE WOMAN HAS A FLASHBACK:

POLAND 1943:

SHE IS A CHILD WATCHING OUT THE WINDOW. NAZIS ARE BEATING OLD PEOPLE ON THE HEAD, SHATTERING JEWISH STORE WINDOWS AND THE WINDOWS IN HER HOUSE. THEY SCREAM "JUDE! JUDE! JUDE!" (SUBTITLE: JEW! JEW! JEW!) THE NAZIS ALSO SING "WHEN THEIR BLOOD RUNS ON THE KNIFE, WE WILL BE FREE" (FROM THE GERMAN NATIONAL ANTHEM OF THE TIME, "HORST WESSEL SONG")

BACK TO THE PRESENT:

A STONE SHATTERS HER WINDOW, LEAVING A LARGE, GAPING HOLE. SHE HEARS, "JEW BLOOD! WHATTA, WE WANT? JEW BLOOD!" SHE SCREAMS AND JUMPS THROUGH THE HOLE IN HER WINDOW TO HER DEATH. IT SEEMED TO HER THAT SHE WAS BACK IN POLAND. THE MOB IGNORES HER, AND SOME STEP ON HER AS THEY PASS.

9:45PM: A GROUP OF BLACKS ASSAULT AN OFFICER, PUNCHING AND KICKING HIM.

10:30PM: A CROWD HOLDING AN OFFICER WHILE OTHERS ASSAULT HIM.

PRESIDENT AND UTICA STREETS. MAN APPROACHES POLICEMAN.

MAN:

I'm Rabbi Spielman, father of two men in the car that struck the Cato children. What can I do to help?

POLICEMAN:

We can't hold the street and guarantee the safety of Jews. About 250 of you here facing about as many Blacks. I advise you to urge your people to leave.

HASID SCREAMS "NO!"

RABBI WAVES TO HASIDIM TO FOLLOW HIM AND THEY DO.

BLACK:
(YELLING AFTER THEM)

You can't go far enough!

11:00PM: A LARGE BLACK CROWD STILL AT PRESIDENT AND UTICA. A TALL BLACK MAN STANDS ON A CAR.

TALL BLACK MAN:
(SHOUTING TO CROWD)

Do you feel what I feel?! Do you feel the pain? What are you going to do about it? Let's march to Kingston Avenue. We're taking the block!

NARRATOR:

The crowd surges down President Street, breaking windows, and overturning cars. One car is burned. The mob then divides, one part to Eastern Parkway and another to Carrol Street. At 11:17pm, the group on Carrol Street overturns a car, throwing rocks and bottles at the windows of homes. The group assaults several people. A 32-year-old Jewish man is surrounded by a group of about 15 black males on Carrol Street between Brooklyn and Kingston Avenues, struck by bottles and tocks and kicked, as his assailants shout, "Jews, get outta here!" On Kingston and Carrol, another Jewish man is being beaten and robbed. Channel 5 and Channel 9 Television vans arrive and are attacked by a black mob. At 11:20pm, ten to fifteen black youths attacked a 29-year-old Hasidic man. He is stabbed four times. The mob flees as police arrive. At 11:35pm, a policeman at City Hall answers the phone.

POLICEMAN:

City Hall, Police Desk.

NARRATOR:

Rabbi Spielman is in the hospital with the driver involved in the accident His name is Lifsh.

RABBI SPIELMAN:
(TO POLICEMAN IN CITY HALL ON PHONE)

Bands of Blacks are rampaging through Crown Heights. They stabbed a man, a young scholar from Australia who came to study with us.

THE SCENE SHIFTS TO ANOTHER PERSON ANSWERING THE PHONE.

PERSON ON THE PHONE:

Lubavitch Headquarters.

RABBI SPIELMAN:
(ON OTHER PHONE)

I suppose it's all quiet now.

LUBAVITCH MAN:

They caught one of the bums, a 16-year-old, Lemrick Nelson. Has nothing better to do than attack a son of survivors.

RABBI SPIELMAN:

I'll call Herbert Block...

LUBAVITCH MAN:
(SARCASTICALLY)

The Mayor's assistant for services to the Jewish community? I don't know who he's assisting, but it's not us. With all the Mayor is doing for us, he needs an assistant. They do nothing anyhow but sit around at VIP luncheons being important, discussing racial harmony.

RABBI:
(CALLING)

Block?...You know what's going on here?! And not even enough policemen?!...what do we pay them for? Giving traffic tickets., pushing pencils, talking? Do something!

NARRATOR:

Midnight, a large unruly crowd at Albany Avenue from Carrol to Crown Street surges to Troy and Schenectady, breaking windows. They veer south on Troy to Empire Boulevard, set fires to cars, smash car windows, and throw rocks at homes on Lefferts between Troy and Schenectady. 25 Black teenagers are shouting, "Jews, Jews, Jews!!" A 17-year-old fires a gun at a cop without hitting him. Another youth drives his car at a group of cops without hitting them. At

2:00 am, 75 to 250 Black youths occupy Yeshiva Chanoch Lenaar's Courtyard at Albany and Eastern Parkway. The Yeshiva van is set on fire. 150 Hasidim gather across the street. A line of police officers, mostly without helmets, stand between the groups to keep them apart.

AT THE HOSPITAL: RABBI CALLS LUBAVITCH HEADQUARTERS.

LUBAVITCH MAN:

Lubavitch.

RABBI:

His parents survived the Nazis. Yankele couldn't survive Lemrick Nelson.

LUBAVITCH MAN:
(HANGS UP, DESOLATE)

Will any of us?

YOUTHS IN THE YESHIVA COURTYARD ARE THROWING BOTTLES, INJURING SEVERAL POLICE OFFICERS, AND A POLICE CAR. THE CAR IS BURNING A BLOCK AWAY.

4AM: BLACK MARCHERS DISPERSE AS POLICE BARRICADE LUBAVITCH HEADQUARTERS.

Scene 5

TUESDAY. FOLLOWING MORNING. TV REPORTER IS TALKING TO A POLICEMAN.

REPORTER:

I see you've loaded the area with social workers; you, for one, Sergeant Caramovitch Community Affairs Officer, I believe.

CARAMOVITCH:

We had Richard Green of Crown Heights Collective down here, and Assemblyman Clarence Norman, all talking to the group that did the rioting.

FLASHBACK: MAN TALKING TO CROWD OF BLACK YOUTHS.

MAN:
(TO CROWD)

Cool it now, boys. We know how you feel, but this way only means more trouble. C'mon boys, you know we're all friends.

ONE OF THE CROWD:

We hear you.

THEY TURN AND LEAVE.

REPORTER:
(TALKING TO COP)

Chief Borelli, you didn't seem to be engaged in any visible activity last night. Rather surprising, to say the least, considering a .357 Magnum was fired at police officers, among other things. Are we a war here or what?

A GROUP OF POLICEMEN IS TALKING TO BORELLI.

POLICEMAN:

We're sitting ducks out there. We're ready to hand in our badges, and you better find a big bucket out there to hold them all. We're not cops, we're targets...wimps...

BORELLI PICKS UP BASKET AND SLAMS IT ON FLOOR. A PAUSE.

BORELLI:

Top Brass had conferred on this and decided this is just a spontaneous eruption in response to an accident and it'll wind down for sure. They believe we've shown sufficient force and broken the back of the demonstrators. We all know incidents of this nature are not altogether unusual in this area. The last eruption we had here the Jews marched on the station house with the same complaint...300 of 'em. Two Blacks beat one of 'em. Happens every day. We supposed to be watching them every minute? Politicians tell me they wish those Jews would get the hell out. Enough already with these guys.

ONE BADGE IS THROWN IN THE BASKET.

POLICEMAN:
(AS HE IS LEAVING)

Liebowitz, Chief, Badge number 17. No way he "stands idly by his brother's blood."

TV REPORTER:
(TO AUDIENCE)

The Mayor's staff convened early this morning in an hour-long meeting at City Hall to sort through information and advise strategy. In addition to Mayor Dinkins were Deputy Mayor Lynch, Herbert Block, Mayor's Liaison to the Jewish Community, Milton Mollen, Deputy Mayor for Public Safety, Police Commissioner Brown, Assistant Police Chief Thomas Gallagher, Chief of

Patrol Selvaggi, Abdi Allah Adesanya, assistant to the Director of African American Caribbean Affairs and Press Secretary Leland Jones.

FLASHBACK: OFFICE OF THE MAYOR OF NEW YORK, DAVID DINKINS. THE MAYOR IS BLACK.

MAYOR DINKINS:

I've instructed several city agencies, including the City Hall Community Assistance Unit, Human Rights Commissioner, and Department of Juvenile Justice to set up headquarters in P.S 167. They'll work with community leaders in crown heights to restore calm.

THE MAYOR'S SECRETARY ENTERS.

SECRETARY:

Rabbi Hecht is on the phone. He says it is urgent he speak with you immediately.

THE MAYOR PICKS UP THE PHONE.

RABBI HECHT:

The police are not reacting. Our community is under siege. We called the governor to contact the National Guard. He says the Guard cannot be called without your permission.

DINKINS:

The city is doing everything it can.

HE HANGS UP.

Scene 6

NEWS REPORTER:
(ON RADIO)

Mayor Dinkins went to Kings County Hospital in Brooklyn last night, where both Yankel Rosenbaum and Gavin Cato had been taken around midnight. Cato died shortly after he reached the hospital. Rosenbaum died hours later. The mayor went with Cato's family and then with Rosenbaum while the young man was dying.

LATER:

DINKINS:
(TO TV REPORTER)

We've decided to focus the dissemination of information and community outreach. In keep with this approach, Deputy Mayor Lynch will convene a meeting to dispel rumors and bring the two sides together.

LATER: REPORTERS OUTSIDE P.S 167. EACH SIDE, BLACKS AND HASIDIM, IS GOING THEIR OWN WAY AND LOOKING ANGRY.

REPORTER:
(TO HASID)

Did you make any headway towards peace?

HASID:
(NODDING HEAD TOWARDS BLACK)

Ask him. The whole thing was a farce...just a forum for expressions of anger by the Black community. Nonsense...at the top of their voice, and I assure you it won't end there. The mayor and all his fancy advisors ought to leave Grade Mansion and spend the next few nights at Utica and President.

Scene 7

AT PRESIDENT AND UTICA, A BLACK CROWD GATHERS AND MARCHES TO THE 71ST PRECINCT. AT THE SAME TIME, HASIDIM DEMONSTRATE AT EASTERN PARKWAY AND KINGSTON AVENUE.

       HASIDIM:
       (SHOUTING)

Where are our police? Have they forgotten, even when they see us robbed, murdered, killed? Our blood is still cheap?! And our mayor forgers we elected him?!

       NARRATOR:

When the Black marchers reach Kingston Avenue, the two groups clash, throwing rocks and bottles at each other. Some of the Black marchers split off and roam nearby streets. They throw rocks at cars and houses and chant "Death to the Jews!" Others scatter, throwing objects at Jewish residents. Police stand by, assigned to fixed posts.

 FLASHBACK: EARLIER IN THE DAY.

     ASST. CHIEF THOMAS GALLAGHER:
       (TO THE POLICE)

You are commanded to exercise restraint, as I believe aggressive police action will worsen the situation.

REPORTER:
(ON TV)

A crowd of Black teenagers pelted Hasidim. They retaliated with a barrage of rocks from Hasidic store owners; bricks coming out of the sky like raindrops.

HE WALKS OVER TO BLACK MAN IN STREET.

REPORTER:
(TO MAN)

Reverend Sharpton, since you were there, I suppose you can give us a clear picture...

SHARPTON:

Rocks flew but I'm not sure who started it. I saw Black youths throw bricks through windows and I ran for cover. The leaders of the march were caught off guard.

REPORTER THENS TURNS TO ANOTHER BLACK MAN.

REPORTER:
(TO MAN)

Reverend Daughtry, perhaps you can enlighten us as to the facts.

DAUGHTRY:

I'm not certain who threw the first rock, but I am certain the police took stronger action against the Black marchers than the Jews. As the rocks and bottles were flying, the police waded into the marchers, beating, and cursing them even as they fled. I saw several Hasidim with what appeared to be broom handles, chasing and beating the marchers. The Hasidim's bottles and rocks were thrown from behind police lines, and there was little or no police action to prevent them. While Blacks were arrested, not a single Jew met the same fate.

REPORTER APPROACHES A POLICEMAN.

REPORTER:
(TO POLICEMAN)

Seems like you're not doing your job, or not doing it fairly.

(TO DAUGHTRY)

I don't think that's fair treatment either is it, Reverend?

MEANWHILE:

RABBI HECHT:
(ON PHONE)

This is Rabbi Hecht. I demand to speak to the Chief of Police immediately. Bottles are being again hurled at windows; people are being attacked. We've been besieging 911 with calls demanding police protection. There is none now in the area. Help us.

POLICEMAN:

We understand your problem...

HECHT:

I want to speak...

POLICEMAN:

Another call coming in...

THE POLICEMAN HANGS UP.

NARRATOR:

Later, a woman is on her way home with three small children on President Street Near Utica. She is surrounded by a group of black youths who block her way shouting, "Heil Hitler!" and "Kill the Jews!" Policemen are standing nearby.

WOMAN:
(TO POLICEMEN)

Please help me. I just want to go into this building with my children.

CHILDREN CRYING, "I WANT TO GO HOME. PLEASE, MR. POLICEMAN, HELP MOMMY TO TAKE US HOME. WE LIVE HERE." THE CHILDREN POINT TO THEIR HOME.

POLICEMEN STANDING BY DOING NOTHING. THE WOMAN PUSHES HER WAY PAST THE BLACK YOUTHS AND ENTERS HER HOME. BRICKS AND BOTTLES COME FLYING THROUGH HER WINDOWS. SHE IS HIT BY A ROCK AND SHOWERED BY SHARDS OF GLASS. THE MOB OUTSIDE STARTS BANGING ON HER DOOR, TRYING TO ENTER.

THE WOMAN'S CHILDREN ARE FRIGHTENED. THEY ARE CRYING, "MOMMY, THEY'RE COMING IN!" SUDDENLY, BANGING STOPS. SHE HEARS, "AAAH, TO HELL WITH YOU" AND LAUGHTER AS THEY LEAVE.

5:00PM: DEMONSTRATORS THROW DEBRIS AT 100 BESIEGED POLICEMEN.

VOICE:
(ON BULLHORN TO POLICEMEN)

This is Chief Gallagher. Orders are that you are to withdraw to the building line for your safety.

A WOMAN CALLS POLICE EMERGENCY NUMBER, "911."

911 OPERATOR:

911.

WOMAN CALLER:

They're headin' down to my house. They're breakin' the windows...Utica and President. Please come. They're in front of my house! Please get the police here!

911 OPERATOR:

What is your address, ma'am?

WOMAN CALLER:

Utica and President...President. Please. They're breaking my windows.

WE HEAR A CRASH OF GLASS BREAKING. THE WOMAN SCREAMS.

911 OPERATOR:

All right, Miss.

5:06PM: WOMAN CALLER TO 911 AGAIN

WOMAN:

Where are they? At my...they're going in my...my...the Blacks, they're on my neighbor...my block...President. They're breaking all the windows on my block!

911 OPERATOR:

President?

CALLER:

Rochester and Utica!

911 OPERATOR:

Just calm down.

THE WOMAN HANGS UP.

5:07PM: THE WOMAN CALLS 911 AGAIN.

WOMAN CALLER:
(TO 911)

Where are the police?

911 OPERATOR:

Utica and President?

WOMAN CALLER:

Yes?

911 OPERATOR:

They're breaking all your windows?

WOMAN CALLER:

Are you kidding? Not just mine. All the damn windows!

911 OPERATOR:

What's your last name, ma'am?

WOMAN CALLERS HANGS UP IN DISGUIST. WE HEAR GLASS BREAKING AND PEOPLE SHOUTING.

5:08PM: WOMAN CALLER, IN PANIC, CALLS AGAIN.

WOMAN CALLER:

Name! Why aren't they here?! Why are they stalling? I'm sick of this!

911 OPERATOR:

Police are on the way, ma'am.

WOMAN CALLER:

I don't see them!

911 OPERATOR:

The police are on their way.

WOMAN CALLER:

I'm sick of living like this.

911 OPERATOR:

OK ma'am.

WOMAN CALLER:

What are you doing to us?

911 OPERATOR:

Calm down, ma'am.

5:09PM: WOMAN CALLS 911 AGAIN.

WOMAN CALLER:

The blacks are rioting. They're on my street. They gotta gun. They about two shots. I am not gonna live like this.

911 OPERATOR:

What's the address there?

WOMAN CALLER:

Corner of Utica and President. We're in between Rochester and Utica.

911 OPERATOR:

What's your last name!

WOMAN CALLER:

I'm not gonna say!

CALLER HANGS UP. TWO GUNSHOTS ARE HEARD THROUGH WOMAN CALLER'S WINDOW. SHE CALLS 911 AGAIN.

5:12PM:

WOMAN CALLER:

Two gunshots flying. Do something!

911 OPERATOR:

OK, the police are on their way. Okay?

A HASIDIC MAN ENTERS HIS HOME. THE DOOR FALLS OFF IT'S HINGES. ONE OF HIS FOUR CHILDREN RUSHES TO HIM. THE CHILD IS CRYING.

CHILD:

Tottie, they wanted to kill us. A whole bunch of them, banging and banging.

MAN:
(EMBRACING WOMAN AND CHILDREN)

Thank God you're safe!

HE PICKS UP DOOR.

It was held on by only a dead bolt. They almost broke it down.

WOMAN PUTS BOTH HANDS ON HER EARS. THE CHILDREN DO, TOO, FOLLOWING HER AND CRYING.

WOMAN:

They're banging now. Can't you hear them?

MAN:

No door, see?

HE GOES FORTH ILLUSTRATING.

CHILD:

I hear them. Tell them to stop.

FATHER TURNS TO DOORWAY AND TALKS AS IF THE DOOR IS STILL THERE.

FATHER:

Stop, you hear and go away!

ALL TAKE THEIR HANDS AWAY FROM THEIR EARS. A PAUSE. HE EMBRACES THEM ALL.

FATHER:

It's quiet now, you see. The bad boys are gone.

CHILD:

Tottie made them go away.

A HASIDIC MAN CALLS HIS WIFE FROM HIS OFFICE. HIS 12-YEAR-OLD SON IS WITH HIM.

MAN:
(TO WIFE)

It's all right now, I guess.

WIFE:

It's dangerous.

MAN:

A man can't walk on his own street with his own son?!

WIFE:

We just celebrated his 12th birthday. We won't live to see his Bar Mitzvah if you don't put a step in the street.

HE LEAVES HIS OFFICE AND, IN THE STREET, HE HAILS A CARE SERVICE. BUT WHEN THE CAR ARRIVES AT HIS BLOCK, IT CAN'T GET IN. POLICE OFFICERS AND POLICE VANS AT CANAL AND SCHENECTADY ARE ON BOTH SIDES OF THE STREET, SO HE LEAVES THE CAR TO WALK HOME.

MAN:
(TO POLICEMAN)

It is safe to walk down the street?

POLICEMAN:

No problem.

HE CROSSES THE STREET. 50 BLACKS WERE THERE, CARRYING BRICKS, BATS AND STONES. THEY THROW THEM AT HIM. SOMEONE TRIES TO HIT HIM WITH A BAT IN THE HEAD BUT MISSES. THEN, A BRICK STRIKES HIS HEAD AND HE FALLS ON TOP OF HIS SON, WHO'S TRYING TO PROTECT HIM. THE MOB SWARMS AROUND THE MAN AND BEATS HIS SON, TRYING TO PULL HIS SON OUT FROM UNDER HIM. ONE OF THE MIB TRIES TO CUT THE MAN WITH A RAZOR, BUT ONLY HIS SHIRT IS CUT. POLICE STAND BY AND DO NOTHING. A WOMAN SEES THIS ALL FROM HER WINDOW.

WOMAN:
(SCREAMING TO POLICE)

Help them! How can you just stand there?! Do something! They'll kill him!

POLICE JUST STAND THERE. A BLACK MAN RUSHES AND SHIELD'S THE HASID'S PROSTRATE BODY.

> MAN:
> (TO MOB)

Look here, I'm Peter Noel, Amsterdam News, and I'm telling you stop this! The man is down already.

CLOCK: 6:25PM: A POLICEMAN IS HEARD ON THE PHONE.

> POLICEMAN:

911? Police officer requesting code 10-85. There are emergency needs here for more cops. About 70 people throwing bottles...I'm on the phone 'cause I don't have a radio! Hurry!

HE POINTS TO HASID'S BODY ON THE GROUND.

Call an ambulance. His head was bashed in.

> NARRATOR:

From Eastern Parkway to Montgomery Street, people are being assaulted with bricks and bottles.

AT PRESIDENT AND UTICA:

> WOMAN CALLER:
> (TO 911)

I been callin' for the past two hours. You promised the police comin'. I ain't seen one yet and it's almost 7! A major riot goin' on. You gotta send in...

> 911 OPERATOR:

Where's the emergency?

> WOMAN CALLER:

President and Utica.

> 911 OPERATOR:

President and Utica Avenue?

WOMAN CALLER:

You have to send the National Guard. They're going crazy out there...

911 OPERATOR:

Ma'am, slow it down...

WOMAN CALLER HANGS UP.

ON SCREEN: THE SNEAKER KING AT PRESIDENT AND UTICA.

SCENE: MOB PULLS THE GATE OPEN AND RUNS IN AND OUT OF THE STORE, GLEEFULLY CARRYING JEANS, SNEAKERS, ETC. MANY POLICEMEN ARE AT THE SCENE, STANDING IN RANK AND BEING INSTRUCTED BY THEIR SUPERIOR OFFICER

SUPERIOR OFFICER:
(TO HIS MEN)

You are ordered to stand fast and not break ranks. Any officer who moves is threatened with suspension.

NARRATOR:

For three hours, the store is looted while police stand by. On the same block, the Utica Gold Exchange store is looted and firebombed. New York Fried Chicken and Eli Jamaica Gold being looted at the same time, while police just stand by. No one is arrested. From Eastern Parkway to Montgomery Street, people are assaulted with bricks and bottles.

MEANWHILE:

8:00PM: A REPORTER AND HIS CAMERAMAN ARE ON UTICA AVENUE AND UNION STREET. A BLACK MAN APPROACHES.

BLACK MAN:
(TO REPORTER)

Turn off your camera.

REPORTER:

It is off.

BLACK MAN PICKS UP BICYCLE AND STRIKES REPORTER WITH IT SEVERAL TIMES.

BLACK MAN POINTS TO ANOTHER REPORTER AND SHOUTD, "TIMES, TIMES," THEN SHOUTS, "KILL HIM!" 15 TO 20 PEOPLE CHASE REPORTER. HE FALLS AND THEY BEAT HIM, STEAL HIS WALLET, AND ASSAULT HIS CAMERAMAN.

REPORTER IN HOSPITAL.

DOCTOR:

I'm afraid you'll have to lead a boring life for a while. You have some broken ribs, among other things.

NARRATOR:

At 9:30pm, a 45-year-old cab driver is pulled from his vehicle and robbed at Union and Schenectady. At 11:30pm, a 46-year-old is beaten by 10 assailants after he pulls into his driveway at Montgomery and Albany Ave.

A HASIDIC MAN IS APPROACHED BY A BLACK MAN.

BLACK MAN:
(TO HASIDIC MAN)

I'm gonna shoot you!

POLICE OFFICER STANDING NEARBY DOES NOT COME TO HASID'S ASSISTANCE. MOB OVERTURNING POLICE CARS, BREAKING COPS' WINDSHIELDS. SIX ARE DAMAGED AND TWO ARE SET ON FIRE.

7:00 TO 9:00PM: CALLS MADE TO 911 ON TUESDAY NIGHT BY MEMBERS OF OTHER ETHNIC GROUPS.

MAN CALLER:

There are some guys stoning Jews on the corner of Lexington...stoning the Jews!

911 OPERATOR:

What are they doing? They're stoning the Jews?

CALLER:

Yes! They're throwing a lot of stones at the Jews.

911 OPERATOR:

This is on Lexington and what?

CALLER:

Lexington between Troy and Albany.

911 OPERATOR:

Do you have an address?

CALLER:

No, I ain't giving you my address...flinging all those stones in Jews' windows... that's how you know...

911 OPERATOR:

How many people are there?

CALLER:

Five.

911 OPERATOR:

Black, White, or Hispanic?

CALLER:

Black, okay?

911 OPERATOR:

Okay, sir.

8:26PM:

MAN CALLING 911:

In the back of the Community Center driveway between Brooklyn and Kingston Avenue.

911 OPERATOR:

What is the emergency?

CALLER:

Back of the Community Center driveway, these guys are beating up this Jewish lady.

911 OPERATOR:

In the back of the Community Center?

CALLER:

In the driveway!

911 OPERATOR:

About how many males?

CALLER:

I don't know…about five of them.

911 OPERATOR:

Five male blacks?

CALLER:

Uh-huh.

911 OPERATOR:

Okay. And this is in the back of the Community Center driveway?

CALLER:

No, the community driveway. It goes through like the back of the houses.

911 OPERATOR:

Oh.

CALLER:

It goes like from Brooklyn to Kingston.

911 OPERATOR:

Do you know if they have any weapons?
A WOMAN IS HEARD SCREAMING.

CALLER:

Um, I hear a lady screaming.

911 OPERATOR:

You don't know if she's hurt right?

CALLER:

No.

911 OPERATOR:

Do you have any descriptions of the persons who are…you know…beating her up?

CALLER:

There are five black males.

911 OPERATOR:

Okay, ma'am, do you care to leave your name and telephone?

CALLER:

No, I don't.

911 OPERATOR:

Okay. The police are over there.

CALLER:

Okay.

911 OPERATOR:

Bye, bye.

8:39PM: 911 OPERATOR PLUGS IN ANOTHER CALL.

911 OPERATOR:

What is the emergency?

WOMAN CALLER:

On Utica Avenue, they're tearing up the stores.

911 OPERATOR:

Utica Ave and what, Miss?

CALLER:

Utica Avenue and Union Street?

911 OPERATOR:

And what did you say they're doing, Miss?

911 OPERATOR HEARS NOISE OF RIOT IN STREET.

CALLER:

They're tearing up the stores. Tearing 'em off. And they're starting a fire in the middle of the street and everything. Do you hear a noise?

911 OPERATOR:

Yeah. They're tearing up the stores?

CALLER:

Yeah. They're tearing up the stores and there's fire in the street! They are starting fires in the street!

911 OPERATOR:

How many people are out there?

CALLER:

How many people?

911 OPERATOR:

Yes.

CALLER:

Maybe a thousand.

911 OPERATOR:

One thousand, right?

CALLER:

Probably a thousand people out there. A thousand. They are tearing up. Starting a fire!

911 OPERATOR:

Your last name, Miss?

CALLER:

Jenkins.

911 OPERATOR:

Miss Jenkins, what's your phone number please?

CALLER:

Huh? I don't want to give my telephone number 'cause I don't want to get involved.

911 OPERATOR:

I see. Oh, let me give you the Fire Department.

A FIRE DEPARTMENT DISPATCHER PICKS UP THE PHONE.

FIRE DEPARTMENT DISPATCHER:

Fire Department.

CALLER:

They're starting a fire over here on Utica Ave, behind the riots.

FIRE DEPARTMENT DISPATCHER:

Yeah, well...we are unable to come there.

CALLER:

You're unable to come?

FIRE DEPARTMENT DISPATCHER:

That's right. That's on President and Utica, right?

CALLER:

Yeah.

FIRE DEPARTMENT DISPATCHER:

Unable to respond right now, but we'll get there as soon as we can.

CALLER:

Okay thank you.

FIRE DEPARTMENT DISPATCHER:

You're welcome.

SCENES DURING POGROM...

A HASIDIC MAN AND HIS TEENAGE SON ARE AT THE FRONT STOOP OF HIS HOME, ABOUT TO GO UP, WHEN HE IS ATTACKED BY SEVERAL BLACK YOUTHS ON THE STOOP. HE THROWS HIS SON INTO THE HOUSE AND CLOSES THE DOOR. THE MAN IS STABBED AND BLUDGEONED REPEATEDLY. HIS SON FENDS OFF

THE GROUP OF ASSAILANTS BY THROWING BOTTLES AT THEM FROM A WINDOW. THEY RUN OFF, SHOUTING, "WE'LL COME BACK AND BURN YOUR HOUSE DOWN!" SEVERAL HASIDIC NEIGHBORS ATTEMPT TO PURSUE THE ATTACKERS, BUT ARE STOPPED BY POLICE OFFICERS, WHO MAKE NO ATTEMPT TO PURSUE THE ATTACKERS.

MEANWHILE, REV. SHARPTON IS IN THE STREET, SHOUTING.

> SHARPTON:

Who do we want? Jews! Whose streets? Our streets!

LATER:

> HASIDIC MAN:
> (TO REPORTER)

I have multiple stab wounds in my legs, but thank God, I'll be able to walk again.

FATHER IS HOUSE HEARS MOB APPROACHING DOWN THE STREET FROM HIS WINDOW. HE SEES GLASS BEING SHATTERED BY A MOB THROWING STONES AND SHOUTING, "KILL THE JEW! GIVE US SOME JEW BLOOD!" THEN, THE MOB IS AT HIS DOORSTEP.

> FLASHBACK: POLAND 1940
>
> NAZIS APPROACH FROM DOWN THE STREET, HURLING STONES AND SMASHING GLASS. MOTHER IS HOLDING HIM COSE. HE IS 9 YEARS OLD. NAZIS COME CRASHING IN, TEAR HIM AWAY FROM HIS MOTHER, SHOOT HER BEFORE HIS EYES AND LEAVES.

BACK TO PRESENT: A YOUNG MAN, AGE 28, RUSHES INTO HIS HOUSE, NARROWLY OUTRUNNING A MOB SHOUTING, "GET HIM!"

> FATHER:
> (GRABBING HIM)

Yitzie! Thank God you're safe, my son.

HE HEARS THE MOB RUNNING DOWN THE STREET AGAIN. HE CALLS 911.

This is the 5th time I've called you about mobs running past the houses and destroying...

> 911 OPERATOR:

...we know what's going on.

FATHER HANGS UP.

THE MOB COMES RUNNING BY AGAIN, SHOUTING AND SMASHING. YITZIE, A GENTLE, QUIET YOUNG MAN GOES INTO A BACK ROOM, HUDDLES THERE WITH HIS WIFE AND SMALL CHILDREN.

FATHER IS IN THE KITCHEN IN THE FRONT OF THE HOUSE.

> FATHER:
> (TO HIS SON)

You can come here, now. I think they are gone. You'll have something to eat.

YITZIE, PETRIFIED, IS SILENT.

> YITZIE'S WIFE:

I'm going to see...

SHE RISES. YITZIE PULLS HER BACK, TERRIFIED.

> YITZIE:

No, not the front. We have to stay here in the back.

FOLLOWING MORNING: ALL HUDDLED TOGETHER IN BACK ROOM OF FLOOR. YITZIE AND HIS WIFE WAKE UP.

YITZIE'S FATHER ENTERS.

> FATHER:

This is not Russia, not Germany, not Poland and it's happening again.

> YITZIE:
> (WITHOUT ANGER OR RAGE, GENTLY)

If this is not safe, there is no safe place.

8:52PM: A FEMALE IS ON THE PHONE.

FEMALE:

This is the 911 Operator.

FEMALE CALLER:

You need to send some police back around Union and Utica, 'cause these people are going crazy out there!

911 OPERATOR:

A unit for Union and Utica Ave.?

CALLER:

Every car that comes down the block they're bombing 'em. They, they've got this one man down. They're pulling him out of his car!

911 OPERATOR:

Union and Utica? And what they doing with the car?

CALLER:

All the Jews that come down the block, they takin' 'em out of the car and beating 'em up.

911 OPERATOR:

Miss, anyone injured?

CALLER:

All these people don't even know what the hell they out there for. It don't make no damn sense.

911 OPERATOR:

How many people out there now?

CALLER:

I ran inside. An army out there!

911 OPERATOR:

Police out there. You go speak to one of them.

CALLER:

I just came from outside!

911 OPERATOR:

Anyone out there get injured?

CALLER:

How do I know?

911 OPERATOR:

Okay, bye.

TV REPORTER:

Six people called 911 about looting and robberies from 5:16pm to 9:45pm. A full five hours after the first call, four people were arrested for looting Sneaker King. No one was arrested for looting, robbing, and firebombing the other stores.

REPORTER SPEAKING TO POLICEMAN.

REPORTER:

Chief Gallagher, we've been informed by several officers that their superiors forbid their taking any action...making any arrests.

GALLAGHER:

Not true. They were told not to take independent action. Anyhow, Chief Borelli is convinced it's all over.

REPORTER:

The situation in Crown Heights is out of control, and nothing will change 'til it's police take back the streets. That all this destruction can occur with almost no police response is shocking. I drove around the area with a police patrol, and I can tell you it's a tinderbox. Seems to me, some aggressive action is indicated.

GALLAGHER:

Aggressive police action will worsen the situation. That's why we must exercise restraint.

TUESDAY NIGHT: TV REPORTER INTERVIEWING A MAN.

TV REPORTER:
(TO AUDIENCE)

With me now is Council Noach Dear from the Crown Heights Area.

(TO DEAR)

This situation seems to call for some serious action. If it's the kind of thing you can't tell our audience, I'm sure we'll understand.

DEAR:

I'm planning to meet with the mayor for some talks.

LATER: COUNCILMAN DEAR ENTERING A BUILDING TO MEET WITH THE MAYOR. A MAN THROWS A ROCK AT HIM. HE PICKS IT UP. MAYOR DINKINS IS WAITING FOR HIM. HE SHOWS THE ROCL TO THE MAYOR.

DEAR:

Al Sharpton out there. One of his followers just missed me with this.

NO COMMENT FROM MAYOR.

TIM MOLLOY:
(CHANNEL 11)

It's escalating. There is no sign it will cool off.

GONZALES:

(REPORTER, NARRATING)

I am horrified by what I am witnessing. I told Lynch many times that the situation is out of control and the police are not reacting.

REPORTER:
(TALKING TO DEPUTY MAYOR LYNCH)

It would seem that a deputy mayor would be out there leading police action to restore order. I realize the buck does not stop with you, Mr. Lynch, but you're the mayor's closest advisor, and I should think a word from you might help.

WE SEE DEPUTY MAYOR LYNCH LATE AT NIGHT, ON A PARK BENCH ALONE.

LYNCH:
(WEARILY NARRATING)

I haven't slept for hours. I hoped my aides on the street would cool things off. We're not sitting here wringing our hands. It's not easy. Where there are people who are hell bent on confrontation, the thing is quote unquote out of control. You see we have to deal with the root causes of anger...

HIS CELL PHONE RINGS.

Yes, Mr. Mayor...

MIDNIGHT. A HEAVY RAIN CLEARS THE STREETS.

Scene 8

WEDNESDAY MORNING. AT CITY HALL, THE MAYOR IS MEETING WITH HIS ADVISORS, LYNCH, AND MOLLEN.

MAYOR:

Where do I come in to help the situation? I've got to know from you gentlemen where I come in? I want specific suggestions. This thing must be solved, and you have to help me. And don't tell you understand, election is coming up.

MOLLEN:

We've discussed this and decided that you should go to P.S 167 to meet with community members, visit the Cato residence and then speak to leaders of the Jewish community.

MAYOR:

No Hasidim. They're only a minority of a minority.

PHONE RINGS. MAYOR PICKS UP.

(TO GROUP)

Rabbi Hecht.

RABBI HECHT:

The violence here will intensify. It's not going to end. A crowd is already forming at President and Utica.

MAYOR:

Dennis De Leon, you know him, our commissioner for the Human Rights Commission, told us early this morning he decided to have his staff of about 15 people wear their red Human Rights jackets and walk with volunteers from other agencies. They're to tell people who had been arrested and to pass out "Keep the Peace" flyers." I've scheduled a meeting for 2pm, which you're welcome to attend, at the National Headquarters for the Furtherance of Jewish Education. That's all I can say for now.

MAYOR HANGS UP.

2PM: RABBI HECHT, POLICE COMMISSIONER BROWN, POLICE CHIEF BORELLI, POLICE CHIEF SELVAGGI, RABBIS BUTMAN AND MOLLEN.

HECHT:

A crowd is gathering, and it looks like they will march on Eastern Parkway.

MOLLEN:

The city will respond effectively, I assure you.

RABBI POTRELL:

We have a list of specific streets where violence is particularly intense, and we need a 24-hour police protection there.

MAYOR:

I assure you we will restore peace to the area.

RABBIS:

How?!

BROWN:

I want to make it very clear. No one ordered police to refrain from making arrests.

3:30PM: A MEETING OF THE JEWISH COMMUNITY RELATIONS COUNCIL.

RABBI POLTRELL:
(TO MOLLEN)

Jews are being attacked and property destroyed because they're Jews! Police are not intervening. We need the National Guard!

MOLLEN:

The city knows what's going on and will act accordingly. I'm going to the 71st Precinct now, the command post for this area, to meet with you all the religious, community, and elected officials in this area. I know that Black militants plan a march at 4pm, and I can assure you we will be on top of the situation.

RABBI BUTMAN:

And we, on the bottom. Three funerals were held this morning...

SHOW SCENES WHILE HE SPEAKS.

Yankele Rosenbaum, the poor woman who jumped to her death, and the baby who died before it could take it's first breath. The services were held in front of Lubavitch Headquarters at 770 Eastern Parkway. About 1200 Hasidim attended. They set up microphones after prayers and made speeches. Approximately 500 Hasidim followed the hearse on Kingston Ave., past the 71st Precinct, en route to Kennedy Airport. We thought it would be a simple funeral cortege, but it turned out to be much more...and we're asking why you were not at Rosenbaum's funeral.

MAYOR:

The marchers are charging that the police were overly aggressive in handling Tuesday's demonstration. We have the police well in hand now, and tension will be resolved for sure.

CATO'S FUNERAL:

ANNOUNCER:

(ON RADIO)

This is WLIB. The funeral of Gavin Cato is going on now, and we bring you a live broadcast at the scene of this tragedy. Rev. Sharpton is delivering a sermon at the gravesite. A huge crowd and our Mayor are there.

SHARPTON:
(ADDRESSING THE CROWD)

Don't just talk about the jewelry store on Utica Ave. talk about the Jew Oppenheimer, in South Africa, sends diamonds straight to Tel Aviv. The issue is not anti-Semitism, the issue is apartheid. We will deal with what is real. Yes, they want us to fight with each other and let them escape in the middle of the fight...we must not reprimand our children for their outrage. Now let us pray.

A MOMENT OF SILENCE.

ANNOUNCER:
Time is now for the rap song that says it all, "No justice, no peace, let's take it to the streets."
HASID:
(ON PHONE WITH MAYOR)

Please Mr. Mayor, we beg you! Give us more police!

NARRATOR:

400 demonstrators march through the streets and arrive at Lubavitch Headquarters. Violence erupts. The building is pelted with rocks and bottles. People are shouting "Heil Hitler" and burning an Israeli flag. 100 Hasidim gather and throw rocks and bottles at them. Police, in riot gear, keep the two groups apart. An 18-year-old Black throws rocks at a police officer, and Blacks throw bottles at police from rooftops. At Eastern Parkway and Utica, a group overturns a police car.

5:11PM: THE MARCHERS REACH SCHENECTADY AVENUE AND EASTERN PARKWAY, JUST AS COMMISSIONER BROWN, A BLACK MAN, ARRVIS AT THE INTERSECTION AND GO TOWARDS A BUILDING MARKED P.S 167.

GROUP:
(SCREAMING TO BROWN)

Get out!!

>BROWN:
>(SHOUTING)

The Mayor is coming to speak to you!

A GROUP CONVERGES ON HIS CAR AND PELTS IT WITH ROCKS. A FEW OFFICERS ARE IN FRONT OF THE SCHOOL. THE COMMISSIONER FLEES INTO THE SCHOOL TO ELUDE THE CROWD. THE FEW OFFICERS IN FRONT OF THE SCHOOL RETREAT THROUGH THE GATE AND INTO THE SCHOOL ITSELF.

>COMMISSIONER:
>(TO COP)

Issue a 10-13 will you for my car! We need reinforcements! It's an emergency!

>OFFICER:
>(ON RADIO)

10-13 for Commissioner's car at P.S 167.

AN ARSENAL COMES OUT OF THE CROWD, BANGING AGAINST CAMERA TRUCKS, ASSAULTING CAMERAMEN, BREAKING CAMERAS, AND ASSAULTING POLICEMEN.

POLICE OFFICERS ARE SEEN RUNNING AWAY FROM A GROUP OF YOUTHS.

>ONE COP:
>(TO THE OTHER)

I don't know what to do. I've never been like this, disorganized and scared, chaos in our ranks. We're not gonna make it.

>OTHER POLICEMAN:

There's gonna be another march down these streets…us! They expect us to take this stuff?! What are we? Jews?!

BOTTLES AND BRICKS STRIKE BOTH OF THEM.

. . .

6:15PM: THE MAYOR IS ADDRESSING THE CROWD THROUGH A BULLHORN. THE CROWD IS HOSTILE.

>CROWD:
>(YELLING TO MAYOR)

We don't want to hear no talk. We want action. Yeah, yeah!

>MAYOR:

Will you listen to me, please?

CROWD SHOUTS "NO!" THEY BOO AND THROW THINGS AT MAYOR.

>MAYOR:

We will have justice, but we will not get it through violence.

CROWD THROWS MORE THINGS AND BOOS LOUDER.

AT THE SAME TIME, A 31-YEAR-OLD MAN IS DRAGED FROM HIS CAR AT UTICA AND EASTERN PARKWAY, BEATEN BY 20-30 PEOPLE, AND A PATROL CAR IS ATTACKED BY A LARGE GROUP AND PELTED WITH ROCKS AND BOTTLES.

BACK TO THE MAYOR:

>CROWD:
>(SHOUTING)

We want the Jew driver arrested!

THE MAYOR IS TRYING TO TALK BUT IS DROWNED OUT BY THE CROWD. BOTTLES ARE THROWN AS HE LEAVES FOR THE CATO HOME.

6:55PM: POLICE CARS ARE OVERTURNED BY MARCHERS. THE MAYOR'S ADVISORS ARE WITH HIM.

>MAYOR:
>(TO HIS ADVISORS)

I want to walk to Cato's home.

MOLLEN:

I wouldn't advise it.

MAYOR:

It's only four blocks.

MOLLEN:

In a war zone, one step can be your last.

THE MAYOR STOPS.

POLICEMAN:
(TO MAYOR)

We've made arrangements for a detail to escort you there by car.

THE MAYOR NODS HIS HEAD "YES." A POLICE CAR ARRIVES AND TAKES HIM TO THE CATO HOME. MANY POLICE IN THE CROWD MONITORING THEM. MAYOR'S CAR PULLS UP THE CATO HOME. SECURITY JUMPS OUT OF THEIR CARS AND STARTS SCURRYING TO GET INTO POSITION. THE CROWD STARTS RUNNING TOWARD THE CATO HOUSE. SOME START THROWING THINGS AT THE MAYOR AND SECURITY MAKES THEM STOP. MAYOR ENTERS THE CATO HOME.

MEANWHILE, COMMISSIONER BROWN IS TOURING THE NEIGHBORHOOD AND RETURNS TO THE 71ST PRECINCT.

BROWN:
(TO POLICEMAN)

I want to speak to First Deputy Commissioner Kelly.

POLICEMAN LEAVES ROOF TO GET HIM. KELLY APPEARS.

BROWN:
(TO KELLY)

I must tell you that I saw the police poorly deployed and not positioned to pursue roving bands. I praise you for your restraint, but I think at this point, tactical changes are necessary.

NARRATOR:

In the nearby 77th Precinct, people are being assaulted in cars. Two individuals are shot and a firehouse is attacked.

In the 71st Precinct, a crowd of 500 demonstrators cause destruction on Utica Avenue from Eastern Parkway to President Street. Mobs of people attack 5 police cars and 3 civilian vehicles.

At 9:45pm, a sniper wounds 8 officers with a shotgun blast from a Schenectady Avenue rooftop.

SUPERIOR:
(TO POLICE)

Okay now. For the first time, since all this mess started, I want you to order your men to make a significant number of arrests. We're gonna restore order around here.

10PM: ABOUT 100 POLICE OFFICERS MARCH DOWN UTICA AVENUE.

LATER: AS MAYOR LEAVES CATO'S HOME, HE IS MET BY COMMISSIONER BROWN IN HIS CAR.

BROWN:

I just met with the delegate from the Policeman's Benevolent Association. They are threatening job action and have issued this letter.

BROWN HANDS MAYOR THE LETTER.

LETTER ON SCREEN:

> "To all officers: We urge you to use your nightsticks and firearms if attacked."

MAYOR:
(TO DRIVER)

Kings County Hospital.

(TO BROWN)

I want to show those men I care...those eight poor cops wounded. Mollen, you'll come with me. You too, Commissioner.

. . .

MIDNIGHT: MAYOR ON WARD. SOME ARE SLEEPING. OTHERS SEE HIM COMING, TURN THEIR BACK ON HIM, PRETEND TO BE SLEEPING. WHEN HE PASSES THEIR BED, THEY OPEN THEIR EYES AND GLARE AT HIM BEHIND HIS BACK WITH HATE.

MAYOR TALKING TO DOCTOR.

>DOCTOR:

A narrow escape, but they'll be alright.

LATER:

>MAYOR:
>(TO BROWN)

I'm questioning the effectiveness of your tactics so far, and I think further steps have to be considered. What do you intend to do to immediately end the violence? I think your approach was appropriate for a peaceful demonstration, but not civil unrest, if I may say so. I'm calling first Deputy Commissioner Kelly to assume responsibility for devising more appropriate tactics.

THURSDAY MORNING: KELLYS MEETS WITH CHIEFS.

HE SHAKES HAND WITH EACH CHIEF.

>KELLY:

Chief Borelli, Chief Selvaggi, Chief Gallagher. Be seated, gentlemen.

THEY SIT DOWN.

>KELLY:

Well, gentleman, at last a new strategy. We'll divide the area into 4 zones, each under a hand-picked Commissioner, saturate the area with mobile patrols, and we're telling the men in no uncertain terms: "Make arrests! Disperse crowds at the first sign of trouble."

>TV REPORTER:

The new police tactics were successful. They moved quickly against unruly people, arresting those who refused to disperse, and relative order was restored after 1,800 officers were assigned to the area and a considerable number held in reserve.

ON SCREEN:

THE GOVERNOR ORDERED A REPORT BY NEW YORK STATE'S DIRECTOR OF CRIMINAL JUSTICE, RICHARD GIRGENTI.

GIRGENTI:

After extensive research, we found that the Crown Heights disturbance represented the most extensive racial unrest in New York City in over 20 years and differed from most since it was directed at one segment of the population, and was systematic, intense, and injurious.

REPORTER:
(TO NOACH DEAR)

Mayor's going to take action against Sharpton for that attempted assault on you, isn't he?

DEAR:

No action taken, and none expected to be.
A MAN IS STANDING IN FRONT OF A VACANT, BURNED-OUT STORE IN CROWN HEIGHTS. A CHARRED SIGN ON THE STORE READS, "FRIED."

MAN:
(NARRATING)

This was once Fried's grocery. That's me. I'm Fried.

FLASHBACK: 1987, CROWN HEIGHTS.

KAHANE:

A Black explosion against Jews is inevitable. Arm yourselves.

MAN:

Never!

NARRATOR:

A week later, man pulled out of store by Black mob and the store is set afire. He flees. Black shoots after him and misses.

BACK TO PRESENT:

MAN:

Kahane was right.

MAN, NOW CARRIES A GUN.

MAN WALKS AWAY. SIGN FALLS AND BLACK MAN PASSING BY KICKS IT INTO THE GUTTER.

Scene 9

1992:

>   MAN:
>   (ON RADIO)

This is Gary Byrd show live from the Apollo, with a live audience here in the theater, the first anniversary of the death of Gavin Cato. The Reverend Sharpton will speak about the upcoming trial of Lemrick Nelson.

>   SHARPTON:

We've had another case of white police brutality visited on our Black brother...

>   AUDIENCE:
>   (YELLING)

...Kill 'em! Kill 'em! Fight!

>   SHARPTON:

We're gonna have a march in Crown Heights tomorrow, August 19th, the anniversary of the <u>murder</u> of Gavin Cato!

PHONE CALL TO STATION. BYRD PICKS UP THE PHONE.

>   WOMAN CALLER:

What about the white people murdered by Blacks? Maybe <u>we</u> should take to the streets each time one of <u>us</u> is savagely mugged! For 20 years, in Crown Heights, white people are being robbed, mugged, and killed in our hallways.

MAN:
(ON PHONE)

This is Brother Abdul suggestin' that Black start shootin' these cops. When you start killin' them, blowin' their brains out, then they will understand!

BYRD:

I'm sure everyone understands the feelings. Brother Sharpton, how do you deal with this situation?

SHARPTON:

Whatever violence comes down, it's been incited by the white police's misconduct.

ONE MONTH LATER:

RABBI:
(TO GROUP)

This is the first meeting of leaders of the major Jewish organizations since the pogrom in Crown Heights. It is incredible to me that there have been no demonstrations of marches to show that we are together in protesting this assault on us as a people.

ONE OF THE GROUP:

I don't think anyone would come.

RABBI:

I fail to see justifiable outrage in any one of you!

ANOTHER ONE IN GROUP:

We prefer dialogue.

RABBI:

Dialogue with our supporters is unnecessary...and with our enemies...

(HE DESCRIBES IT WHILE IT BEING SHOWN)

KHALID MUHAMMAD:

The Jews "dialoguing" with us sayin, "Ve, ve, ve suffer like you. Ve, ve, ve marched with Dr. Martin Luther King Jr. Ve, ve, ve were in Selma, Alabama. Ve, ve, ve were on the front line of Civil Rights marchers. Ve always supported you." And I'm dialoguing' saying...

HOLDS UP BOOK.

You see this here book, "THE SECRET RELATIONSHIP BETWEEN BLACKS AND JEWS." And what is this secret? To control our destiny, that's what...put our entertainers in their hip pocket, our athletes in the palm of their hand, our politicians in the white man's hand, but particularly in the palm of the <u>Jewish</u> white man's hand.

BACK TO RABBI.

RABBI:

No such scorn and derision for anyone but us. I think some honest dialoguing with <u>ourselves</u> is indicated.

ANOTHER ONE IN THE GROUP:

Blacks are not anti-Semitic.

RABBI:

I said honest dialogue.

ANOTHER ONE IN THE GROUP:

I say "to Hell with 'em. Let's stay on the sidelines like everybody else."

RABBI:

Better, but still not honest enough.

ANOTHER MEMBER IN THE GROUP:

"Georgia hates the Negro...Harlem hates the Jew," to quote the Black writer James Baldwin, 1948.

RABBI:

At last, an honest man. Now, we can begin to dialogue...with ourselves.

ALL NOD IN AGREEMENT.

Scene 10

AUGUST 19, 1992:

      COLIN MOORE:
      (ON WLIB)

In Lemrick Nelson's upcoming trial, the Hasidim will be receiving preferential treatment, as the District Attorney Hynes will be representing Jewish interests. Art Whaley of WLIB has a question.

      WHALEY:

But Hynes was the one who joined us in prosecuting Whites who killed Blacks, isn't he?

      MOORE:

His mindset is identical to those of the Hasidim. When they think of Crown Heights, they don't think of little Gavin Cato under the wheels of a car driven by Hasidim. They think about it as an anti-Semitic pogrom.

      MAN CALLER:

This is for Mr. Whaley. You obviously set up Moore to give that answer. Have to wipe out from the minds of your audience that Hynes is known to be a fair man, and thereby erase any appreciation for his efforts.

ANOTHER CALLER:

The killer of Gavin Cato sneaked out of the country and fled to Israel. Why can't we get him back here?? Put him on trial! Gt him the hell in prison where he deserves and take care of him ourselves! He's the murderer...not Nelson. Nelson's a martyr that's what he is.

ANOTHER CALLER:

You know, Mr. Moore, your listeners never seem to get the facts straight. I guess you don't, either. Cato was killed in an accident and a predominately Black jury, deciding not to equate accident with a cold-blooded murder did not indict the driver. If every Black fled the country in fear for his life when he killed a Jew, there wouldn't be enough ships, trains or cars to hold them; they'd be leaving every day...so where do you get off playing victims?!

MOORE:

The HASIDIC driver enjoyed, "white skin privilege." He knows he can drive a car into Gavin Cato, kill him and walk blithely into some kind of ambulance or something.

Scene 11

THE TRIAL

SEPTEMBER 24, 1992:

ON SCREEN: THE LEMRICK NELSON TRIAL.

A LINE IS WAITING OUTSIDE THE COURTROOM IN THE HALL, WAITING TO GO IN. TWO YOUNG BLACK WOMEN STANDING NEXT TO A WHITE WOMAN ARE ON LINE DISCUSSING PRIOR TESTIMONY.

BLACK WOMAN:

You could tell the cop was lying. They framed an innocent boy...

WHITE WOMAN:

...What about the bloody knife in Nelson's pocket? The blood matched Rosenbaum's.

OTHER BLACK WOMAN:

The cop planted the knife on Lemrick. They stuck it in the wound and planted it in the boy's pocket.

Scene 12

OCTOBER 19, 1992:

BYRD:
(ON RADIO)

Welcome to WLIB. Our guest, Attorney Alton Maddox. Mr. Maddox.

MADDOX:

The trial is a lynching of Black people. You have a young man, on trumped up charges, in a kangaroo court, before a hanging judge.

OCTOBER 22:

BYRD:
(ON RADIO)

This is WLIB. Our guest today, Sonny Carson. Sonny.

CARSON:

The media and the police have misrepresented the events of Rosenbaum's murder. The cops will come out of this looking the way they're supposed to look. They're crack dealers, they're Klansman, don't live in our community and think we're animals.

CALLER:

The cops didn't murder Rosenbaum!

CARSON:

He provoked his own murder by assuming a karate stance when he saw those Black kids coming down the street.

CALLER:

I guess you could say he was about to kill 20 people with that posture.

BYRD:

Now. Let's see what our political figures are saying about us.

A PICTURE OF GOVERNOR CUOMO APPEARS ON SCREEN.

BYRD:

Governor Cuomo?

CUOMO:

I have nothing but praise for WLIB's parent company, INNER CITY BROADCASTING, as a source of strength and guidance for the African American Community.

MAYOR DINKINS APPEARS ON SCREEN.

DINKINS:

I urge the station to keep up the good work.

MALE CALLER:

This is Rabbi Stein. You can add to this disgraceful list Charles Rangel, Robert Abrams, Elizabeth Holtzman, David Patterson, Percy Sutton, Jesse Jackson and the Dinkins family, who continue to own shares in ICB, the parent company, and have yet to condemn the hate and lies you're spewing!

BYRD:

Come, come Rabbi...you and I both know that those who speak the truth are often maligned.

RABBI:

Hitler also flattered himself with those very words.

Scene 13

OCTOBER 29:

POLICE CHIEF:
(TO MEN)

If Nelson gets his just desserts, we'll need to beef up security and put on riot gear, in and outside the courtroom.

THE POLICE PICK UP RIOT GEAR AND BARRACKS TO BEEF UP SECURITY.

LATER:

TV REPORTER:

Hundreds of police are stationed around the courthouse and in the Crown Heights neighborhood. The jury consists of six Blacks, four Hispanics, and two whites...both non-Jews. The courtroom is full of Hasidim, Blacks and police. The prosecutor alleged Rosenbaum identified Nelson as his assailant before he died, and a detective said Nelson confessed. The defense alleges Nelson was the victim of a police frame-up. There's a long line of people waiting to get into the courtroom. There's Norman Rosenbaum, the victim's brother, here from Australia, and Eric Breindel, reporter for the New York Post.

(TO ROSENBAUM)

Seems like there are strong arguments on both sides.

ROSENBAUM:

We'll win. Jew's blood is not cheap.

AN HOUR LATER: POLICE ON DUTY OUTSIDE THE COURTROOM. ONE COP WHISPERS TO ANOTHER "THE VERDICT IS IN." POLICE BEGIN LOOSENING THEIR RIOT GEAR AND SECURITY GUARDS COME DOWN, IN THE COURTROOM AND OUT.

IN THE COURTROOM, PEOPLE ON LINE WHISPERING, "THE VERDICT IS IN...ACQUITTAL." HASID WAVES HIS BAND, DISMISSING THE RUMOR. SOMEONE YELLS FROM THE BACK OF THE LINE, "VERDICT!"

RIOT GEAR AN BARRICADES COME DOWN. ROSENBAUM PULLS NERVOUSLY AT THE BACK OF HIS PANTS.

ALL ENTER THE COURTROOM. JUDGE ENTERS AND SITS ON BENCH.

JUDGE:

Before the verdict is read, I must warn you I will tolerate no outbursts from anyone in this courtroom.

(TO JURY)

Have you arrived at a verdict?

FOREMAN STANDS.

FOREMAN:

Yes, your Honor.

NELSON IS SITTING ERECT AND MOTIONLESS.

FOREMAN:

Murder in the first degree...not guilty.

Murder in the second degree...not guilty.

Murder in the third degree...not guilty.

Murder in the fourth degree...not guilty.

NELSON TAKES A DEEP BREATH AND EXHALES ONLY ON THE FOURTH "NOT GUILTY." BEHIND HIM, HIS FATHER, LEMRICK NELSON, SR. PUMPS A CLENCHED FIST IN THE AIR, CLOSES HIS EYES, KNEELS, CROSSES HIMSELF AND BURSTS INTO TEARS.

ON THE HASIDM, THERE IS A SEA OF OBEDIENT, SILENT FACES. OTHERS SOB OPENLY AND OTHERS POUND THEIR FISTS ON THE BENCH BACKS IN FRONT OF THEM. ONE ANGRY HASID VOICE RINGS OUT.

HASID:

There is no justice for Jews in this country.

ROSENBAUM SPEAKS TO A TV REPORTER OUTSIDE COURTROOM.

ROSENBAUM:

In the same way Lemrick Nelson has the blood of Yankel Rosenbaum on his hands...now the jury has the blood of Yankel Rosenbaum on their hands!

JURY FOREMAN IS TALKING TO TV REPORTER

FOREMAN:

Too many inconsistencies in the police statements.

REPORTER:

Such as...

FOREMAN:

I don't want to talk about it.

TV REPORTER:

9 police from 9 different precincts and they all lied?! You dismissed their testimony like that?!

REPORTER SNAPS HIS FINGERS.

FOREMAN:

Yes!

ALL OTHER JURORS AGREE, SAYING, "YES," TOO.

ANOTHER JUROR:

We decided not to indict the driver, didn't we?

ROSENBAUM:

So, you have an excuse to let my brother's murderer go free?!

> ON SCREEN: THE NIGHT NELSON IS ACQUITTED, CURTIS SLIWA, THE LEADER OF "THE GUARDIAN ANGELS," A GROUP PLEDGED TO PROTECT INNOCENTS ON THE STREETS, IN THE SUBWAYS, IS ESCORTING SOME OF THE HASIDIM HOME. SOME BLACKS ARE SEEN PASSING BY.

BLACKS:
(TO SLIWA)

Ey, what are you walking with the Jews for? We're not going to lump them down. Our boy is free. But if they'd locked the brother up, we would've turned (POINTING TO HASID) this mother upside down.

NEXT DAY: SLIWA BEING INTERVIEWED BY A BLACK INTERVIEWER ON TV.

INTERVIEWER:

You were at the Lemrick Nelson trial. I assume you have a fair judgement of the events since you're neither Black nor a Hasid.

SLIWA:

I'm concerned that the jury was so demoralized by the WLIB version of events that it was set to find the brother innocent, regardless of the evidence.

INTERVIEWER:

That's the white man's justice, not ours.

SLIWA:

This time he wasn't doing the judging.

THE DAY AFTER THE ACQUITTAL, ALL ARE IN A RESTAURANT. NELSON, HIS LAWYER, AND THE JURY ARE HAVING A VICTORY CELEBRATION. THEY ARE TOASTING, CONGRATULATING, BACKSLAPPING, HUGGING AND SHOUTING, "TO VICTORY!" SUPERIMPOSED ON THIS SCENE IS THE VICTIM, ROSENBAUM, SCREAMING "COWARDS!" AT NELSON AND 20 OTHERS AS THEY'RE SURROUNDING HIM AND NELSON STABS HIM. THE GAYETY GOES ON WHILE THE CROWD IN THE SUPERIMPOSED IMAGE SCREAMS, "KILL THE JEW!"

BREINDEL:
(ON SCREEN)

The life of Yankel Rosenbaum has just been declared worthless.

FLASHBACK: 1991

TV REPORTER:

Lemrick Nelson's attorney, Colin Moore, spoke to reporters today.

COLIN MOORE:

This trial is a facedown between the oppressed black community and the influential Jews.

NARRATOR:

The present, a round table discussion on TV with Black host and Eric Breindel, Lemrick Nelson Sr., Dr. Howard R. Garber, Republican Central Committee Member from California, Isaac Sapeistein, freelance journalist, Rabbi Feinstein, David Susskind, well known host of TV Talk Show (a Jew), Abraham Foxman, ADL, Dr. Leonard Jefferies, Black CCNY Professor.

BREINDEL:

The Nelson case, which rested largely on police testimony, stood virtually no chance of getting a fair hearing from a predominately non-white jury. Public officials and activists who encourage hatred or police bear some responsibility for this verdict.

BLACK HOST:

I would have done the same...voted for acquittal. My experience with cops is the same as Nelson's.

BREINDEL:

Unrelenting cop bashing will continue to be dangerous to both groups.

BLACK HOST:

C'mon. Cops kill you if you put your hand in your pocket, then say you has the gun they put there...excusing themselves for what they did. We and the Hispanics distrust cops. I see no reason why we should now have a man's life depend on their word. A liar is a liar.

BREINDEL:

A major factor at work, here, too, is having little influence and no power. It's highly unlikely that a Black and Hispanic jury would convict a Black accused of killing a white Orthodox Jew. Not even if, like Nelson, the defendant is apprehended carrying the blood smeared weapon. Not even if, like Nelson, he is identified by the dying victim. Not even if, like Nelson, he actually confesses to the crime. Hasidic Jews, everyone knows, are not about to stage a riot. So, for them, justice is almost unattainable.

BLACK HOST:

We have to make up for all the time Whitey sent us away for nothing.

BREINDEL:

This circumstance will endure 'til the victims refuse to put up with it.

ISAAC SAPERSTEIN:
(TO BREINDEL)

Now, you know, Whitey profited, exploited, enslaved, and tortured Blacks for years. Their argument is not with any specific group. I think Jewish paranoia is showing, and a chip on the shoulder knee jerk reaction.

BREINDEL:

A pogrom, which saw Jews cowering in 1991 New York, behind locked doors, as if they were back in Czarist village, represents one huge assault on Jewish lives and sensibilities...rather than a figment of the imagination.

SAPERSTEIN:

You're making too much fuss over a few Jews.

BREINDEL:
(TO SAPERSTEIN)

In all likelihood, the verdict was also related to the high rate of anti-Semitism among Blacks and Hispanics, well documented in recent studies and ignored, as usual, by most Jews.

SAPERSTEIN:

Nonsense! People of good will on both sides have to accept the verdict of a jury or the problem will not disappear.

BREINDEL:

That's laughable, in view of what was said after a white jury acquitted Whites.

LEMRICK NELSON, SR.:

I have no hatred against Norman Rosenbaum.

BREINDEL:

There's something obscene about the remark. Rosenbaum, after all, suffered the loss of his brother. Why should you, of all people, hate Rosenbaum? The ultimate irony, a rabbinical student, coming to America to research the Holocaust, is himself murdered by a Black Nazi in the "Land of the Free and Tolerant."

NELSON, SR.:

My son was forgiven by God.

BREINDEL:

Why is it necessary for an innocent man to be forgiven by God? Those who should ask forgiveness are the ones who added a celebratory dinner to the pain inflicted on the aggrieved.

SAPERSTEIN:

Nobody fair?! The jury, the lawyer, the restaurant? Not even God?! Lemrick's father, who has seen his poor son's suffering come to an end, and he's not even supposed to be happy?!

RABBI:

An accidental death is not the same as an attack by a murderous mob and yet, Mr. Saperstein, they're equated by you people in the media. A white mob attacks a Black and demands are made for all their heads. Not a word here for a Jew by our Civic leaders, politicians, religious leaders. And why is there no mention in the media, Mr. Saperstein, of the burning anti-Semitism in Crown Heights? Where is the pain, anger, and outrage, the marching and yelling in the streets by our rabbis and prominent organization leaders when of our own is destroyed? Where are we? And sadder yet, where were we...to feel the pain of our brothers as the Blacks feel for theirs.

SAPERSTEIN:

A Black expression of righteous indignation is what you're seeing. A revolt whose time has time.

GARBER:

Face it. The nation has been adapting to Black violence and anti-white racism as if it's unsolvable and even worse...justified.

BLACK:

All this fuss over one guy killed who probably brought it on himself.

GARBER:

The public shares your attitude. It is indifferent to violence against Jews and the media treats "Burn, Baby, Burn" ...which translates into our cities in flames...as a justified Black revolution. A Black was killed, and there was national outpouring of protest, yet, when Israel Rosen was beaten to death two weeks later by six Blacks on a New York subway station, no full-page articles, no rallies, no evidence of an outraged nation.

SAPERSTEIN:

We've been close; fought and died together.

GARBER:

Being a man of the media, I'm amazed at your focusing on yesterday's news, Mr. Saperstein. The Blacks now support the PLO, Israel's archenemy, change their names and convert to Islam, a religion which favors destruction of Israel, and for years, our nation has watched, in virtual silence, the ongoing catastrophe in the decay of our inner cities where "babies have babies."

BLACK:

You want genocide of the Black people! Have no babies at all...is what you'd like! Well...we're not obliging!

GARBER:

And if one condemns Black crime and gang warfare, they are sure to be charged with white racism. And I ask, is it racial...or is it factual?

SAPERSTEIN:

Eradicate the underlying causes...

GARBER:

...it's time for all of us to stop rationalizing black lawlessness and racism.

BLACK:

Whitey don't give a damn about our suffering, so why should we care about yours? I say, make Whitey suffer. Let 'em know how it feels to be afraid...of us... this time...not the other way around. Let Whitey have the upper hand and it'll be the other way around...again.

GARBER:

Will Blacks continue to be immune from hate crime laws or will our future be one of lawless anarchy?

DAVID SUSSKIND:

Two very oppressed groups in history shouldn't be fighting each other.

MOSHE STERN:

The oppression of Jews is only in history? I see you're a Jew who's never worn a yarmulke in public.

FLASHBACK: STERN IS PUNCHED IN THE FACE, GIVEN A NAZI SALUTE AND CALLED A KIKE.

BACK TO PRESENT:

MOSHE STERN:

This is oppression because it goes on daily. No one does anything to stop it and the only defense is violent action.

DAVID SUSSKIND:

You really are in favor of this conflict going on, aren't you?

MOSHE STERN:

Whether or not Blacks and Jews should be fighting each other is always a question posed to Jews. For some strange reason, you denounce anti-Semitism to Jews. That's good. I'll try not to be anti-Semitic, and I'd appreciate Blacks extending a similar effort.

SAPERSTEIN:

I'd say anti-Jewish and anti-Israel sentiments have developed only in recent years.

MOSHE STERN:

JDL knew was what going on. You didn't. Rabbi Kahane knew what was going on. You didn't. and why? Because he put a foot in our streets while you were marching around in Selma...certainly not for the oppressed Lubavitch. I'd say Jew hate developed in 1967, when you were so active in Civil Rights, marching, fighting, dying for Blacks...and...for us...neglect, indifference shame. at most, pleas for moderation and dialogue. Not one Jew on the Lemrick Nelson jury. Blacks and Hispanics <u>our peers</u>? Would <u>they</u> accept a <u>Jewish</u> jury for one of <u>their</u> defendants? Can't you see? War is being waged against us?!

DR JEFFERIES:

You Jews are greedy and sneaky, hiding behind good works, but we know better now. You're to blame for the slave trade, and Jewish doctors are spreading the AIDS virus among our people.

RABBI:

It's incredible that Black rioters were running through the streets of Crown Heights screaming "Heil Hitler!" I think it's time for you to teach your people some history. Hitler had as much hate and contempt for Blacks as he did for Jews.

STERN:
(WITH BITTER IRONY)

And the NAACP was founded will Jewish help.

JEFFERIES:
(TO RABBI)

Hitler was a great man.

RABBI:

Unfortunately, this kind of talk is dismissed as the ridiculous ravings of crackpots, but your charges and opinions are coming from people like you, with legitimate academic credentials, who are respected in the academic community. And it also hasn't helped matters that mainstream Blacks leaders have not denounced you...especially as recent surveys show that Blacks are twice as likely as the rest of the population to have anti-Semitic views.

ABRAHAM FOXMAN:
(TO STERN)

In spite of what you say, the truth is that Jews do feel differently vis a vis the Black community. There is a kinship, and it goes beyond nice sounding talk. Look, there's never going to be a crisis in Irish-Black relations or Italian-Black relations because they have no relations, as we do.

STERN:

So let them start relating and we start separating. At this point, it seems like a one-sided relationship. They're insulting, mugging, killing us, and we're lying down and saying it's okay. I suspect no one else but us is willing to have that kind of relationship, and they know it. Sharpton lives in New Jersey. He crossed state lines to incite a riot in Brooklyn. No charges, Federal or otherwise, were made. And from you, the silence is deafening. We must become militant to survive with dignity. That's our problem...not the relationship.

Scene 14

CROWN HEIGHTS: A BLACK WHO OWNS A NEWSPAPER STAND IS SHOUTING AT A HAID AS HE PASSES BY.

BLACK:

You not even buyin' a paper from me no more? We still supportin' you Jews, buying everything from you, and you givin' us no business.

HASID IGNORES HIM AND WALKS ON.

BLACK:

Whenever you Jews act up, nobody bothers you. You raise plenty of hell and nobody say nuthin'. That's not fair. If Black people did that, there'd be plenty of trouble.

HASID TURNS AROUND AND SHOUTS.

HASID:

I have no store. What you buying from me? The ashes you left when you burned it down?!

BLACK:

Look what happened the first time justice was served for a Black man, Lemrick acquitted, you all screamin' "Jewish blood ain't cheap." Well, ain't nobody talkin' about that little boy who got killed!

HASID:

And <u>you're</u> talking about Rosenbaum? The only time you give him a second thought is when you can't sell me a paper. Then you blame him for hurting business.

BLACK:

What you Jews really want is to buy everything and <u>push</u> Black people out of the neighborhood!

HASID:

100,000 of you, 20,000 of us, we'd have to do a lot of pushing. And how do we do that from the hospitals and the graves where Black muggers and killers have <u>pushed us</u>?

SCENE 83

1991: A MAN IS PASSING EASTERN PARKWAY SYNAGOGUE. A PICTURE OF IT IS SHOWN, A LARGE AND MAJESTIC TEMPLE.

MAN:
(NARRATING)

This was once the center of a large, Jewish area, and it's now on the border between Jewish and Black areas. It's main hall, once magnificent, is now musty and seldom used. It's once grand steps are inelegantly closed with iron gates. There's now a very small room used as a temple inside. We call it a shtiebel, a tiny temple, like they used to have to the pogrom days in the ghettoes in Europe, and the Depression says in America. Despite vandalism and hostility from the outside, the shtiebel has a loyal congregation that's struggling to keep it's doors open and it's lights on. Two years ago, in 1989, I was a guest of one of the congregants at afternoon prayers in January on a Saturday. There was no heat in the building, so my two- and one-half-year-old son and I wore overcoats during the Service, and I then decided to go to the library to look over the books.

FLASHBACK: MAN AND HIS SON LOOKING AT BOOKS IN TEMPLE LIBRARY.

CHILD:
(TO MAN)

I have to go to the bathroom.

ANOTHER MAN STANDING BY HEARS CHILD.

OTHER MAN:
(TO CHILD'S FATHER)

He can't use the one up here. Junkies removed most of the plumbing fixtures. You have to go downstairs.

DOWNSTAIRS, A LINE OF CLOSED LAVATORIES WITH SIGNS ATTACHED, "OUT OF ORDER." ONLY TWO ARE FUNCTIONAL. TWO BLACK MEN APPEAR, ONE IN AN EXPENSIVE FULL-LENGTH LEATHER COAT AND OTHER IN A SHABBY, CHECKERED JACKET.

MAN:
(NARRATING)

I tried hard not to be suspicious, despite the strong scent of liquor, and, trying to dismiss my feelings of suspicion, I assumed they were stranded motorists asking for assistance.

BLACK:
(IN LEATHER COAT, WITH STRAINED POLITENESS)

Perhaps you could do us a favor...

(HE PULLS OUT A GUN)

Give us your money!

FATHER:
(NARRATING)

I wasn't carrying any money or anything else because of the Sabbath, so I moved my hands toward my pockets to show him I had nothing.

THE MAN IN LEATHER OVERCOAT STIFFENS AND REACHES FOR HIS GUN.

FATHER:

Don't worry. I don't have a weapon.

THE LITTLE BOY IS GETTING RESTLESS.

> FATHER:
> (TO SON)

Don't worry Nachum. Everything is going to be okay.

(NARRATING)

I was about to add, "with God's help," but we were in the bathroom where, according to Jewish law, one does not pray or even mention God's name.

> THE BLACK IN THE LEATHER COAT:
> (TO FATHER)

Take off your coat and shirt. There's money in there. Gotta be.

FATHER REMOVES HIS COAT AND SHIRT AND BACK PATS HIM DOWN LIKE HE IS A PRISONER.

> THE OTHER BLACK:
> (TO HIS PARTNER)

Let's get out of here! He ain't got nuthin'.

> BLACK IN LEATHER COAT:
> (TO MAN)

You count to 100. If you move from here before you finish counting, I'll blow your son away.

ONE WEEK LATER:

BOTH BLACK MEN ARE IN A LINEUP.

> FATHER:

I do not recognize them.

> POLICEMAN:
> (TO ANOTHER POLICEMAN)

I know he spotted them.

POLICEMAN:

You think he's crazy?! At the time of the robbery, he was in the process of moving his family to the other end of Crown Heights, which is very close to where these guys live.

BLACK MAN IS SEEN SWAGGERING DOWN THE STREET IN HIS LEATHER COAT WHILE FATHER LOOKS AT HIM, ENRAGED.

FATHER:
(NARRATING)

Every day, I see him! Every day!!

TWO YEARS LATER:

CROWN HEIGHTS: SCENE OF RIOT. FATHER IS ON THE STREET. RIOTERS ARE BREAKING HIS WINDOWS. POLICE ARE LOOKING ON.

FATHER:
(TO COPS)

Do something! That's my house!

POLICE STAND THERE, DO NOTHING.

Scene 15

NINETEEN DAYS AFTER THE NELSON VERDICT:

TV REPORTER:

Several hundred Jews from around the city gathered at the headquarters of the Anti-Defamation League for a conference on "Confronting Anti-Semitism: Practical Responses." For nearly two hours, the crowd sat in virtual silence as the assembled experts responded in reasoned, measured tones to the prodding of the moderator. Norman Podhoretz, the well-known journalist, gave us the following report on the proceedings.

    FLASHBACK:

MODERATOR:
(TO CROWD)

I think we can best deal with this if we create a fictional situation and ask ourselves how we would go about handling the problems that arise. Imagine a housing project where there is a series of escalating anti-Semitic incidents.

BACK TO PRESENT:

TV REPORTER:

The Reverend Guy Massie of Brooklyn, Chairman of a group called "Jewish-Catholic Dialogue," glowingly detailed the role his church would play.

Lieutenant Thomas Burke, head of the Bias Unit, talked about how the police would respond, and the State's Human Rights Commissioner, the City's Human Rights Commissioner, the Deputy District Attorney and other made their contributions.

FLASHBACK:

MODERATOR:

Now the floor is open for questions. I think the panel and I can safely assume you've all been pleased with our presentation, since you've been listening attentively and quietly, taking it all in without objection.

TV REPORTER:

It would have been no surprise to find everyone sleeping, but, as you shall soon see, they were only lying in wait.

FLASHBACK:

MAN IN AUDIENCE:
(GRABS MICROPHONE AND SHOUTS)

When there was a pogrom in Brooklyn, when a person who killed only because he was a Jew...

MODERATOR:

Excuse me, but that is not what this meeting is about. Please limit your...

ANOTHER MAN IN AUDIENCE:

Let him speak!

ANOTHER MAN:
(SHOUTING)

Don't silence him!

MODERATOR:
(PLEADING)

We are not here to discuss Crown Heights...

MIDDLE-AGED MAN:
(SCREAMING)

...That's what we came for! That's what you should be dealing with now. Jews are being beaten and killed. That's what...

A SECURITY GUARD WITH A GUN BULGE IN HIS POCKET MOVES TOWARD MIDDLE-AGED MAN AND WRAPS HIM IN A BEAR HUG, LIFTS HIM AND IS ABOUT TO CARRY HIM OUT WOMAN STARTS YELLING.

WOMAN:

Leave him alone! Don't touch him! Don't you dare! This is not Berlin! Put him down!

MAN IS PUT DOWN.

AN ORTHODOX WOMAN RISES. SHE IS QUAKING WITH EMOTION.

WOMAN:

I was a prisoner in my house for 72 hours, forced to hide in the bedroom with my six children. My house was attacked twice, and the police wouldn't come to our aid. My children have been traumatized.

PRESENT:

TV REPORTER:

It went on like this for 45 minutes, some on the verge of hysteria. One by one, they came to the microphone and pleaded for answers, help, reassurance.

WOMAN:

What can you do when bottles and bricks are flying through the windows of your house, and both times you hear...

FLASHBACK: NOISE OF SHATTERING GLASS IS HEARD. WOMAN CALLING 911.

911 OPERATOR:

This is 911. Would you like a police officer to take a report about broken glass?

PRESENT:

      WOMAN:

No one came to help us.

     ANOTHER MAN:
      (SHOUTING)

I don't care about anti-Semitism. The problem is anti-Semites. All I want is to be protected from attack.

Scene 16

TV REPORTER:

In our studio today, Mr. Norman Podhoretz:

NORMAN PODHORETZ:

One of the problems of dealing with this situation, if it can be dealt with all, is that lies are told. You get the impression, from most of the coverage of Crown Heights, that these groups hate each other equally, and you have to dialogue to heal wounds. I regard this as a lie. What you have is an aggression coming from Blacks against Jews. This is not an even-handed dispute in which both sides are guilty, both sides at fault. So, all these calls for dialogue are beside the point. I think there is a serious problem in the Black community, and it has to be addressed as such. Most people know it in their hearts, but very few say it.

Scene 17

1992:

    BLACK SPEAKER:
    (TO AN AUDIENCE)

I'm delighted to have been invited to a dialogue between the followers of Mr. Farrakhan and you Jews…and I will get to the point immediately.

HE HOLDS UP A BOOK.

This book, "THE SECRET RELATIONSHIP BETWEEN BLACKS AND JEWS" compiled by the Nation of Islam's research department, calls Jews key operatives in the crime of Black enslavement and accuses them of monumental culpability in the Black Holocaust.

    BLACK AUDIENCE MEMBER:
    (INTERRUPTING)

I demand to know why the Jews have not apologized to the descendants of the African kings and queens. Never mind books! I want action!

    SPEAKER:
    (TURNING TO WOMAN ON PODIUM)

Ms. Kantrowitz, the Jew woman who organized this event, can best answer that question, I should think.

KANTROWITZ:

I know I speak for a lot of Jewish people in this room when I say, "I'm sorry. We're ashamed..."

MAN:
(INTERRUPTING)

None of us Jews would debase ourselves like that. Who is speaking for the Jewish people in this room? Is it me...or that woman there? If it's me, raise your hands.

JEWS RAISE THEIR HANDS.

ANOTHER BLACK SPEAKER ON PODIUM:

Why should the Melanie Kaye Kantrowitzes of the world, whose ancestors survived Czarist pogroms and the Nazi Holocaust, be the most hated among us Blacks? You know who asked that question? A famous black professor at Harvard. Time you asked the same question, Ms. Kantrowitz.

KANTROWITZ:

Simple. Because we were close to them, helpful and kind, too...more than anyone was...so, they feel they can be more open with us than anyone. I don't think that's really hate at all.

OTHER BLACK SPEAKER:
(TO KANTROWITZ)

Time you faced the fact of Black-Jew hate and be ashamed you're so blind, deaf, and forgive me, dumb.

ANOTHER BLACK MAN:

What are you sayin', man? Don't you know the Jews get special treatment? They want to control everything, and the government gives them too much say-so.

HASIDIC MAN:

Even if it were so, which it is not, that's an excuse for killing people?! It took 17 months for Mayor Dinkins to meet with us Hasidim, though in the Crown Heights riot, a dozen Jews were stabbed or assaulted, hundreds of car windows broke, businesses and home shattered. Thousands heard "Kill the Jew!" and "Heil Hitler" in front of their homes directed at them...

RUMBLING HEARD IN AUDIENCE TO DROWN HIM OUT. HE SHOUTS LOUDER.

HASIDIC MAN:

And the reaction among Jews, Ms. Kantrowitz, is like yours, denial, excuse, and avoidance. And worse, the disaster of murder of an innocent man was equated by some with an automobile accident; the recommended solution, "Dialogue!"

BLACK:

Can't bear to hear the truth, can you?!

HASID:

(SHOUTING LOUDER)

Anti-Semitic insults and attacks continue on a daily basis, and Blacks are still out on the street passing out leaflets about a Hasidic conspiracy.

BLACK:

...Getting your just desserts. The party's over for you guys. You takin' pain now...what you've been givin' us.

HASID:

That the Black is a victim of oppression is no excuse for his oppressing another victim.

Scene 18

1992: CROWN HEIGHTS:

TUESDAY A.M:

TV REPORTER:

Phyllis Lapine, a 37-year-old mother of 4 was brutally murdered in her home in Crown Heights. She was stabbed 30 times. When her 5-year-old son and a neighbor found her, her dress was pushed up around her waist and her 2-year-old daughter was hiding under a bed.

JDL BOYS NOW CALLED "KAHANE CHAI" (KAHANE LIVES), ARE AT THE POLICE PRECINCT.

BOY:
(TO POLICEMAN)

We want a permit to demonstrate, to demand that someone do something to find the murderer of a defenseless mother of four children.

POLICEMAN:

Denied. You're trouble.

ON RADIO:

"KAHANE CHAI appealed to the ACLU, who was able to obtain a permit for them."

KAHANE CHAI LEADER:
(TO GROUP)

Before we march for Hasidim, I want their leader's permission, or they won't follow.

LATER: THE SECRETARY OF RABBI SCHEERSON, LEADER OF LUBAVITCH HASIDIM, SPEAKS TO KAHANE CHAI LEADER IN THE RABBI'S OFFICE.

SECRETARY:

The Rebbe will give you a special audience.

THE GROUP IS FACING THE RABBI, WHOSE BACK IS ON TO US. WE ONLY HEAR THE REBBE'S VOICE.

RABBI SCHEERSON:

I bless you all and wish you luck.

THE GROUP LEAVES.

TUESDAY P.M: THOUSANDS OF HASIDIM, HUNDREDS OF OTHER JEWS, AND YOUTHS LED BY KAHANE CHAI MARCH THE 71ST PRECINCT. THEY CARRY SIGNS SAYING, "WE DEMAND PROTECTION."

WEDNESDAY A.M:

A HASID AND HIS WIFE ARE WALKING IN THE STREET. A BLACK MAN PASSES AND SAYS, "HEY, JEW, GIVE ME YOUR WALLET." ANOTHER BLACK MAN SLAMES THE HASID ON THE HEAD WITH A BASEBALL BAT WHILE THE FORMER GRABS THE WOMAN FROM BEHIND AND STRIKES HER TWICE IN THE HEAD BEFORE TAKING HER PURSE.

MEMBERS OF KAHANE CHAI ARE STILL DEMONSTRATING WITH SIGNS THAT READ "THE LIST OF VICTIMS IS GROWING." THEY ARE SHOUTING, "JEWISH BLOOD IS NOT CHEAP." (SEE PICTURE ON FOLLOWING PAGE) THEY'RE WEARING FULL MILITARY GEAR. LATER, BLACKS THROW ROCKS AND BOTTLES FROM BUILDINGS AT THE KAHANE CHAI MEMBERS. JEWS

CHARGE THE BUILDINGS AND APARTMENTS FROM WHERE THE ROCKS AND BEING THROWN. POLICE FORM A HUMAN CHAIN TO PROTECT THE BLACKS.

WEDNESDAY A.M: KAHANE CHAI DEMONSTRATORS ARE PEACEFULLY STANDING AT THE INTERSECTION OF CROWN AND ALBANY. ENRAGED POLICEMAN CHARGE THEM.

> POLICEMAN:
> (TO ANOTHER POLICEMAN)

Smash the Jews!

> ANOTHER POLICEMAN:
> (SHOUTING TO KAHANE CHAI)

The Nazis didn't kill enough of you!

DEMONSTRATORS ARE BEATEN, HOSPITALIZED AND ARRESTED FOR NO REASON. (PICTURE)

LATER:

> KAHANE CHAI LEADER:
> (TO GROUP IN STREET)

Welcome. We'll patrol the streets at night.

THEY HAND OUT POSTERS AND PLASTER THE STREETS WITH THEM.

> KAHANE CHAI MEMBERS:
> (SHOUTING)

Ten thousand dollars reward for finding the murderer of Phyllis Lapine!

> KAHANE CHAI LEADER:
> (TO GROUP IN STREET)

And we ask that you join our self-defense classes.

TWO DAYS LATER:

KAHANE CHAI YOUTH IN STREET SHOUTING, "JOIN DEFENSE CLASSES. SHOW THEM JEWISH BLOOD IS NOT CHEAP." PEOPLE SEEN SIGNING UP FOR CLASSES. (SEE PICTURES ON FOLLOWING PAGE.)

THE MARCH: Members of Kahane Chai.

Kahane Chai recruiters signing up Hassidic Jews to join self-defense classes in Crown Heights.

FOLLOWING DAY:

ON SCREEN:

"A BLACK HAITIAN, AGE 23, WITH A CRIMINAL RECORD, WAS ARRESTED FOR THE MURDER OF PHYLLIS LAPINE."

JEWISH MAN:
(TO MAYOR DINKINS)

You are going to Lapine's funeral. We have made arrangements.

MAYOR:

She was only a murder victim, not the victim of bias crime and there are 6 homicides here every day.

MAN:

We didn't burn down stores, riot or put police cars on fire. And I guess, for that reason, there's no respect, even for our dead. There were as many homicides when Cato died, and you went to his funeral.

HE LEAVES.

LATER: JEWISH MAN IS SEEN WALKING ON STREET WHERE THERE IS SIGNING UP FOR DEFENSE CLASSES BY KAHANE CHAI.

KAHANE CHAI BOY:

We have a hundred signatures already!

MAN:

That's all?! A million and a half Jews and a pittance here signing?!

YOUNG MAN:
(SHOUTING)

Sign up here! Defend yourselves. Show them Jewish blood is not cheap!

MAN:

White sneaker polish is worth more than our lives?! Where are all the politicians, white and Black, shrieking themselves hoarse, like they did when someone allegedly sprayed that stuff on a Black face. Where are the righteously indignant Jews and angry politicians shouting, "No Justice, No Peace?"

BOY:
(SHOUTING)

Jewish blood is not cheap.

MAN:
(ANGUISHED)

I'm afraid it is.

MAN SIGNS UP.

     WOMAN PASSING BY:
      (TO MAN)

Don't you think these boys are over-re-acting?

      MAN:
    (SHOWING NUMBER ON ARM)

The last time we thought it would go away, it didn't.

Scene 19

1992: COLUMBIA UNIVERSITY CAMPUS.

STUDENTS ARE ENTERING THE AUDITORIUM. KHALID MUHAMMAD ARRIVES IN A BURGUNDY ROLLS ROYCE AND IS WEARING A FUR COAT. BLACK STUDENTS ENTERING THE AUDITORIUM ARE SEARCHED BY BEING JUST PATTED DOWN BY BLACK GUARDS, WHILE WHITE STUDENTS ARE SUBJECTED TO A DEGRADING AND INVASIVE FRISK. ONCE INSIDE WILLMAN AUDITORIUM, STUDENTS ARE SURROUNDED BY UNIFORMED BLACKS WHO ARE SEEN ASSAULTING SEVERAL WHITE MEMBERS OF THE AUDIENCE. THEN, THE AUDITORIUM DARKENS. THERE IS SILENCE AND THEN A SPOTLIGHT ON STAGE. A ROAR IS HEARD, "KHALID, KHALID, KHALID!" MUHAMMAD APPEARS AND QUIETS THE CROWD, SIGNALING WITH HIS ARMS FOR SILENCE. THERE ARE LOUD CHEERS BEFORE THE AUDIENCE QUIETS DOWN.

MUHAMMAD:

I am honored to have been invited to speak on the life and legacy of Malcolm X...a great leader...gone...but never forgotten. First, however, before we talk about our friends, we have to be aware of our enemies...the Jews...who claim to practice Judaism, but in reality, practice a dirty religion.

CHEERS FROM THE AUDIENCE.

There is a long standing organized Jewish conspiracy to oppress Black people. Zionism and racism are one, and they are foolish and silly people for not admitting it.

CHEERS.

WHITE STUDENT:
(JUMPS TO HIS FEET, SHOUTING)

We created the NAACP and worked our fingers to the bone for your freedom...

MUHAMMAD:

You did all that so you could use Black people as cannon fodder to pursue your racist agenda and...

STUDENT:

You're cursing up and we're still giving you money. You don't want us and we're still giving you money...You're hurting us and we're still...

MUHAMMAD:

The Jewish community in America was the primary financier of the slave trade. You're just giving us back the money you owe us.

(TO BLACK STUDENTS)

Are they the bloodsuckers of the Black community? Or are they suckers anyway?

BLACK STUDENTS RAISE THEIR FISTS AND PUNCH THEM IN AIR.

MUHAMMAD:

Jews are scared to death some Black man or woman is going to knock them in the head and take our money back that they rob from us all day long.

CHEERS AND LAUGHER FROM AUDIENCE.

They drive their tractor-trailer full of money from our neighborhood to their neighborhood, and ours gets poorer and poorer, while theirs gets richer and richer.

A WHITE BOY RISES.

WHITE BOY:

Since you're so full of the truth, why don't you say your real name, Harold Moore Vann? It is because you were in jail for fraud, which is what you're perpetrating now, having learned nothing from your time in jail apparently. And you've even gone so far as to suggest blowing up gas stations and pulling whites out of cars at stop lights. Anybody here gonna join me shouting loud and clear, "Muhammad, get outta here! You're disgracing the University and us!"

SILENCE. A PAUSE. BLACK STUDENTS GRAB WHITE STUDENT, BEAT HIM UP AND THROW HIM OUT. FIRST BOY WHO SPOKES RUSHES TO HELP HIM AND IS ALSO ASSAULTED AND THROWN OUT.

FOLLOWING DAY: FIRST BOY WHO SPOKE GOES TO DEAN'S OFFICE.

BOY:
(TO SECRETARY)

I want to see Dean Jack Greenberg.

SECRETARY:

Do you have an appointment?

BOY:

I want to talk to him.

THE SECRETARY PICKS UP PHONE AND CALLS THE DEAN. THE SECRETARY TALKS TO THE DEAN.

SECRETARY:
(TO BOY)

About what?

BOY WALKS INTO DEAN'S OFFICE AND STARTS TALKING TO DEAN.

BOY:

I'm shocked and dismayed that the Black Student Organization at Columbia would invite a monster like Khalid Muhammad to speak, much less applaud him. What is even more appalling is the University Administration has turned a blind eye to the situation.

DEAN:

You are here without permission and are requested to leave.

BOY:

You have a responsibility to see that Columbia students are treated with respect and dignity on their own campus...

DEAN:

...You are not the teacher. I am! And I will not accept instruction by you...

BOY:

...It has a responsibility to ensure that student dollars do not go to support hateful bigots. Most importantly, you have a responsibility to speak out on these issues when, for two hours, our people were constantly degraded by a speaker on a college campus who belongs in a sewer...not the hallowed halls of a University!

DEAN:

Academic freedom demands we remain silent and permit the exercise of free speech. Now, leave voluntarily or be forced out.

BOY:

Apparently, the freedom of speech is not extended to me!

TWO MEN PULL HIM OUT OF THE DEAN'S OFFICE.

THAT NIGHT: BOY IS WRITING A LETTER.

BOY:
(READING LETTER)

To the Black Student's organizations, I hope that someday, the Black student at Columbia will understand that the Jewish community supports your demands for full participation in America life. To the Black community, I have one simple request: Please don't attack me anymore. I know what it means to suffer, and I only want to be your friend.

Scene 20

1993:

ON SCREEN: STATE UNIVERSITY OF NEW YORK, ALBANY, NEW YORK. A STUDENT IS ADDRESSING OTHER STUDENTS IN A HALL.

STUDENT:

In the last 12 months, 5,000 of us Jewish students have been forced to contribute 64 dollars each. And for what? To provide the Black student organization on campus with 22,000 dollars to bring Black Jew haters here to speak. A ratio of 2,000 Blacks to 5,000 of us and they're making policy! Democracy, where art thou? Jew haters like Leonard Jefferies, Sister Souljah, Kwame Toure, (FORMERLY KNOWN AS CARMICHAEL) invited here and our President remains silent! When he was an administrator at Temple University, he was accused of bias against Jews and favoring Blacks, to the detriment of the school. Now he's doing the same here.

BOY:
(SHOUTING)

Governor Cuomo put him in. and he knows more than you. You're a troublemaker. JDL, I bet.

SPEAKER:

Scene 20

The Blacks are passing out monthly leaflets asking the student body to "Smash Zionism," and our President remains silent. Even worse is the book they're handing out, "The Secret Relationship Between Blacks and Jews," full of dangerous lies against us. And the President remains silent.

ANOTHER STUDENT RISES.

STUDENT:
(SHOUTING)

Talking and doing nothing, as usual. Waste of time, all of it.

SPEAKER:

Where were you when we tried to confront the ones handing out this poison...?

STUDENT:
(SARCASTICALLY)

...I never saw or heard anything of the kind...

SPEAKER:

We were blocked by faculty...

STUDENT:

I'll believe you when I see some action.

SPEAKER:

We're holding a memorial for Yankel Rosenbaum tomorrow. Then, we'll plan a strategy. I'll believe _you_ if I see you there.

THE FOLLOWING DAY: JEWISH STUDENTS IN TEMPLE, HEADS BENT IN PRAYER. THEN THE RABBI SPEAKS.

RABBI:

Yankel Rosenbaum was a man of peace, love and learning. Gone from our midst is an irreplaceable loss. Our hearts still grieve for him. He graced the world with his presence and let us bereft in his absence. God in...

BLACK STUDENTS RUSH IN SHOUTING, "CA-TO! CA-TO!" THEY THROW PRAYER BOOKS AROUND, TEAR YARMULKES FROM HEADS AND SHOUT, "JEW BASTARD IS WHAT HE WAS" AND LEAVE. YARMULKES ARE PUT BACK ON HEADS. THE CANTOR SINGS A MOURNING SONG. THEN, THE PRAYER BOOKS ARE PUT DOWN AND THE STUDENTS FILE OUT SADLY AND SOLEMNLY. OUTSIDE, A GROUP FORMS AROUND THE LEADER.

LEADER:
(TO GROUP)

I'm going to speak to the President about this right now.

AN HOUR LATER: LEADER RETURNS TO GROUP AND SHAKES HIS HEAD.

LEADER:
(TO GROUP)

No. I was invited to leave. We know what we have to do.

UNBELIEVING STUDENT:

The answer to that is "nothing." Strutting, posturing, attention getting and that's about it.

THE FOLLOWING DAY: LEADER READS A LETTER HE WROTE TO THE PRESIDENT.

LEADER:

To H. Patrick Swygert: The leadership of the Jewish student body, with the approval of the entire group, has decided to invite Rabbi Meir Kahane son, Binyamin Kahane, to speak on campus about the peace process in the Middle East. To publicize this event, we are putting up posters and would appreciate funding for this event.

THE GROUP PUTS UP POSTERS (ON SCREEN) THAT READ, "THE LATE, MATYRED RABBI KAHANE CALLS UPON JEWS TO PROTECT THEMSELVES. NEO-NAZIS, MUSLIM FUNDAMENTALISTS, AND FARRKHAN...JEWS MUST MIGHT THESE ENEMIES WITH GUNS, KNIVES AND FISTS!"

. . .

FOLLOWING DAY: JEWISH STUDENTS ARE MILLING AROUND NEAR THE POSTERS. SWYGERT, WHO IS BLACK, CONFRONTS THEM IN RAGE.

PRESIDENT SWYGERT:

You are haters! I pity you! Remove those posters now!

LEADER:

I seem to recall that, when Kwame Toure said, "the only good Zionist is a dead Zionist," you said absolutely nothing. And when white students, particularly Jews were being attacked, you were stony silent.

BLACK STUDENTS APPEAR SHOUTING, "SMASH ZIONISM." SWYGERT IS SILENT.

SWYGERT:
(TO JEWISH STUDENTS, ENRAGED)

Before I attacked your deplorable actions, I contacted the local ADL, the Jewish Federation, Mayor Ed Koch, and Rabbi Avi Weiss, and they specifically abhorred the signs.

LEADER:
(TO SWYGERT, AS HE POUNDS KAHANE'S POSTER)

And he specifically abhorred them!

SWYGERT:

Remove that poster!

LEADER:

Not till you remove them!

LEADER IS LOOKING FIRMLY AT BLACK STUDENTS AND POUNDING. BLACK STUDENTS LEAVE. JEWISH STUDENT REMOVE POSTER.

CYNICAL JEWISH STUDENT:
(TO JEWISH GROUP, BITTERLY)

Cowards.

THEY LEAVE WITH POSTER.

LATER: LEADER IS IN HIS ROOM ALONE. HE PUTS ON HIS YARMULKE AND PUTS PICTURES OF JEFFERIES, FARRAKHAN, SHARPTON AND DAUGHTRY ON HIS WALL. LEADER SHOOTS DARTS AT THEM, WHILE SAYING THE NAME OF EACH.

LEADER:

And If I had more of these, they'd be for Koch, Weiss, and you, Mr. Foxman, from the ADL, who doesn't know when a Jew is being defamed. You all killed Yankele, betraying us to them, appeasing our enemies, destroying our friends.

LATER THAT NIGHT: STUDENT WHO MOCKED JEWOSH STUDENT LEADER IS BANGING A POSTER ON TREE AND GIVING A SPEECH TO NO ONE.

STUDENT:
(POUNDING POSTER)

This, Rabbi Meir Kahane, is your speech, the one we should have heard. "If we are victims because we are not armed and dangerous, let it be different. Laughing at our timidity and confidently beating us for it...let it be...every Jew a 22!"

A GUARD SEIZES HIM AND TEARS DOWN THE POSTER.

GUARD:

You'll be suspended for this!

STUDENT:

Nothing would please me more. I wouldn't accept a diploma from this so-called college. It would shame and dishonor me.

HE TURNS AND PUNCHES GUARD SO HE FALLS. THEN, HE HANGS POSTER BACK ON TREE.

Scene 21

1993:

                TV REPORTER:

A movie about the Holocaust, "Schindler's List," was shown to Black high school students in California, so they could be sensitized to Jewish suffering. One of the scenes shown was of a Jewish woman being murdered by Nazis, just for the fun of it. The reaction of the students to this scene:

FLASHBACK: THE STUDENTS BURST INTO RACOUS LAUGHTER AND APPLAUSE. THEATER MANAGER APPEARS ON STAGE.

                THEATER MANAGER:

We cannot continue the show. I must ask you all to leave.

A FEW DAYS LATER: A ROUND TABLE AT WHICH DOZEN MEN ARE GATHERED. ONE MAN RISES AND SPEAKS.

                MAN:

Gentlemen, gathered here today are representatives from Jewish organizations, the Oakland Unified School District, and the City Government, to discuss a Holocaust Education Program which would prevent the student behavior we witnessed at our first attempt in this direction. Steven Spielberg, the producer of the movie, agrees with me that the students were not to blame, as they've been, and I quote, "desensitized to violence."

HEADS ARE BOBBING IN AGREEMENT.

> MAN:
> (RISING)

What would your attitude have been if Jewish students laughed at brutality visited on Blacks?

> CHAIRMAN:

You're out of order. Please be seated.

Scene 22

1993: CROWN HEIGHTS

>ON SCREEN: IN STREET, SOUND OF SCREECHING BRAKES IS HEARD, BLACK CHILD IS DARTING OUT. SHE IS HURT, BUT NOT BADLY. A BLACK MOB DESCENDS ON THE HASIDIC DRIVER AND OTHER HASIDIC DRIVES WHO HAVE NOTHING TO DO WITH THE INCIDENT. THEY ARE BEATEN, ROCKS AND BOTLES HURLED AT THEM. SOME BLACKS ARE HEARD SAYING "GOD DAMN JEWS. WE'LL GET EVEN." WITHIN MINUTES, 60 OFFICERS APPEAR IN RIOT GEAR.

OFFICER:
(TO ANOTHER OFFICER)

Let's try to appease this bunch or else…

OFFICER NODS AND REMOVES HASID AND HIS FIANCEE IN HANDCUFFS.

BLACK WOMAN:
(TALKING TO ANOTHER BLACK WOMAN)

If it were my family or relative, I would have done something violent. But it isn't, so I'm staying neutral.

. . .

SEVERAL HOURS LATER: INTERVIEWER ON TV WITH MAYOR DINKINS AND HASIDIC RABBI.

INTERVIEWER:
(TO MAYOR DINKINS)

Mayor Dinkins, after the accident, just a short time later, several Jews were stabbed and nine shot. Two have died.

DINKINS:

Let me assure you, this violence was not related to the auto accident and did not exceed normal levels.

HASIDIC RABBI:
(TO DINKINS)

You don't care that we live under constant threat. When the driver is Hasidic and the victim is black that's just cause, it seems, for a riot. The New York Times, it seems, is also delusional, as always.

HOLDS UP HEADLINE: 2 SIMILAR ACCIDENTS, 2 DIFFERENT RESULTS.

Nonsense! Attitudes have not changed. Blacks still hate us. Anything we do can still inflame them...and sometimes we don't have to do anything but be kind. Shmuel Graybar, a Hasid artist, a very gentle man...

THE RABBI IS NEAR TEARS.

FLASHBACK:

GRAYBAR:
(IN HIS STUDIO, NARRATING)

I paint peace murals to bring Black and Jewish children in Crown Heights together...artwork to unite and guide. Here's a beautiful one we did together.

HE SHOWS MURAL.

LATER: HE IS PAINTING A NATURE SCENE IN HIS STUDIO. NINE BLACK YOUTHS RUSH IN, DESTROY THE MURAL, AND BEAT HIM MERCILESSLY.

BACK TO PRESENT:

RABBI:
(TO DINKINS)

Your own son is involved with WLIB, where Jew hate is spewed any hour of the day, every day. So much for your racial harmony routine.

DINKINS:

You misunderstand the phrase entirely. It means simply that the other group feels the interests and concerns each group feels.

RABBI:

It means that, when Jewish interests conflict with Blacks, it's always understood who interests must suffer.

Scene 23

1994:

A MEETING HALL WITH PICTURES OF AL SHARPTON RUNNING FOR MAYOR. A BLACK MAN STEPS TO THE PODIUM. THERE ARE HUNDREDS OF PEOPLE IN THE AUDIENCE. ALL OF THEM ARE BLACK.

      MAN:

I'm Bob Law, ladies and gentleman...you've heard me on the radio.

APPLAUSE FROM THE CROWD.

Some black leaders didn't take care of their own people, because they were too busy, "Driving Miss Daisy" and then checking with her to find out who they can support and who they must repudiate.

      WOMAN:
      (YELLING)

Teach!

      MAN:
      (YELLING)

Tell it, brother!

SHARPTON STEPS TO THE PODIUM. THE CROWD EXPLODES, CHEERING. SHARPTON IS WELL DRESSED, THINNER AND IS WEARING A SHIRT AND TIE.

SHARPTON:
(BELLOWING)

No justice!

CROWD:
(ROARING)

NO PEACE!

SHARPTON:
(IMPLORING)

What do we want?

CROWD:

Sharpton!

SHARPTON:

When do we want him?

CROWD:

Now!

SHARPTON:

I will run for the United States Senate!

CROWD:
(SHOUTING)

Sharp-ton! Sharp-ton! Sharp-ton!

ETHNIC CLEANSING

MERCHANTS

Scene 24

1994:

HEADLINE: NEIGHBORHOOD UNDER SIEGE. VIOLENCE RULES THE STREETS AND THE CITIES.

TV REPORTER:

The area of Flatbush Avenue, Brooklyn that runs from Church Avenue to Empire Boulevard, between Flatbush and Nostrand Avenue, a Jewish area, is now going under. Black gangs of armed youths roam the streets, preying on residents and shopkeepers.

MERCHANT:

We open our stores for business in fear every day. We've all been held up at least once, some, four or five times, most at gunpoint. We all know shopkeepers or store employees who've been shot, stabbed, robbed.

> FLASHBACK: STREET SIGNS SAY, "ROGERS AVENUE." SIGN ON STORE SAYS, "IVI'S GROCERY." BLACK GANG ENTERS, SHOOTS AND KILLS OWNER.
>
> A AND B FURNITURE STORE OF CHURCH AVENUE. BLACK GANG ENTERS, SHOOTS AND KILLS OWNER. CUSTOMER LEAVING STORE IS ROBBED OF HER PACKAGE.

NOSTRAND AVENUE CHECK CASHING SERVICE. BLACK GANG ENTERS, SHOOTS AND KILLS OWNER.

BACK TO PRESENT:

More of us businessmen are giving up and walking away, no longer willing to risk our lives trying to make a living in this section of Flatbush.

A WOMAN, IN PANIC, IS RUSHING HOME AFTER SHE LOOKS AT HER WATCH. SHE ENTERS THE HOUSE. HER HUSBAND IS WORRIED.

HUSBAND:

Where have you been? I nearly died from worry. You know that after 6 o'clock, you don't dare walk the streets.

WOMAN:
(STILL GASPING)

I passed the grocery. To my surprise, he was still open, so I ran in the get some milk, wandered around for some things, and didn't realize how time was passing. Before I turned around, a hald hour passed and I ran home as fast as I could.

SHE COLLASPES ON HIM, CRYING.

WOMAN:

Oh, Herman, what are we doing here?

HERMAN:

We're paying the only rent we can afford.

TV REPORTER:

Our guest today, Mr. Adam Walinsky:

WALINKSY:

How long can decency survive if our only answer to violence is day to day surrender? We should confront danger ourselves. Legal offices, laundromats, beauty shops, discount stores, a community in Flatbush is dying; children given money to bribe thugs; children left alone to face wild ones at 3pm.

A SIGN ON A DOOR SATS, "BARRY'S LAW OFFICE." THE LAWYER IS SEEN INSTALLING PLEXIGLASS IN HIS LAW OFFICE.

SIGN ON STORE: ED'S CANDY AND TOBACCO.

ED:

I've been robbed five times and assaulted three times. I've enclosed my entire shop in Plexiglass. Every day two to three businesses are robbed. Police have increased their patrols, but we live in fear that the robberies will go on anyhow.

TV REPORTER:
(TO POLICEMAN)

You should have a cop on every corner...

POLICEMAN:

We don't have enough men.

ONE YEAR LATER:

MERCHANT:

All we struggled to build...to provide for everyone from birth to death...baby needs, charities, temples, funeral homes...and it was no use. Kahane was right. "Every Jew a 22." We didn't listen...and our community died.

Scene 25

FLASHBACK:

1970:

KAHANE:
(NARRATING)

There is Jew hatred today, and in alarming doses, from totally unexpected and unorthodox sections of the American public. In no way should we refuse to see and correctly assess the very real local danger to Jews that comes, not from white, but from Black Jew hatred...of epidemic proportions. It was the Rosenwald Foundation, established by the Sears magnate, that predominantly financed black colleges, literature, and science, at a time when whites made it all but impossible for blacks to receive a decent higher education. In its struggling years, before Congress agreed to help, Howard University survived only because of men like Rosenwald.

ON SCREEN:

1994:

HOWARD UNIVERSITY, FEDERALLY AND SOMETIMES CALLED THE "HARVARD OF BLACK COLLEGES." BLACK STUDENTS AND SOME WHITES ARE IN THE AUDITORIUM.

ANNOUNCER:
(TO STUDENTS)

We are proud to present one of our top students, Malik Zulu Shabazz.

SHABAZZ APPEARS.

> SHABAZZ:
> (SHOUTING)

Who caught and killed Nat Turner?

> STUDENTS:
> (SHOUTING)

Jews!

> SHABAZZ:

Who controls the Federal Reserve?

> STUDENTS:

Jews!

> SHABAZZ:

You're not afraid to say it, are you?

> STUDENTS:

Jews! Jews!

> SHABAZZ:

Who controls the media and Hollywood?

> STUDENTS:

Jews!

> SHABAZZ:

Who has our entertainers, our athletes, in a vice grip?

> STUDENTS:

Jews!

SHABAZZ:

Am I lying?

STUDENTS:

No!

ANOTHER SPEAKER TAKES THE MICROPHONE WHILE THE YELLING FROM THE AUDIENCE GOES ON.

MAN:

Let's junk "We Shall Overcome" and replace it with a new anthem, "We Shall Not Sell Out to Jews!"

AUDIENCE CHEERS.

LATER:

A REPORTER IS INTERVIEWING A WHITE MAN EXITING FROM THE HALL.

REPORTER:
(TO WHITE MAN)

I'm from the Washington Post. Interesting, isn't it, hearing their current viewpoints.

MAN HAS A FLASHBACK. (SEE PICTURE)

MAN:

Reminds me of Nuremberg, 1935, students hearing and cheering an anti-Jewish tirade.

MAN RUSHES AWAY, VERY DISTRAUGHT.

THE WAY IT WAS: *Nazis parade through Nuremberg on the way to a party rally in 1935.*

FOLLOWING DAY:

MAN IS FRANTICALLY SEARCHING THROUGH THE WASHINGTON POST AND FINDS THE ARTICLE HE IS SEARCHING FOR.

MAN:

Ah, here it is.

HE STARTS READING.

In a speech by a law student at Howard University last night...

HE GOES ON READING SILENTLY ONCE, THEN AGAIN.

MAN:
(IN SHOCK)

Not a word about the Jew baiting?!

HE DROPS THE PAPER, PUTS HIS FOOT ON IT, THEN RETRIEVES IT. HE SETS THE PAPER ON FIRE, THEN THROWS IT IN A PAIL. HE SITS DOWN WEARILY AND HAS HIS ARM SLUNG OVER A CHAIR. WE SEE A NUMBER TATTOOED ON THE ARM AS THE FLAME RISES NEARBY.

END OF PART THREE

Part 4

Scene 1

DECEMBER 31, 1994:

TV INTERVIEWER:
(ON SCREEN)

A conflict is raging in Harlem. A dispute between a Jewish landlord, FREDDY'S FASHION MARKET, a clothing store, and his Black tenant, Sikhulu Shange, of Record Shack. The owner of Freddy's, Mr. Harari, is here. Morris Powell, who heads the 125th Street Vendor's Association and the Buy Black Committee is also with us today.

HARARI:

I must make one thing very clear. Record Shack is only a sub-tenant of mine. The landlord of both of us is a Pentecostal church, "THE HOUSE OF PRAYER FOR ALL PEOPLE." It was founded by Bishop C.M (Sweet Daddy) Grace in the 1920's, and is one of the largest Black landlords on 125th Street. We are both refusing to renew the lease...

POWELL:

...We are not going to stand by and let a Jew interloper remove this brother so he can expand his business. We're gonna picket this Jewish landlord 'til he gets the hell out.

TV INTERVIEWER:

You've had problems with Mr. Shange yourself, Mr. Powell. He tipped over your vendors' tables, refused to let them set up in front of his store and threatened one with a machete, saying he stole bootlegged tapes and hurt his business. Strange, you're defending him.

HARARI:
(TO POWELL)

So why did Mr. Shange, who hates vendors, go to you, of all people for help? Because he knew the truth and so do you, Mr. Powell. The church wasn't going to help him. Prices soaring. They wanted more rent. He wouldn't pay. And besides, his business was dusty and poor looking, would not fit the 4.5-million-dollar renovation the church was planning in the area. I heard Mr. Shange himself had a feeling the church doubled-crossed him.

POWELL:

City got some of that 350 million dollars the Federal government gave to Harlem, and the first thing they do is come after our vendors, moving them to the side streets, claiming they're hurtin' business cloggin' main streets. Roland Smith, a vendor, and I are fightin' this tooth and nail! And what's this got to do with creating a Harlem with Black business only? Never happen with whites drivin' us out. We're gonna see that this cracker suffers! And Reverend Sharpton is with us.

FOLLOWING DAY: MORRIS POWELL, SHARPTON, AND OTHER PICKETING FREDDY'S.

POWELL AND SHARPTON:

Jew stores gotta go!

PEOPLE BEHIND THEM:

Yeah! Go! Go! Go!

POWELL:

Where do we want Jews?

OTHERS:

Out!

SHARPTON:

When do we want them out of our neighborhood?

OTHERS:

Now!

SHARPTON:

When?

OTHERS:

Now!

ON SCREEN: MONTHS LATER.

THE PICKETING IS STILL GOING ON. PROTESTORS START MAKING MOTIONS OF STRIKING A MATCH AND THROWING IT ON OUTSIDE CLOTHING DISPLAYS OR IN DOORWAY OF STORE.

PICKETER:
(TO FREDDY'S BLACK SECURITY GUARD)

Cracker lover! You'll get yours as a traitor to our race!

(TO ANOTHER PICKETER)

Hey Shabazz, just this morning the cops ask this guy to sign an affidavit saying we're troublemakers around here and he signs...big as life... "Kareem Brunner." Give it to 'em, will ya! He's getting me goin' to jail! Cops showed me the paper when I got to the summons.

SHABAZZ ENTERS FREDDY'S STORE AND PUSHES GUARD AND MANAGER.

SHABAZZ:
(SHOUTING TO MANAGER)

I will be back to burn this Jew store down...burn, burn, burn...if you ain't the hell out soon.... Ya hear me, Mr. Manager? Very, very soon! And I mean quick!

MANAGER:

I'm tired of this going on for months. You come in here like this again and I'll...

SHABAZZ:
(LOOKING EVEN MORE VICIOUS)

You'll what?

(SHABAZZ SHOVES HIM AGAIN)

I'll be back tomorrow.

SHABAZZ LEAVES.

THE FOLLOWING DAY: SHARPTON IN THE STREET LEADING A BOYCOTT RALLY IN HARLEM AGAINST FREDDY'S.

TV REPORTER:
(TO SHARPTON)

You've made no mention of the Black church wanting the Black tenant out and pressuring Freddy's to get him out.

SHARPTON:

Freddy's is not our community and kicked nothing back to Harlem. We are spending over 50 billion today but not with us. We're actually boycotting our own business.

REPORTER:

But the church is refusing to renew the lease on a Black business.

SHARPTON:

We can't sit back and allow Freddy's injustice to go unanswered. Brother Felder chastised us for wasting money on holiday fineries and making them Jews rich. I remember a year ago, Brother Felder...

FLASHBACK: FELDER ADDRESSING A BLACK CROWD AT A SHARPTON RALLY.

FELDER:

I'm tired of hearing the Jewish people accuse Minister Farrakhan, Reverend Al Sharpton, and other Black leaders, of anti-Semitism. I'm serving notice on the Jewish community...

(LOUD APPLAUSE)

That if you don't stop, we will marshal 6 million men and women and boycott every Jewish business throughout the United States.

BACK TO PRESENT:

SHARPTON:

The threat of such boycott now will silence the Jews, because nobody loves money more than greedy Jews.

REPORTER:

You don't think the church is greedy? Never heard you use that word to characterize them.

SHARPTON:

We're trying to close down Freddy's...not our church.

DECEMBER 7, 1995: HARARI IN HIS LAWYER'S OFFICE

HARARI:

I want to apply to the Supreme Court for some legal action against this harassment of me. And Shange knows I'm doing this. I hope this will get him out and off my back at last. He asked to speak to my attorney, so I gave him your name and you should expect a call from him. Maybe he wants to strike out some sort of bargain.

HARARI LEAVES.

LATER: ATTORNEY PHONES HARARI.

ATTORNEY:

Mr. Harari, I just got a call from Shange. He says you're tampering with something for which you'll be sorry, that you're opening up a can of worms which you never close anymore.

MAN ON PICKET LINE:

We're going to come back here with 20 niggers and loot and burn that Freddie bastard. We hollerin' and hollerin' and he ain't goin nowhere. Lousy, blood suckin' Jew!

SHARPTON HEARS AND SAYS NOTHING. ROLAND SMITH IS SEEN AMONG THE PICKETERS.

DECEMBER 8:

BLACK MAN WALKS INTO FREDDY'S FASHION MART. IN THE STORE ARE WHITES, HISPANICS, AND BLACKS. BLACK MAN PULLS OUT A GUN, ORDERS ALL BLACKS TO LEAVE, WITH THE EXCEPTION OF THE BLACK GUARD, KAREEM BRUNNER, WHO IS ORDERED TO STAY. MAN THEN SPILLS PAINT THINNER ON SEVERAL BINS OF CLOTHING, SET THEM AFIRE, LOCKS WHITES, HISPANICS, AND GUYANESE INSIDE, AND TURNS GUN ON SELF.

HEADLINE IN PAPER ON SCREEN:

"MASSACRE AT FREDDY'S IN HARLEM"

TV REPORTER:

Roland Smith, a Harlem resident with a criminal record going back 30 years, killed 8 people, setting a fire fueled by anti-Semitism. He was part of a group of picketers led by Al Sharpton and Morris Powell. The only Black killed in the store was the guard at Freddy's who was accused of betrayal by the picketers and threatened.

FOLLOWING DAY: MAN READING NEW YORK TIMES ALOUD

MAN:

Roland Smith was a man of principal, hard-working, a little criminal, but sort of spiritual.

MAN, STUNNED, SHAKES HIS HEAD IN DISBELIEF.

HARLEM NEWSPAPER HEADLINE:

AMSTERDAM NEWS ON SCREEN:

"ROLAND SMITH SETS FREDDY'S ABLAZE BECAUSE HE WAS HOMELESS AND UNEMPLOYED."

FOLLOWING DAY: TV REPORTER IS INTERVIEWING MORRIS POWELL AND SHARPTON WHO ARE NOW PICKETING BARGAIN WORLD, A JEWISH STORE IN HARLEM.

POWELL:

It was just one of those crazy things like an earthquake or tornado or something.

REPORTER:

You don't think that what you're doing now might provoke another tornado?

SHARPTON:

There is no link between the protests and the fire at all.

REPORTER:

But you're accused of setting the climate that led to racial arson.

SHARPTON:

I heard no anti-Semitic, anti-White or any other expression of racism. We never said we were going after Whites or Jews. We were protecting businessmen in our community.

REPORTER:

Questions that remain open: Enraged at being pressured to move by Freddy's, did the sub-tenant Shange pay Shabazz to viciously harass the store's manager? Why didn't Mr. Shange open his open at the usual time that day?

SHARPTON:

It's time for healing and dialogue with Jewish leaders, I'm thinking.

REPORTER:

Isn't fear the final arbiter in these cases? Fear...of riots...fear of burn, burn, burn?

FOLLOWING DAY:

SIGN ON BUILDING: SLAVE THEATER. IN FRONT OF BUILDING, POWELL, BETTY DOPSON, AND OTHER BLACKS ADDRESSING BLACK AUDIENCE AT A STREET RALLY HONORING SMITH, THE KILLER AT FREDDY'S.

DOPSON:

The Harlem incident was caused by the Jew, not the brother who had the psychological breakdown. He was a hero and a martyr....

AUDIENCE MEMBER:

Like Colin Ferguson...doing his thing on the Long Island Railroad.

POWELL:

A cracker is a cracker is a cracker...stealin' our dollars. In Roland Smith's honor, we're holding a memorial tomorrow in front of Freddy's!

CHEERS FROM AUDIENCE.

A FEW DAYS LATER: SMITH'S FUNERAL: WOMAN GIVING EULOGY.

WOMAN:

Roland was not a criminal. He was not deranged; he was...like many of us, frustrated by the treatment of African people.

TV REPORTER:

In the open casket, Smith wore African attire, with a Black Panther symbol pinned over his heart.

Scene 2

1995:

> REPORTER ON RADIO:

A Million Man March on Washington is being planned by Nation of Islam leader Farrakhan, who does not hesitate to show his contempt for Whites and Jews and considers Hitler a great man.

OCTOBER 15.

A WEEK LATER: WASHINGTON D.C

FARRAKHAN IS ON THE PODIUM, ADDRESSING A HUGE BLACK CROWD AT THE CORNER OF 4TH AND JEFFERSON. ONE BLOCK FROM THE PODIUM, TWO MEN APPROACH THE POLICE WILL TWO SIGNS. ONE SAYS, "FARRKHAN AND DAVID DUKE...TWO SIDES OF THE SAME COIN," AND THE OTHER SAYS, "THE NATION OF ISLAM IS A NATION OF HATE." BOTH MEN ARE WEARING YARMULKES. BLACK SURROUND THEM, SPITTING ON THEM AND THREATENING "WE RE GOING TO GET YOU," AND SAYING "HILTER SHOULD HAVE FINISHED YOU OFF."

> POLICEMEN:
> (TO SIGN HOLDERS)

You have every right to demonstrate, and we will protect you.

. . .

FOLLOWING DAY: THE TWO MEN AGAIN APPEAR WITH THEIR SIGNS.

> BLACKS IN THE CROWD:
> (TO THE SIGN HOLDERS)

You better get outta here!

BLACKS PULLING THE SIGNS OUT OF THEIR HANDS WHILE THE POLICE STSND BY AND DO NOTHING.

> POLICEMAN:
> (TO THE TWO MEN)

You must leave.

> MAN:
> (WITH SIGN)

You're violating our First Amendment rights.

> POLICEMAN:

Inciting to riot is violating our rights. Now get out, or you'll be arrested!

> BLACKS:
> (SHOUTING AT TWO MEN)

Jews control the world, but you can't control our day. You better watch your back. We're comin' to get you and no one gonna help you.

> POLICEMAN:

You're in danger. You better go.

> ONE MAN:
> (TO OTHER)

He's right.

AS THEY ARE LEAVING, THEY ARE FOLLOWED BY OVER 50 BLACKS WHO KEEP THROWING OBJECTS AT THEM WHILE THE POLICE WATCH AND DO NOT INTERFERE.

Scene 3

1995. CROWN HEIGHTS.

AN 11-YEAR-OLD BLACK GIRL AND A GROUP OF HASIDIC BOYS BEFORE A JUDGE IN A COURTROOM.

> GIRL:
> (TO JUDGE, HYSTERICALLY)

One of them (POINTING TO HASIDIM) called me a "nigger" and slapped me, and two of them other grownups with the curls all came to hit me, too.

THREE DAYS LATER: A HASIDIC DRIVER HAS HIS WINDSHIELD BROKEN BY A GROUP OF ROCK-THROWING BLACK YOUTHS. HE RUSHES OUT OF THE CAR AND BEATS ONE OF THE ASSAILANTS. POLICE PASSING BY ARREST HIM.

> HASID:
> (WRITING AND READING A FLYER)

Rabbi Spielman, Chairman of Crown Heights Jewish Community Council, urges all the members of the Crown Heights community to report any grievance to the police or our agency, rather than take the law into their own hands.

> POLICEMAN:
> (TO PRESS)

The cases involved the two Black children will be handled by the Chief himself, as well as other top brass.

HEADLINE IN BLACK NEWSPAPER ON SCREEN:

"HASIDIC FAMILY MAULS 11-YEAR-OLD IN FRACAS."

SHARPTON:

We're coming down Eastern Parkway, where those people have their headquarters, on this case. We're not going to let them beat up on our children. In fact, I'm going to hold another rally from headquarters on Saturday!

RABBI SPIELMAN:

Desecrating the Jewish Sabbath.

BLACK MAN ON RADIO:

This is WWRL. Reverend Del Shields. Today's message is simple and to the point. Too many children are being beat up by gangs of Hasidim. The attorney representing one of their victims is asking you to pack the courtroom so as to make an example of the Hasid.

A WEEK LATER: RABBI SPIELMAN BEING INTERVIEWED BY REVEREND DEL SHIELDS ON RADIO.

SPIELMAN:

You ask why racial tensions have reemerged in Crown Heights; obviously, because certain people are trying to create tensions.

DEL SHIELDS:

I'm very troubled by the fact that members of your community have purchased at least three homes in ours...the Cambria Heights community.

SPIELMAN:

Anyone has the right to live wherever they want.

DEL SHIELDS:

Very few Blacks in the Crown Heights community compared to years ago. You'll do the same to Cambria Heights.

SPIELMAN:

Blacks in Crown Heights, 100,000. Jews...20,000.

DEL SHIELDS:

You have influence with the Mayor, the city and state.

SPIELMAN:

The State Assembly and City Council members representing Crown Heights are Black.

DEL SHIELDS:

Now, members of the audience, we await your calls.

DEL SHIELDS RECEIVES A CALL FROM MEMBER OF THE AUDIENCE.

AUDIENCE MEMBER:

The Jews want to own everything. The rabbi insulted the Black community!

DEL SHIELDS:

It is rather strange that 20,000 people can rule, influence, and control 100,000.

SPIELMAN:

Standard anti-Semitic language...we have power...we have control. The same talk was heard on Black radio just before the Crown Heights riots 4 years ago.

LATER:

HEADLINE ON SCREEN:

"HASIDIC MAN WAS STABBED IN CROWN HEIGHTS TODAY FOR NO APPARENT REASON."

ETHNIC CLEANSING

ROCKAWAY, NEW YORK

Scene 4

FLASHBACK: 1984

KAHANE:
(ADDRESSING A CROWD)

The neighborhood is changing. I have seen what the word means in other Jewish areas. A synonym for "about to go under." If Black muggers, rapists, killers, put a foot in your street, your *shule, your home, to slay you, slay them first! Never Again, sit home and wait for death to break in the in-door!

PEOPLE IN CROWD:

Boo!

MAN:

Racist!

PRESENT: 1995:

THE ABOVE MAN IS IN HIS ROOM IN A WHEELCHAIR SITTING IN THE DARK. THE LIGHT, COMING IN THROUGH THE WINDOW FROM THE MOON, SHINES ON PART OF HIS FACE, SO HIS FEATURES CAN BE SEEN. HE IS LISTENING TO THE RADIO. SYMPHONY MUSIC IS PLAYING AND HE IS WAVING HIS ARMS

ABOUT LIKE HE IS THE CONDUCTOR. THE PROGRAM ENDS, AND A TEMPLE IS CONDUCTING FRIDAY NIGHT SERVICES.

FLASHBACK: WOMAN AND MAN WELL DRESSED. HE LOOKS LIKE A YOUNGER VERSION OF THE MAN IN THE WHEELCHAIR. SHE IS RUSHING.

WIFE:

We have to hurry, Ben, or we won't be on time. First time ever we'll be late for services. The rabbi won't like it. He's a nice man. I don't like to upset him.

BEN STOPS HER AS SHE'S RUSHING TO THE DOOR.

BEN:

I don't want another first. We go out together, as always.

HE PUTS HER ARM AROUND HIS ELBOW. OPENS THE DOOR WITH A COURTLY GESTURE. THEY LEAVE.

WALKING DOWN THE STREET, THEY PASS BEAUTIFUL STORES IN A LOVELY NEIGHBORHOOD. EVERYONE IS DRESSED FOR SABBATH. THE TEMPLE IS A MAGNIFICENT ONE. THEY ENTER.

LATER: RABBI ON THE PODIUM.

RABBI:

Our lovely synagogue, DERECH EMUNAH, is with us 91 years and we hope our children and our children's children will be sitting in these seats for 120 years and beyond. This temple is built to last...like us. Strangers among us now. We welcome them. Our community will be a shining example of integration, neighborliness, brotherhood!

BEN AND HIS WIFE ARE SMILING.

BACK TO PRESENT:

PEOPLE ARE LEAVING THE TEMPLE. STONES ARE THROWN AT THEM BY BLACKS SHOUTING "JEW MOTHER..." BLACK GANGS ROAMING THE AREA ATTACK THE CHILDREN. THE STORES THAT WERE ONCE BEAUTIFUL ARE NOW BOARDED UP. MOVING TRUCKS LINE THE STREETS, "FOR RENT" AND "FOR SALE" SIGNS ARE ON ALL THE HOUSES. THE AREA LOOKS LIKE A SLUM, NOW...AND THERE ARE BLACKS ON THE STREET

COMING AND GOING. ONE MAN IS BOARDING UP HIS STORE. BEN STOPS TO TALK TO HIM. BEN IS THE MAN WHO CALLED KAHANE A "RACIST."

BEN:
(IN A WHEELCHAIR)

You're leaving too?!

MAN:
(BANGS NAILS IN RAGE)

My son mugged, my father robbed, and now, my brother was here watching the store for a week (A SOB IN HIS VOICE) and he...he was...murdered.

THE MANS BANGS WILDLY ON THE BOARDS NOW, STOPS, DROPS HAMMER AND COLLASPES ON STREET. HE JUST SITS THERE.

BEN:
(GASPS IN SHOCK)

I didn't know. Just came out of the hospital again. (HE SHAKES HIS HEAD SADLY) Good man...your brother. (STARING OFF) My wife forgot to lock the door. Four big black men rushed in. we sat in a corner cowering, while they took the little, we had, then hacked our bed to shambles...looking for money in the mattress, I suppose. After they left, she was still trembling. I held her in my arms on the floor. There was no place to put her to make her comfortable. She died of fright. She was all I had. I went looking for them, but they found me. One of them broke my legs, and the other said, "So you'll stop lookin'." The next Black man I saw was in the hospital...in a bed next to mine. He suddenly became four in my eyes.

FLASHBACK:

BEN:
(SCREAMING AT HIS HALLUCINATION)

I want an accounting...of how many of us you've raped, mugged, robbed, killed, forced to flee our homes, schools, temples. Count them! Everyone!

BACK TO PRESENT:

MAN:

They count when they're <u>born</u> in our doctor's hands…not when we <u>die</u> at theirs. You should come with me…. or are you a fool like the others? Can't leave the *shule.

BEN WHEELS ANGRILY AWAY.

THAT NIGHT: BEN LOOKING OUT OF THE WINDOW. A HUGE FIRE IS SEEN IN THE DISTANCE, AND AN ANGUISHED CRY IS HEARD, "THE SHULE!" BEN TURNS ON THE RADIO.

RADIO ANNOUNCER:

A bulletin just in from Far Rockaway, New York. The magnificent Derech Emunah Synagogue has been torched. The rabbi says, "With the help of others, we will repair and rebuild."

BEN:

Thank God.

ON SCREEN: EIGHT MONTHS LATER. ANOTHER HUGE FIRE IS SEEN FROM BEN'S WINDOW.

BEN IS LISTENING TO RADIO.

NEWS REPORTER:

Derech Emanuel Synagogue has been torched again. The rabbi says, "We will repair and rebuild."

BEN:
(NARRATING)

'Til they came, my house was full of neighbors, Mrs. Scharf, Mrs. Rosen, the lady in black and red. Widows on pension, all of them. They used to cook for me and I would help them do a little of this, a little that. Wonder where they went. The few neighbors that are left are afraid to walk down the hall. We telephone each other…the man and I next door…or he pounds on the wall. After my last mugging, my head is not so good…and I'm afraid…even here…so I sit and watch the door to make sure no one comes in…only the nice lady who brings me my food. We have a signal. She knocks three times. It's getting dark. I leave the radio on so they'll know I'm home and won't rob me. And I never take my eyes off the door. That's what protects me…watching my four locks.

Scene 4 471

A SUDDEN POUNDING ON THE DOOR. IT IS SMASHED IN, ONE LOCK AT A TIME. FOUR HUGE BLACKS STORM IN, KNIFE HIM, RIFLE THE ROOM, AND STEAL THE RADIO ON THEIR WAY OUT.

A KNOCK IS HEARD ON THE WALL. AFTER REPEATED KNOCKING, NEIGHBORS COME RUSHING IN. BEN IS DYING. HE WHISPERS, "KAHANE WAS RIGHT." THE STORE OWNER WHO BOARDED UP HIS SHOP COMES RUSHING IN WITH THE POLICE. HE JOINS BEN SAYING, "KAHANE WAS RIGHT," AS DO THE OTHERS.

Scene 5

1995: FAR ROCKAWAY, NEW YORK. SCENE IS OF A SENIOR CITIZENS' RESIDENCE. CLOCK ON SCREEN SAYS 7:30. SNOW, SLUSH AND ICE ARE ON THE GROUND. A HEAVY WIND IS BLOWING. IT IS MORNING, BUT BARELY LIGHT OUT. TWO OLD WOMEN WEARING SNOW JACKETS, WOOLEN CAPS AND BOOTS, ARE SITTING IN A MAKESHIFT SYNAGOGUE ON PLASTIC CHAIRS AND PEERING OUT THE WINDOW. AN EMPLOYEE PASSES WITH A BROOM, SWEEPING.

OLD LADY:
(TO EMPLOYEE)

It's freezing in here.

SHE IS TREMBLING WITH COLD.

I'm going to organize all these old ladies and make a fuss!

EMPLOYEE:

Same complaint every day, Mrs. Rosen.

(TO OTHER LADY)

Tell her, Mrs. Scharf. She don't listen to me.

SCHARF:
(TO ROSEN)

You know it's much too early for the heat to be coming up. Put on another sweater!

ROSEN:

And I told you I don't have any!

SCHARF:

Go to your room and get your blanket!

ROSEN:

I don't want to miss the policeman.

SCHARF:
(STARING OFF)

Remember how beautiful it was here, once? Such a fancy beach resort. The summer bungalows...how lovely they were. And now...these ugly dinosaurs filled with all of us on Social Security and projects filled with young people on Welfare. Those beautiful stores, all boarded up. Some burned to the ground. The beach has no bathers. And the streets...I wouldn't dare put a foot. I used to enjoy a little walk to the market or take a bus somewheres. But... (SHE SHOWS BRUISES) It still hurts...where they knocked me down. Two Black kids...high like this.

(SHE ILLUSTRATES)

A little one like me...you can imagine. I'm surprised I'm still here. I don't even know what for. To wait for the policeman?

ROSEN:

I have also bruises. Here.

(SHE SHOWS LEG)

I fell on the bus. Snow on the stairs. Slippery. And here.

(SHE SHOWS HER OTHER LEG)

I fell the next day on the sidewalk.

SCHARF:

I can never say I'm sick without hearing you're worse. <u>You</u> were stupid. <u>I</u> couldn't help it, so I'm still ahead. Today is my turn…my day to complain and get sympathy.

FLASHBACK:

1990: A MEETING OF THE OLD LADIES WITH A POLICEMAN WHO IS ON THE PODIUM.

ROSEN:
(TO POLICEMAN)

You don't really care what happens to us. Nobody does. We're afraid to go out and afraid to stay in. If we go out to buy bread, we don't know if we will come back. And if we don't go out, we starve. I tell you I'm going, and if something happens, it happens, but I can't stand anymore an empty refrigerator. I need milk for my bones.

A RUMBLE IN THE GROUP, "SHE'S RIGHT!"

POLICEMAN:

I promise a big 12-seater van will go around to 12 different locations beginning at 8am sharp and pick up anyone who wants to go to the supermarket.

BACK TO PRESENT:

CLOCK ON SCREEN: 8:30AM A POLICE VAN PULLS UP TO THE BUILDING. SCHARF HURRIES FROM HER CHAIR.

SCHARF:

Hurry! We have to get in the first load!

ROSEN IS RUNNING, ANXIOUS AND BREATHLESS.

ROSEN:

We'll never make it. He'll leave before we get out there. No use hurrying.

SCHARF REACHES THE DOOR FIRST AND BRACES HERSELF FOR THE WIND. POLICEMAN IS OUTSIDE WITH THE DOOR OPEN.

ROSEN:

I didn't hardly recognize you. Where were you last week? Why didn't you come? We waited from 7 o'clock to after 10 and nobody came. Why can't you tell us you're not coming? Then we wouldn't have to wait so long.

POLICEMAN:

I tell the guys in charge of van operation to do that, and they just don't.

SCHARF:

I'm 76 years old and I have no food. Eating nothing but toast and coffee since no one came last week.

POLICEMAN:

I feel really lousy about the bad service.

A RUSH OF SYMPATHY FROM THE WOMEN. THEY PAT HIM ON THE SHOULDER AND SAY WARMLY, "IT'S OKAY" ...AND THEY BEAM WITH DELIGHT.

POLICEMAN:
You outta write to your congressman.
ROSEN:

My son, that I never see, he did me a favor. I can't write.

(SHE SHOWS HER TWISTED FINGERS)

Arthritis. He wrote letters to everybody that made us promises before the election. I never saw they should send me back even a form letter with another empty promise. Nothing with nothing.

THE VAN STOPS TO PICK UP OTHERS IN ANOTHER SENIOR CENTER. THE OLD LADIES ARE WAITING IN THE LOBBY, PROPPED UP AGAINST THE WALLS.

LADY IN BLACK DRESS AND RED HAT:
(TO POLICEMAN)

We're here for hours waiting like this! I have no bread; I'm eating matzoh for a whole week! But I won't do this again, I don't think. It's not worth the waiting and worrying for a little shopping. I'll take a bus and the van will take me home. But something should be done!

SCHARF:

While you're waiting in the cold for a bus, you should hold up a poster that says, "No Bread." We'll all hold posters. Then, they'll hear us.

(TO LADY WITH RED HAT)

You with me? And how about the rest of you?

SILENCE. LADY WITH RED HAT FRIGHTENED NOW.

LADY WITH RED HAT:
(TO MRS. ROSEN)

I'm grateful, very grateful for whatever the government can give me. You remember Ben, our neighbor in the wheelchair? I still worry about him. If he were here, he'd be grateful, too. It's, at least, better than where he is. Thank God, we're here.

MRS. ROSEN:

Kahane was right.

(SHE POINTS THUMB AND FOREFINGER LIKE GUN.)

If we did what he said, we'd still be there.

(OTHERS AGREE, NODDING HEADS VIGOROUSLY.)

Scene 6

FLASHBACK:

1972: NEW YORK CITY

MAYOR LINDSAY:
(ADDRESSING HIS POLITICAL GROUP)

I'm glad to see so many members of our party here to discuss my plan. I propose to build housing for the Black poor outside of their ghettoes; the first one in the solidly middle class, predominantly Jewish, and of course, predominantly Liberal, Forest Hills in Queens.

MAN:

They won't like it. We promised them a place for the Jewish poor in that area.

LINDSAY:

We can expect no resistance. On the contrary, full cooperation. As for promises, we can handle that, can't we?

UNAMINOUS APPLAUSE

LINDSAY:

Then I'll go full steam ahead.

. . .

FOLLOWING WEEK: FOREST HILLS, QUEENS. JEWISH PEOPLE IN THE STREET CARRYING PICKET SIGNS SAYING, "SENIOR CITIZENS ONLY," "KEEP THIS A MIDDLE-CLASS COMMUNITY. NO PROJECT." BLACKS CARRYING PICKET SIGN SAYING, "WHITES AGAINST A LOW-INCOME HOUSING PROJECT CAUSE THEY'RE RACIST!"

BOTH GROUPS ARE SHOUTING AT EACH OTHER.

JEW:

This will destroy a middle-class community!

A JEW IS POKING A FINGER INTO A BLACK, WHO IS POKING A FINGER INTO HIS CHEST. BOTH ARE ENRAGED. (SEE PICTURE ON FOLLOWING PAGE)

BLACK:

You Jews for integration as long as it's somewhere else!

RADIO COMMENTATOR:

After an 11-hour debate in City Hall, and a sit-down protest of Forest Hills residents, which has tarnished their image around the country to their everlasting shame, the mayor has called upon Mario Cuomo, a prominent attorney in Queens, to affect a compromise, give the Blacks their rightful due, and prevent White flight.

FLASHBACK:

KAHANE:
(ON PHONE)

...I recall you saying bullets were too good for us.

(HE HANGS UP AND TURNS TO JDL BOY)

One of those "Respectables" in Queens calling to find out if JDL can bomb the low-income housing the city is preparing to build in their neighborhood. Nowhere to be found when we needed them.

At City Hall hearings on the Forest Hills Project in 1972, police had to separate opponents and proponents of the developement.

THE "RICH JEW"

AND

ETHNIC CLEANSING IN HOUSING

Scene 7

MAN ON PODIUM WITH CHIEF OF POLICE.

MAN:
(TO FOREST HILLS CROWD)

Ladies and gentlemen, I'm Mario Cuomo, here in Forest Hills to work out an equitable solution to a painful problem. I understand the concern of all of you who are currently residing in Forest Hills, a beautiful community you've struggled to build, and I equally feel for the grievances of our Black citizens who deserve an equal chance to partake of our society. Borough President Mannes and I are therefore proposing we make the whole project into the city's only low-income CO-OP. the city will contribute, as well as Blacks and Jews, and pride of ownership will have positive results...a clean, safe, secure environment for all, especially since we're scaling the building down from 24 to 12 stories.

JEWISH MAN:
(IN AUDIENCE)

Without security from police 24 hours a day, we don't want nothing!

POLICEMAN:

Even more, if necessary. If you have problems, don't hesitate to contact us.

THE FOLLOWING DAY, THERE ARE NO PROTESTS.

CUOMO:
(TO LINDSAY)

I think we can proceed now. The protestors have been quiet all weekend.

ON SCREEN: 1992: MAYOR GUILIANI ON A PODIUM WITH POLICE COMMISSIONER BRATTON ADDRESSING AN AUDIENCE OF BLACKS AND JEWS IN FOREST HILLS CO-OP.

GUILIANI:

I've received a friendly reception here today, which means things have gone as expected when this place was built...racial harmony and peace. Four car thefts in 9 months were the only major crimes here. Housing police working together with our men in the precinct...that's the ticket...that made this place safe and will continue to do so as long....

JEWISH MAN:
(INTERRUPTING)

...Passing the buck is what you're doing. Break-ins, robberies, beatings and nobody knows nothing.

BLACK MAN:

Outside maybe, but not here. I have no trouble.

ANOTHER JEWISH MAN:

We live in fear so much, we're afraid to complain and use our names. If we do, we'll be punished by the city, thrown out of here with nowhere else to go, or drug dealers may come after us...

BLACK MAN:

...Lies! Makin' up stories to keep us out of here when an apartment comes up.

ANOTHER JEWISH MAN:

Three months ago, three Black guys with guns pushed their way into our apartment after they knocked on the door and I opened it. They tied me up, stabbed me, hit me on the head, took an electric iron and burned me on the leg. They were equipped with walkie-talkies and were informed by someone that another person was coming to my floor. My sister-in-law arrived with her kids. They grabbed her, robbed her, too, and fled...but not before they tied us all up. An hour later, we broke loose, my mother, uncle, sister-in-law, and me. The kids were too young to do anything but cry.

BLACK MAN:

More lies. You didn't report that to the police because it never happened.

JEWISH MAN:

Security is very poor. The back door is left open. The elevators are used as bathrooms, it's disgusting!

BLACK MAN:

White man trying to keep us in slums!

JEWISH MAN:

I'm on the tenant selection committee. The New York City Housing Authority requires us to take 75 percent white and 25 percent others. I have never once been sent an application to interview who is Caucasian, Indian, Jewish, Gay or Lesbian. This place will become 100 percent Black, racial tension in the area will increase, and we'll become crime infested like the South Bronx. What we were afraid of 20 years ago and made to appear like the KKK, has unfortunately come to pass...and...like everywhere else that this has happened, no one will hear our cries.

POLICE CHIEF:

We're listening and hearing.

JEWISH MAN:

But what will you do? We go home and...you go home. Danger lurks in our hallways, does it inn yours?
SILENCE.

MAYOR:

I guarantee you that heads will roll. This situation will not be tolerated.

. . .

LATER: JEWISH PEOPLE GOING TO THEIR APARTMENTS, TERRIFIED AND WATCHFUL IN THE HALLWAYS, AND CLOSING THER DOOR, ONCE THEY'VE RUSHED INSIDE, WITH A SIGH OF RELIEF, AND BOLTING, SEVERAL LOCKS. A KNOCK IS HEARD AT ONE OF THE DOORS. A NEIGHBOR IS OUTSIDE WITH A PURSE.

NEIGHBOR:

It's Mel. Your wife left her purse.

NO REPLY. HE KEEPS KNOCKING AND KNOCKING. MEL IS INSIDE BUT IS AFRIAD TO OPEN THE DOOR AS KNOCKING CONTINUES.

Residents say that the 108th St. Project has become dangerous.

At City Hall hearings on the Forest Hills Project in 1972, police had to separate opponents and proponents of the developement.

Scene 8

FLASHBACKS:

1970:

KAHANE:
(NARRATING)

The new housing quotas will dispossess the so-called "rich" Jew. The Jewish poor will get poorer...ill fed...ill clothed and now, very ill housed. HUD, the government's Housing and Urban Development Program will not be housing us. But we will fight on, no matter what.

1990: WILLIAMSBURG

HASID:
(NARRATING)

For the past 20 years, housing restrictions were instituted in deference to Black and Hispanic applicants to "even the score" in their favor and the Hasidim were ignored and disenfranchised, though nearly half of the Jewish population of Williamsburg lives at or below the poverty level.

1993: BLACK AND HISPANIC PROTESTORS MARCHING IN FRONT OF A SIGN THAT SAYS, "BARRY HOUSING PROJECT."

THEY CARRY POSTERS THAT SAY, "HASIDS OUT. BLACK AND LATINOS IN."

HASID:
(TO LATINO)
65 percent of us were displaced to build this place. We're supposed to get priority and we're not even getting that!

LATINO:

Our goal is to make sure you Jew get nothing!

(CHANTING WITH OTHERS)

Kikes out! Jews out! Hasids out!

HASID:

With the exception of us, <u>whites</u> are out. Fled from here like the plague was after them. We're here due to our high birth rate and our dependence on our religious institutions. They're our life. We built them. They're all here. We're not asking for much, just 12 apartments out of 150!

LATINO:

You got plenty money. Move to park avenue. You don't have to live here. We do! C'mon. get off it. We the ones got nuthin'.

HASID:

They had Legal Services led by Jews fighting for them, 10 million from the Federal Government, hundreds of thousands in state dollars, discrimination suits funded by Federal HUD grants, it's research done by nothing...got nothing. So many restrictions put in our path, we stopped applying.

Scene 9

FLASHBACK: 1992

NAME ON SCREEN: KHALLID MUHAMMAD

MUHAMMAD:

The Jewish community in America was the primary financier of the slave trade. You just giving us back the money you owe us. Jews are the bloodsuckers of the Black community.

1996: WILLIAMSBURG

HASIDIC WOMAN:
(TO HUSBAND)

I'm pregnant, Moishe, with twins.

HUSBAND:

*Nu, God's will.

HASIDIC WOMAN ENTERS A BUILDING, ON WHICH IS ENGRAVED, "NEW YORK HOUSING AUTHORITY." SHE ENTERS OFFICE MARKED "MISS PECK" AND SITS DOWN. A LINE FORMS BEHIND HER. PECK IS A BLACK WOMAN WHOSE FACE LOOKS LIKE A PIECE OF ICE.

HASIDIC WOMAN:
(BEGGING)

Please, we already have 4 children, a two-room apartment, a curtain dividing one room, so we call it two. Our oldest is 5 years old. She's sleeping in the bathtub.

PECK:
(ARROGANTLY)

Sorry. Next!

HASIDIC WOMAN RISES TO LEAVE.

HASIDIC WOMAN:
(PLEADING)

Where will I find a place for the twins?

PECK DISMISSES HER WITH A WAVE OF THE HAND. HASIDIC WOMAN TURNS TO PECK ONCE AGAIN, WITH PLEADING EYES. IT IS TO NO AVAIL. A COLD HAND DISMISSES HER AGAIN.

THE NEXT WOMAN ON LINE IS A LATINA. SHE CANNOT SPEAK ENGLISH. SHE HANDS PECK A PIECE OF PAPER. THE LATINA IS PREGNANT. PECK CALLS HER ASSISTANT ON THE PHONE. SHE SMILES AT THE WOMAN.

PECK:

I need help.

ASSISTANT ENTERS.

PECK:
(TO ASSISTANT)

Tell her we have one bedroom for her family in the project.

ASSISTANT TRANSLATES. THE WOMAN SPEAKS TO THE ASSISTANT IN SPANISH. ASSISTANT TRANSLATES TO PECK.

ASSISTANT:

She says she'll need another bedroom for her first baby. It's her dream.

> PECK:
> (SMILING)

We'll see what we can do.

THE ASSISTANT TRANSLATES. THE WOMAN IS BEAMING.

A MONTH LATER: IN THE HOSPITAL. A NURSE IS TALKING TO THE HASIDIC WOMAN.

> HASIDIC WOMAN:
> (TO NURSE)

Both of them…miscarriage?

NURSE SADLY NODS, "YES." THE HASIDIC WOMAN SOBS. HER HUSBAND COMES IN. THE NURSE LEAVES. SHE MEETS ANOTHER NURSE IN THE HALLWAY.

> NURSE:
> (TO OTHER NURSE)

I don't know why she's so upset. Too many children already.

> OTHER NURSE:

No matter; a tragedy for them when they miscarry.

SHE POINTS TO A ROOM ACROSS THE HALL.

> HASIDIC WOMAN:
> (HEARD TALKING TO HUSBAND)

Next year, God willing, we'll have what we lost, two beautiful twins.

Scene 10

FLASHBACK: CROWN HEIGHTS, 1991

SHARPTON:

Get the diamond merchants outta here!

FLASHBACK: 1992

KHALLID MUHAMMAD:

They drive their tractor-trailers full of money to their neighborhoods and our neighborhoods ger poorer and their neighborhoods get richer and richer.

1996:

A SIGN ON A DOOR IN AN OFFICE BUILDING SAYS, "METROPOLITAN COUNCIL FOR JEWISH POVERTY." A HASID, VERY SKINNY, UNKEMPT, RAGGEDY ENTERS, HE SPEAKS WITH AN ACCENT.

MAN:
(TO PERSON AT DESK)

I just want to be warm for a while, then I'll go.

SOCIAL WORKER:

You don't want to go home?

MAN:

I live in a cardboard box.

SOCIAL WORKER:

No family?

MAN:

Holocaust survivors living in a shelter. They just couldn't...couldn't...
HE BREAKS DOWN SOBBING.

SOCIAL WORKER:
(PUTS ON COMFORTING HAND ON HIS SHOULDER)

We're here to keep you warm from now on...and your family.

MAN LOOKS TO HIM WITH GRATITUDE. ANOTHER MAN ENTERS.

SOCIAL WORKER:
(TO HASID)

You'll go with our volunteer, Mr. Epstein. He'll get you a winter coat, then a place to stay.

(TO MR EPSTEIN)

You'll tell the other volunteer to take some food to Mr. Stein and his family.

LATER: METROPOLITAN COUNCIL VOLUNTEER IS VISITING THE STEIN HOME WITH A BAG OF GROCERIES. A MAN GREETS HER AT THE DOOR WITH HIS THREE YOUNG CHILDREN. THEIR MOTHER IS IN BED, SICK.

VOLUNTEER:

I'm so sorry I'm late, Mr. Stein.

Scene 10

THE CHILDREN SURROUND THE VOLUNTEER LOVINGLY. SHE PUTS CONTENTS OF BAG (BREAD, FRUIT, ETC.) ON TABLE.

(татo CHILDREN)

And a lollipop each.

THEY EAGERLY GRAB POPS.

Minnie any better?

MAN:
(TO VOLUNTEER)

My wife is sleeping. She'll be so upset she missed you.

VOLUNTEER:

I have some medicine for her.

THE VOLUNTEER GIVES HIM MEDICINE.

MAN:

And I have...something. Here's ten dollars. I'll give you more as soon as I can. We must give, even as we receive. So many people here without a mattress, a meal, a coat, or a safe place to live.

VOLUNTEER:

Our nightmare is those we can't find or those who can't find us.

MAN:

I'm lucky.

MET COUNCIL SOCIAL WORKER:
(NARRATING)

More than 180,000 of us are at poverty level, another hundred thousand at near poverty. More than 5,000 applications were received for a residence for our senior citizens. Only 180 poor elderlies won the lottery to get in.

ELDERLY LADY:

We were lucky.

Scene 11

FLASHBACK: 1987:

KAHANE:
(TO CROWD)

There is trouble in Crown Heights, real social and religious hatred. Jews are regularly terrorized, mugged, and robbed, while the social Workers and Sociologists, the Community Relations people and well-groomed and manicured Establishment types, rush to soothe and repeat their usual nonsense before running back to Manhattan's East Side, or Westchester's or Long Island's gilded ghettoes. An urgent appeal to Crown Heights...have a powerful defense patrol or get out and go home to your Land!

MAN:
(SHOUTING)

The police are our <u>defense</u>, and this is our <u>land</u>!

CROWN HEIGHTS: APRIL 1996:

WOMAN AND HER EIGHT CHILDREN SITTING IN A ROOM CRAMPED WITH BOXES, TALKING TO A REPORTER. THERE IS A PICTURE OF HER HUSBAND AND FAMILY ON THE WALL. (SEE PICTURE ON FOLLOWING PAGE) REPORTER TAKES OUT CAMERA.

Scene 11   497

REPORTER:
(WHO SHOUTED AT KAHANE)

Mrs. Seldowitz, my paper would like a picture of you and the children. So, if you don't mind...

SHE AND CHILDREN STAND STILL WHILE HE SNAPS PICTURE. MRS. SELDOWITZ IS A VERY GENTLE WOMAN.

MRS. SELDOWITZ:

I never want to see that picture. I don't want my husband to come back here. I want to leave here and not be reminded...

HER VOICE CHOKING TO KEEP BACK TEARS, SHE CANNOT GO ON.

A CHILD POINTS PROUDLY TO THE PICTURE ON THE WALL.

CHILD:

That's Tottie!

FLASHBACK: FEBRUARY 1996:

MRS. SELDOWITZ IS IN THE BACK BEDROOM WITH HER TWO YOUNGEST CHILDREN. IT IS MORNING. THE DOOR IS OPEN FOR THE CHILDREN TO BE GOING OFF TO SCHOOL.

DEREK WILLIAMS, A BLACK, AGE 29 SLIDES IN WHILE SHLOME, THE HUSBAND IS SITTING ON THE COUCH. WE HEAR MRS. SELDOWITZ SHOUTING TO THE CHILDREN FROM THE BEDROOM.

In happier times: Shlome Seldowitz with his wife Sara and family. *Richard Levine*

MRS. SELDOWITZ:

Hurry, you'll be late for school!

SHLOME:
(TO WILLIAMS)

I think you may have the wrong house.

BLACK MAN TURNS AS IF TO LEAVE, THEN LEAPS ON SHLOME, HITTING HIM REPEATEDLY, BLACK MAN THEN GRABS HIS WALLET AND LOOKS INSIDE. HE FLINGS IT BACK.

WILLIAMS:

Nothing but a driver's license!

THE BLACK MAN FLEES.

LATER:

POLICEMAN:
(TO MRS. SELDOWITZ)

Tell me all you can about the man who did this. What he looked like, what he was wearing, whatever.

MRS. SELDOWITZ:

I was way in the back, the children and I shouting. It all happened so fast. By the time I came in here, Shlome's head was...

(SHE LETS OUT AN ANGUISHED CRY)

Why couldn't it be me?! If only...if only I did something!

POLICEMAN:

Nothing you could have done, Mrs. Seldowitz. I'm afraid pleading, reasoning, crying and begging, which are your only weapons, would only have meant more victims...you...your children. Did your husband do something to protect himself, scratch the man's face, maybe? We'd have something to go on.

MRS. SELDOWITZ:
(SHAKING HER HEAD "NO")

Shlome is a very gentle man.

BACK TO PRESENT:

REPORTER AGAIN INTERVIEWING MRS. SELDOWITZ.

. . .

TWO WEEKS LATER:

IN HER APARTMENT, A HAND LETTERED, "WELCOME HOME TOTTY" SIGN HANGS OVER THE DOOR.

> REPORTER:
> (POINTING TO IT)

He'll like that.

> MRS. SELDOWITZ:

Since I saw you, he's been in the hospital and a Convalescent Home. He suffered a concussion, a broken arm, and many cuts. He still has swelling on the brain, dizziness, memory loss, nausea, memory lapses and slurred speech. He's not himself. It's even hard for him to walk. It's very frustrating for him. He wants to be home with us, but this apartment has no space for Shlome's wheelchair, walker, and therapy with a visiting nurse. So now, he's in a room in his parent's apartment. He works at a computer, trying to salvage his new business, which has developed 36 Hebrew typefaces for reprinting the Talmud and other texts. He rests. He prays. He prays for hours. We have no car, so we talk for hours on the phone several times a day. And he learns, reviewing now, the writings of Maimonides. But he doesn't want to meet visitors in person or talk to them on the phone, yet. Now, our door is always locked. It was open then because the children were leaving for school. And the *mezuzah was found to be defective for some reason, so we replaced it immediately, of course. We moved here two weeks ago. It's two blocks away from where we were. We were left with no income, so some of our agencies are helping us.

> REPORTER:

Makes you wonder sometimes about having faith in God. I do.

> MRS. SELDOWITZ:

Hasidim believe everything that happens is for the good. As for me, it's part of my lot of life. The children are still frightened. It's Passover. Shlome will be here for the first night. They're very excited. The chair at the head of the table is empty. It will not be, for the first time. But our Seder night will be different from most holiday nights. No guests. They would exhaust him. We always had lots of guests. Shlome loved guests. He might not be able to concentrate on the entire Haggadah, but we're still happy that he'll be here physically.

> REPORTER:

I'm afraid I have to go now.

REPORTER RUSHES OUT. HE LEANS AGAINST A WALL AND WIPES THE TEARS FROM HIS EYES.

FLASHBACK: REPORTER REMEMBERS KAHANE'S SPEECH.

KAHANE:

If our neighborhoods are prey to muggers, rapists, and robbers, because it's well known we have no guns, let it be changed. If we are victims of hoodlums and hooligans because we are not armed and dangerous, let it be different. Laughing at our timidity and confidently beating us for it...let it be...Every Jew a .22!

REPORTER:
(THINKING ALOUD)

If all the Shlomes would defend themselves...they'd be studying Maimonides in peace. Kahane was right.

FLASHBACK: 1991

JDL GROUP:
(CHANTING)

Never again! Never again! Never again!

BACK TO PRESENT:

HASIDIC RABBI:
(SADLY)

Again, Kahane was right. "Every Jew a .22!"

Scene 12

ON SCREEN: GLENWOOD HOUSES: A POOR HOUSING COMPLEX IN BROOKLYN.

AN 8-YEAR-OLD BOY, WEARING A YARMULKE, COMES OUT TO PLAY IN FRONT OF ONE OF THE BUILDINGS. THREE YOUNG BLACKS APPROACH. THEY ARE ALL IN THEIR TEENS.

> BLACK BOY:
> (TO JEWISH BOY)

Get out of here, you Jew. We were playing here before you.

HE KNOCKS THE YARMULKE FROM HIS HEAD. THE JEWISH BOY'S PARENTS COME OUT.

> MOTHER:
> (TO BLACKS)

What's wrong? My boy only wants to play with you.

HER SON, PETRIFIED, NODS HIS HEAD.

> MOTHER:
> (TO HER SON)

Now, shake hands.

HER SON THRUSTS OUT HIS HAND TO SHAKE HANDS WITH THE BLACK, WHO OFFERED A LIMP HAND.

MOTHER:

Ah...now be friends. Play nice.

BLACKS LEAVE AND MOTHER AND SON RETURN TO THEIR APARTMENT.

TEN MINUTES LATER: TWENTY BLACK YOUTHS COME TO THE BUILDING LOOKING FOR THE FAMILY.

BLACKS:
(SHOUTING)

Come down, or we're coming to get you!

MOTHER COMES DOWN TO THE LOBBY. THEY MEET HER AND BEAT HER UNCONSCIOUS. A MAN RUSHES OUT TO HELP HER AND HE IS ATTACKED.

BLACK ATTACKER

Jew! Kike! Bastard!

ANOTHER BLACK:

Give it to him!

LATER: MAN IN HOSPITAL. ADMITTING CLERK IS INTERVIEWING MOTHER.

CLERK:
(TO MOTHER)

Relation to you?

MOTHER:

My brother.

CLERK:

Occupation?

MOTHER:

Shoemaker.

CLERK:

Where was he born?

MOTHER:

Russia.

CLERK:

How long is he here?

MOTHER:

Two months.

LATER:

NURSE:
(TO MOTHER)

His left eye socket is broken, and two ribs fractured.

MOTHER:

He has a little one-man business. He must go home soon. He speaks very little English and depends on what he earns each day.

NURSE:

He'll have to close it for a while.

MOTHER:

The family will starve. They brought very little money from the Soviet Union. Please, can't you…

NURSE WALKING AWAY.

IN POLICE PRECINCT:

SERGEANT:
(TO POLICEMAN)

I see that one of the mob in Glenwood was arrested. Good. Bias crime, I guess.

POLICEMAN:

Not at all!

SERGEANT:
(TO POLICEMAN)

A reporter's finally come out with the truth about all this. We can't pretend anymore that we don't know that the attackers are Black, and the victims are white.

POLICEMAN:

Well, the papers are pretending it's not so, the victims are pretending they can just take it and it'll disappear, why can't we pretend...or they'll call us "racists."

SERGEANT:

Whites'll get good and mad, you'll see. They'll be some action around here.

MOTHER:
(TO CHILD)

I found your yarmulke in the drawer.

BOY:
(TREMBLING)

I'm scared, Mommy.

(HE LOOKS LONGINGLY OUT THE WINDOW.)

I'll never go out to play with my yarmulke and I don't want to go out at all. My friends are staying inside, too. Too scared to come out and they hid their yarmulkes.

MOTHER:

Not even in the house, you'll wear it?

BOY:

If I go out and forget...and they see it...

THE BOY IS NEAR TEARS. MOTHERS PUTS YARMULKE BACK IN DRAWER.

Scene 13

OLD RABBI ON PHONE.

RABBI:
(TO POLICEMAN)

Officer, this is Rabbi Brienda. I live in apartment that is above my small synagogue with about 40 members. Last night, two Black youths came in and hit me, so I fell down and hurt my hip and the few dollars I managed to save were stolen.

POLICEMAN:

Didn't I tell you before to get a burglar alarm system?

RABBI:

The congregation can't raise the money.

LATER: DETECTIVE INTERVIEWING ONE OF THE BLACK MUGGERS, AGE 16.

DETECTIVE:

Housing police saw you coming out of Rabbi Brienda's place. He insists it's a bias crime. We still think you're just hoods hittin' what's around.

MUGGER:

We planned it that way. It's a pact we made. Only white people, 'cause they're easy ones. Get away with it 'cause nobody cares. Whites don't do nuthin', especially them old Jews.

DETECTIVE:

Suppose it was the other way around. Whitey hit each one of your grandmothers.

MUGGER:

Burn, baby, burn.

BLACK TEENAGERS ARE STANDING BEHIND A BUILDING ON ONE CORNER. ANOTHER GROUP OF BLACK TEENAGERS IS WAITING OUTSIDE A SYNAGOGUE. A GROUP OF OLD LADIES COMES OUT OF THE APARTMENT BUILDING. THE TEENAGERS GRAB THE WOMEN AROUND THE NECK FROM BEHIND, PUNCH THEM AND THROW THEM TO THE GROUND.

A FEW HOURS LATER: OLD LADIES COMING OUT OF THE SYNAGOGUE ARE ALSO ATTACKED IN THE SAME WAY.

A MONTH LATER:

NEWSPAPER ARTICLE ON SCREEN:

"THERE HAS BEEN A MONTH-LONG SPREE IN GLENWOOD HOUSES OF YOUNG TEENAGERS MUGGING OLDSTERS."

DETECTIVE:
(READING ARTICLE)

Still calling these bums nice names. "Teenagers' makes them seem like a ball club and still no mention that they're Black. If no one is yelling "Bias crime," why should we? I can hear the press now, screaming "Racist." It should die down soon as these bums find another way to amuse themselves.

OLD WOMAN IN HOSPITAL.

DOCTOR:
(TALKING TO NURSE)

Looks like the attacks are growing more violent at Glenwood. This poor soul is in critical condition, her hip broken...

HE EXAMINES X-RAYS.

Her skull was shattered while they were grabbing her handbag, which, I think, contained the heavy sum of two dollars and three cents.

NURSE:

It wasn't too wise of her to resist. We tell them not to.

DOCTOR:

Even the Planarium worm is known to put up a little struggle when it's attacked. It has some pride.

MAN:
(ON PHONE WITH DOCTOR)

Officer, I'm living in Glenwood. The Housing Police can't protect us. We need a real policeman who knows what to do.

POLICEMAN:

You've called before and we told you we can't send anybody down there. We don't have enough men.

FLASHBACK:

KAHANE:
(NARRATING)

Where the police don't have enough men, we have to be men.

Scene 14

1997:

BLACK ORATOR:
(TO AUDIENCE)

We all know who controls us in Crown Heights, don't we? Jews, that's who. Jew power...that's what!

AUDIENCE ROARS IT'S APPROVAL.

FLASHBACK: 1991:

NAME ON SCREEN: ERIC BREINDEL.

ERIC BREINDEL:

If the victim in this case would have been Black, and he'd been pursued by a mob of 20 or more Whites yelling, "Get the Blacks," there's no chance whatsoever that only one person would have been arrested, no chance that the Jew would have been acquitted on each and every count, and no chance that the Federal authorities wouldn't have been called immediately to Crown Heights to seek justice for the victim of a racial killing by a mob. So much for Jewish power, a people now rendered weak and dismissible.

BACK TO PRESENT:

NEWS STORY ON SCREEN:

"After six years, a Federal civil rights case was made against Lemrick Nelson. He received a 19-year sentence, which is being appealed. The others involved in the murder are still at large and no investigation was or will be made.

Scene 15

NEWSPAPER ARTICLE ON SCREEN:

"Intellectuals will be holding a meeting at Hunter College today to discuss crime. We expect, at last, a rational, calm approach and analysis, a liberal, rather than an extremist position on the issues. Laymen, Black and White will also be on the podium airing their views.

FOLLOWING DAY: HUNTER COLLEGE AUDITORIUM. MASTER OF CEREMONIES IS SPEAKING.

MASTER OF CEREMONIES:

With us today are Dr. Ruth Wisse, Professor of Yiddish and Literature at Harvard University, Ann Rolphe, a well-known author and liberal, and Elliot Abrams, Conservative. Also, Mr. Sherman, Democratic Party, Mrs. Jones, Liberal, Mr. Travis, Republican, and Mr. Goldstein, a Survivor.

EACH ONE RISES AS THEY ARE INTRODUCED. SHERMAN, JONES AND TRAVIS ARE BLACKS. THE OTHERS ARE WHITES.

WISSE:

Unlike other minority groups who confront the established order, Jews are always adjusting to power. They don't rock the boat when there are critical issues to be faced. Jewish leaders cringed when Rabbi Kahane threatened and confronted. Most of them opted for ADL, not JDL. Very few shed a tear when he was murdered or cared when his assassin was freed. Liberal Jews are still embarrassed by anyone who stands up for them in an assertive, effective, confrontational way.

BLACK MAN ON PODIUM:

He blamed us for crime. We all know who is to blame for our crime rate...White America. And what is the Whites rulers planning to do? More police. Jails, tyranny and neglect!

ANOTHER BLACK MAN ON PODIUM:

All we do is search for ways to avoid using the words, "Personal Responsibility."

BLACK WOMAN ON THE PODIUM:
(SHOUTING AT ABOVE BLACK MAN)

We don't make the guns or grow the cocoa!

SECOND BLACK MAN ON PODIUM:

Who pulls the trigger? Who smokes the crack? Or is all this hootin' and hollerin' to drown out those questions from even bein' asked in your heads?

FIRST BLACK MAN:

We need massive Federal aid!

SECOND BLACK MAN:

Come close to accusin' America of genocide, then turn around and beg for help. For neglecting our homes, schools and children, Black America is payin' a heavy price. Even white Liberals are gettin' disgusted with all this pap we keep repeatin'.

JEW IN AUDIENCE:
(SHOUTING)

I'm a Jewish Liberal and proud of it! The answers are education, jobs, tolerance and understanding! That's what I thought we'd be talking about...not this! I'm shocked!

ELLIOT ABRAMS:

The reality of Black anti-Semitism amazingly escapes the notice of most Jews. Liberal politics have, unfortunately, triumphed over your self-interest.

ANN ROLPHE:

With dealers and armed gang members, I say, "We need martial law." Bring in the army and clean them out. When a man has his hand on your throat, you don't read him constitutional rights. Many might die in such a war, but there would be a clear choice…be a dead thug or live student, wage earner, father, and husband.

JEWISH LIBERAL:
(SHOUTING)

The innocent will die with the guilty…Blacks and Jews…and we'll have Fascism in the country…or anarchy…the Wild West all over again…where all life is cheap…and our rulers are not those who are kind or smart, but those are fast on the draw!

JEW ON PODIUM:

I grew up among Holocaust survivors who told me of piles of corpses, and you'd never see a rifle sticking up out of them. Jews did not carry guns to the gas chambers, unfortunately. In the bible, the Jews of Persia killed 30,000 attackers to save themselves. We deserve the same right today.

AUDIENCE CHEERS HIM.

FLASHBACK:

FARRAKHAN:
(SHOUTING TO CROWD)

Hitler was a great man. The Jews deserved the Holocaust and if they continue to oppose me, they will, once again, be exterminated!

CHEERS AND APPLAUSE.

FARRAKHAN

"JUDAISM IS A GUTTER RELIGION"

Scene 16

JULY 1991:

MAN ON RADIO:

The Nation of Islam speaks...and repeats the truth. If you want to know it, we must repeat...repeat...repeat..." "Judaism is a gutter religion...tryin' to put us there..." And we're tellin' them... "We're not goin'."

BOROUGH PARK, BROOKLYN. MORNING. A HASIDIC ELDERLY COUPLE IN THEIR KITCHEN. SHE IS PRAYING. THEN, WHEN SHE FINISHES, SHE IS SEARCHING FOR A PAPER.

WOMAN:

I can't find the list. What will I do without it?

MAN:

That list is getting longer and longer.

WOMAN:

You worry too much. I'll rest when I get to the bungalow. So peaceful there.

SHE PULLS THE LIST OUT OF HIS POCKET.

MAN:

All those orphans need help?

> **VOICE OF NOI:**

Judaism is a gutter religion. Was, is and will always be.

> **WOMAN:**
> (CHECKING LIST)

Here's one that needs money for a nice wedding. Her parents passed away when she was 17 and left 10 children. She'll need food, clothing...

SHE CHECKS THE LIST AFTER SHE READS EACH ITEM.

> **MAN:**
> (TEASING HER GOOD NATUREDLY)

A down payment on a house...

> **WOMAN:**
> (REPEATS WHILE SHE ADDS TO THE LIST)

...A down payment on a house.

(SHE CHECKS THE LIST)

When I started the orphan's fund, I didn't think I could do all this, but people have been so generous...beyond my wildest dreams. I even have some to give the yeshivas so the children can learn the Torah, and as soon as I get some more money, I help the orphans with rent and Bar Mitzvahs.

LATER IN TEMPLE:

RABBI IS INTONING THE KADDISH (THE MOURNING PRAYER) WITH CONGREGANTS WHO HAVE LOST DEAR ONES RECENTLY. OF THOSE WHO ARE STANDING, THERE ARE MORE CHILDREN THAN ADULTS. AFTER KADDISH, RABBI SAYS:

> **RABBI:**

Once, there were more adults than children mourning with us. Now, there are more children who are here crying for their parents. It is heartbreaking.

MAN IS SITTING IN AN AISLE SEAT. A YOUNG BOY IS LOOKING FOR A SEAT. MAN PUTS HIM ON HIS LAP.

> **MAN IN NEXT SEAT:**

You're complaining always about pain in your legs. This won't help. Every *Shabbos, another boy sitting on them and you're hobbling out.

MAN:

He's tired.

MAN IN NEXT SEAT:
(SKEPTICAL)

Tell me another story.

MAN:

Maybe's he an orphan, so he needs, for a little while, a father. His pain is always worse than mine. Mine, it goes away. Not his. My son Benjamin, I always put on my lap. So here, I put somebody else's. I think He wants me to.

THE MAN LOOKS TO HEAVEN.

MAN IN NEXT SEAT:
(EXTENDS HIS ARMS TO BOY)

Give him to me.

HE PUTS THE BOY ON HIS LAP.

VOICE OF NATION OF ISLAM:

Repeat: "Judaism is a gutter religion." Repeat after me and keep repeating...'til I know you know what I know...robbin' from us...then prayin'...that's the Jew gutter. Them prayers ain't going to Heaven, they're going into the gutter... where they belong!

FOLLOWING DAY:

9AM: WOMAN IS PREPARING LUNCH FOR MAN BEFORE LEAVING. THEN, SHE PUTS IT IN THE REFRIGERATOR.

WOMAN:
(TO MAN)

I want to see an empty plate when I get home.

SHE RETURNS AT 6PM AND OPENS THE REFRIGERATOR. HIS LUNCH IS STILL THERE. SHE SITS DOWN AT THE TABLE. HE TAKES OUT HIS LUNCH AND EATS IT.

FOLLOWING DAY:

A VAN FULL OF PEOPLE IS TRAVELING ON A COUNTRY ROAD AND TURNS AT A SIGN THAT SAYS, "KIAMESHA LAKE." IT STOPS AT A BUNGALOW AND COUPLE GOES IN. IT IS GROWING DARK. SHE IS UNPACKING. HER PURSE IS ON THE TABLE.

AN HOUR LATER: IT IS DARK. THERE IS A KNOCK ON THE DOOR. SHE OPENS IT. A BLACK MAN ENTERS.

> ANTHONY BURTON:
> (AGE 22)
> (TO WOMAN)

Need some work done?

HE LOOKS SEARCHINGLY AROUND ROOM. MAN IS SITTING NEARBY ON SOFA.

> WOMAN:
> (CAUTIOUS)

So nice of you to come by and ask...but no.

SHE CAN SEE OUT THE WINDOW.

Oh, my neighbor is coming.

BURTON RUNS OUT THE DOOR. NEIGHBOR ENTERS. THE WOMEN HUG EACH OTHER.

> NEIGHBOR:

I know that man...Anthony...Anthony Burton. He lives a few blocks away from me in Crown Heights. He did work for me once and complained, said we Jews are his neighbors and God said a Jew should "love thy neighbor as thyself," and we don't do anything of that kind.

> WOMAN:

I'm afraid in the city, but here, I don't even lock my door. The bungalow is safer than Borough Park.

NEIGHBOR:
(ON HER WAY OUT)

See you tomorrow. Lock the door.

SHE LEAVES. WOMAN TRIES TO LOCK DOOR. THE LOCK IS NOT WORKING. SHE LEAVES THE DOOR OPEN AND SHUTS THE LIGHTS. A LONG PAUSE. BURTON TEARS INTO THE HOUSE. THE MAN AND WOMAN ARE BOTH SLEEPING ON THE SOFA. THEY AWAKE SUDDENLY, PANICKED. HE STRIKES THEM BOTH WITH A HAMMER. THE ROOM IS FULL OF BLOOD. BURTON GRABS PURSE FROM TABLE AND LEAVES.

FOLLOWING DAY:

NEWSPAPER HEADLINE ON SCREEN:

"ELDERLY HASIDIC COUPLE BRUTALLY MURDERED IN BUNGALOW. THOUSAND EXPECTED AT FUNERAL. CONDOLENCE CALLS HAVE BEEN COMNG IN FROM AS FAR AWAY AS RUSSIA. THE PAPIERS WERE HOLOCAUST SURVIVORS AND HAD LIVED IN BROWNSVILLE AND CROWN HEIGHTS BEFORE COMING TO BOROUGH PARK.

THEIR SON IS IN CHAPEL, COMPLETING HIS EULOGY.

SON:

In my parent's memory, the family has decided to perpetuate the good deeds for which they were known. Next week, there will be a graduation ceremony at the Yeshiva. No music, as my parents requested, because there are so many orphans. And...we will take care...as they did. Our tradition, our precious religion...demands that of us...and we demand it of ourselves.

BURTON'S VOICE:

You understandin' now what I'm sayin'? The Jew, his so-called religion.... the gutter! One and the same!

THE FOLLOWING WEEK:

SON AND HIS FRIEND ARE IN HIS PARENT'S HOME SORTING PAPERS.

>   FRIEND:

Here's your mother's list, Benjamin.

BENJAMIN TAKES THE LIST. THE LIST APPEARS ON SCREEN WITH THE TITLE "ORPHAN'S LIST." HE WRITES HIS NAME, "BENJAMIN," AT THE END OF THE LIST. A TEAR FALLS.

ON SCREEN:

> A MONTH LATER, AUGUST 1991:

>   WOMAN'S FRIEND IN BUNGALOW COLONY:
>   (WITH IRONY)

Crown Heights...neighbors...as in "love thy..."

A BLACK MOB IS SCREAMING.

>   MOB:

Jew blood! Jew blood! Give us some!

>   VOICE IN MOB:

Repeat! Repeat!

>   MOB:
>   (REPEATING)

Jew blood!

Eliezer and Miriam Papier, O.B.M.

Scene 17

1996:

ON SCREEN:

    AN AUDIENCE OF THOUSANDS LINE 47TH STREET IN NEW YORK, FROM SECOND TO FIRST AVENUE, AROUND THE CORNER FROM THE JEWISH ANTI-DEFAMATION LEAGUE HEADQUARTERS. NEW YORK NATION OF ISLAM LEADER, CONRAD MUHAMMAD, IS ADDRESSING THE AUDIENCE. ABOVE HIM IS A BANNER. IT READS, "MINISTER LOUIS FARRAKHAN SPEAKS, WORLD DAY OF ATONEMENT, UNITED NATIONS, OCTOBER 16, 1996."

                MUHAMMAD:

This event will be broadcast live to 11 cities and beamed by satellite to other countries.

FARRAKHAN SALESMAN ARE GOING THROUGH THE CROWD SELLING BOOKS TITLED, "THE UGLY TRUTH ABOUT THE ADL AND THE JEWISH ONSLAUGHT." THEY ARE WELL DRESSED, WEARING SUITS AND BOW TIES.

Scene 18

A FEW DAYS LATER:

A BLACK WOMAN IS IN HER PARLOR, WEARING A NURSE'S UNIFORM AND LISTENING TO THE RADIO. FARRAKHAN IS SPEAKING.

FARRAKHAN:

And now, the truth about the Jew...slave traders...bloodsuckers! Jew doctors invented and spread the AIDS virus to eliminate us. It's nuthin' but a gutter religion, a rich, rich gutter and we tendin' their babies, scrubbin' their floors and they exploiting us while they're prayin', enslavin' us while they're prayin', and callin' that...abomination...religion. I say, we leave the prayin' to us and the slavin' to them for a change, so they know what hypocrisy their Jew-da-ism really is. Oh yeah, and I forgot to mention...they don't like their hair, they don't have to sit around straightening or curling, just hit the old bank account for lotsa bucks and buy whatever hair you're in the mood for at that time.

WOMAN:

Right on, Brother!

SHE IS TALKING TO RADIO.

First day on the job. Hope I don't have to deal with those people. Who they kiddin'? their prayer shawls wrapped around all the money they steal from us. The little boxes on their heads are for secret communicatin' how to steal more.

All that mumblin' and shakin' they doin' is talking to their God...money. You think I'm gonna go to that Jew hospital healin' them, so they can hurt me? No way!

A DOCTOR IS TALKING TO A PATIENT IN HIS OFFICE. THE PATIENT IS ORTHODOX, A GENTLE MAN WITH A BEARD AND CURLS, A HASIDIC JEW.

DOCTOR:

Rav Horowitz, you have two years, maybe three.

RAV HOROWITZ:

Please don't tell anyone about my illness. They might become upset hearing the news.

DOCTOR:

You'll have to tell. We need to...amputate...your right arm.

RAV HOROWITZ:

Doctor, I am very stringent regarding our Laws of putting on Tefillin. It's written that a right-handed individual wraps the Tefillin around his left arm. But with me, there is a question whether I may also be left-handed, so it's written that I must be careful to put the Tefillin on my right arm as well.

(HE LETS OUT A CRY FROM THE DEPTH OF HIS SOUL.)

What will happen to my putting on Tefillin?

(CALMER)

It is surely a decree from Heaven. I accept it with love.

TWO YEARS LATER:

HOROWITZ IS NEAR THE OPERATING ROOM. A NURSE ENTERS. SHE IS THE FARRAKHAN SUPPORTER.

RAV HOROWITZ:
(TO NURSE)

You're new here. Welcome.

NURSE:
(HARSHLY)

Agency sent me. I'm new here, so I take what I can get.

HIS WIFE APPEARS HOLDING A *TALLIS (PRAYER SHAWL.) NURSE STARTS TO WHEEL HIM INTO THE OPERATING ROOM.

RAV HOROWITZ:
(TO NURSE)

Stop, please. I can't enter the operating room until I fulfill a good deed.

HE BECKONS TO HIS WIFE. SHE PUTS THE SHAWL AROUND HIM. THE NURSE IS STUNNED.

RAV HOROWITZ:
(TO WIFE)

Tefillin.

(SHE HANDS HIM TEFILLIN. HE WRAPS THEM AROUND BOTH HANDS SAYING "THE LAST TIME" AS HE WRAPS IT AROUND HIS HAND. HE TELLS HIS WIFE, "I MUST DO IT NOW.")

NURSE:

We have no time for that stuff. The doctor is waiting!

HE MUMBLES PRAYER. WIFE REMOVES SHAWL AND TAKES TEFILLIN.

NURSE:
(TO HOROWITZ)

That's pretty shrewd. Asking God for a favor thing now...when He's sure to be listening.

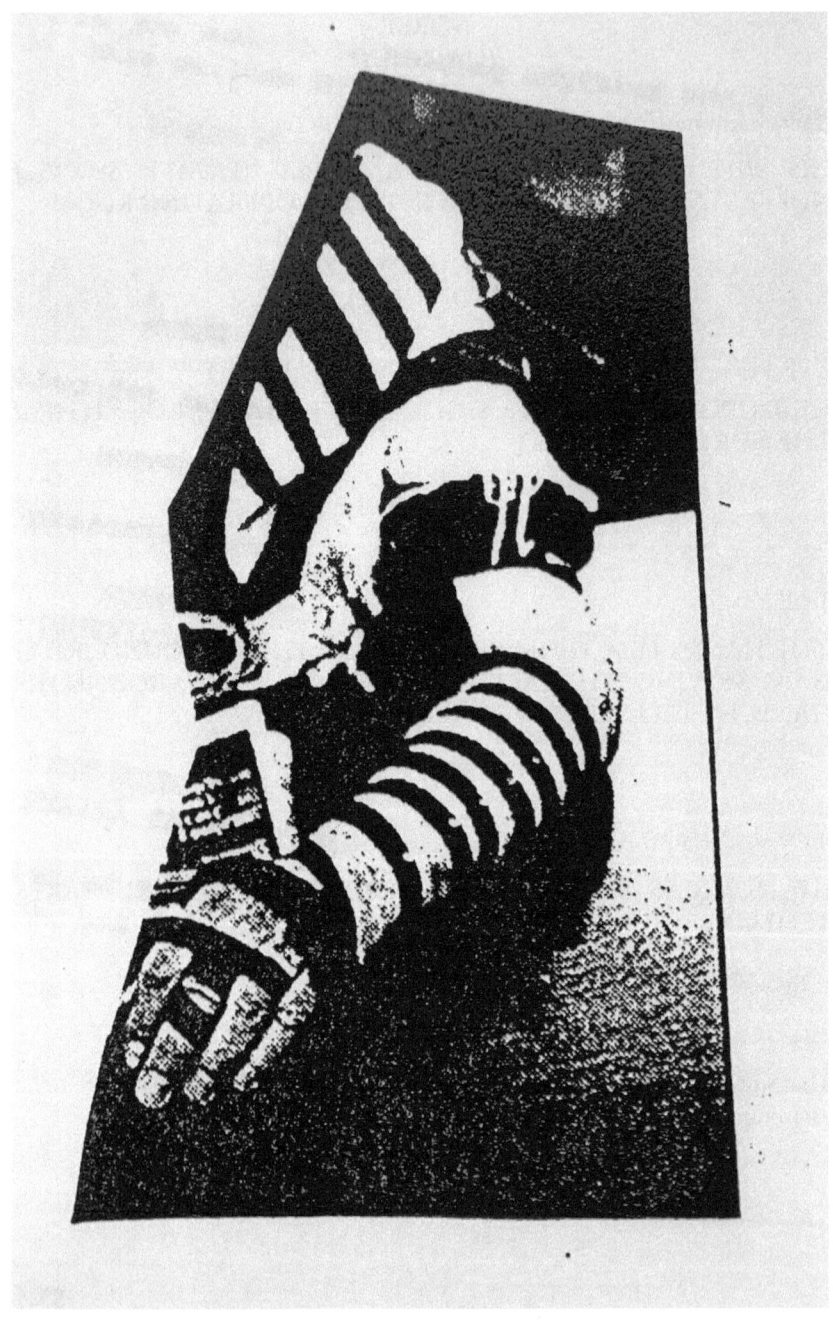

HOROWITZ:

I thanked Him for what he gave me already.

(HE REPEATS PRAYER IN ENGLISH)

Praised be thou, O Lord, King of the Universe, who has sanctified us by thy commandments, and has instructed to wrap ourselves in prayer shawls to remind us of all the commandments of Thy Torah.

NURSE IS STOPPED. SHE WHEELS HOROWITZ INTO THE OPERATING ROOM.

HOURS LATER:

THE OPERATION IS OVER. HOROWITZ IS IN HIS BED.

RAV HOROWITZ:
(TO HIS WIFE)

The *siddur. Give it to me.

NURSE ENTERS AS WIFE IS HANDING HIM THE BOOK.

NURSE:

Stop it! Not now! You're too weak to be holding anything and I don't want to be responsible! Make me lose my job!

HOROWITZ:

I'll say it from memory.

HE MUMBLES PRAYER IN HEBREW.

NURSE:

Don't tell me you not asking for sumthin' now.

HOROWITZ:

I'm giving...thanks...for preserving me.

NURSE:
(SUSPICIOUS)

Say it in English!

> HOROWITZ:
> (SAYING PRAYER IN ENGLISH)

Blessed art thou, O Lord, Ruler of the Universe, Who, in bestowing Good upon man, beyond his deserving, has dealt graciously with him.

NURSE IS STOPPED.

TWO YEARS LATER:

RAV HOROWITZ IN BED IN THE HOSPITAL. HIS WIFE IS BY HIS SIDE. BLACK NURSE ENTERS. SHE HEARS HIM TALKING TO HIS WIFE.

> RAV HOROWITZ:
> (TO HIS WIFE)

I don't see too well now, but...even if I'm blind, they have books where I can teach Torah with my fingers!

(WITH JOY)

You see, Hashem takes care.

NURSES PUTS JUICE ON TABLE AND LEAVES. IN HALLWAY, SHE TALKS TO HEAD NURSE, WHO IS BLACK.

> NURSE:

What's with them, anyhow?

(NURSE LOOKS TO HOROWITZ' ROOM)

That guy in there needs to have rabbis bringin' him food, Christian stuff not good enough for him. He talks words I don't understand. All this fuss over him and he's talkin' stuff behind all our backs. Never know what those people are up to!

> HEAD NURSE:

Telling me?!

> NURSE:

I gotta get goin' home.

HOROWITZ' WIFE PASSES. SHE SMILES AT NURSE. NURSE GLARES AT HER.

LATER:

NURSE AND WIFE ARE LEAVING THE HOSPITAL.

WIFE:
(TO NURSE, SYMPATHETICALLY)

You seem so angry. Not good for you to be mad always.

WIFE IS VERY RELIGIOUS WOMAN WHO WEARS A WIG. NURSE GRABS THE WIG FROM HER HEAD AND FLINGS IT ON THE SIDEWALK.

NURSE:

I can't afford store bought'n hair like you!

WIFE GASPS. SHE PUTS HER WIG ON AGAIN QUICKLY. SHE IS PALE AND TREMBLING.

WIFE:

It's my religion. I have to cut my hair.

SHE LOOKS AT HER WATCH.

I have to run now...my children...

NURSE:

Don't tell me there's no one like me around in your place to take the children off your hands when you feel like...doin' plenty of scrubbin' besides, while you're sittin' around chattin' on a phone!

WIFE HURRIES AWAY.

FOLLOWING DAY:

RAV HOROWITZ IS DYING. HIS RABBI AND WIFE ARE NEAR HIS BED.

RAV HOROWITZ:

                        (TO HIS WIFE)

Please see that our children are taught Torah and led along the path of service and fear of Hashem.

HE DIES.

FOLLOWING MORNING:

                        BLACK HEAD NURSE:
                            (TO NURSE)

You'll be passing by Horowitz' place on your way to the bus.

(SHE PICKS UP A SMALL PLASTIC BAG CONTAINING HIS THINGS)

Some stuff he left here.

SHE TAKES BAG GRUDGINGLY.

                            NURSE:

She'll have to come down and get it. I'm not obligin' her.

                          HEAD NURSE:

I don't care how you do it. Stuff left here takes up room we don't have. She lives on the first floor. You can rap on the window and leave it on the sidewalk, for all I care. I just don't want folks comin' round here sayin' we stole somethin', understand?

LATER:

NURSE ARRIVES AT A DILAPIDATED BUILDING, DARK AND DINGY HALLS WITH CRACKED WALLS. SHE KNOCKS ON DOOR. A 12-YEAR-OLD GIRL LETS HER IN TO A SMALL ROOM. THE ROOM IS FULL OF BEDS, A RICKETY TABLE, CLOTHES HANGING ON LINES, PILES OF CLOTHES SCATTERED AROUND ON THE FLOOR, AS THERE IS NO PLACE TO PUT THEM. THE WALLS ARE DINGY, IN DIRE NEED OF PAINTING. THE CEILING HAS HUGE YELLOW MARKS FROM LEAKS. THE PAINT IS PEELING, THE WALLS ARE BULGING, THE FLOOR HAS OLD LINOLEUM THAT IS CRACKED AND BLACK FROM WEAR. THE WINDOWS ARE

WITHOUT CURTAINS AND OLD SHADES WITH CRACKS THAT ARE YELLOWED WITH AGE. THE NURSE IS SHOCKED.

CHILD:

Please sit down. You want some tea?

NURSE:
(SHAKING HEAD NO)

Thank you.

WIFE IS SITTING ON ONE OF THE BEDS MOURNING.

CHILD:

I remember you from the hospital. My mother says you took good care of *Tottie.

NURSE:
(NEAR TEARS, THEN, FIRM AGAIN)

I do my job.

(SHE LOOKS AROUND AT THE BEDS AND CLOTHING)

You have brothers and sisters. Lots of 'em, I see.

CHILD:

Only 10. My friend has 13. They're all with grandma now.

(CRYING ON BABY IS HEARD)

Except…You wanna see?

(CHILD TAKES NURSE BY THE HAND TO THE BATHROOM. A BABY IS IN THE BATHTUB ON A MATTRESS)

She's two months old.

NURSE PICKS UP BABY AND HOLDS HER CLOSE. SHE STOPS CRYING. MOTHER COMES IN AND TAKES HER GENTLY FROM NURSE, WHO HELPS THEM BOTH BACK INTO BED.

THE NURSE BECOMES SLIGHTLY SUSPICIOUS AGAIN.

NURSE:

(TO CHILD)

By the way, what does...

(SHE MISPRONOUNCES THE WORDS, "TORAH" AND THE "A" IN HASHEM LIKE THE "A" IN CAT)

"TOREY" AND "HASHEM" mean?

CHILD:

Torah means our "Bible" and Hashem, means, means "God."

(SOBBING NOW AND LOOKING TO HEAVEN)

Why did you take Tottie?

NURSE HOLDS CHILD CLOSE AND SITS HER DOWN GENTLY ON BED, THEN SQUEEZES WIFE'S SHOULDER WARMLY AND LEAVES.

LATER:

IN TEMPLE. RABBI AT PODIUM, ABOUT TO SAY THE EULOGY. NURSE SLIPS IN QUIETLY, NOT TO DISTURB AND SITS DOWN.

RABBI:

Rav Horowitz passed away at the age of 38. He devoted his life to the teaching of Torah, despite crushing poverty. He accepted his lot with joy and perfect faith in the Almighty. His wife and 11 children, age two months to 12 years, lived in a tiny, cramped apartment consisting of three small rooms. He refused to borrow, even for necessities, concerned he might not be able to pay his debts. His short life, one of deep spiritual achievement, and of the greatness of Judaism. (SEE PICTURE FOLLOWING PAGE)

CANTOR SINGS YISKOR.

LATER: THE NURSE IS AT HOME. SHE TURNS ON RADIO.

VOICE ON RADIO:

This is the Voice of the Nation of Islam. Who is our enemy? The Jew. Who is tricky, conniving, and who knows him best? Our brother...Minister Farrakhan who's here with us today.

FARRAKHAN:

The Jew...

NURSE SNAPS OFF RADIO ANGRILY. THE GENTLE VOICE OF RAV HOROWITZ IS HEARD.

VOICE OF HOROWITZ:

I want to thank the Almighty for preserving me.

TEARS FALL FROM HER EYES.

ABSENT-MINDELY, SHE TURNS ON RADIO AGAIN.

VOICE ON RADIO:

Ladies and gentlemen, the voice of the Nation of Islam continues. "The Jew knows how to dupe and ensnare, to play saint to hide the devil, touch our hearts with kindness, so we trust and believe, then shatter and betray us when we're not looking.

SHE TURNS HIM OFF ANGRILY, THEN TURNS HIM ON AGAIN.

FARRAKHAN:

The Jewish Pilgrim fathers used to kidnap Black Africans more than any other ethnic or religious group in New World history.

SHE SNAPS OF RADIO AGAIN, THEN SNAPS IT ON AND OFF AGAIN...THEN ON AGAIN.

FARRAKHAN:

The immense wealth of the Jews was acquired by the brutal subjugation of Black Africans.

HER FACE HARDENS. SHE SHOUTS, "RIGHT ON" WEAKLY, WITHOUT THE FORMER SPIRIT.

A Young Tzaddik Torn From Our Midst

"Please don't tell anyone about my illness. They might become upset upon hearing the news."

Scene 19

1999:

KHALLID MUHAMMAD:

I want 100,000 Black youths to come to my rally in Harlem. They chose me by mandate to speak for them. If the Mayor says he won't accept a rally in Harlem, then we'll go to Eastern Parkway in Brooklyn. 10,000 Orthodox Jews living there, and we want to scare all the yarmulkes and rabbis to death. We want to take this right to the area that slapped us in the face by killin out little baby, Gavin Cato. We'd love to take a million Black people to Eastern Parkway and just kick it to these crackers, have a direct confrontation with the Jews who have misused and abused our people for so long.

RABBI:

You're some examples of an "abused people." A 140,000-dollar Rolls Royce you have your office in, a second Rolls you drive around in, 10,000 dollars a speech you get from universities, living in a million-dollar house with 5 bedrooms, 6 bathrooms, which will be adorned with expensive fabrics and statues.

FLASHBACK: 1993:

NEWSPAPER HEADLINE ON SCREEN:

"ON DECEMBER 7, 1993, COLIN FERGUSON, A BLACK, SHOT SIX PEOPLE AND INJURED 19 ON A CROWDED RUSH HOUR LONG ISLAND RAILROAD CAR."

BACK TO THE PRESENT:

MUHAMMAD:

I want to kill the enemy, not just say it...all the Whites. That's why I understand the mass murderer Colin Ferguson. I mean, goddamn it, we're supposed to have at least <u>one</u> Colin Ferguson. I would be embarrassed if we couldn't point to one Colin Ferguson that decided one day to catch some train or walk in some place and just kill every goddamn Cracker he saw.

RABBI:

I'd be humiliated if one of us ever talked like that. You're lucky you're here. Black crackers in Africa, where you come from, never treated you so well.

MUHAMMAD TEARS PICTURE OUT OF HIS POCKET.

MUHAMMAD:

This picture is from 1800...that's how long you people tormenting us!

(HE POINTS TO PEOPLE IN PICTURE)

A Black man hanging from a tree and these angry looking men in work clothes around him...they're not workers at all...they're rabbis.

RABBI:

I know that's rubbish, but when you showed that to Black youngsters in college...<u>they</u> didn't. when you had trouble with your own people, you fled to a fancy, white Jewish condominium and recuperated, playing tennis and swimming. No one as much as put a finger on you. If the situation were reversed, a Jew spewed the rot you've been mouthing, he would not live and hour in a Black building.

MUHAMMAD:

Can't help it if White people are stupid. In Harvard, when I took a course there, I met tough Blacks. We'd have meeting and White folks would come in from different corporations and Black folks would beat the hell out of them, but the White folks kept writing us big checks anyhow and left all kinds of donations. Throughout my life, Jews have helped me, but I can't bring myself to associate with the devil. The government killed my heroes, and the government is a representative of White folks and Jews. I have to hate all of them, especially the hook-nosed Jewish bloodsuckers. Jews are bloodsuckers who deserved Hitler. All the White people deserve him. I call for genocide of all whites.

RABBI:

I understand you've been on fundraising trips with Farrakhan where you become well acquainted with Libya's Qaddafi...who harbors terrorists and hates Jews and obliges you by killing them. You addressed the United Nations on behalf of Farrakhan, where you referred to them as, "Jew-nited Nations."

MUHAMMAD:

Not one of them protesting. Not one of them nations saying I was out of line.

RABBI:

Our leaders would never stoop to maligning or degrading, but yours, some in the high ranks of academe, accuse us of worldwide conspiracies, greediness, sneakiness. We would like to say these are ravings of crackpots, but, and I quote the eminent Black Professor, Henry Louis Gates Jr., "Sad to say, the statements come from respected people in the Black community, campus lecturers and community activists writing treatises, not mumbling slurs." I thank God he teaches at Harvard, not you. With a professor like him, the school deserves it's reputation. My faith is that voices like yours will "strut and fret their hour upon the stage and be heard no more."

Scene 20

1999:

REPORTER ON TV:

A militant Jewish organization is protesting the appearance of Dr. Leonard Jefferies, the anti-Semitic City College professor, and asking students to join them. He has spoken at the College of Staten Island before.

JDO STUDENT:
(TO DR SPRINGER)

The Jewish Defense Organization is calling for a protest outside your home to show our disdain for Dr. Jefferies, in the hope that you will cancel his appearance.

DR. SPRINGER:

I am aware of your militant and unruly tactics and advise you, here and now, that I will not respond to your threats.

STUDENT:
(TO SPRINGER)

Many of us disapprove of Jefferies' visit, particularly the 1,000-dollar speaking fee that we are paying.

ANOTHER STUDENT:
(TO JDO STUDENT)

But most of us call JDO tactics and embarrassment and bad publicity for Jews.

Scene 21

NEW YORK, 1999:

KHALLID MUHAMMAD IS ON THE PODIUM WITH OTHER BLACK SPEAKERS. BEHIND THEM IS BANNER THAT READS "MILLIONS YOUTH MARCH."

MASTER OF CEREMONIES:

Our next speaker is Sister Warrior Woman.

SHE APPEARS AND IS GREETED WITH ENTHUSIASTIC APPLAUSE. ALL SPEECHES OF FOLLOWING SPEAKERS ARE SIMILARLY GREETED.

SISTER WARRIOR WOMAN:

We have to be ready for the revolution. We have to start revolting against the snake...the Jew. And now, Brother Muhammad.

MUHAMMAD:

Stop asking me about the Jews being the bloodsucker of the Black nation, the no-good bastards. They are the bloodsuckers of the Black community.

MUHAMMAD STRETCHES HIS ARM OUT TO BROTHER ODEH AND SAYS HIS NAME. ODEH TAKES THE MICROPHONE.

ODEH:

You think Brother Khallid is wrong? You think Brother Khallid is mean? You better do every single thing this man demands your wicked white ass do, because you're gonna have to deal with me, and I ain't askin' no questions, and I ain't takin' no prisoners. I'm shootin' in the back. I'm shootin' in the face. I'm aimin' for the heart, and I ain't pleadin', and I ain't askin' for a soul to like it. Let me tell you about Jerry Springer. He's a big crooked-nose, bagel-eatin', wicked, penny pinching, ruthless, wicked slime, low-slime-of-the-earth ass Jew... and now...Malik Shabazz.

SHABAZZ:

Whether you call yourself a nigger, you call yourself a Cip, you call yourself a Blood, <u>you</u> are the chosen people of God. I don't care what the Jews say; you are the only people that have been in bondage for over 400 years. You are the <u>true</u> Chosen people of God, and it is not the so-called Jews... Cops say we have to stop at 4 o'clock. I say "Hell, no!"

TV REPORTER:

The Million Man Youth March was terminated at 4PM by orders of the Mayor, and firm police action.

SISKEL AND EBERT

"THE 'ARTS'... JEWS IN THE GUTTER"

Scene 22

1997:

SPEAKER ON PODIUM IN A HALL. AUDIENCE PRESENT. BANNER ON WALL SAYS, "JEWISH FEDERATION OF WEST HARTFORD, CONNECTICUT."

SPEAKER:

We are proud to introduce film critic Gene Siskel. He and his partner, Roger Ebert, of the TV film review program, "Siskel and Ebert," have been household names for 22 years. Their thumbs are celebrities. Thumbs up (SPEAKER SMILES), approval. Thumbs down...

(SPEAKER FROWNS AND SHAKES HEAD DISAPPROVINGLY)

SISKEL APPEARS. AUDIENCE ENTHUSIASTICALLY APPLAUDS.

SISKEL:

As you know, my topic for today is "JEWISH IMAGES IN FILMS," which receives a (POINTS DOWN WITH HIS THUMB) from me. I'll discuss clips from six films, which were all directed or written by Jews and show us in a derogatory way. The first clip, from the 1994 movie, "NORTH," directed by Rob Reiner, and featuring Jewish actor Jason Alexander of "Seinfeld." A pivotal scene shows several inspectors in a factory. One of the inspectors is a Hasidic Jew who is trapped in a soundproof glass cubicle and beats his chest with his fist for the "Al Chet" prayer, which is a confession of sins on our holiest day, Yom Kippur. On the wall behind him are a Torah scroll, which he regards as sacred, and a menorah that is lit on holy days. Both here are merely designs on the wallpaper.

AUDIENCE MEMBER:
(SHOUTING)

They're nuts and embarrassing. I don't care how they show them.

SISKEL:
(SHOCKED)

A confession of sins?! This is presented as humor?! This film pushed me over the wall, and I began to deal openly on my show with the problem of Jewish identity. The Hasid is the most religious Jew. If he's viewed as a joke, then so is our religion, and I won't have that.

ANOTHER AUDIENCE MEMBER:

I'd rather the world laugh with us than at us.

SISKEL:

In "City Slickers: The Legend of Curly's Gold," written by Billy Crystal, the Shallowitz brothers were stereotypical Jews, wimpy, scared, and trying to please the wrong people. And that's how Hollywood sees them.

AUDIENCE MEMBER:

What's wrong with showing us decent and kind?

SISKEL:

I have three brothers. They're not like that. Where's pride? I don't see it. Where's the Jewish Spike Lee?

AUDIENCE MEMBERS:

Steven Spielberg.

SISKEL:

I'm not looking for films about victims. I remember my father praying before he went to work every day. Where are those scenes in the movies?

AUDIENCE MEMBER:

I can see that in temple and I'm not interested. That's not what I go to movies for.

SISKEL:

In "The Simple Wish," a children's film with actor Martin Short, who plays a magician, Short bungles an attempt to turn a horse into a rabbit. Instead, it turns into a giant rabbi, complete with hat, tallis and beard. The magician tells the scared child, "If it spits, we're goners," and they run away. Why would a rabbi spit? Because he's to be feared. The Jew or his holy garments are not respected.

AUDIENCE MEMBER:

We don't need all those trappings. We live in America. Let's look and behave like Americans...not like strangers and freaks...even in our temples.

SISKEL:

In the film, "The Bird Cage" by Mike Nichols, one character admits his homosexuality with great pride, but shuns his Jewishness. Why do you want to hurt and destroy your beautiful ancestry and Jewish values?

ANOTHER AUDIENCE MEMBER:
(ABOUT THE ONE ABOVE)

He doesn't know them himself! Ignorant!

SISKEL:

That's the problem.

HASID:
(NARRATING)

I lost my wife and 11 children to the Nazis, but they could not take my faith or my pride. In an academic institution in America, State University in New Paltz, New York, a play called "Whiplash: Tales of a Tomboy" written by Shelley Mars, a Jew callously and cruelly made a mockery of my torture and suffering and degraded me, and all those like me, who went to a horrible death because we are what we are. On the stage, the author beat a man dressed as a Hasid with a whip, made him crawl on all fours, forced him to the ground with his pants lowered and proceeded to simulate a sex act that Hasidic Jews believe is immoral. She then whopped him off the stage. Also included in this performance was the rape and brutalization of a Hasidic man by a self-proclaimed Mafia prostitute. The audience wildly cheered. And I have this to say to the author: Having seen what lack of faith can do to the morality and sensibilities of a human being, my religion remains, as always, my pride and my strength, untouched by the likes of Shelley Mars.

FLASHBACK:

KAHANE:
(NARRATING)

The day must come when it will dawn on someone that we've gone too far.

PRESENT:

ON SCREEN:

MOVIE IS SHOWN IN WHICH HASID, IN HIS CLOTHING, BLACK HAT AND COAT, RAPES HIS BROTHER'S WIFE.

JEWISH FORWARD NEWSPAPER ARTICLE ON SCREEN:

"Reform Judaism is set to turn towards Jewish tradition. New vision embraces ritual and Torah study. Moving away from strictly rational and modern rational and modern religion to ritual observance, and the language of commandment and holiness."

ETHNIC CLEANSING

JEWS

BY

ARABS

Scene 23

1975:

FLASHBACK:

KAHANE:
(NARRATING)

Though Hebron is the city of Patriarchs and Matriarchs of the Jewish nation, where lived and died Abraham, Isaac, Jacob, Sarah, Rebecca, and Leah, Jews were evicted from the city for 50 years. Even though we liberated Hebron in the Six Day War in 1967, Jews are not permitted to enter the old city by the Israeli government, which fears to offend the Arab who calls it "Occupied" ...a city which, to us, is second in holiness to Jerusalem. I protested by entering a building in Hebron and was ordered to prison before trial for my so-called "offense." One morning, at 6am, Sarah Nachson wakes and finds her 5 ½ year-old son not breathing. She calls a doctor. He arrives too late. The baby is gone. She cradles her sons in her arms, saying...

FLASHBACK:

SARAH:

I'm going to bury him in the old Jewish cemetery in Hebron. I want my child to open the eye and heart of the government, so they should let us back in the area that belongs to the Jewish people.

. . .

LATER: SARAH AND SEVERAL YESHIVA STUDENTS DRIVING TO THE CEMETERY IN HEBRON. THEY ARE STOPPED AT A CHECKPOINT BY ISRAELI SOLDIERS.

SARAH:
(TO SOLDIERS)

I'm here to bury my son.

SOLDIER:

You have no permission to bury him in Hebron. The commanding officer told em the government wants to give it back to the Arabs. Go bury your child in Jerusalem.

SARAH:

I'll sit here 'til you let me in.

THREE HOURS LATER, SHE IS STILL THERE. NIGHTFALL IS APPROACHING. THE DEAD INFANT IN HER ARMS, SHE BEGINS TO WALK TOWARD THE CEMETERY AND, BESIDE HER, ARE THE YESHIVA BOYS, WHILE THE SOLDIERS ARE FEVERISHLY TALKING ON THEIR PHONES.

SOLDIER:
(ON PHONE)

Commander, the woman will not be stopped. And even if she could, we will not do it...

(CRYING NOW)

A crime for a Jewish woman to bury her baby on our sacred ground? What have we become?!...Thank you...I will...right away...Well if he won't... you sure he won't?

(CRYING AGAIN, HANGS UP)

LATER: SOLDIER RUNS AND CATCHES UP WITH SARAH.

SOLDIER:

The Minister of Defense gave his permission!

AT THE CEMETERY, THE SOLDIERS ASSIST HER WITH THE BURIAL. SOLDIER TAKES PRAYER BOOK. HE LOOKS AT HER QUESTIONINGLY.

SARAH:

His name is Abraham.

Scene 24

FLASHBACK: 1979:

HEADLINE ON SCREEN:

"ISRAEL NEGOTIATING RETURN OF THE SINAI TO EGYPT. PEACE NOW!

                 SARAH NACHSON:
                  (TO GROUP)

This means it's only a matter of time before the government also gives away Hebron. With no Jews living in the city, there'll be no obstacles to the government making a deal for more so-called peace, so we have to occupy a building in Hebron and stay there.

FOLLOWING NIGHT: 3AM

FIFTEEN WOMEN, SOME PREGNANT, AND 35 CHILDREN, STILL IN THEIR PAJAMAS, ARE CARRYING BROOMS, MATTRESSES AND A LADDER TO A BUILDING SEEN IN THE DISTANCE. ISRAELI SOLDIERS ARE ON PATROL ON THE ROOF OF THE BUILDING IN THE FRONT OF IT, SO THE WOMEN SNEAK AROUND TO AN ALLEY IN THE BACK, CUT THROUGH THE BARBED WIRE, CLIMB UP THE LADDER AND INTO A WINDOW. INSIDE, THE BUILDING IS FULL OF DEBRIS. THEY CLEAN FLOOR. ONE OF THE WOMEN SNAPS A LIGHT SWITCH. THERE IS NO LIGHT.

ANOTHER TURNS A TAP FOR WATER. NO WATER. THEY PUT THE MATTRESSES ON THE FLOOR AND GO TO SLEEP. IN THE MORNING, THE CHILDREN, WHEN THEY ARE AWAKE, SING, "V'SHAVU BANIM L-GVULAM" ("THE CHILDREN HAVE RETURNED HOME.")

SOLDIERS HEAR THEM AND RUN DOWN.

SOLDIER:

How did you even get in here?!

CHILD:
(TO SOLDIER)

Jacob's Ladder.

SOLDIER:

You must all leave now!

SARA NACHSON:

Tell Prime Minister Begin we are not moving!

PRIME MINISTER MENACHEM BEGIN:
(TO COMMANDER)

I am not in favor of their settling in the city, but I will not physically expel them. The building is to be surrounded by police and soldiers, and nothing, including food and water, is to be allowed in Beit Haddish.

THE FOLLOWING DAY:

SECRETARY:
(ON PHONE TO BEGIN)

Rabbi Moshe Levinger to see you...

RABBI LEVINGER:
(TO BEGIN)

My wife Miriam and many of my children are inside Beit Hadassah.

BEGIN:

Against my orders.

LEVINGER:

When the Israeli army surrounded the Egyptian army in Sinai during the Yom Kippur war, we gave the enemy soldiers, who killed ours, food, water, and medical supplies. We can, at least, send our women and children in Hebron the same.

BEGIN NODS IN AGREEMENT.

BEGIN:

With one condition: No one is allowed in and anyone leaving will not be able to return.

TWO MONTHS LATER IN BEIT HADASSAH BUILDING:

A TEN-YEAR-OLD BOY:
(TO HIS MOTHER)

I have a toothache.

MOTHER TAKES HIM TO SOLDIER AT GATE.

MOTHER:
(TO SOLDIER)

My son has to go out. He needs to see a dentist.

BOY IS LET OUT. TWO HOURS LATER, HE RETURNS.

SOLDIER AT GATE:

You know the rules. Once you go out, you can't come in.

BOY:
(CRYING)

I want to see my mother.

ON SCREEN: BEGIN IS IN SESSION WITH HIS CABINET. A NOTE IS RELAYED TO BEGIN. BEGIN READS NOTE.

NOTE ON SCREEN:

"A LITTLE BOY IS CRYING OUTSIDE BEIT HADASSAH BECAUSE HE WASN'T ALLOWED BACK IN."

AN HOUR LATER:

SOLDIER RECEIVES A NOTE.

NOTE ON SCREEN:

"FOLLOWING A DISCUSSION BY THE CABINET, THE LITTLE BOY IS PERMITTED TO RETURN TO HIS MOTHER IN BEIT HADASSAH."

INSIDE THE BEIT HADASSAH BUILDING:

GROUP OF WOMEN HAVING DISCUSSION.

> WOMAN:
> (TO A WOMAN WHO IS PREGNANT)

One of the children came down with hepatitis. Without water nor sanitary facilities, we advise you to leave, or you'll come down with the disease.

> PREGNANT WOMAN:

If I cannot return, I will not leave, even if I have to give birth here.

8 MONTHS LATER:

> BEGIN:
> (TO SOLDIER)

There has been so much pressure on me that I want you to dispatch a messenger to the pregnant woman in Hebron with a written permit allowing her to return there following the birth.

SOLDIER GIVES PERMIT TO WOMAN. SHE READS IT AND RETURNS IT TO HIM.

> WOMAN:

This let me return, but it doesn't state that I can bring my baby with me.

BEGIN:
(ON PHONE)

...I'll issue a new permit.

A MONTH LATER: WOMAN AND BABY IN BEIT HADASSAH BUILDING WITH GROUP OF WOMEN.

WOMAN:
(TO GROUP)

It took two months, but we won. Now, we can leave and return.

ANOTHER WOMAN:

But no one else is allowed in.

WOMAN:

They will be soon. You'll see.

A YEAR LATER:

REPORTER ON TV:

For the past year, women and children are still occupying the Beit Hadassah building in Hebron, a hospital for Jews and Arabs, built and manned by Jews 'til the 1929 Arab riots, when Jews were brutally and horribly slaughtered by those to whom they'd been kind. The building has been abandoned for many years, and here is still a standoff between the women and the government. The government has remained unbowed, though some of the women were forced to give birth inside Beit Hadassah. Life has been grueling there. Still no light or running water all this time. Yeshiva students and families provide food, water, and other essentials. They are permitted in for a brief time.

ON SCREEN: FRIDAY NIGHT:

YESHIVA STUDENT:
(TALKING TO OTHER STUDENTS)

Let's go to Beit Hadassah and give the women a good Shabbos. We'll go sing Sabbath songs to them.

THEY SING OUTSIDE THE BUILDING.

ON THE WAY, THEY'RE AMBUSHED BY ARAB TERRORISTS WHO OPEN FIRE FROM A ROOFTOP AND THROWN HAND GRENADES.

TV REPORTER:

Last night, six Yeshiva students were killed and 20 injured by Arab terrorists. They were singing songs to their loved ones.

ANNOUNCER:
(ON RADIO)

Our Prime Minister is with us today. He is devastated by the news and wants to say a few words to us all. Ladies and gentlemen, Menachem Begin.

BEGIN:

The boys can be buried in Hebron, and I want the women to be given light and water. I want them to be told that, for the first time in 50 years, our people can come back to their home in Hebron.

Scene 25

1994:

NEWSPAPER HEADLINE ON SCREEN:

"Two parties outlawed in Israel, Kach and Kahane Chai, calling them now terrorist groups, the new ban makes it a crime to give these groups financial or even verbal support. Wearing their t-shirts or carrying cards bearing their emblem is prohibited. Any person caught with these contraband faces jail without trial. Freedom of speech is also banned, as those caught lauding these groups publicly will be jailed, their meeting places shut down and their property confiscated. Anyone charged with these offenses can be sentenced up to 20 years in prison.

KAHANE:
(NARRATING)

Why hasn't the Communist Party of Israel, which advocates the overthrow of any democratic government and has close ties with the PLO, whose covenant calls for the destruction of Israel, been outlawed?

Scene 26

1929:

A POGROM IS IN PROGRESS IN HEBRON. ARABS BURNING THE SYNAGOGUE TO THE GROUND, AND AN OLD JEW IS SEEN BRAVING THE FIRE TO RESCUE A TORAH SCROLL. HE SAVES ONE FROM THE FLAMES AND IS RUSHED TO A HOSPITAL, STILL HOLDING THE SCROLL. IN THE HOSPITAL, THE OLD MAN, WHO IS DYING OF HIS WOUNDS, HANDS TORAH SCROLL TO A MAN IN THE ADJOINING BED.

OLD MAN:

Please...see that this is returned to Hebron when we go back there.

ON SCREEN:

THE TORAH IS WRAPPED IN A MANTLE THAT SAYS, "SAVED FROM THE POGROM OF 1929. RETURN TO HEBRON."

HEBRON, 1996:

MILITARY OFFICER:
(TO SETTLERS)

You have no permission to be living here. The Arab Mayor of this town is very upset. He's bitterly attacked your presence here, and we have no alternative but to move you out to an Army camp. You will not be permitted to leave or return without any permission. Visitors are absolutely forbidden, and those wishing to speak with any of you must stand outside the gate. We'll be coming back soon to move you out. Start packing.

HE LEAVES.

SETTLER:
(TO ANOTHER)

We're now recognized by the government as an official force, Haim!

HAIM:

The government caved to Arab pressure and is afraid of world opinion.

1997:

NEWSPAPER HEADLINE ON SCREEN:

"SETTLERS RETURN TO HEBRON AFTER GOVERNMENT AGREES TO GIVE 80% OF CITY TO ARABS AND 20% TO SETTLERS. AGREEMENT WAS CONCLUDED AS A BOMB EXPLODES IN TEL AVIV, KILLING 4 ISRAELIS AND WOUNDED 40. MORE RIOTING ERUPTED WHEN JEWS WANTED TO BUILD A SETTLEMENT NEAR JERUSALEM.

ON SCREEN: HEBRON:

ARABS THROWING FIREBOMBS, ROCKS, STONES AND BOTTLES. ISRAELI SOLDIERS ARE WATCHING. ONE HAS HIS JAW SMASHED BY A STONE. SOME ARABS ARRESTED AND QUICKLY FREED WHEN SOLDIERS ATTACHED BY A BARRAGE OF STONES.

ARAFAT:
(TONGUE IN CHEEK TO PRESS)

I urge Palestinians to shun violent protests and my 30,000-member police force to prevent clashes.

HAIM:
(TO SETTLERS)

The grandson of the man who saved one Torah scroll in the 1929 pogrom has it in his possession and wants to bring it to Hebron. We've been given permission by the army. Preparations have already been made to bring it here!!

(THEY EMBRACE EACH OTHER WITH JOY)

A KNOCK AT THE DOOR. THEY OPEN IT. A SOLDIER ENTERS AND HANDS SETTLER A PAPER. HE READS.

SETTLER:

The Army orders us not to bring the Torah here.

ANOTHER SETTLER:

Our Arab mayor fears a Torah scroll? Hasn't wiped us out enough? Or does it reveal a secret...that we were here once before...murdered once before...and before that...and maybe...just maybe...we belong here...and he doesn't! The Torah is ours! We'll bring it here ourselves!

SOLDIER:

You have no choice but to obey.

TV REPORTER:

In the matter of the Hebron Torah, Shiek Jabri, Mayor of Hebron, rejoices and enjoys the popularity with his people for his victory over the Jews.

SETTLER:

The government ought to be ashamed...retreating before an Arab.

ANOTHER SETTLER:

What does the Torah mean to a Leftist? They'd rather the Arab win. If the army retreats and runs from Arab stones, what is it for them to run from us? But in time, it will be ours. God will see that.

MAN WHO OWNS TORAH SCROLL IS LOOKING AT IT AND MUSING.

MAN:

Will this be the future of Israel?

HE PUTS HIS BAND ON THE SCROLL.

All that will be left? Maybe...not even this.

ETHNIC CLEANSING

JEWS

BY

JEWS

Scene 27

HEBRON, 1997:

A PLAYGROUND IN A DAY CARE CENTER. ARABS ARE THROWING STONES AT CHILDREN IN THE PLAYGROUND. AN ISRAELI SETTLER GRABS AN ARAB. AN ISRAELI SOLDIER THEN GRABS THE ISRAELI AND BEATS HIM BRUTALLY. MORE SOLDIERS ARRIVE WITH A FENCE TO SEPARATE ARABS FROM ISRAELIS AND PROCEED TO PUT IT UP. THE ISRAELI TEARS IT DOWN, AND ANOTHER ISRAELI CARRIES A SIGN SAYING, "YOU WILL NOT MAKE A GHETTO OUT OF ISRAEL." THE SETTLER SHOUTS THE WORDS AS WELL.

ISRAELI SOLDIER:
(SHOUTING ON A BULLHORN)

You have 10 minutes to put down your signs. Those still protesting will be arrested. Stop shouting nonsense and go home.

ISRAELI SETTLER:

We're to be fenced in like animals, while Arabs roam free in our land?! They kill us and we have our weapons confiscated if we defend ourselves?!

SOLDIER:

Your name is on the list.

(POINTING TO A GUN IN THE SETTLER'S POCKET)

Hand it over.

ISRAELI SETTLER:
(GIVING UP GUN)

The list will be too long to carry very soon.

FLASHBACK:

THE WHITE HOUSE LAWN, 1994. ARAFAT IS SHAKING RABIN'S HAND.

ARAFAT:

The Oslo "Land for Peace Process," which we have signed today, will bring an end to terror and war.

LATER: RABIN IS BACK IN ISRAEL TALKING TO HIS PEOPLE.

RABIN:

We will give up Jericho and Gaza first, as an experiment to see if giving away land will indeed bring peace.

LATER: ARAFAT IS TALKING TO HIS PEOPLE.

ARAFAT:

This is the first step to a Palestinian state, with Jerusalem as it's capital!

CHEERS FROM AUDIENCE.

KAHANE:
(NARRATING)

Gaza and Jericho...where our forefathers walked from the beginning, their holy names in our beloved Torah. A Palestinian state is a tragedy. A state intent on war, that is chillingly near our population centers, boxing our Air Force in, exercising control over the Mediterranean shore, and importing weapons for our destruction. Yossi Sarid of the Meretz Party has this say:

YOSSI SARID:
(MERETZ PARTY)

Palestine now!

BACK TO PRESENT:

HEBRON SETTLER:

Mr. Sarid's Leftist Party is blind and deaf to our cries that we are being killed now! Gaza and Jericho are a refuge for terrorists committing crimes in Hebron. Housebreaking, burglary, and auto theft have skyrocketed. Thousands of cars are stolen and reused in Gaza and the 7 cities there are now under Arab control.

FOLLOWING DAY:

RABIN'S OFFICE:

POLICEMAN:
(TO RABIN)

We must be forceful. This a crime wave going on now.

RABINS WAVES HIM AWAY.

RABIN:

To be expected.

POLICEMAN LEAVES.

IN STREET: ISRAELI DEFENSE FORCE SOLDIERS AND ISRAELI CIVILIANS ARE BEING PELTED WITH CEMENT BLOCKS AND FIRE HOSES BY ARABS. IDF SOLDIERS RUN FOR COVER. THEN, BEING SHOT AT BY PALESTINIAN ARAB POLICE, IDF SOLDIERS RAISE THEIR GUNS.

IDF COMMANDER:
(TO SOLDIERS)

Hold your fire!

SOLDIER:

But they're shooting at me with guns our government gave them!

COMMANDER:

You heard me!

ARABS CONTINUE FIRING. SOME IDF BOYS ARE KILLED. OTHERS RAISE THEIR GUNS AGAIN.

COMMANDER:

Those not holding fire will be court-martialed.

A SOLDIER FIRES. HE IS ARRESTED BY OTHER SOLDIERS.

A WEEK LATER: HE APPEARS BEFORE THE JUDGE.

JUDGE:
(TO SOLDIER)

You defied an order of your commander.

SOLDIER:
(TURNING HIS EYES TO HEAVEN)

I was obeying Another Who orders us to defend the life and land of a Jew. In this case...mine. Rabin and Peres brought this calamity on us by following the appeasers...the radical left...your politics, as well, Your Honor. The Arabs can blow us up, shoot us, stab us, firebomb us with impunity. Suicide bombers, drive-by machine gunning, throat slashing of young women, shooting of young schoolgirls...of no importance to the peaceniks.

JUDGE:

Ten years.

(TO BAILIFF)

Take him away.

SOLDIER:
(SHOUTING)

Must we suffer the ignorance and incompetence of political hacks like you, who shouldn't even be street sweepers?!

. . .

Scene 27

TWO MONTHS LATER:

TWO 23-YEAR-OLD GIRLS ARE HIKING. THEY ARE LAUGHING, RUNNING, PLAYING CATCH WITH THEIR DOG. SUDDENLY, ARABS ATTACK AND BRUTALLY MURDER THEM.

FOLLOWING DAY:

NEWSPAPER HEADLINE:

"PRIME MINISTER NETANYAHU IS SHOCKED."

ANOTHER NEWSPAPER HEADLINE ON SCREEN:

"SEVEN ISRAELI 12-YEAR-OLD GIRLS SHOT TO DEATH, AND SIX WOUNDED, BY A JORDANIAN SOLDIER. HE HAS BEEN ARRESTED."

JORDANIAN SOLDIER IN ISRAELI PRISON.

GUARD:
(TO JORDANIAN)

You have a visitor.

ARAB ENTERS. JORDANAIAN IS FRIGHTENED.

VISITOR:

You have nothing to worry about. Hundreds of Jordanian lawyers have volunteered to defend you free of charge.

A YEAR LATER:

NETANYAHU:
(TO HIS SECRETARY)

A letter to Jordanian Crown Prince Hassan: Prime Minister Netanyahu requests the honor of your presence at a memorial for the girls.

THE FOLLOWING DAY:

SECRETARY:
(TO NETANYAHU)

Crown Prince Hassan refuses.

NETANYAHU:

This'll pass. Things will get better.

SECRETARY:

Now I'm shocked. When Jewish witnesses saw the killings in the death camps and managed to escape to tell their brethren, they were either not believed or told, "It'll pass. Things will get better."

SHE LEAVES.

Scene 28

7:30AM THE FOLLOWING DAY:
A VAN CARRYING WOMEN TO HEBRON:

          ONE WOMAN:
          (TO ANOTHER)

At your age, you must be babysitting a long time, huh?

          OTHER WOMAN:

I just started here. It's my second job. I hope the lady likes me.

          FIRST WOMAN:

Mine doesn't, but I'm a good babysitter, so what can she do, eh?

          OTHER WOMAN:

She can throw you out 'cause she's jealous, the baby likes you more than her.

(STARING OFF)

How I loved that little one.

SCENE SHIFTS TO OUTSIDE. A TERRORIST IS SPRAYING VAN WITH MACHINE GUN FIRE.

          . . .

LATER:

IN HOSPITAL. OTHER WOMAN IS VISITED BY A FRIEND.

FRIEND:

They should bullet proof everything.

OTHER WOMAN:

Remember what happened in Gush Katif? School children in a bullet proof bus, so they used a car bomb. They know they can get away with it. No one will hunt them down or catch them, so why not?

HEADLINE ON SCREEN:

> "DOZENS OF JEWISH SETTLERS ARE ORDERED TO TURN IN THEIR WEAPONS, THOIGH WARNINGS OF TERROR ATTACKS CONTINUE."

FLASHBACK:

KAHANE:
(NARRATING)

Jews need a couch.

Scene 29

1997:

ON SCREEN:

ISRAELIS, FULFILLING ANOTHER COMMITMENT IN THE OSLO PEACE PROCESS WITH ARAFAT, HAVE WITHDRAWN FROM HEBRON, RETAINING ONLY 20 PERCENT OF THE CITY SO THEY CAN PROTECT THE 540 JEWISH RESIDENTS LIVING IN THE MIDST OF 25,000 ARABS. BEIT HADDASH HOUSE 54 JEWISH FAMILIES. IT IS A HEAVILY GUARDED COMPOUND. HEBRON IS THE ONLY CITY WHERE JEWS ACTUALLY LIVE AMONG ARABS, RATHER THAN IN SETTLEMENTS NEAR ARAB TOWNS.

PALESTINIAN:
(NARRATING)

I am a Palestinian...a freedom fighter. These Jews are on our land. They must get out! Those metal spikes they put on the road in front of their house to prevent car bombs and drive by shootings won't help. Sandbags and barriers around their houses won't help. The military post near their door won't help, and neither will the buses taking the children to school with metal grates on their windows, accompanied by Army jeeps, keep us from our task. They will die at our hands no matter what they do. We are always one step ahead...until the inevitable happens...Hebron is ours, Jerusalem...is ours, Palestine is ours... once again.

AN ISRAELI SOLDIER IS TALKING TO A WOMAN. SHE IS WEARING VERY RELIGIOUS DRESS (SEE PICTURE ON NEXT PAGE.)

ISRAELI SOLDIER:
(TALKING TO WOMAN)

I wish you people would get out of here. It's hell for us being around you, with all the problems you're causing. We never know when we'll be next. Go live somewhere else. You're hurting yourself and your children...for what?

WOMAN:

Hebron is in my heart...in my soul. I could never live anywhere else, even though terrible things are happening. My brother was stabbed coming home from prayer. Arabs threw rocks, bottles and gasoline bombs near my door. My son was hit with a rock getting off the school bus. There he is now, marching into the Purim parade...surrounded by soldiers in riot gear...but...no matter what...he knows to hold onto our traditions. Living here has taught my children values. Holding on to biblical land, the dream of 2,000 years, in Hebron, Jerusalem. Schechem, and Tiberias...the land of our Bible.

SOLDIER:

People like you are extremists who threaten the peace process. You're contemptible...stopping the advance of history...making Israel a secure place to live. You are a simple-minded fanatic, Jews from Brooklyn...gun toting...Arab hating, religious fanatics. You've got seven children, for God's sake. Don't you care what happens to them?!

WOMAN:

You want comfort, a Western style capitalist country, spiritually empty.

SOLDIER:

Why give our lives for a bunch of old graves?

WOMAN:

Some day you'll see. There's more to life than materialism and instant satisfaction. You don't understand what we're doing anymore...why we returned to Israel at all. Much of the idealism has faded away. Meaning and purpose all gone.

HER 18-YEAR-OLD SON IS SEEN COMING HOME PALE AND HIS SHOULDER SLUMPED. SHE PUTS AN ARM AROUND HIM AND THEY ENTER THE HOUSE. SHE HAS A SMALL SPARTAN APARTMENT. SON TURNS TAP TO GET SOME WATER. THERE IS NONE.

WOMAN:

We had some this morning. I don't know when it'll come on again...but...better sometime...than never.

SON:

I just got off a bus that was attacked and two people killed. More friends gone and tomorrow I go to the army.

WOMAN:
(RUSHING OUT)

I have to get the bodies off and clean the bus of what remains of those poor souls!

A MAN CONFRONTS SEVERAL ARABS WITH A GUN. HE SHOOTS AND KILLS TWO OF THEM.

MAN:

One for each of my people whose lives you took on that bus.

THE REST RUN AWAY. ARAB OWNER OF NEARBY VEGETABLE MARKET CLOSES HIS SHOP AND RUNS AWAY. ISRAELI MAN PUTS A SIGN ON HIS SHOP IN HEBREW AND ENGLISH. IT READS, "THIS MARKET WAS BUILT ON JEWISH PROPERTY STOLEN BY THE ARABS AFTER THE 1929 MASSACRE."

FLASHBACK:

KAHANE:
(NARRATING)

As it's written in the Bible...God's word..."and you shall pursue your enemies and they shall fall before you by the sword. And five of you shall pursue a hundred and a hundred of you shall pursue 10,000, and your enemies shall fall before your sword."

BACK TO PRESENT:

ARABS THROW STONES AT ISRAELI SOLDIER (SEE PICTURE ON FOLLOWING PAGE) HE RUNS AWAY. THEY WATCH HIM, LAUGHING, AND THROW MORE STONES WHILE HE RUNS.

FLASHBACK:

KAHANE:
(NARRATING)

But should we run from the enemy, the warning of God in the bible... "I will scatter you among the nations and will draw out the sword after you. And those who are left alive, I will bring a fear into their hearts in the land of their enemies, and the sound of a fluttering leaf will chase them, and they shall flee from a sword, and they shall fall when none pursueth."

"COME FROM BROOKLYN AND NEW YORK ARE THE WORST," SAYS AN ARAB. "THEY HAVE NO RIGHT TO THIS PLACE, NO RIGHT, AND THEY ARE THE CRAZIEST."

New Jersey expatriate David Wilder is Hebron's official Jewish voice; settler Shani Horowitz has a tight grip on her 2-year-old daughter.

Top, Palestinian rock-throwers taking aim last week; bottom, men and boy outside Hebron's Beit Hadassah.

Scene 30

1997:

NEWSPAPER HEADLINE ON SCREEN:

"HEBRON BURNS. 500 FIREBOMBS THROWN BY ARABS IN THE PAST THREE WEEKS."

ARAFAT:
(ON PHONE)

The Israelis are threatening to reoccupy Hebron. Tell your men to restore calm and make arrests if necessary.

FLASHBACK:

1990:

KAHANE:

Israeli Arabs are a cancer in our midst. They are the same as those outside terrorists. Killed 16 Jews on a bus in Jerusalem. I was jailed in Israel for daring to say what they are...a disease that is killing us.

PERES:

An Arab with Israeli citizenship is a loyal Israeli. All he wants is to live in peace with his neighbors and share equally will his neighbors.

REPORTER ON TV:

An Israeli policeman was attacked by Israeli Arabs in a settlement. They shouted "Death to the Jews" in Hebrew. An Arab member of the Knesset and President Weizmann are with us today at the scene.

ARAB KNESSET MEMBER:
(ENRAGED)

We must understand the frustration and pain of our Arab brothers on stolen land.

PRESIDENT WEIZMANN:

We cannot permit ourselves to give in to more rage on both sides. My mission is to calm tensions.

SETTLER:
(ENRAGED)

We have a full-scale riot here today because we were building on our land. Where was the army to stop the riot and arrest the leaders?!

ISRAELI POLICE ARREST SETTLER.

WEIZMANN:

We are here to hold negotiations with the rioters.

SETTLER:

In other words, encourage them to kill us. No rioter ever died from negotiations, but we are.

POLICEMAN:
(STRIKING SETTLER)

Shut up!

ANOTHER SETTLER:
(SHOUTING)

Let's negotiate…in Hebron, where an elderly rabbi was murdered in his own bedroom by a knife wielding Arab murderer who easily escaped.

WEIZMANN:

Shouting and condemning is not negotiating. That's why you're in trouble, antagonizing and rushing into judgement.

POLICE ARREST SETTLER.

ANOTHER SETTLER:

Let's <u>negotiate</u> where was woman was shot near her home and bullets riddled a Jewish car.

ARAB:

We have our stories too!

SETTLER:

Let's <u>negotiate</u>.... where an explosion injured 11 Jewish soldiers, and Arab policemen and perpetrators slipped away.

WEIZMANN:

We are here to increase understanding on both sides, and you are not helping.

SETTLER:

You are here to delude us into thinking there are good Arabs who live in Israel, and Arab terrorists who come from outside who are evil. We back down and negotiate and they know terror pays...those outside and...inside.

ARAB:

Let's be clear. They are political revolutionaries fighting for our rights. We could let them go on as they are with our blessing, but we choose to be reasonable and you are, to say the least, far from grateful.

Scene 31

1998:

SOLDIER ON PODIUM ABOUT TO ADDRESS A CROWD OF SOLDIERS AND OTHERS. BEHIND HIM IS A BANNER SAYING, "PEACE NOW."

SOLDIER:

A member of the Knesset is with us today, Naomi Hazan. Let's welcome her.

SHE APPEARS. THERE IS NO APPLAUSE.

HAZAN:

I will go straight to the point. Soldiers should refuse to carry out orders to destroy Arab structures that our government calls "illegal." To the Arabs, they are legitimate, as they feel this is their land, not ours. We must respect that. Soldiers are behaving like Nazis when you raise the house of an Arab to please the Orthodox, who are a horrible evil in our midst.

ORTHODOX MAN IN CROWD:
(SHOUTING)

That Israel has survived with leaders like you is proof we are right. God exists! Your party depends on Arab votes, so you support them. You are fooling nobody. But they are fooling you. Before this so-called "peace process," Israeli Arabs were careful to define themselves as Israeli Arabs. They didn't want to be counted as Palestinians. Now, all of a sudden, they're <u>Palestinians</u> who were <u>forced</u> to accept Israeli citizenship…and live well with every benefit we can give them, incidentally. The ones we educated for nothing in our colleges are screaming the loudest, "Kill the Jew" …which doesn't stop us from paying for the next course…or their Jewish professors from praising <u>them</u> and attacking <u>me</u>! In spite of our giving up more land, our home-grown Arabs said was theirs, and it was nothing of the kind, they exploded two car bombs in our midst, just so we wouldn't forget we owe them every grain of sand we're sitting on. When will he hear God's plea, "Hear, ye deaf; and look, ye blind, that ye may see"?

HAZAN:

We must give peace a chance. Settlers running about and arming themselves every time an Arab builds a house for his family, legal or not is provocative, beyond the limits of reason, and understandably provokes violence. The settlers must quiet down on their own, or we'll have to force them to see the light.

(SHOUTING)

Peace now!

ARMY OFFICER:

We are being turned into cannon fodder. It's forbidden for us to react. If we do, we're put on trial. Arabs from Hebron attacked. We were injured and we just stood there. Some of us removed our uniforms, refusing to serve in an army that's not a defense force, but a death trap.

HAZAN:

You must listen to your commanders who know how to resolve problems.

SOLDIER:

In Hebron, ours just abandoned us.

SEVERAL SOLDIERS DROP GUNS.

SOLDIERS:

What do we need these for?

Scene 32

1999:

JEWS ARE PROTESTING THEIR BEING FORBIDDEN TO PRAY AT THE TEMPLE MOUNT, JUDAISM'S HOLIEST SITE. LAST WEEK, THEY SAT DOWN AT THE TWO OF THE GATES OF THE TEMPLE. NOW, 100 JEWS WILL ATTEMPT TO ENTER TO PRAY. THE ARABS HAVE A MOSQUE THERE AS WELL, BUILT LONG AFTER THE TEMPLE MOUNT.

TV REPORTER:

We have been assured by the leaders of the demonstration that this will be a peace protest. No trouble is expected.

ISRAELI POLICE OFFICER:
(TO HIS MEN)

We don't want to disturb the Arabs, so we're positioning the Elite Border Patrol at the gate, where we'll be waiting for the religious fanatics with a ratio of two of us to one of them. Remember, we must teach them a lesson.

FOLLOWING DAY: PROTESTORS WEARING PRAYER SHAWL APPEARS.

LEADER:

(TO POLICEMAN GUARDING TEMPLE)

We're here to pray.

OTHER POLICEMAN APPEAR, WEARING SKULL CAPS. THEY ENTHUSIASTICALLY PROCEED TO BEAT THE PROTESTORS USING EXTREME FORCE. HEADS ARE SMASHED INTO WALLS AND TWISTED TO A BREAKING POINT AS THEY ARE PASSED ALONG POLICE LINES, AND THEIR FACES GROUND INTO MUCK.

TV REPORTER:

Eight protestors were arrested, handcuffed in pairs, and taken on foot to the notorious Kishle Jail.

THEY APPEAR IN COURT.

JUDGE:

You are charged with assaulting Police officers, disturbing the peace and rioting.

Scene 33

ON SCREEN:

> FOLLOWING DAY: A SOCIALIST SCHOLAR, MR STEN, IS ADDRESSING SOCIALISTS AND OTHERS ON THE POLITICAL LEFT IN AN AUDITORIUM.

> MR. STEN:

Though I'm for a Palestinian state and the peace process, I do not feel that the Israelis and Zionists are equally responsible with the Arabs and the Palestinians in all areas of conflict...

> AUDIENCE MEMBER:
> (FULL OF HATE)

You should be ashamed. We are fully to blame in every conflict. What do you mean...equal?! We are the aggressors...

> ANOTHER AUDIENCE MEMBER:

Israeli Zionist Nazi! You don't belong here anymore!

> STEN:
> (SHOCKED)

Such hatred for your own country?! For Israel?! For Zionism?! For me?!

AUDIENCE MEMBER:

Mr. Sten, I want to remind you that Amos Oz, who won our top literary award, accuses protesters like the Temple Mount group of being a small, cruel cult wanting to impose a blood ritual on us, and says they're the same as the Arab terrorists Hezbollah. Mr. Barak, head of the Labor Party said that, if he were a young Palestinian today, he would be a terrorist. A sculptor, whose work was selected for placement at a museum for our Holocaust victims, stated that, when he looked at the people who protested at the Mount, he could understand Hitler. And we have programs on Tv that celebrate Arab terrorists. They can't all be wrong!

AUDIENCE APPLAUDS HIM.

FLASHBACK:

KAHANE:
(NARRATING)

The artistic Liberal types come out of their holes of ego and self-importance to prattle and preach "love" and "peace" to us mere mortals who die at the enemy's hands. The artist flies to embrace an arch murderer, Arafat, and in so doing spits in the graves of hundreds of thousands of our people massacred and murdered by so-called "Palestinians," who are frantically laying the groundwork for a similar fate for many more of us.

A HASIDIC MAN JUMPS ON STAGE, SUDDENLY, THE RELIGIOUS MAN ON THE PODIUM SHOUTS.

MAN:
(SHOUTING)

May God avenge the blood of Shlomo and Harel!

THERE IS SILENCE IN THE HALL.

MAN:

Two of our dearest students, Shlomo Liebman, age 24, and Harel Bin-Nun, age 20, were murdered by Arab terrorists while guarding the Jewish settlement of Yitzhar. Shlomo loved the Yeshiva. He was there from 6 in the morning 'til 10 at night. Often, while standing, he would cry out, "Yosef! Yosef!" and would answer the phone, "Od Yosef Chai," stressing that Joseph still lives. Shlomo was with us since he was 16. Harel Bin-Nun also came to the Yeshiva at a young age and was wounded by Arab bullets fired at a bus he was riding. Searching for a place of truth and idealism, he came to Yitzhar. He labored day and night, building houses and a farm to establish the Jewish claim to our land. Shlomo and Harel studied Torah together whole on patrol guarding the settlement every night from 11 to 12. At 11:30pm, terrorists ambushed and murdered these two saintly men. The next day, the Israeli government was giving more land to the PLO and freed more Arab terrorists from prison. Thousands of Jews who attended the funerals wept openly. I ask only that you let a few tears fall.

MASTER OF CEREMONIES:

Get off stage!

MAN DOES NOT MOVE.

MASTER OF CEREMONIES:

You heard what I said!

MAN DOES NOT MOVE. AUDIENCE MEMBERS ARE SHOUTING AT HASID.

AUDIENCE MEMBERS:

Vulgar baboon!

Snake!

Greedy, domineering vulture!

Evil!

Primitive!

Corrupt!

Parasites!

Horrible monster!

Sadists and murderers!

Committing crimes against humanity!

MAN IN AUDIENCE:
(RISES)

I am here representing leading journalists and professors. In response to the opening of a religious kindergarten you're planning to build, we say, "Exterminate all of you at birth!"

ENTHUSIASTIC APPLAUSE.

FLASHBACK:

KAHANE:
(NARRATING)

The media...weapons of self-hate, corrupting our normal sense of self-preservation. In their hands, the murderous Arab becomes our innocent victim. Our professors...well...there are two kinds of fools...arrogant and stupid. They fall into both categories.

STEN:
(TO AUDIENCE)

You sound like Nazis!

MAN IN AUDIENCE:

What else can a Nazi like him understand?! We should storm their settlements will machine guns and mow them down!

MASTER OF CEREMONIES:
(TO HASID)

You'd better leave before you start a riot, and we have you arrested!

BEARDED RELIGIOUS MEN WEARING BLACK SUITS AND HATS ENTER THE HALL, PUT ON TALLISIM AND START TO PRAY.

MAN IN AUDIENCE:

I would tie all your beards together and light a match! Who let those people in here anyhow?!

ONE OF THEM:
(REPLYING)

God.

THEY ARE SPIT UPON AS THEY ENTER THE DOOR.

HASID:

In Russia, I could not talk! Here, I cannot talk. There, I talked and went to jail. Here, I go to jail, too, but first, I talk.

MASTER OF CEREMONIES:

Be brief and get out!

HASID:

The Bible tells us, when the Jewish people were not unified, it was a sin, and they were not forgiven. But, when they were unified, they were forgiven. The mitzvah "*V'ahavta l-reacha kamocha" tells us we must love our neighbor as ourselves, our fellow Jew as ourselves. We must give respect to those who thinking is different from ours...

MAN IN AUDIENCE:

...I would cast the first stone in an intifada against you.

HASIDIC MAN:

A story is told of a rabbi who was to attend a meeting at which an adamantly irreligious government leader was going to be in attendance. All the Hasidim were concerned what would happen between the rabbi, who was an uncompromising and outspoke defender of Torah and this man. To their surprise, the rabbi walked over and hugged him. The man became a lover of torah. And so, I hug all of you.

MAN IN AUDIENCE:

If we really loved our neighbors, we'd get rid of our chauvinism and our fascistic nationalism, get rid of an anthem, "Hatikvah," that talks about a Jewish soul. Don't our Arab neighbors have souls? Change the country's name, make it a bi-national state, then you'll be talking about love for neighbor.

HASID:

God did not give this land to the Arabs. And "Love your enemy" is not a Jewish commandment...loving ourselves is...and, unfortunately, here we are seriously lacking.

MAN IN AUDIENCE:

You should all be suspended on an electric pole!

STEN:
(TO ABOVE MAN)

Let him talk! Shut up!

HASID:

Israel's radical Left, many of you here, are at war on two fronts...with the Arabs...a war which is called "peace" and at war with the Jewish state...your goal being...No state and no Jews. Rabbi Meir Kahane, of blessed memory...

AUDIENCE MEMBER:
(SHOUTING)

...Don't mention that name. It offends our ears!

STEN:

And Arafat doesn't?! We're behaving like Fascists here ourselves. If a Jew can't speak to a Jew, who can he speak to? Kahane certainly couldn't!

FLASHBACK: HASID TELLS WHAT HAPPENED WHILE WE SEE SCENE.

ISRAEL: KAHANE IN A COURTOOM BEFORE A JUDGE.

JUDGE:
(TO KAHANE)

You are charged with being a threat to our democracy...a menace that must be stopped...a...

KAHANE INTERRUPTS, AND WHILE'S HE'S TALKING, JUDGE SHOUTS PERIODICALLY DEMANDING HE BE QUIET.

KAHANE:

...People who banned a Knesset member, me, from appearing on State TV and radio for four years; people who banned a movement that was supported by hundreds of thousands...mine; people who forbid debating my Bills in the Knesset...

KAHANE LOOKING HARD AT JUDGE.

...then appoint judges like you to keep themselves in power, have the nerve to talk about democracy?! Hypocrites! All of you! I...

JUDGE BANGS GAVEL. KAHANE IS SILENT.

JUDGE:

Revolutionary incitement! Guilty as charged!

HE IS LED AWAY.

BACK TO PRESENT:

HASID:

Kahane reminds us...so we are proud of, appreciate, and fight for our land... I quote: "In the annals of world history, there may never have been an event as astounding and miraculous as the rebirth of the Jewish state...the real-life drama of the Jews, a stubbornly, sublimely obstinate people who refused to die in the face of a thousand, more powerful enemies determined to eliminate them from the face of the earth. There is no more fantastic and improbable drama that that of a people ripped from their land swept by the winds of oppression and persecution into the four corners of the earth, and who returned, in blood and fire, to the land of their forefathers..."

AN AUDIENCE MEMBER RUSHES ON STAGE AND SPITS ON HASID. ANOTHER AUDIENCE MEMBER GRABS HIM AND PULLS HIM FROM STAGE.

ANOTHER AUDIENCE MEMBER:
(SHOUTING TO MAN WHO SPIT ON HASID AND RUSHED ON STAGE)

Shame on you!!

HE IS EJECTED FROM THE HALL.

HASID:

...Kahane goes on to say, "People mocked and ridiculed his way of life; he was the butt of cruel humor and worse, from east to west and north and south, they spat upon the Jewish gabardine...as now...in the land of the Jews...they spit on mine."

A PAUSE.

Isaiah, the prophet, who most of you know nothing about and pride yourself in your ignorance of his holy words, said, "Woe unto them that call evil good, and good evil; that put darkness for light and light for darkness; put bitter for sweet and sweet for bitter."

HE TURNS TO LEAVE.

AUDIENCE MEMBER:

I want to hear more. Let him stay! We all believe in Relativity. No absolutes. Good, evil...these judgements depend on circumstances. Let him make a fool of himself.

ANOTHER AUDIENCE MEMBER:

He said he'd be brief. Enough of this nonsense!

MASTER OF CEREMONIES:
(TO HASID)

What is good and what is evil...un-answerable questions.

HASID TURNS BACK TO ANSWER.

HASID:
(SHAKES HIS HEAD "NO")

The answers are in the Torah, but we don't hear, we don't see, we don't listen.

FLASHBACK:

KAHANE IN COURTROOM BEFORE ANOTHER JUDGE.

JUDGE:
(TO KAHANE)

You are charged with destroying the youth...returning them to feudalism, tyranny, medievalism...and I quote: "This Land is the Land for each and every child to bask in its holiness and sanctity. Without study of Torah, how can our children know how to behave, what is forbidden, what is obligatory. Without Torah, how can you teach them the Higher Law, how can you understand its structure, its commandments, it's spirit, and if you don't, how can they? The Holy Land of the Holy people becomes more and more a moral cesspool, filth, and perversion of sacred values in a people that once prided itself on its chosen ness."

KAHANE:

It can only get worse.

JUDGE:

Guilty as charged! Take him away!

BACK TO PRESENT:

1999:

HASID:

Yesterday in Tel Aviv when evil was evil...Kahane's nightmare...50,000 young people from the best families, high on marijuana, ecstasy, and LSD.

THEY ARE BRANDISHING RINGS FROM EVERY VISIBLE PART OF THEIR BODY, EARS, NOSES, LIPS, BELLY BUTTONS, DANCING WILDLY TO A MIND-NUMBING 150 BEATS PER MINUTE TO THE MUSIC, WHICH IS A CROSS BETWEEN NEO-HIPPIE AND RAPID-FIRE, COMPUTER-GENERATED BASS LINES.

AUDIENCE MEMBER:
(SHOUTING)

This is frightening!

HASID:

The trendy elites in academia, education, the arts and politics are busy proving that the religious are degenerate to the core, the tradition is tribal, out of date, anti-humanitarian, racist, the Bible, only a fable. And this is counterculture, drugs and all, for the next generation of which they approve.

SOUNDS OF SHOCK AND HORROR IN THE AUDIENCE.

AUDIENCE MEMBER:

Many of us were there. Joined in and had lots of fun. It's just a way of getting in touch with themselves. A passing fad if you will.

HASID:

Well, yes, if you regard the destruction of Zionism and Jewish values a passing fad. And now, the good...Kahane's dream...

FLASHBACK:

TV REPORTER ON SCENE:

A mass prayer is being held to protest the High Court's decision desecrating the Sabbath...making it a workday, like any other. Jews are standing at the entrance to the Holy City, many crying "*Shema Yisrael" (THE LORD OUR GOD, THE LORD IS ONE")

POLICE STAND BY HOLDING CLUBS AND GAS CANNISTERS. THEY DROP BOTH AND JOIN THE PEOPLE, CRYING OUT "SHEMA YISRAEL." SECULAR MEN, BAREHEADED, BEGGING RELIGIOUS MEN TO WEAR YARMULKES.

SECULAR MEN:

Please, give us yarmulkes, so we can join in saying, "Shema Yisrael." We never have before, but we want to now.

BACK TO PRESENT:

HASID:

A rabbi at the gathering has received many phone calls from men telling him that they have since started to put on Tefillin.

(HE RAISES HIS EYES TO HEAVEN)

"Shema Yisrael," Kahane's dream...that we would not raise an arm to each other, that we respect our traditions, our Judaism ourselves. That we are, at last, united as one.

FLASHBACK:

KAHANE:
(NARRATING)

Praying is not enough. For centuries, we were set afire in our temples. During the thousands of years of our torment, the Jew dreamed of return to Zion where his children could walk tall and proud and free and above all, unafraid. But now, in his own land he is afraid...because a dangerous and absurd equation is made by his government. And I say, to our so-called leaders, "The Jew who picks up a gun and uses it to defend himself against an Arab terrorist is not the same as a Jew hater who picks it up to murder him. The Jew who patrols the streets of a frightened and troubled Jewish neighborhood with a gun is not the same as the hoodlum-rapist-mugger who carries a gun." The time is long overdue to say, "The difference makes a difference." Violence against evil is not the same as violence against good, and sometimes violence is needed to preserve all that is true and beautiful in the world, and Jews who protect other Jews with violence are <u>right</u>.

PRESENT:

TV REPORTER:

Kahane was loved by the man in the street. They hugged and kissed him. By the "ruling class" he was reviled. Was it because they feared his message? Are they afraid he is still a threat because he was a messenger who told the truth? Are they afraid because now we hear, "He was right"? And I'm beginning to think, "Maybe he was."

KAHANE:
(NARRATING)

I was arrested tens of times in Israel, but that could never dim the love for my people and my land. My entire life has been one of ideas that were eventually taken up by people and became acceptable. I consider that, in this sense, I have won. But one of my main concerns <u>was</u>, and still <u>is</u>, the underlying theme in my struggle, which can be summed up in one sentence: "If the Jew does not learn from history, he is doomed to repeat it." And I have tried, with every fiber of my being, to prevent a repetition of our tragic history...that has been, unfortunately too often repeated. And I ask that you put these burning questions to yourselves, now. What are we are about to be repeating? What have we not learned? And I beg you, answer them now!

KAHANE'S PICTURE (SEE NEXT PAGE) IS SUPERIMPOSED OVER THE FOLLOWING:

SOUNDS OF "SHEMA YISRAEL" ARE HEARD THROUGHOUT THE AUDIENCE. SEVERAL PEOPLE ARE SAYING, "KAHANE WAS RIGHT." THE WORDS RISE CRESCENDO AS MORE AND MORE PEOPLE JOIN IN. THEN, THE SONG "A SPECIAL MAN" IS PLAYED.

THE END.

Rabbi Meir Kahane was arrested approximately 70 times throughout his lifetime. In Israel alone, around 60 times, and the rest in the United States. Most arrests happened in the 1970's. He spent around 5 years of his life in jail. During that time, he continued to write and study.

Rabbi Meir Kahane

1968...age 36
November 4, 1990...died....age 58

My task, I considered, to report a great historical figure to the advance guard of humanity for emulation.
Brecht, "Letter to the Theater Union"

www.ingramcontent.com/pod-product-compliance
Lightning Source LLC
Chambersburg PA
CBHW060347080526
44583CB00012B/204